Emily Post's

THE GIFT OF
Good Manners

OTHER BOOKS FROM

THE EMILY POST INSTITUTE

Emily Post's Etiquette

Emily Post's Wedding Etiquette

Emily Post's Wedding Planner

Emily Post's The Etiquette Advantage in Business

Emily Post's Entertaining

THE GIFT OF
Good Manners

A PARENT'S GUIDE TO
RAISING RESPECTFUL, KIND,
CONSIDERATE CHILDREN

Peggy Post and Cindy Post Senning, *Ed.D.*

HarperResource

An Imprint of HarperCollins*Publishers*

EMILY POST'S THE GIFT OF GOOD MANNERS. Copyright © 2002 by
The Emily Post Institute, Inc. All rights reserved. Printed in the United
States of America. No part of this book may be used or reproduced in
any manner whatsoever without written permission except in the case of
brief quotations embodied in critical articles and reviews. For information address HarperCollins Publishers Inc., 10 East 53rd Street, New
York, NY 10022.

HarperCollins books may be purchased for educational, business, or
sales promotional use. For information please write: Special Markets
Department, HarperCollins Publishers Inc., 10 East 53rd Street, New
York, NY 10022.

FIRST EDITION

Designed by Richard Oriolo

Printed on acid-free paper

LIBRARY OF CONGRESS CATALOGING-IN-PUBLICATION
DATA HAS BEEN APPLIED FOR.

ISBN 0-06-018549-X

02 02 03 04 06 WBC/RRD 10 9 8 7 6 5 4 3 2 1

We dedicate this book to our parents,
who so generously shared "the gift" with us.

Acknowledgments

IT IS WITH A DEEP APPRECIATION that we acknowledge the following people for their contributions to this book.

Martha DuBose for her research, invaluable assistance, and hard work. We can't imagine how we would have completed this book without her.

Julia Martin, Fred DuBose, Peter Post, and Elizabeth Howell for their creativity and assistance.

Toni Sciarra and Greg Chaput of HarperCollins for their insights and attention to detail that helped bring focus and clarity to the book.

Katherine Cowles, our agent, advisor, and friend who always asks us the hard questions, guides us through our answers, and supports us in so many ways.

To our advisory group whose creativity and knowledge of parents and children helped form the vision from start to finish for this book:

Sara Barrett, M.Ed.
Jeanne Bataille, MS, SLP
Alex Houston, M.Ed.
Cindy Lyons, M.Ed.
Lucy VonHollebeke, MS, CFNP

Our families—husbands, children, siblings—and friends who have supported and encouraged us throughout this project.

And the legacy of Emily Post, whose generosity of spirit and timeless wisdom live on to serve as the foundation for this book.

Contents

Foreword

AS WE VISIT CITIES AND towns across the United States, we hear a troubling question repeated over and over again. It comes in different forms, but it boils down to "Why do children today have such poor manners?"

Experience tells us that today's children and young people are not as ill mannered as people may think, yet the persistence of the question indicates problems. The letters that pour in every month to the Peggy Post manners advice columns in both *Parents* and *Good Housekeeping* magazines tell us that parents really do want their children to be considerate and well mannered. But many parents feel that they are fighting a losing battle. How can they compete, we are asked, when films and television programs exalt bad behavior and a "me first" mindset prevails? Where are the positive role models whose public behavior supports and affirms a parent's efforts to teach good manners? How can parents in a two-income or a single-parent household find the time to teach manners?

Admittedly, educating children and teenagers in etiquette may not be as easy as it was forty years ago. But it's not as difficult as parents may believe, and the lifetime benefits are nearly limitless. That's why we decided to write *The Gift of Good Manners: A Parent's Guide to Raising Respectful, Kind, Considerate Children*—the first new Emily Post publication for parents and children in more than a quarter of a century. Working closely with our advisory board of experts in the fields of education, communication, child and adolescent health, and human development, we've developed a guide that parents and children can confidently turn to for sound information, helpful advice, and unwavering encouragement. *The Gift of Good Manners* includes not only the correct manners to teach but also the when's, how's, why's, and what-if's of etiquette education.

The structure of this book is unique: Manners education is presented within the context of normal childhood development. The study of the developmental process has come so far since the 1950s that it now provides us with a virtual roadmap to effective teaching. *The Gift of Good Manners* is not a developmental text; instead, it employs developmental knowledge as a fundamental framework. Understanding children's developmental capabilities and emotional needs helps parents to set realistic etiquette goals and expectations. There is also focus on the exceptional influence parents have as role models and teachers of good behavior. As well, the book aids parents with their own issues—answering everyday etiquette questions and addressing the fine points of courteous interaction with other parents and adults.

A vital concern has been to make *The Gift of Good Manners* relevant for everyone who is raising children today, whatever the form of their families. For convenience's sake, we use the words "parents" and "caregivers" most frequently throughout the book, but we regard these terms as all-inclusive. A parent or primary caregiver can be anyone—biological parent, adoptive parent, stepparent, grandparent, guardian, or foster parent—who has taken on the responsibility of nurturing, loving, and educating a child to maturity.

Back in the late 1930s, when the country was being drawn into World War II, Emily Post wrote *Children Are People* (1940), a groundbreaking etiquette guide for parents. Three decades later, Elizabeth Post wrote *Please Say Please* (1972). Both these periods were marked by turbulence, and many people believed then—as some do now—that etiquette was of little concern in times of war and social upheaval. Emily and Elizabeth Post knew otherwise, and they wrote forcefully about the positive consequences of raising mannerly children. Learning manners, they said, builds character through the promotion of values including:

- Consideration for the sensibilities of others
- Respect
- Honesty
- Self-control
- Trustworthiness
- Fairness and sportsmanship

These qualities, they said, enable men and women to face whatever the future may bring with strength, courage, and integrity. We wholeheartedly agree. Isn't strength of character what we want for all children today? Many of the rules of etiquette and methods of teaching have changed since *Children Are People* and *Please Say Please* first appeared, but the fundamentals of good manners and good character have not. *The Gift of Good Manners* is a modern guide for modern parents and children. It is also part of a long tradition. So with a grateful salute to the past and an enthusiastic nod to the future, we begin.

—Peggy Post
Cindy Post Senning

A Gift for a Lifetime

MOST PEOPLE KNOW THAT MANNERS must be taught and learned, but how many consider etiquette itself to be a gift? The principles of etiquette and mannerly behavior are passed on from one generation to the next in the knowledge that good manners are fundamental to a good life. We give our children life and love, but we cannot make the future for them. So we give the tools that will enable them to build useful and satisfying lives, and we teach them etiquette and polite manners to make their futures brighter and better for themselves and others.

Etiquette has been described as society's *glue*—the element that enables individuals to live and work together harmoniously. The rules of etiquette change as people adapt to new circumstances, but the underlying principles of self-respect and respect for others remain the same. There are some today who challenge the need for etiquette—an old-fashioned idea, they say, and past its prime in an age of hustle, bustle, and "anything goes" competition. But they are vastly outnumbered by those who value civility, courtesy, and consideration as the outward expressions of fundamental human decency. In fact, there are many who believe these characteristics are more important in today's complex world than ever before.

Not only does etiquette have a place in our own twenty-first-century culture; it is unquestionably necessary for every child's lifelong confidence and success. As a parent or caregiver, you naturally want your child to be fully prepared for independent adulthood. You will save and probably sacrifice so that he receives the best education possible. You will encourage his talents and ambitions and help him develop a positive self-image. You will provide him with the moral, spiritual, and ethical structure that will enable him to distinguish right from wrong, make sound choices, and act with integrity. And you will teach him good manners.

Etiquette education is inseparable from the other things parents must do to rear responsible, self-sufficient adults. It's not a kind of add-on that can be attended to after the schoolwork and the soccer, ballet, and French lessons are done. Etiquette reinforces all the higher values and ideals that you impart to your child and makes it easier for him to learn from others when he begins his formal education. Teaching and modeling good manners are integral to daily family life.

Because you care about your child's manners, you may sometimes feel like a voice crying in the wilderness. But you aren't alone. Consider the fact that major American companies in the last decade have found it necessary to provide etiquette education for their employees, including senior management. Consider that college and university career planning officials must now instruct many of their students in the most basic manners—arrive on time, dress neatly, listen respectfully, and follow instructions—before these young adults head off to job interviews. There is a world of people and institutions crying out for higher standards of behavior and manners education.

The Challenge of Teaching Manners

ETIQUETTE CAN BE DEFINED IN a few lines of dictionary text as the set of rules and procedures that regulate behavior in social and official life. Good manners are the behaviors that follow the rules; bad manners are the behaviors that don't. What could be simpler? Yet why do so many parents have such difficulty teaching etiquette to their children? And why does our modern world seem overpopulated with young people who lack the basic social skills?

Part of the answer is that good manners have often become disconnected from other aspects of daily behavior. The causes for this break range from the time constraints on busy parents to a disapproval of societal restrictions on individual behavior that began in the late 1960s and continues today. For one pervasive example of the difficulties parents face, you need look no further than the television set and the movie theater. Understandably, concerned parents worry about sex and violence in the media, but far less attention has been paid to the modeling of social manners. Think about how manners are portrayed in mass entertainment. Even children who watch "family-friendly" television programs see countless examples of disrespect for elders, gross behavior, and poor mealtime manners portrayed as cute and funny. Too many sports and music "heroes" throw tantrums on and off the public stage, and too often their behavior is excused or ignored.

Fortunately, parents are in the best position to counter negative outside influences. You are your child's first teacher and role model. Peers, other adults, and the media will exert considerable influence as your child grows up. However, children and adolescents respect their parents, need parental approval, and are inclined to conform, sooner or later, to the examples and teachings of their parents. Etiquette education begins with you, the parent or caregiver. With persistence, patience, understanding, discipline, and large doses of love, you can teach, exemplify, and promote appropriate behavior and raise mannerly children.

What Does "Mannerly" Mean?

MOST PEOPLE CAN SPOT A well-mannered individual within minutes of first meeting. A mannerly person is the kind of person others want to be around, enjoy working and socializing with, and probably prefer to deal with in times of conflict. The signs may be seen in the genuine warmth of a greeting or the way the person puts others at ease. But whatever the external cues, mannerly people actively live by the Golden Rule and share the following characteristics and values:

- **Self-confidence.** A mannerly person knows how to behave and how to interact in most social and business situations and has the confidence to navigate comfortably through unfamiliar circumstances. Her self-confidence is not boastful or pushy. Rather, she is secure with herself in a way that tends to inspire confidence in others.

- **Consideration for others.** A mannerly person is always sensitive to others. He *notices* other people and does what he can to meet their needs. He also understands that his behavior often reflects on others including family, teachers, and employers, and for their benefit, he wants to be a thoughtful and courteous representative.

- **Respect.** A mannerly person understands that other people have rights, and she respects their rights. Because she values other people and their experiences, she can be deferential when appropriate—to elders and people who have attained positions of high rank, for example—without kowtowing or behaving obsequiously.

- **Common sense.** A mannerly person is a practical problem solver. He facilitates good relations by adapting to the needs of others without sacrificing his integrity. He knows which battles are worth fighting and how to take a stand without demeaning others.

- **Tact.** A mannerly person values honesty but also understands that brutal frankness is not always a virtue. She can set aside her personal opinions and biases. She thinks before she speaks or acts because she knows how easily thoughtless words and deeds can hurt others.

- **Flexibility.** While a mannerly person values tradition, he isn't rigid. He is comfortable with solutions and changes that make sense in the context of modern life. But he will want better reasons for change than personal convenience and expediency. He also understands that etiquette is an expression of broader cultural and social values. He finds it relatively easy to modify his manners to accommodate the traditions and etiquette of other cultures.

Mannerly adults fill the personality spectrum. They can be passionate and assertive or soft spoken and sedate, jolly or serious, highly focused or absentminded, self-effacing or self-promoting. Good manners do not limit anyone's ability to think deeply or act boldly. As an adjunct to individual character, good manners can actually have positive effects on personality traits—helping to temper an aggressive personality; encouraging a shy person to overcome her reserve in unfamiliar settings; enabling the boisterous individual to use tact in situations that require sensitivity. Good manners allow people to disagree agreeably; in the workplace alone, good manners have steered many a successful employee through the storms of office politics and corporate upheavals. Good manners may be most important in personal relationships and within families, where respectful and considerate behavior cements the bonds of love and affection.

The mechanics of good manners can be learned at any age, but when the learning process begins in childhood, mannerly behavior eventually becomes natural. It's always easier to prevent the formation of habits than to change habits that become ingrained. An early start takes advantage of children's instinct to learn, to master new skills, and to win the approval of the people around them.

The Gift of Good Manners *Distinction*

THE GIFT OF GOOD MANNERS is intended as an ongoing source of reference and ideas that you can turn to with confidence throughout your child's first eighteen years. Although this book is chiefly for parents and caregivers, the latter chapters also include information specifically for preteens and teenagers.

The Gift of Good Manners is organized around two key principles:

- That it is best to model and teach etiquette virtually from birth and throughout childhood and adolescence (although it's never too late)
- That education in manners is most effective when geared to a child's developmental capabilities

Of course, *The Gift of Good Manners* includes the specific rules of mannerly behavior—how to set a table, tips for writing thank-you notes, basic telephone manners, and so on. But what distinguishes this book is the emphasis given to etiquette education in the context of a child's total development. The sections that follow are divided into stages from birth through the high school years. From chapter to chapter, etiquette issues and teaching methods are geared to children's normal capabilities during those years. This focus on linking etiquette training to development will enable you to determine when to teach principles and manners, how best to teach in relation to your child's readiness to learn, and what your child can be expected to learn and to do.

This emphasis on *process* will add to your confidence to serve as teacher (you don't have to teach all the manners at once) and alleviate worries. When parents have reasonable expectations, children can reach age-appropriate goals throughout childhood and adolescence, take pride in their accomplishments, and then build on what they have learned. By integrating etiquette education into general development, treating the teaching of manners as a gradual and continuous process, and focusing on how well a particular child learns (rather than setting exact deadlines for learning), parents will find that teaching etiquette is not the struggle they may have anticipated. In fact, it is a source of pleasure and pride for both parent and child.

This developmental approach benefits children by encouraging parents to set reasonable goals and flexible time limits. It is in no way a precise timetable for expectations and achievements because development cannot be pinned down with absolute certainty. Each child will progress at his own pace, sometimes achieving skills ahead of schedule and sometimes acquiring abilities late in the developmental range. It is up to parents to recognize and respect their own child's unique developmental patterns and to adjust their teaching accordingly. Children can be held accountable for what they should reasonably be expected to understand but not held to standards beyond their physical, emotional, and intellectual capabilities.

How to Use The Gift of Good Manners

EACH OF THE SIX SECTIONS of this book is divided into five chapters that deal with the following core manners topics:

- **Values and ethics** chapters address ways to clarify, teach, and model the fundamental moral and ethical values that are the foundations of good manners. Key concerns include the difference between right and wrong, truth and lies, thoughtfulness and thoughtlessness, kindness and cruelty. These chapters include guidance for parents on effective methods of discipline and conflict resolution, as well as means to encourage a child's independence, empathy, and personal responsibility.

- **Respect for self and others** chapters deal with the why's and how's of respectful attitudes and manners, beginning with parental modeling and progressing through respectful treatment of other adults, siblings, and peers. Attention is given to the means by which parents can instill and model respect for authority figures including teachers, school personnel, coaches, employers, and public officials. There is emphasis on teaching youngsters to share and cooperate and also to respect personal property—others' as well as their own.

- **Spoken and written communication** chapters examine how parents can teach and encourage their children to use language effectively. This includes traditional manners such as greetings and making introductions, telephone manners, invitations, and thank-you notes. The book also covers etiquette concerns related to new technologies including the Internet and cellular phones.

- **Table manners** chapters include the mechanics of gracious table manners and broader issues of social interaction including appropriate conversation, sharing, and consideration for others at mealtimes. "Dining-out" etiquette—from having dinner at a friend's home to restaurants and formal social occasions—is discussed. Tips for polite entertaining and the responsibilities of well-mannered hosts and guests, whatever their age, are found throughout the book.

- **Out-and-about** chapters examine behavior in social situations outside the home. These chapters cover a wealth of situations, from a child's first rides in the car or on a plane to dating and employment. Help is also provided for parents and teens dealing with social pressures that can lead to dangerous behaviors including alcohol and drug use and unsafe driving.

Specific etiquette issues may be emphasized at some stages and given less attention at others. For instance, table manners, when taught consistently during the preschool years, are usually pretty well established during a child's elementary school years. But with the onset of puberty, many children seem to forget their once-acceptable behavior, and parents have to reestablish and reinforce expectations in terms appropriate for early adolescence. So chapter by chapter, the information on table manners and other key issues is presented in the way most likely to assist parents and children as they move from one developmental phase to the next.

Special Features

Brief essays at the end of each section highlight topics that are not age specific. These features offer suggestions and manners guidelines on a variety of topics: children with special needs, the changing structure of the modern family, parent-to-parent interaction, excessive pressure on children, and school problems. The concluding feature on "Getting to College" focuses on the etiquette essentials of college application and admission for high school students and their families.

The Gift of Good Manners is full of short features, including questions from parents, which may highlight an etiquette point or provide advice on situations ranging from the everyday to the exceptional. These special features include several recurring topics:

- *Health and Safety* points out some of the more commonplace concerns parents have for their children's physical well-being and safety. This book is not a medical guide and should not be used as a substitute for the advice of qualified medical professionals. Healthy and Safety features are intended only as a heads-up for parents and caregivers, and in every instance, they are advised to consult with competent, professional health-care providers.

- *Toys, Games, and Activities* offers ideas for selecting and using playthings and activities for your child, with an emphasis on reinforcing manners instruction in an enjoyable, age-appropriate way.

- *For Grandparents* looks at issues and opportunities unique to the child–parent–grandparent relationship and at ways grandparents can make positive contributions to the etiquette education of their grandchildren.

- **Parent-to-Parent** features will help parents in their relations with other parents. These features explore issues such as what to do when other parents' rules and expectations are different from yours.

A Happy Gift

MORE THAN A CENTURY AGO, American essayist Ralph Waldo Emerson said about etiquette, "Manners are the happy ways of doing things."

These "happy ways" are among the most extraordinary gifts you can give to your child. Good manners will play a considerable role in the happiness and contentment of your child and the many people he encounters. For eighteen years, you and your child will travel a long and sometimes rocky road together. Learning and practicing good manners will often make the journey easier for you both. By the time your child is ready to tackle the world on his own terms, he will have your gift of etiquette to smooth his way.

As a parent or primary caregiver, it is your responsibility to make the manners connection—letting your child know by your teaching and example that good manners are part of a good life. When etiquette is taught in conjunction with all other aspects of a child's intellectual, moral, and ethical development, the child learns that manners are the *sincere, considerate,* and *sensible expressions* of important values in everyday life. There is no institution or organization that can adequately substitute for your influence and guidance. And there's no time like the present to begin. Whether you are preparing for your first baby or seeking more effective ways to teach your youngster the etiquette principles, you can begin today, with *The Gift of Good Manners* as your reliable and supportive companion.

Waking to the World: Birth to Twelve Months

N O W ' S   T H E   T I M E   T O . . .

- Model basic values and behavior

- Build trusting relationships

- Demonstrate respect for yourself and others

- Promote early communication skills

- Include babies at the family table

- Establish basic limits and routines

- Demonstrate considerate manners outside the home

WHEN A BABY ARRIVES, THE whole world changes. A new human being, full of promise, has come into your life. The challenges may seem daunting in the early days and weeks, but the rewards will more than compensate as you watch your baby grow, learn, and transform from the helpless infant in your arms to the bright, curious dynamo he will be by his first birthday.

While you won't yet be teaching etiquette in any formal way, you will be your baby's first and most influential model of social behavior and respect for others. You are the center of his universe, and the bonds of love and trust you forge this year will be the underpinnings for his future learning. By loving and respecting your baby and treating others with respect, kindness, and consideration, you will set standards for your child to emulate and eventually adopt as his own.

Children are never quite what we expect; they develop on their own schedules and fill everyone's days with surprises. During his first year, you will come to know your baby's temperament—the starting point of personality—and to appreciate his individuality. The parent–child relationship is complex, and as in all relationships, mistakes will be made. But as long as you love and cherish your baby, respond to his physical needs, and guard his safety, there's little you can do to impede his natural development at this stage. So relax, and trust and care for yourself as well as your baby.

Parenting is an awesome responsibility, but the pleasures of rearing a child are sublime. You and your child are beginning a great adventure together. In this first year, you will be marking the pathway that will lead him through childhood and adolescence, and into the world as a responsible, respectful, courteous, and socially assured adult.

Building the Foundations

AT SOME POINT—USUALLY BETWEEN six and twelve weeks—your baby will look at you and smile. As days and weeks go by, she will learn to greet you with expressions of both recognition and pleasure. These are among her earliest forays into the parent–child relationship. She is learning to trust you and to depend on your presence in her life. As she wakes to the world, her trust in you forms the bedrock for all her experiences to come.

Over her first twelve months, your baby will acquire an astonishing array of physical and mental skills, progressing from an almost totally reactive being who responds instinctively to physical stimuli (an empty tummy, a wet diaper, a sudden noise) to one who makes deliberate choices. She will begin to master her body and start to manipulate her environment—grasping objects she wants, for example. She will learn to distinguish her primary caregivers and cling to them. Around five or six months, she will become delightfully sociable. She will begin to sense herself as a separate being and learn to recognize her name. She will be driven to explore by her limitless curiosity. From birth to twelve months, a baby is an incredibly busy little person.

You're the Model

YOU WILL NOT ACTIVELY TEACH the principles or guidelines of etiquette for several years to come. But from the day she is born, you will be helping your child build her foundations for life. As babies develop, they increasingly learn through imitation. *What you do* will provide the example of how people act and interact. By your example and with the introduction of a few limits in the second half of your child's first year, you begin to establish patterns that will eventually translate into appropriate manners, conduct, and concern for the well-being of others.

By meeting your baby's physical and safety needs and giving her the fullness of your affection and attention, you are establishing *trust* and *love*—the two great pillars of teaching and learning. Whatever the form of your nuclear family—two parents, single parent, grandparents or other guardian as principal caregiver, adoptive or blended family—you are the central figure in your infant's life and will be for many years. With your love and attention now, your child will be well on her way to becoming a loving, attentive, and considerate member of the human race.

Visits and Gifts

BECAUSE HOSPITAL STAYS AFTER AN uncomplicated birth are as short as a day or two, it's fairly easy to put off visitors until you return home. The problem with the early homecoming is that a postpartum mother often feels far from well yet, and both mother and father are coping with their new duties. Hopefully, family and friends will be both sensible and sensitive.

Most people will phone before coming to visit. If you are not up to receiving guests, you can explain and suggest alternative days and times. If people drop by unexpectedly, you can't turn them away, but you can set some limits. ("Gosh, it's good to see you. We just got the baby to sleep about twenty minutes ago. Let's visit for a while, but if she doesn't wake before you leave, we can plan another time." Your friend will get your message.)

Young Visitors

Young children or any child who is ill should not visit a home with a newborn. If friends call in advance, you can head off a problem. ("We'd

Baby showers are usually given before a birth but may be given after your baby arrives. Co-workers, for example, may host a shower after new parents (dads as well as moms) return to the job. Showers for adopting parents can be held before or after the legal process is completed. Invitations to a shower never include gift suggestions. (*A gift—any gift—is always the choice of the giver.*) You can provide the hostess or host with a list of items you may need so that she can advise anyone who asks for a gift recommendation. If you provide a list, be conscious of the financial capabilities of the guests. Send a thank-you note to anyone who gave a gift but did not attend, including those who contributed to a group gift.

A grandparents shower is hosted for new grandparents by their friends. Although gifts are given to the grandparent for the new grandchild, it is the parents' responsibility to write thank-you notes.

---

love to have little Charlie over, too, but our pediatrician insists that the baby shouldn't be around other children for a few weeks yet. Tell Charlie that we'll miss him this time.") If parents with young children show up unannounced, your best tactic is to put your baby in her room or yours immediately. Your uninvited guests may think you're being overly protective, but as long as you are polite, they will have no reason to complain.

Deflecting Visits

A grandparent or other close adult may be able to run interference and deflect inconvenient visits. Also, let your home phone answering machine take calls during your busiest times, and you won't be caught by surprise when someone asks to drop by. You should return the calls as promptly as possible, but the answering machine gives you time to collect your thoughts and avoid a flustered response. Requests to visit will probably ease up after a few weeks. Your baby's christening, *brit* or *brit bat,* or other observance will satisfy most people's desire to see the baby and congratulate you in person.

Thank-You's

When you feel capable, use your spare time to complete thank-you notes and calls. While you should respond to gift givers as soon you can,

Don't forget to thank people who have given gifts that are not tangible—the hostess of your baby shower, the neighbor who babysat your older child when you rushed to the hospital, the friend who cleaned your house on the day you returned home. A warm note is in order, or even a suitable gift—something that reflects the interests and tastes of the person but is not too expensive or elaborate. Don't offer payment to a friend who has done you a sincere kindness, but do reimburse any expenses.

people are generally understanding about short delays, especially in the weeks just before and after a baby's birth. But for gifts sent by mail or delivery service, phone the givers as soon as possible to let them know that their presents have arrived. (E-mail will work if you know that the person will understand the casual nature of your message.) Then follow up with a thank-you note.

Writing thank-you notes can be done by both parents. If you have older children, it will be a good lesson for them to see you thanking the people who have been so kind to the new baby.

The Building Blocks

THIS IS A YEAR FOR fundamentals as your baby assembles the building blocks for a lifetime of attitudes and behaviors. It's time to consider several of the most important basics—issues that affect your child's emotional, intellectual, and physical growth and her later development as a respectful and considerate social being.

Respect Her Individuality

One of your earliest challenges will be to accept and appreciate your infant's individuality. Your child comes equipped with her own *temperament*—an inborn element of personality. Long before she can express herself in words, she will become adept at giving you clues and cues to her personality. Even the newest newborn displays "style," or her own way of responding to and dealing with the world around her, and it doesn't take long for parents to discern that style. Infant temperament can generally be classified in these broad categories:

- The baby with an *easy* temperament is ready to adapt to routines and also to accept changes, such as lengthening the time between feedings or adjusting sleep schedules.

- The baby with a *difficult* temperament seems to have a mind of her own and is less likely to settle into routines or take changes as they come.

- The baby with a *slow-to-warm-up* temperament is shy and wary of change.

- The baby with a *combination* temperament reacts differently to various situations; she may be easy about most adjustments but difficult about her feedings.

By respecting a newborn's temperament, parents can ease their own anxieties significantly. You haven't caused your child to be willful or shy. That is just the way she is. Feed your infant on demand if necessary. Accept the fact that you both may not be sleeping through the night quite as soon as you expected. You and your baby will be much happier if you are willing to bend in the beginning.

When Baby Rules the Roost

Sometimes, parents can be too adaptive—literally re-creating their own lives to suit their infant. A home in which an infant, through no fault of her own, rules the roost is likely to be chaotic, and no one is happy. One vital lesson babies begin to learn during the first year is how to regulate themselves—to take their longer sleep at night, for example. Parents who respond instantly to their baby's every whim and whimper are demonstrating a lack of self-respect and may be depriving their child of the rudiments of self-control.

By showing respect for her personality and her instinctive preferences in this critical first year and by imposing limitations appropriate to your child's safety and development, you demonstrate the fundamental principle of concern for others that is the basis of positive social interaction. All the fine points of etiquette stem from respect for and consideration of others. Appreciate your baby for who she is, find joy in her uniqueness, and you will be modeling the values that underlie considerate manners.

Birth announcements may range from strictly formal to charmingly imaginative. Whether you choose a traditional printed announcement, create something unusual, or post the news on your website, the basic information should include the name(s) of the parent(s) and the child (full name if parents are known by different surnames or if you plan to use a double surname for your child) and date of birth. You may want to include the place of the birth and your baby's weight and length at birth. For example:

Mr. and Mrs. Robert Simpson
are happy to announce
the arrival of
Jessica Leigh
September third, 2002

William Shelton-Brown
Born June 21, 2002
to joyful parents
Sharon Shelton and Edgar Brown
at Community Women's Hospital
Seattle, Washington
Seven pounds and 14 ounces; 20 inches

Single, divorced, and widowed mothers follow the same form but do not include the father's name. In a formal announcement, single mothers should use the title (Mrs., Miss, or Ms.) that they prefer.

To announce an adoption, you can follow a variation of the above styles whether the child is an infant or older:

Mr. and Mrs. Julian O'Brian
are happy to announce the adoption of
Katherine Louise
born May 15, 1998
and welcomed into our family on February 5, 2002

A card tied with a pink or blue ribbon can be helpful when the baby's name—Lee or Hilary, for instance—is not gender specific. You can include your home address on the announcement, especially if you're sending the news to friends and relatives who live in different locations or if you've moved recently. In any case, your home address should appear on the mailing envelope.

If you have the time to design your announcement, feel free. There are also attractive preprinted cards (just fill in the information), or you can consult with your local print shop. If you choose a preprinted card to announce the adoption of an older child, be sure the card is not designed for newborns.

Avoid announcements that are too elaborate; people want to share your happiness but probably not watch a ten-minute videotape of your baby sleeping. It's delightful for family and friends to receive a photograph of your child, though you might want to take your own shot; hospital photos of newborns are rarely flattering.

Birth and adoption announcements are sent to family and good friends and are not intended to solicit gifts. Most people know that gifts are not expected, so don't hesitate to send your announcements. If you do receive a baby gift, assume that it is given in joy and affection and simply thank the giver with a personal note.

Unless there is a close personal relationship, announcements are not sent to business associates or casual acquaintances, although you may want to send an announcement to your office or post it in an appropriate communal spot. In the workplace, however, it is often enough to tell one or two associates about your baby's arrival and ask them to spread the word.

- *Personal notes.* If your mailing list isn't long, you may want to write personal announcement notes. Just keep in mind that you will be very busy in your baby's first few weeks, so don't take on more work than you can handle.

- *Newspaper announcements.* If you want to announce the birth in your local press, look at other birth announcements in the paper for guidance on the information and wording. Newspapers once published announcements as a courtesy, but many now charge for the service, so check on your newspaper's policy. Other avenues include church bulletins, school and college alumni publications, and company newsletters; call the editors to ask about their requirements.

- **Internet announcements.** These can be lots of fun, but not everyone is plugged into a computer, so you probably want to mail announcements to those people who are not routinely online.

---◄←

Actions Beget Reactions

ONE OF A BABY'S EARLIEST lessons is that actions cause reactions—the essence of social interactions. When a baby cries because she is hungry and immediately starts nursing or is given a bottle, she is learning to associate the reaction of the adult who provides her nourishment with the satisfaction of her needs. It's not conscious association. It takes countless repetitions of this cry-and-response scenario for the baby to realize that an action on her part leads to a reaction on the part of her caregivers.

Through cry and response, the baby begins to associate her comfort with the adult who most often meets her needs, whether a biological parent, adoptive parent, or other caregiver. She can distinguish this person's touch, smell, and voice and soon recognize her caregiver's face. By around the middle of her third month, she will show signs of anticipating her caregiver's actions.

Later, the baby learns that other actions produce reactions. Her smiles bring loving touches. Her baby noises elicit imitations of her sounds from adults. Her physical attainments are greeted with enthusiasm and excitement. Some of her actions earn negative responses. If she reaches for a dangerous item, she or the item will be moved with a firm "no," and the baby will sense that the reaction was unpleasant.

After six months or so, a baby becomes fascinated by cause and effect in her environment. She drops her rattle or pushes her ball and watches intently to see where it goes. She loves to bang anything that makes noise. Your baby is learning that she can make things happen. In a crude way, she is starting to think in a manner that will eventually lead to genuine problem solving and decision making—another critical building block in the construction of a well-mannered individual.

Setting Limits

ETIQUETTE IS A CODE OF behavior that provides guidelines for social interaction, and one of the first things infants learn in the school of etiquette is to live within limits. Most parents begin to guide and limit infant behavior during the first three months. When a baby has her days and nights reversed (taking her longest sleep during the day), parents will adjust feeding times or take other steps to gradually shift the baby to a more convenient schedule. Gentle, early regulating means that the parent is taking charge in ways appropriate to the situation. As the baby develops, parents find themselves setting limits in increasingly diverse ways.

For much of your child's first year, setting limits is a matter of adjusting your routines and environment for your baby's safety and comfort, and the very young baby will simply accept most limitations. As the attachment between parent and child grows and the baby's range of activities expands, she may literally look to you for limits. A crawling, exploring seven- or eight-month-old will sometimes turn to a parent before venturing into a new space or putting an object in her mouth. She wants to see your reaction before she proceeds.

A Question for Peggy and Cindy

Our baby was very premature and spent several months in the hospital before we could bring him home. He has some health problems, but his doctors are now confident of his survival. We would like to send birth announcements. Is it too late?

By all means, send your announcements. Your friends will be overjoyed to receive the news. Though you probably don't want to go into the medical details, you might note that your baby is now at home with you. If you have the time, you could send personal notes to close family and friends. Be sure to save a copy of your announcement; someday it will mean a great deal to your child to see that you love him so much that you wanted to share the news of his arrival.

First Playthings

You can't dictate what toys others give to your baby, but etiquette allows you to make suggestions when asked. If Grandpa wonders whether the baby would like a giant teddy bear, gracefully recommend that some of the following toys will be more fun for an infant and improve vision and motor skills:

- A simple floor gym

- An unbreakable mirror to secure onto the crib at the correct distance for baby's range of vision

- A mobile that features the basic elements of the human face

(If the oversized toy arrives anyway, be grateful and put the item on display, unless it could be dangerous.)

An older baby will want chewing toys, plastic key rings, and rattles. (To prevent choking, no toy should be smaller than 1½ inches in diameter.) As motor skills and hand-eye coordination develop, he'll enjoy blocks, balls, and rattles that he can throw, drop, push, and roll. Sturdy household items such as pots, pans, unbreakable plastic spoons and cups, and cardboard boxes will also enrich a baby's early play.

Understanding "No"

By her first birthday, your baby will probably understand the intention of "no" and that her actions—even contemplated actions—can be stopped or interrupted by her caregivers. She wants approval, and she will usually try to avoid negative responses. If you firmly say "no" and then move your baby to another room when she tries to touch the hot stove, she will begin to grasp that "no" is a signal not to do something. Too many "no's," however, can undermine her self-confidence; a baby will react to a "no" long before she understands your reasons for limiting her behavior.

Fear of Separation

Around six months, a baby begins to sense that she is separate from her primary caregiver and capable of independent action. But if she is independent, then her caregiver can go away. This new *separation anxiety* is scary for an infant and can be difficult for parents. She may cry forlornly whenever you leave the room or move out of her line of sight. She may wake in the night and cry out. It's important that she begin to understand the nature of separation: first, that you are there for her whether she can see you or not, but second, that you do not necessarily respond instantly to her every beck and call. Your willingness to wait even for a minute before answering her cries could be called baby's first real-life lesson in the fact that other people have needs that may not coincide with hers—a concept fundamental to respectful manners later on.

Crying It Out

By around eight or nine months, babies may cry to get attention, and parents face the crying-it-out dilemma. Assuming that the baby's physiological and safety needs have been met, should you react immediately or let her cry? Letting her cry for a few minutes won't cause her any harm. When a baby wakes and cries during the night and the cry doesn't signal discomfort or difficulty, you may want to delay going to her for several minutes. The crying often stops as the baby settles back to sleep. But if it continues, you can go to her crib and let her see you. Speak soothingly, give gentle pats, and maybe sing a lullaby. But don't pick her up, and don't play. You are being considerate of your baby's needs but also demonstrating one of the basics of social behavior—that she cannot have absolute control over other people's reactions and responses. You will be teaching an important lesson about delayed gratification— another fundamental for the mannerly child and adult.

As difficult as it is to hear a baby cry for even a short time, the delay can be an important first step toward the development of a considerate child. By consistently rushing in at the first peep, parents set up an expectation that any demanding cry will result in cuddling, rocking, playing—attention. This pattern can set the stage for constant interruptions of your life and lead to selfishness and self-centeredness in your child.

A Safe and Warm Environment

PLANNING AND CREATING A PLEASANT place for a baby is a natural part of the nesting instinct. But environment involves more than a place;

Babies need and want structure in their lives. Structure is a kind of security—a pattern of habits that can be trusted. By structuring aspects of your baby's life now, you are fostering the sense of emotional security that will eventually help him become both self-regulating and socially confident.

Structure can be provided in any number of ways, but establishing routines and regulating daily activities are among the most successful. Observing set times for eating, napping, bathing, sleeping, and other activities is comforting for babies. For example, you can signal that bedtime has arrived by following a consistent routine—a final feeding, a bath if that is calming, a fresh diaper and clean sleeping suit, a favorite sleep toy or blanket, a lullaby or story, some cuddles and rocking time—and a clear good-night and leave-taking. You'll probably find yourself and your baby looking forward to rituals like this, not to mention the benefits of routines when you begin leaving your baby with other caretakers.

Establishing routines and setting limits is a gradual process. Structuring activities should never be so rigid that it impedes your child's desire to explore and experiment. Yes, babies want and need structure. But within the limits of safety and convenience, wise parents always give their children plenty of chances to try, fail, and try again.

it is an expression of your values and respect for your child. Doubtless, your objectives include creating a warm, loving atmosphere and a safe setting. You want a place that is comfortable for your baby and you and that is stimulating and encourages learning.

Child-rearing books and magazines and your health-care provider will help you choose safe, age-appropriate furnishings, accessories, and playthings for your baby. As you prepare your baby's room, remember that it will be some time before she can see more than a few inches beyond her face. The focus of her visual attention will initially be human faces—not wallpaper designs or motorized mobiles. Trust your common sense as you purchase items. Your child's room can evolve as she grows, and when she's older, you can enjoy furnishing it together.

The Child-Safe House

Get a head start on accident prevention while the baby is still too small for much movement. Look at the world through his eyes. Anticipate his actions, and remember that he can acquire physical capabilities seemingly overnight. Before he begins to roll or crawl, you should get down on the floor and see what's there. Before he can walk and climb, look at your entire house and its environs from the perspective of one to three feet off the ground. By around the middle of his first year, your child will have nearly full use of his five senses—and no sense of danger. Whatever your baby can see, he will want to touch, rub, grab, poke, shake, punch, push and pull, climb, sniff, taste, and probably eat.

When he is too small to move around, give him plenty to look at by shifting the position of his infant seat and taking him from room to room throughout the day. When he begins to reach for, grasp, and play with objects, supply toys that enable him to exercise his new skills. When he begins to roll, scoot, or move about in any manner, clear the decks and let him roam under your watchful eye. Guard his safety first; then consider his changing capabilities and give him some room for trial and error.

You will begin setting limits when your baby begins to move under his own steam. Bearing in mind that "no" is just another sound to a baby until near the end of his first year, you can effectively limit early explorations by blocking off certain areas, distracting his attention to an equally interesting activity, or removing him from any dangerous situation. Because he trusts you, he will eventually get the message that some things and places are off-limits. These early limits are your baby's first exposure to the concepts of respect for property, respect for privacy, and concern for the safety and comfort of others.

First Lessons in Respect

A NEWBORN IS A TOTALLY self-centered being; his needs are entirely those that will guarantee his physical survival. He must learn the "higher" emotions—love, sympathy and kindness, respect, generosity, and consideration for others—from his parents and the other adults with whom he most consistently spends his time. So whether he learns to treat others with kindness and respect or to be self-focused and selfish is largely determined by the examples he sees.

Siblings as Rivals

IF THERE IS AN OLDER child in your family, you're no doubt worried about sibling rivalry and how it will manifest itself. Your baby is unlikely to feel any need to compete, but older children can be vulnerable to jealousy, resentment, and acting out. By respecting all your children and their feelings as you manage early sibling conflicts, you may be able to ameliorate later difficulties.

The closer your baby is in age to siblings, the more problems you are likely to encounter. Because newborns spend so much time sleeping, young siblings (under age two and a half) may hardly seem to notice the baby's presence until the infant becomes mobile. A sibling between two and a half and four years of age may feel resentment from the start, especially if she is a first child. Children over four years old generally cope better, largely because their interests are focused less narrowly on their parents.

A crawling, walking, exploring baby requires a high level of parental attention. In addition, the baby's natural inquisitiveness leads him into an older sibling's things. He may share an older sibling's room, depriving the older child of privacy and even access to the room during nap times. In short, the mobile baby can be a huge pain for his sibling. (See the recommendations in Chapters 7 and 12 for helping older children adjust to a new baby.)

Parents need to understand that older children don't automatically love their new siblings and that some degree of jealousy and resentment is normal. Your role is to make the change as easy as possible for your older child or children, respecting their needs and providing the extra doses of love and reassurance that older siblings need most.

Other Adults

A BABY'S INTEREST INITIALLY CENTERS on his primary caregiver and then gradually widens to include other adults who are routinely present. By around six months, babies begin to display increasing sociability. They like attention and love to perform. Even shy babies learn that their smiles and babbling delight adults and win more attention.

But you may also notice that when a stranger appears, the baby who is so gregarious with the people he knows is suddenly hesitant. He doesn't smile instantly but looks to you for guidance. If you react well to this unknown person, your baby is likely to become his usual sociable self. But if you show hesitation, he may reach for you and perhaps whimper. All babies experience stranger anxiety to some degree and may progress to crying or withdrawing at the sight of an unknown person.

Comfortable Meetings

You can help your baby and the adults get through a bout of stranger anxiety with minimal upset by preparing the grown-ups before they meet your child and then stage-managing the meeting.

A Passing Phase

Even grandparents aren't immune to a baby's stranger anxiety. It's fairly common for a baby of seven or eight months to cry wildly when visited by adoring grandparents whom the infant hasn't seen regularly. If grandparents are not prepared, they will probably feel rejected and wonder what they've done to cause the baby fear or pain. But don't worry. Stranger anxiety is a natural phase and will usually pass as grandparents spend more time with their grandchild.

- *Tell visitors in advance*—before they come or when they arrive at your home—that your child is going through a fear-of-strangers phase. Inform the guest of the best way to greet your baby. If your baby is inclined to cry around strangers, don't take him to the door unless the visitor is well known to him.

- *Introduce the new person gradually.* The visitor should come into the baby's presence quietly and acknowledge the baby with a smile and a soft word or two. If the stranger rushes forward, touches, or talks excitedly, the baby is likely to withdraw or start crying.

- *Behave normally.* Talk with your guest. Let the baby observe your reactions and give him time to size up this strange person.

- *Encourage the guest to make gradual overtures* as the baby becomes more assured—gently voiced comments and small gestures. Your baby may warm up to your guest or maintain a guarded attitude, but you will have avoided a scene and done your best for the comfort of both your visitor and your infant.

Variations on this technique work well whenever you introduce any new person—babysitter, nanny, or housekeeper, for instance—into your home. If possible, arrange one or several meetings at which you are present. Let the baby become accustomed to the caregiver; then leave them alone together for short periods, increasing the length of time you are out of sight as your baby becomes more comfortable.

If you will be leaving the baby in someone else's home or in day care, this process of gradual introduction also allows the baby to adjust to the new surroundings. It may seem time-consuming, but the results should be worth your efforts. You will demonstrate your concern for the new caregiver's feelings. You'll also help your baby learn that the stranger is a friend and that you can be trusted to return every time you leave.

You can't control every situation. If a friend approaches you in the mall and your baby bursts into tears, your only recourse is to explain the baby's reaction and make it clear that your friend has done nothing to cause the problem. Also, remember that your baby's anxiety is genuine and normal. Don't scold or become upset with him. If a parent overreacts to what is really a very minor embarrassment, the baby may become confirmed in his suspicion of strangers, and you will have difficulty with later teaching of good meeting-and-greeting manners.

Playgroups and Other Children

ORGANIZED CLASSES FOR BABIES UNDER one year are often too structured and can be stifling for a baby, whose primary interest is exploring his environment in his own way and at his own pace. But informal, unstructured playgroups with children of similar age can be stimulating for babies and parents alike. Your baby is introduced to the concept of a group activity, and he sees adults interacting in a positive social situation. Probably more important, mothers, fathers, and caregivers can share information, wisdom, and concerns.

Until they are about three years old, children don't interact with peers. Babies may be interested in other babies in the same way they are curious about a new toy or their own reflections in a mirror, but parents shouldn't be fooled into thinking that deliberate play is taking place. You cannot begin to teach concepts such as fairness, selflessness, and sharing to a baby in the first year. Not until the parent–child bonds of love and trust are firmly cemented will any youngster become genuinely interested in his peers.

When you start a group or join an existing group, it's important to clarify the etiquette ground rules for all members. The following guidelines won't interfere with the informality of the group, but they will help make the time together more rewarding for everyone:

- **Never leave infants unsupervised.** Ideally, supervision means one adult per child, and no fewer than one adult for every three or four children. Be wary if older children are part of the group. *Never leave infants alone with preschool children of any age.*

- **Clearly establish the rules about handling the babies.** Except in emergencies, it's better not to pick up or hold someone else's baby unless you are asked to. Conversely, it's inconsiderate to hand off your own child to someone else unless the person clearly welcomes the responsibility.

- **Discuss discipline.** Parents and caregivers may have very different ideas about what to do when babies smack, poke, push, and pull at other infants. Members of the playgroup need to discuss discipline honestly and arrive at mutually agreeable rules. Usually no more is required than distracting the offending infant's attention to something else or moving him. Discipline for toddlers can be a thornier problem, and as the children grow older, your group will need to revise the rules for everyone. (See Chapter 7 for discussion of toddler playgroups.)

- **Avoid comparing and competing.** Everyone suffers if members relentlessly compare their babies' achievements. This is really a matter of individual etiquette, but the group can make its general feelings known regarding excessive boastfulness and competitiveness. (See "Competitive Parenting" below.)

- **Observe arrival and departure times.** This is particularly important if you gather in private homes. It may be acceptable to arrive a bit late, but call the hostess or host if you are delayed or cannot attend. It is never acceptable to leave after the predetermined time, unless you're invited to stay. In a facility such as a church hall or community center, be sure to depart on time as other activities may be scheduled to follow yours.

- **Be clear about who provides refreshments, if any.** Coffee and cookies are sufficient for the adults; perhaps juice for any toddlers in the group. But since most informal playgroups meet for an hour or two at most, refreshments are not really necessary.

- **Bring your own baby supplies.** Don't expect your hostess or host to provide diapers, bottles, baby food, infant seats, strollers, cots, playpens, and the like. Other than tap water, you should come equipped with everything your baby may need.

When Your Baby Is Sick

If your baby is at all sick or you suspect she may have been exposed to illness, be considerate and skip gatherings with other children until she is well and cannot pass on any contagion. Should your child become ill within a few days after a playgroup gathering, notify the other parents and caregivers if your child has something that can be spread.

- **Clean up.** Whether in a home or public place, clean up spills and messes immediately and don't leave anything behind. This is a special concern with dirty diapers and items such as disposable bottle liners, wipe-ups, and baby food containers. It's a good idea to use zip-up plastic bags and dispose of diapers and other trash when you get home. (Keep your plastic bag supply tightly sealed and well away from all children.)

Competitive Parenting

AT TWO MONTHS YOUR NEIGHBORS' baby was sleeping through the night; yours was still waking up at 3 A.M. At five months, your neighbors' baby was crawling; yours was still struggling to sit without support. At twelve months, your neighbors' baby can say a dozen words. You are still waiting for "mama."

It might not be so bad, if your neighbors didn't constantly drop by to tell you about each new accomplishment. Despite reassurances from your pediatrician that your child is progressing quite nicely, you can't help but worry and fret.

You're the victim of competitive parenting—an all-too-common behavior. For first-time parents especially, this kind of competition can be extremely stressful, yet emotional reactions on your part may cause long-term problems. Pushing a baby to walk before he is ready or putting him in highly regimented classes in order to keep up with the precocious tyke next door may impede normal physical, emotional, and intellectual development.

Dealing with Boastful Parents

Remind yourself of the first principles: respect for your baby and appreciation of his unique temperament. Then consider the results of child development research: Normal, healthy children develop their physical, emotional, and intellectual skills *at varying rates*—often widely varying (some babies walk independently at eight months and some at eighteen months, all within the range of normal development). Children tend to surprise us. A child who seem to be far behind his peers in speech at age one, for instance, may well be acquiring an extensive mental vocabulary and begin chatting in complete sentences at age two.

You can listen to competitive parents' boasting politely, but don't be drawn into making comparisons or defending you own baby. If you have questions or concerns about your baby's development, consult your pediatrician or family doctor. Read child development and child-rearing material from qualified authorities. Find like-minded parents with whom you can comfortably "talk babies" and share information.

If they constantly impose on you, you may be forced to deal directly with neighbors who are quick to brag. This kind of conversation is never easy, but unless you prefer to move, it has to be done.

Above all, stay calm. Avoid discussing your children. Tell your neighbors how much you enjoy their visits, but explain that your schedule is stretched thin and you'd like them to call before coming to see you. Assure them that you will do the same because you know they are as busy as you. Keep the conversation friendly and nonconfrontational, but stick firmly to your point that time is the problem. Highly competitive people generally want a receptive audience, so limiting their access to your household may give you some relief and maintain neighborly relations.

Child-Care Etiquette Issues

THE MAJORITY OF PARENTS TODAY are employed, most outside the home. Despite greatly improved conditions including extensions of paid and unpaid maternal and paternal leave, employed parents will sooner or later find themselves facing the day-care decision.

Your baby will form attachments to his outside caretakers, and they will profoundly influence his development and help shape his understanding of personal and social interaction. Child-rearing guides can provide helpful information about how to conduct your search and select the child-care situation that best suits you and your baby.

Once you have decided on your child-care provider, some specific etiquette concerns arise, influenced in part by the type of care and the provider you select.

At-Home Care

Paid at-home care (professional nanny, full-time babysitter, au pair) is usually the most expensive arrangement but is generally advantageous to the baby because it involves one-on-one attention in the baby's home environment. When hiring and employing an at-home provider, you should:

- *Spell out your expectations and requirements in detail and stick to the job description you've created.* This not only is a matter of good etiquette but is absolutely essential for the happiness and security of your child and child-care employee alike. Do not, for example, expect your nanny to do housework or cook for the family unless this is part of her contract. If your sitter is responsible for children in addition to the baby, be sure that she understands the extra duty and is compensated fairly.

- *Be clear about working hours and abide by them.* An occasional late arrival from work may be okay if you call and warn the caretaker. But consistently expecting your nanny or sitter to stay after working hours or not notifying her when you will be late is inexcusable.

- *Give advance notice whenever the caretaker will not be needed.* In all fairness, you should probably pay the provider for any unscheduled time off.

- *Never require your employee to work when she is ill.* It's smart to have a backup plan for times when your at-home provider simply cannot work. If you must stay at home, notify your own employer immediately.

- *Define boundaries for live-in providers.* This applies to both time and territory. Agreed-on days off and holidays must be honored. The caretaker's private quarters and personal property

A well-trained, experienced child-care provider should be regarded as a professional, and like all professionals, she will probably prefer payments in salary or wages rather than gifts and tips. Gift giving is fine for appropriate occasions—Christmas, Hanukkah, birthdays—but you should never substitute a gift for fair compensation. Be wary of offering your employee used clothing or cast-off household items. What an employer regards as generosity is often perceived as demeaning by an employee.

should be sacrosanct. A live-in child-minder will be part of your household, so think very carefully about your house rules. Smoking, alcohol use, noise levels in the house, personal guests, hours or no hours, use of house keys, appropriate dress, transportation—consider everything. The age and experience of your live-in employee may also be a factor, especially if you find yourself in a de facto parental role with a young caretaker. It is all too easy to take unintended advantage of an employee. Before you lay down too many rules—or too few—you should put yourself in the live-in employee's shoes for a while. What would you reasonably expect of your employer?

- **Reimburse your employee's out-of-pocket expenses immediately.** Better still, be sure to provide adequate funds for any shopping that you expect your at-home provider to do for you.

Group Day Care

Group day care offers professional care to a number of children—usually from ages one to five, although some accept younger babies—in a specially equipped facility. Though not as costly as at-home care, group centers are rarely capable of intensive personal attention, and there may be concerns related to the presence of older children, the spread of illnesses, and the lack of scheduling flexibility. If your employer offers on-site day care, this can be a wonderful option because it includes ready access to your child during the workday.

- **Be sure that you understand and accept all the policies and rules of the group-care center.** Don't expect the center to make exceptions for you and your child.

- *Carefully observe the center's hours of operation.* Whether commercial or not-for-profit enterprises, all good day-care centers are run as businesses. Parents who abuse the center's drop-off and pick-up times may soon find themselves without day care. Plan ahead and arrange your backup—a grandparent, friend, or babysitter who can pick up and mind your child when you are late leaving your workplace.

- *Don't hesitate to inform the center's management if you suspect a problem* such as an incompetent child-care worker or a danger in the physical environment. Well-run centers will appreciate your information because the problem, if left unattended, can affect their reputation and bottom line. You may choose to keep your child at home until the problem is resolved. If nothing is done within a reasonable time, remove your child entirely and report the situation to appropriate authorities such as your state's licensing and child protection agencies. Reporting is an act of concern for other parents and children who may not yet have observed or encountered the problem.

- *Always keep a sick child at home.* Out of consideration for the other children, inform the management of the nature of your child's illness and do not return your child to the center until the possibility of contagion has passed. Also tell the center if your child has been exposed to illness, even though your baby may seem perfectly healthy. Your pediatrician can give you guidelines about infection periods and when it is safe to take your baby back to day care.

- *Follow the center's policies on gift giving and tipping.* Tipping may be appropriate if an employee does something for you that falls outside normal duties. But be cautious. Tipping may be regarded as favoritism and cause resentment among other employees.

Home Day Care

Home day care is provided by an individual (often a mother with small children of her own) who minds several children in her home. Home care may be the least costly option, offers a domestic setting, and in the best circumstances provides more individualized attention and flexible scheduling than group care. The etiquette issues here are much the same as with a day-care center. Adhere strictly to drop-off and pick-up times, keeping in mind that the provider probably has other family to care for. Do not take a sick baby or one who has been exposed to a contagious condition to day care. Follow the same guidelines for tipping and gift giving that apply to an at-home caregiver.

Parent's-Day-Out Programs and Part-Time Group Care

These situations are not intended for full-time employed parents. But if you do stay at home with your infant, particularly if you have a home-based business, such services can provide much-needed breaks. Parent's-day-out programs are often offered by local religious and service organizations such as the YWCA and YMCA. Your etiquette concerns will be the same as in group day care.

When you've settled on your child-care arrangement, you'll want to gently and gradually introduce your baby to the child-care provider. (See "Other Adults," page 17.) There needs to be a good "fit" between your infant and the provider. If things do not settle down within a reasonable time or your baby becomes excessively unhappy or fearful, you may have to make a change. This doesn't mean that the child-care provider has done anything wrong; it may be that the nature of the child-care situation itself just doesn't suit your child's temperament. Ideally, you were diligent in your initial search for good child care, know of alternatives, and can make a change fairly quickly.

Respecting Property

IT WILL BE SOME TIME before your baby has any sense of "yours," "mine," or "ours." Right now, all things exist for his entertainment and exploration. Parents, on the other hand, have a finely tuned understanding of property and ownership, and even in the first year, you can begin laying the groundwork for later lessons in respect for property—your child's and everyone else's.

Some new parents do not protect their precious household items, attempting instead to train their baby from the beginning not to touch. Life would be easy if this approach worked, but it doesn't. Things get broken because a baby's innate curiosity is a true force of nature. If the mobile baby is confined to his crib or playpen often or for long periods in order to prevent damage to the home, he will endure terrible frustration and boredom, and quite possibly his self-confidence, creativity, and developing independence will suffer.

If the baby is scolded, told that he is "bad" for touching this thing and that, and hears "no" all the time, he may eventually conform to the judgment and assume that he and his instincts really are bad.

Protecting Possessions

How you handle property issues will be determined by concern for your baby's safety and development. But you will also be adding more building blocks to etiquette principles by balancing his need to explore with limits on what and whose property he can get into.

- *Look at your home from your baby's perspective and anticipate his interests.* Remove and store items that are a threat to his safety or are easily broken or damaged.

- *Protect items that you can't or don't want to store by putting them literally out of the baby's reach.* Be warned: Even before an infant can walk unassisted, he can climb and may be capable of stacking up books, pillows, and the like in order to get what he really wants.

- *Knobs and switches on appliances and electronic equipment are very tempting for the exploring baby.* If knobs are easily detached, keep them in a convenient place until needed. You can also put strong tape over knobs, switches, and openings to VCR, DVD, CD, and cassette players, although the tape itself will probably catch your little one's eye. Once he has a degree of fine motor control, he will try to get the tape off—and you may find mashed banana in your VCR. Investing in a well-constructed, latched or lockable, closet-style entertainment center for delicate equipment and remote controls may be one of your wiser expenditures.

Off-Limits

Some places and things must be declared off-limits. Hook-and-eye latches and door gates will let you secure rooms that you don't want

While your baby may not be wreaking havoc, she knows how to make a mess. To alleviate the problem without stunting her natural need to explore, use common sense. Substitute unbreakable items for the breakable ones. Slipcovers will protect upholstered furniture from the inevitable spills. Use the lower levels of bookshelves for your baby's books and toys. Keep some low drawers and cabinets unlatched and full of baby-safe things your child can find so that she will learn about opening, closing, and putting away. (But be careful: Babies can use open drawers like steps to climb to dangerous heights.) Always supervise your baby's play.

your baby to venture into alone—the bathroom first and foremost, the kitchen unless it is thoroughly childproof, your bedroom, a sibling's room, workrooms, and a home office. Then start teaching your child that some places are off-limits to him. Each time you go into the bathroom with him, show him the latch and explain that this room is entered only with Mommy or Daddy. He won't understand the reason for the restriction, but he will begin to sense that this place is somehow different from his play areas.

An especially difficult property issue involves things that belong to older siblings. A toddler is developing a sense of ownership, especially in relation to "mine." A baby who takes her things is a real threat, and the older child's feelings of infringement are valid. After all, you are teaching the older child to respect other people's belongings; she has a right to expect the same for her own possessions. A parent who repeatedly excuses an infant's behavior or demands that an older child give in is just tossing gas on the fires of sibling rivalry. (See Chapter 7, page 74, for ideas about managing toddler–baby issues.)

Putting Away

You can begin teaching respect for property by initiating "putting-away" routines during your baby's first year.

- **Let your infant watch your clean-up routines** such as putting the clean laundry into drawers and the dirty clothes into the hamper. When he is older, allow him to help with these chores.

Keep a hamper or basket in the bathroom. Even before he can walk, he'll enjoy being held up to drop clothes into the container after a bath or change of outfit.

- **Incorporate a little putting-away time in his bedtime ritual when he begins playing with toys.** Praise him when he hands you an object and later when he actually takes items to his toy basket or box. By allowing him to participate in small ways, you are impressing on him that things have their places and that neatness has a role in his life and yours. It won't be a big impression, but it's a necessary beginning.

The messes a baby creates each day can seem overwhelming, and some parents are tempted to let the chaos rule. But living in perpetual mess becomes dispiriting. Instead of giving up, make some strategic adjustments. You can forget many of the finer points of housekeeping for some time and still maintain a livable home. Ask yourself what you need to do to keep your home safe for the baby and maintain a sense of order. (Consult your pediatrician or family physician and your child-rearing guides for more complete information on home safety.)

If you try to clean up after your exploring infant as he goes through the day, you may inhibit normal inquisitiveness and learning. (Do, however, wipe up food and liquid spills quickly to prevent falls.) Instead, why not straighten the mess a couple of times every day—during your baby's nap and after he goes to bed at night? Putting certain areas of your home off-limits protects your baby and also creates havens for you. By making your own bedroom a child-free zone, for instance, you enable yourself to retreat to an oasis of order at day's end.

CHAPTER 3

The Budding Communicator

PROBABLY NO OTHER SKILL IS as important to a child's ultimate success—in school, career, and all social interactions—as the ability to communicate effectively. Language will also be your fundamental tool for teaching etiquette and appropriate social behavior, and you can start your baby on the path to clear communication by talking to her now.

How Babies Communicate

ALTHOUGH MOST BABIES DON'T DO much intelligible talking in their first year beyond "mama," "dada," "baby," and a few other simple words, they acquire a good deal of verbal comprehension by age one. Your child will know her own name and those of her caregivers. She'll recognize a number of words, associate some words with objects or pictures of objects, and probably be able to respond nonverbally to simple statements and commands.

She will also have a good-sized nonverbal vocabulary. The newborn who cries when hungry is communicating instinctively. The eight-month-old who cries for attention is communicating deliberately. Parents learn rather quickly to distinguish among hungry cries, wet and uncomfortable cries, sleepy and fussy cries, angry cries, and, later, attention and "I need help" cries.

As she grows, your baby will become a master of facial expressions and body language. Smiling and laughing, wiggling, staring, touching, kicking—she will increasingly use her body to signal her feelings and needs. Toward the end of her first year, her gestures will become specific, as when she holds out her arms to be picked up or points to her cup when she wants a drink. Whether the medium is verbal or nonverbal, whenever meaning is shared between the child and the caregiver, real communication is taking place.

First Lessons in Language

Babies hear sounds in the womb and become accustomed to background noise. The newborn will, however, startle at sudden, loud sounds—an innate reflex that disappears around the third or fourth month. She responds to soothing sounds and voices, although even the youngest baby can block out sounds when she wants. Most babies have an early preference for higher-pitched voices and are likely to react to female voices first. As their hearing becomes more acute, they respond to the lower male range.

Newborns make a lot of sounds naturally—sighing, breathing, sucking, and smacking noises. As they learn to manufacture sounds, their range expands to include cooing and gurgling, followed by laughing, giggling, squealing, razzing, and coughing. They begin experimenting with sounds that are basics of language—vowel sounds at first, then consonants. At about six months, babies are sensing that certain words are attached to certain people, objects, and actions. Within another couple of months or so, they will be putting the simple sounds together.

Talking to Your Baby

IT'S NEVER TOO SOON TO start talking to your baby. Though she has no comprehension of what you're saying, she will pick up how language works and how meaning is conveyed by inflection, pitch, tone, and volume. She hears the rudiments of grammar, and toward the end of her first year, she'll probably be able to distinguish between a simple state-

Hearing Problems

Parents often worry about their baby's hearing, especially when a baby fails to respond to sounds or words. But even newborns can block out noises; they may not react to a sound on one occasion but react normally on another. Serious hearing loss is relatively rare, but partial hearing loss and temporary deafness, often related to respiratory infections, are more common. Any persistent problem with hearing is likely to interfere with a child's acquisition of basic communication skills and can cause later learning difficulties. Hearing losses can be difficult to detect in routine physical exams, so if you suspect a problem, talk with your pediatrician about a referral to a pediatric audiologist who can test your child.

---

ment, a question, and a command. If you talk *with*—not at—her, she hears and sees that conversation is a mutual give and take.

If you feel self-conscious talking to your baby—many parents do—keep in mind how important this aspect of parenting is. As your baby begins to respond to your voice and words, talking to her will become enjoyable. One suggestion is to start with a simple running description of whatever you are doing. Other early ways to encourage your baby's communication skills include:

- *Using names for people and objects as often as possible.* Your baby can't even learn her own name unless you address her frequently by name.

- *Asking questions.* ("Patsy, do you have a big burp in there?") Show your interest by giving the baby a chance to respond with her own coos and sounds.

- *Imitating her sounds.* She will eventually begin to imitate yours—an essential part of speech development.

- *Reading to her.* At this early stage, it doesn't matter whether you read the sports pages or *War and Peace,* but you will probably introduce picture books around six months.

- *Reciting simple rhymes and adding simple, repetitive gestures.* "Humpty Dumpty," "Mary, Mary, Quite Contrary," and all the rest of Mother Goose have served generations of parents.

- *Singing to your baby even if you can't carry a tune.* You will never have a more receptive audience.

All word play should be fun for you and your child. When your infant loses interest, she will signal that it's time to be quiet by becoming fussy or just turning away. Follow her cues. Keep in mind that you can't force learning; rather, you are establishing the habits of language and communication.

Baby Talk

Some parents worry about baby talk, but there is a difference between what is known as *parentese* and *babyish* talk. Raising the pitch of your voice for a newborn helps to get her attention and makes sound pleasurable to her. Using nouns helps her to identify and name individuals and objects. Speaking in simple sentences and questions helps her begin to understand language forms and functions. Repetitive rhymes and songs help her master the rhythms of speech. These are all examples of parentese.

Babyish talk involves distorting language by, for example, adopting infantile terms in your ordinary speech. If your language is babyish, your child's will be as well. Some baby words are acceptable, like "kitty" and "dolly"; just don't overdo it. Also avoid treating your child's early words as entertainment. When adults laugh and applaud every time a baby mispronounces a word in a charming manner, the child naturally concludes that what she is saying is correct.

When your baby begins to comprehend language, sometime around six or seven months, encourage her learning by:

- *Speaking clearly and at a normal pace.* Too-rapid speech is confusing for adults, so consider the effect on a baby who is just beginning to sort out words and meanings.

- *Emphasizing the words and objects that are part of your baby's daily life.* Use the correct words for everything in your baby's world—and avoid babyish talk. Say "bottle," not "baba"; "pillow" rather than "pi-wo." Repeat, repeat, repeat.

- *Introducing abstract terms and concepts.* ("This blanket feels very soft." "Zach's block is lying under the kitchen table.")

A baby soaks up all that he sees, hears, and overhears—from incorrect grammar to swearing and angry gestures. He is incapable of making judgments, so if he hears his big brother shouting in the house or sees that everyone pays attention when Uncle Jeff swears, chances are the baby will sooner or later be shouting and swearing as well. Break your own bad language habits now, and you won't have to break your child's habits later.

Begin to describe things by their colors, sizes, and shapes ("the big blue blanket," "the round ball").

- **Continuing to repeat the sounds your baby makes;** she'll be flattered, and the habit of imitation will be affirmed.

- **Beginning to use simple commands.** ("Wave bye-bye." "Give Daddy a hug.") Show your child what you want her to do.

- **Listening to your baby and being responsive.** By nine months to a year, she will probably be trying to form words, but a distracted or inattentive caregiver can miss her efforts at speech, thereby discouraging further attempts. A parent who really listens can become adept at translating a child's first efforts. Don't worry much about pronunciation; your child is likely to have difficulty with certain sounds until she is five or six or even older. If your twelve-month-old manages to verbalize a simple thought such as "babee ju," you can say something like, "That's very good, Samantha. You want a cup of juice," both praising her efforts and giving her a lesson in correct speech. When you give her the juice, she will begin to make the connection between her words and the result she wanted.

Use the "Magic Words" Now

"Please" and "thank you" are the most important words in the etiquette lexicon, so using these courtesies from the beginning will establish the habit with your child. Introduce the magic words by using them often. Even a six-month-old can begin to sense the difference between "Drink your milk" and "Please drink your milk." Thank your child whenever she does something for you ("Thank you for not wiggling") or someone else ("Thank you for giving Daddy your toy"). This early attention is fundamental to the development of a courteous child.

The Reading Habit

LITERACY ENCOMPASSES THE ABILITY TO speak, read, and write in one's standard language. It is essential to all aspects of life in the modern world, including etiquette. Literacy is the portal to ideas and the foundation of education; it is fundamental to success in the workplace.

Your attitudes toward reading and learning now will have a powerful effect on your child's ultimate level of literacy. A parent who approaches reading to his baby as a chore conveys a message. A parent who is seen reading for her own pleasure and education is conveying a quite different message. Even in their first year, children can sense their parents' negative or positive feelings about reading.

A baby's interest in being read to will be variable—her attention span is very short, and she is easily distracted—but her awareness of reading material and how it is used is growing. At six months, your infant will probably chew on a book; by nine or ten months or so, she will open it, turn the pages, and perhaps look at the pictures. By a year, she may be able to point out a few objects in picture books when you say the words. Through early exposure, she gets the *feel* of books and learns that books are entertaining.

Interactive Games and Play

THROUGHOUT YOUR CHILD'S FIRST THREE years, learning and playing are intimately linked. One of the earliest games you play with your infant will probably be Peek-a-boo. Before five months or so, she is most likely to react with interest and often a questioning look. Then her reaction will become giggles, and she may imitate you by hiding her own face. It won't be long before you can vary the game by covering an object with a blanket and letting her find it. Peek-a-boo and other early games are so traditional that parents may not be aware of their learning purpose. But hiding games help to teach that individuals and objects have permanence; they exist even when they cannot be seen—an intellectual concept and a fundamental element of trust building.

Buying Books

Since babies explore with all their senses, infant books should be sturdy and washable (heavy cardboard, laminated cloth, vinyl), be made with nontoxic materials and inks, and have rounded corners that can't cut little mouths. Babies like to exercise their developing fine-motor skills by turning pages, so flat cloth books are not recommended, although padded cloth pages can be fun. Instead of buying expensive books that can only be read with supervision, collect a number of books that your baby can play with and add new books from time to time.

Include reading times in your baby's daily activities—after she's eaten, perhaps, or before nap or bedtime. Be flexible, however. If she'd rather cruise along the couch or play Peek-a-boo, skip the reading until she's more receptive. Forcing a small child to listen will only teach her that reading and books are not fun. And please forget about flashcards and mechanical and computerized word toys that distort normal sounds.

More important, let your child see you reading, and she will come to think of reading as something she wants to imitate. You may not be an avid reader, but let your baby see you when you do read. Hold her on your lap as you thumb through a cookbook. In the car, read road signs and billboards aloud. When you take a carton of milk from the fridge, show her the word "milk" and read it to her. For the budding communicator, every word is part of a great new adventure.

Tried-and-True Games

Playing simple games is fun and also demonstrates key principles including cooperation, sharing, taking turns, and communicating and understanding instructions.

- *Pat-a-cake* allows your child to participate at increasingly complex levels as she learns to bring her hands together and clap and to anticipate the appropriate actions.

- *Eyes, Nose, Mouth* and other body games let you teach your baby the words for her body parts, including genitalia. Parents who are uncomfortable using the correct terms may find their discomfort alleviated through these simple body games. To a baby, after all, words like "penis" and "vagina" have no greater significance than "ears" and "fingers."

- **Action games such as Itsy Bitsy Spider** allow more complicated interplay between words and actions as well as teaching concepts like "up" and "down." Your baby probably won't master the gestures until her second year, but you can guide her through the movements.

- **One, Two, Buckle My Shoe** is a classic counting game that uses numbers in sequence, and This Little Piggy also relies on the concept of things happening sequentially.

Every culture has its learning games, and these traditions are an excellent way to introduce your child to aspects of her cultural and ethnic heritage. Early games stimulate your baby's intellect, enhance her communication skills, and encourage her socialization. When she plays This Little Piggy with a grandparent or older sibling, she is socializing by cooperating with someone else in order to have fun. She is sharing a structured social experience, though she won't comprehend this for some time.

CHAPTER 4

At the Table

TABLE MANNERS USUALLY COME TO mind first when we think of etiquette for children. While a ten-month-old baby lacks the physical coordination and the intellectual capacity for lessons like "soupspoon on the right" and "elbows off the table," his first year is the time to gather the building blocks for later learning. Your concern now is to expose your baby to the basic mechanics of dining and the social side of sharing mealtime with others.

First Meals

WHEN YOU ADD SOLID FOODS to your baby's diet—perhaps around six months or a little later—you are introducing foods and establishing eating habits that are good for his health and growth. In addition, the foods you choose for your infant can affect his eventual eating-out etiquette. Will he be a junk-food junkie by the time he is two? Will he refuse treats that aren't sweets when he is three? Will he embarrass you every time you dine out with his picky eating demands when he is four?

Older children go through a range of bizarre and often annoying eating phases, but you can alleviate some later eating hassles by regulating your baby's earliest experiences with food. Your physician or health-care provider is your best guide about when, what, and how much to feed your child and health issues such as allergies. The following are a few general dietary suggestions that can improve your child's eating etiquette in the future:

- **Vary your baby's diet and introduce new foods regularly.** A child accustomed to a varied diet from the start may be less inclined to turn up his nose at new foods. You won't be able to control his preferences; he may enjoy spinach today and reject it tomorrow. But by varying his choices and offering new foods one at a time, you will help your child prepare for the time when he should not make demands about the foods served at home and away.

- **Never use food as a reward.** If you give a baby something to eat every time he cries for attention, he will begin to equate food with attention and love—a pattern that can eventually lead to serious eating disorders and other behavior problems.

- **Practice what you preach, both in your diet and your manners.** Babies are great imitators, and if they see their caregivers regularly gulping soda pop for breakfast or eating French fries from a cardboard carton for lunch, they will come to believe that such a diet and manners are the norm.

As a baby grows used to solid foods, feeding takes longer and longer, requiring a good deal of patience on your part. Assuming that the baby is still receiving his primary nourishment from breast milk or formula, eating solid foods is as much a source of fun as a necessity. Babies love to play with food. When you put your baby in his chair, he'll wiggle and squirm, grab for the spoon, spit and bubble the food, and somehow get most of the meal on his face, clothes, and anything else in his vicinity. This isn't bad behavior; it's natural exploration. He wants to know all he can about this new stuff. Spread newspapers for the spills, be patient, and remember his new interest in cause and effect. When he pours peas on the floor and watches them scatter, he's not being naughty; rather, he is curious to see the effect of his action.

You can avoid later squabbles by teaching your baby that mealtime is strictly for eating and socializing. Keep distractions to a minimum. Turn off the TV and the radio. Let the answering machine catch your phone calls. And don't let your baby have toys to play with while eating.

You should also begin to differentiate between meals, snacks, and treats. A meal is a seated affair with at least one other person present. A snack is a means to tide a baby over between meals; begin early to schedule snacks, preferably midway between meals. Food treats are special—for example, a slice of birthday cake—and infrequent.

◄┼

A baby's adventure with food is a parent's mess; that's just the way it is. But even these early mealtime experiences are opportunities to learn etiquette.

- *Using a bib* may seem like an exercise in futility, but a bib (large and washable) introduces the concept of neatness that will later be translated into the correct use of a table napkin.

- *Gently wiping your baby's hands with a damp cloth* before a meal or snack and cleaning him up afterward introduce the hygiene routines associated with eating.

- *Using a spoon to feed your child*—though he will use his hands and you'll give him finger foods when the danger of choking has passed—and introducing a cup will teach him to associate eating with utensils. He'll learn to drink from a lidded cup fairly soon and try to use a spoon, but children do not usually master a spoon until around age three.

Mealtime Routines and Rituals

PARENTS NATURALLY WANT TO INTEGRATE their baby into their own routines, but trying to feed a baby when you are having your meals is a losing battle. The better way to introduce your older infant to dining etiquette is to feed him first and then include him in the family circle at your main mealtime. Set him in his high chair, put his bib on, and give him a nonbreakable bowl and spoon and some non-mess-making finger foods. (He'll still throw and drop his food, but fruit bits and bread are relatively easy to clean up.) He may want a taste of your meal—a good way to introduce him to new foods.

Your goal is to introduce your baby to the social side of eating and give him a sense of the rituals associated with meals. Saying grace if that is your custom, passing foods from one to another and saying "please" and "thank you," waiting until everyone is served before beginning to eat, placing and using utensils and napkins correctly, eating and conversing quietly, taking turns, asking to be excused, helping to clear the table—all the routines of table etiquette are opportunities for your baby to observe and learn. (If you are a bit rusty on table manners, it's easy to brush up. See the table manners chapters throughout this book.)

Together at the Table

THESE DAYS, EATING TOGETHER AT the table is a luxury for many busy families, and frankly, that's a shame. A family meal is about sharing and learning as well as eating. It is often the only period in the day when everyone gathers and interacts as a family in an atmosphere of relative tranquillity. It is an especially opportune time for parents to learn about their children's daily activities, interests, and problems.

Parents with conflicting employment schedules and single working parents may not be able to stage a sit-down meal every day, but even the busiest families should strive to have family meals at least once or twice each week. Family meals don't have to be formal. But take-out food warmed in the microwave can be transferred to serving dishes and places correctly set with plates, utensils, and table linens. It's never too soon— or too late—to institute the fundamental habits of gracious dining and good mealtime manners.

In the Larger World

---◂◂

THE WORLD BEYOND HOME IS a classroom for etiquette instruction even in your baby's first year. Getting out into the wider world and among other people is important for her social development and for your sanity. But it also calls for a serious reality check. Parents must understand that there are occasions and places where infants and young children are welcomed and even catered to, but many more places where they are not.

Unfortunately, some new parents become so immersed in their own family unit that they can forget the needs of others. If you have paid to see a movie or a concert, you don't want the performance spoiled by an incessantly crying infant. If you are flying cross-country for an important business meeting, you don't want to sit next to a mother who is diapering her infant. If you have worked for days to host a formal dinner, the last thing you want is to open the door to a couple loaded down with their uninvited baby plus accessories. And neither does anyone else. As the parent of a very young child, you must carefully weigh your need to socialize against the needs of others.

Private Occasions

MOST PEOPLE—EVEN FAMILY MEMBERS and close friends—may be hesitant to tell new parents that bringing an uninvited baby to a private gathering is inconsiderate. There may be real emergencies that necessitate taking a baby to an event or a place that is not normally appropriate. But if parents habitually adopt a "take me, take my baby" attitude, they will soon receive few invitations to adult occasions and find themselves acquiring a reputation for thoughtlessness. Following these rules of etiquette will ensure that other people will enjoy your baby and vice versa:

- *Never assume that babies and children are included in invitations to private functions.* If the host hasn't specifically indicated that children are invited, the deletion is deliberate, and children are not included. As a rule, ceremonial events such as formal weddings and funerals are not appropriate for babies or toddlers.

- *Don't call and ask if your child can attend.* This will put the host or hostess in an embarrassing spot. Before you become comfortable leaving your baby with a sitter, you may have to refuse some invitations, but a missed party is preferable to a bruised relationship with the host.

- *Be especially thoughtful when visiting homes where there are no small children.* People who don't have children or whose children have grown beyond toddlerhood probably won't have childproof spaces. For your mobile baby's safety and to prevent damage to property, give others plenty of advance notice when you plan a visit and always ask if it is convenient to bring your baby.

- *Be prepared when you accept invitations to private homes.* If a friend calls and asks you and your infant to her house for lunch, explain that your baby is now crawling and tends to get into everything at or near floor level. Short-notice invitations often make it impossible for you to get a babysitter, so be prepared with all the equipment you need to manage your baby, including a portable cot or playpen for sleeping. Be sensitive. If your friend seems hesitant, you can suggest an alternative, such as lunch at your home or on another day when you can arrange for a sitter.

In Public Places

YOU WILL TAKE YOUR BABY to many public places during her first year—to the doctor's office or clinic for her checkups, to the grocery store and on other shopping trips, perhaps to her older sibling's school, parks, restaurants, and special events. In her second year, you'll begin teaching the manners for behavior in public places. Right now, it is up to you to see that each out-and-about occasion is fun for your child, comfortable for you, and not an imposition on others.

Plan Ahead

Remember when you could just grab your keys and hop into the car for a quick run to the store when you ran out of bread or milk? Now even the briefest trip requires advance planning. Pack your baby bag with all the things you might need. You may sometimes feel that you are equipping a small army, but if you anticipate needs and always expect the unexpected, you'll be able to cope with whatever arises.

It's also a good idea to plan for quick escapes. In an unfamiliar place, reconnoiter a bit as soon as you arrive—locate the changing rooms, rest areas, and exits.

Scheduling and Timing

Try to schedule out-and-about activities around your baby's routine. If you don't want her to fuss while you shop, go after her lunch or nap. Also, be conscious of time; your baby can only tolerate her carriage or stroller for so long. If you can, take your own car on excursions to avoid the hassles of installing your car seat in someone else's vehicle. With your own transportation, you can leave early if your baby becomes cranky or overly tired.

Basic Considerations

In public places, the basic etiquette requirement for parents with babies is always consideration for others. Practice the Golden Rule and do for others what you hope they would do for you in a similar situation.

- **Eating out.** The average shopping center food mall and family restaurant these days are equipped for babies and small children. But if you plan to dine at an upscale restaurant, ask if it has facilities for babies when you call for reservations. Most restaurants will quickly inform you if children are welcome.

- **Religious services.** Your place of worship may provide wonderful nursery care, but if not, you should carefully consider the risk of disturbing others during services. Your baby is probably more than welcome at the monthly potluck supper, but it can't hurt to check with the organizers.

- **Civic events.** The purpose of most civic gatherings—the regular city council or town meetings, school board meetings, court sessions, professional club meetings—is to conduct business. Babies and young children quickly become bored and fidgety, and their antics or crying distracts adults from the work at hand. Even meetings such as the PTA/PTO session at the local school, where it may seem all right to bring children, can be thoroughly disrupted. Be considerate and leave your little one with a babysitter.

- **The business office.** If you have a home-based business or telecommute, there will be times when you have business-related meetings and conferences with your employer or clients. The etiquette is simple: Don't take the baby. Besides distracting others, you can damage your own professional image by showing up with your baby and all her paraphernalia. There are informal occasions such as employee birthdays or going-away parties when babies are often the center of attention. But always check with your employer or party organizers before taking a baby or children of any age to an office function.

- **Entertainment venues.** Movie houses, theaters, and other indoor performance facilities are rarely good places for very young children. At outdoor events, it's advisable to find seating that is a little distant from the main crowd. Taking babies to large, organized sporting events is usually more trouble for you and irritating for others than it is worth.

No matter how convenient it might seem, never impose child-minding duties on someone else when you are out. The dangers of turning your baby over to a stranger are all too obvious. But even if you are acquainted, it is both rude and wrong to ask a salesperson to watch your baby while you try on an outfit or to expect the receptionist to tend to your child while you have a quick business meeting at the office. Apart from the fact that this person may be unprepared or unsuited for such responsibility, it is unlikely that babysitting is part of her job description.

◄◄

Be Prepared to Leave Immediately

If you do take your baby to an enclosed public area—a theater, museum, or performance hall, for example—be ready to leave the instant your infant starts to grumble or cry. Too many parents try to soothe their babies back into silence, but those two or three minutes can cause real discomfort for others. (Imagine that you are the guest speaker at a special event or an actor in an amateur play and that your presentation is interrupted at a critical point by a crying baby. Even when quiet is restored, the audience will be distracted and the mood of the presentation will be lost.) If the area has seating, take a place at the rear or near an exit—an aisle seat if you can get one—to facilitate a quick getaway.

Religious and Other Special Observances

THE ARRIVAL OF A NEW baby is celebrated in virtually every culture. The christening or baptism is a Christian rite for Catholics and most Protestants. Jews have several ceremonies for newborns including the *brith milah,* or *brit,* for boys and the *brit bat* for girls. The Islamic *akikah,* or birth ceremony, is observed by many Muslims. In the Hindu faith, a naming ceremony, referred to as the "rice-eating ceremony," is often celebrated when an infant reaches the age to eat solid foods, usually between six and eight months. Most of these events are accompanied by a reception for guests. Parents and families may also plan special, non-religious events—a naming day, for example, or a secular reception for family and friends.

To determine how and when to plan religious observances, consult with your clergyperson, rabbi, or spiritual leader. Customs will vary from sect to sect and congregation to congregation.

- **Timing.** Selecting the day and time may be a matter of great importance. For example, the *brith milah*, or "covenant of circumcision," is held on the eighth day after the birth of a healthy boy, though the service can be delayed if the child is under medical care.

- **Location.** Religious rituals can be performed in the place of worship during regular worship services or at a special time, or at home. (Your religious adviser can give you guidance on planning a home ceremony.) Receptions may be allowed at the place of worship, or you may prefer your home, a family member's home, or a convenient club or restaurant.

- **Formal or informal?** The degree of formality or casualness usually reflects local and family traditions. In some Christian families, for example, elaborate christening gowns are passed down from generation to generation, but your baby can just as well be christened in a plain white gown or special outfit. A formal religious ceremony may easily be followed by a pleasantly informal gathering. If you are unsure about the customs in your community or congregation—for instance, whether to serve champagne at the reception following a christening—your minister or religious leader can be of great help.

- **Guest list.** Religious and secular observances are intended to honor the baby, and receptions or parties given in conjunction with the ceremonies are intimate occasions. The guest list is normally limited to family members and close friends. (A trend that should be avoided is the exploitation of important spiritual rites of passage as excuses for lavish entertaining of business associates.)

- **Invitations.** Invitations are usually issued informally—by phone call or personal note—especially when the event occurs very soon after a baby's birth.

- **Gifts.** The giving of baby gifts is associated with most of these observances, but parents should be considerate. It is perfectly all right to tell a friend who has already given a shower gift and a baby gift that a christening gift is unnecessary.

Choosing Godparents

Godparents for your baby may be required by your faith. If so, they should be asked well in advance—often before the baby is born—so that they can consider the spiritual responsibility before accepting. Godparents should be either family members or very close friends. The rules of your church may require that your baby's godparents be of your faith. Being a godparent generally involves certain spiritual obligations as well as taking a special interest in one's godchild, including giving gifts on birthdays and holy days. Contrary to some thinking, however, godparents are not obligated to adopt or financially support godchildren who lose their parents. Because of the responsibilities, think about your choices for godparents with great care. (For instance, you probably want someone who is likely to remain geographically close rather than a friend who lives or may soon move far away.) It is difficult for a friend or family member to turn down a request to be a godparent, so if you do receive a refusal, assume that it was made after much serious contemplation and for very good reasons. The person who is unable to become a godparent to your baby is no less a friend for refusing.

In the Car

LOTS OF BABIES LOVE CARS and other motor vehicles. In fact, riding in a car is one tactic used by parents for soothing a colicky or cranky infant. Newborns seem to enjoy the motion and vibration. Later, they like the change of scene that a car ride provides, and they learn to associate a car ride with going someplace pleasurable, like grandparents' homes or day care. In-the-car etiquette is directly related to safety, so the lessons of the first year are grounded in teaching safe routines that will later become mannerly expectations.

It's generally agreed that children of all ages are safest when riding in the rear seats—not in front with the driver. Get your child in the habit of backseat riding by putting her carrier or car seat there from the start. Early attention to her safety should translate later into automatic use of seat belts and restraints. You may also be able to head off squabbles among siblings (Who gets the front seat?) by accustoming each of your children to backseat riding.

What you do influences your child's behavior, so be sure that you buckle up, even if you are driving just a few blocks. Every car ride can be a learning experience, so why not institute a ritual that teaches your baby the sequence of safe riding? Seat secure, baby buckled up, driver and others buckled up, doors locked, hands inside. Never, even once, allow your child to be held by an adult while riding in a car.

Early Car Manners

Though there is very little you can teach about car and travel etiquette at this stage, you can begin by setting the following limits:

- No messy foods when riding in a car or on public transport.

- No playing with door locks and handles (even if you have safety locks).

- No throwing toys. Your baby will throw things before she learns this lesson, so limit travel toys to soft items.

- No standing or wiggling out of the car seat. You'll probably have to emphasize this rule repeatedly after your baby becomes mobile.

- No screaming or shouting.

Teaching Opportunities

Time in the car is a good opportunity for conversation and word or singing games, though never at the expense of your concentration. As your baby grows increasingly alert, talk to her about what she is seeing through the car window. You will also want to begin teaching your little one that the driver controls the car. Whenever the driver asks for quiet, everyone in the car responds immediately. Your baby probably will not be quiet at this stage, but she will begin to sense that there are times when you cannot and will not respond to her.

When driving, my father sometimes doesn't bother to buckle his seat belt. I'll need him to drive my nine-month-old to the babysitter's now and then. How can I tell him to observe the safe-driving rules without sounding patronizing?

Your father probably began driving before seat-belt use was mandated by law. His failure to buckle up is likely an old habit, and he may not be well acquainted with current laws and information about car safety. Begin your conversation by focusing on your child's welfare, and be honest about your concerns. Discuss the importance of modeling car safety for your child. Enlist your father's assistance in teaching your baby the buckling-up and in-car behavior rituals you follow. Be sure that you provide a car seat whenever your child will ride with your father or anyone else and that your father knows how to install the seat and strap your child in safely. You should be clear that you expect everyone who transports your baby to follow the same rules. Finally, ask for his agreement. Your father will probably be happy to attend to safety matters when he knows the rules and understands how important they are to you.

Breast-Feeding in Public

BREAST-FEEDING IS NO LONGER THE exception it was in your grandmother's time. The medical benefits of breast-feeding for babies are well established. It provides your baby with natural protection against some illnesses and is wonderful for a baby's nutrition and for mother–child bonding.

If you breast-feed, you're right to think it the most normal and convenient activity in the world. However, others don't always share your feelings, and it's important to accept the fact that attitudes differ. Most people will be too polite to make any direct comments, so it's up to you to be sensitive.

Nature's Way

It can be helpful to keep in mind that breast-feeding isn't a movement or a political cause; it's nature's way (though not the *only* way) to nourish the very young. Mothers who can and do breast-feed are making a positive choice for their babies. It's best for both the baby and mother for feedings to take place in a situation that is calm and free of anxiety. If people around a breast-feeding mother and child are uncomfortable or tense, the mother will probably be affected and the feeding may not go well. Thus, the whole point of breast-feeding—to benefit the baby—will be defeated.

Your goal is to be neither ostentatious nor defensive. Many people regard breast-feeding as a private activity and inappropriate in a public setting, and this makes it all the more important to be discreet when breast-feeding around others.

If you don't have to breast-feed in a public place, don't. Should your baby become hungry while you are at the mall or a public building, you can quickly retreat to the rest room or your car for a relaxed feeding. When your baby is older and eating finger foods, you can probably delay the breast-feeding by giving her something else to eat. Unless you are determined not to give your baby a bottle, a supplemental bottle of expressed milk or formula can be an option.

When There's No Choice

If you must breast-feed in a public place, be discreet. Even in a family-style restaurant, you should ask to be seated in a location that is not in the center of attention. A booth or a table that is off the beaten path provides some privacy. On an airplane, ask the attendants if there are empty seats where you can breast-feed. In a private home, you can retreat to a bedroom or other quiet spot. Whatever the circumstances, do your best to avoid a display. A baby blanket or shawl carefully draped over your shoulders is an easy way to cover up. Many breast-feeding mothers love to wear roomy tops that can be lifted up, rather than dresses and shirts that must be unbuttoned from the top.

TOYS, GAMES, AND ACTIVITIES

The First Birthday Party

The day that your baby turns one is a huge milestone for you . . . and just another day for him. As yet, he has no concept of the passage of time in any concrete way, so whatever you plan will be little more than a diversion for your child. If you plan too elaborately—too many guests, activities, and decorations, for too long a time—your baby's first birthday will almost certainly end in tears, frustration, and exhaustion. The watchwords for a successful infant party are "simple" and "short."

- *Invite close family and perhaps a few friends.* You can send written invitations, but phone calls are just fine. One or two little guests of your child's age may add to the adults' pleasure, but don't expect the babies to play together or to participate in organized games.

- *Schedule the party at a time when your child is rested*—an hour after his morning or afternoon nap is usually good. Don't delay a normal meal in hopes that he will eat during the party. He'll most likely be grumpy and quick to cry. As to duration, an hour or 90 minutes is long enough for babies to enjoy the excitement without becoming overly stimulated or bored.

- *Keep the food simple and healthy.* A one-year-old doesn't need or expect a heavily frosted cake and rich ice cream. One or two candles on the cake will do, and beware of joke candles, string foam, confetti, and any party items that might flare up and cause serious injury.

- *Choose simple decorations.* If you want to decorate to a theme, there are inexpensive items featuring characters who may be favorites with your child. Be sure that decorations are safe, nontoxic, and flameproof. Mylar balloons are recommended because small children can easily choke on pieces of popped rubber balloons.

- *Give age-appropriate gifts.* You can't control what others give, but you can limit your own shopping to a few items. If toddlers are included in your gathering, present-opening time can cause difficulties; to minimize grabbing and squabbling, you might provide inexpensive gifts for all the children to open.

There are other birthday party options that meet the simple-and-short rule—a family dinner with cake and kisses for dessert, a visit with grandparents or special friends when presents are opened, a family picnic when the weather is right. If a weekly dinner with extended family is a custom in your household, why not make the family gathering closest to your child's birthday a time for celebration? If your baby is in group day care, you might ask the proprietor if you can supply birthday cookies, juice, and decorated cups and napkins for snack time.

Of course, you will want to take lots of pictures. You will treasure your memories of this landmark celebration forever, and someday your child will delight in the photos and your stories of his first birthday—though he won't remember a bit of it.

Children with Special Needs

THOSE WHO THINK THAT VALUES have taken a tumble might want to consider the dramatic progress made in society's attitudes toward and treatment of children and young people with special needs. Over the past fifty years or so, America has come to place high value on its disabled citizens—supporting broad legal efforts to improve institutional and workplace conditions and open educational opportunities. Compassion is a major factor, but so is the recognition that people with disabilities have a great deal to contribute.

The term "special needs" covers literally hundreds of circumstances including physical and mental handicaps, birth defects, chronic illnesses, learning disabilities, and emotional and behavioral problems that affect millions of American children and adolescents. Depending on individual situations, the socialization and manners education of children with special needs may follow a somewhat different course than that of healthy children but are no less important. At the same time, healthy children need help to understand the special needs of others. Positive role modeling is essential. In addition to the social etiquette discussed throughout this book, the following suggestions should facilitate social interactions.

For Parents of Children with Special Needs

Parents of children with special needs have so many responsibilities; it may seem unfair that they must cope with etiquette issues as well. Yet most people outside your immediate family will look to you as their principal model for considerate behavior. Your own child will turn to you to pave the way for positive, productive relationships with others. These few basics should help you set the standards in most social situations:

- *Inform others.* Even when special needs are evident, others may not know what to do or say. Most people will gladly make adjustments for you and your child, but they need to know what is required. In order for your youngster to enjoy social outings and playdates, for example, you should fully advise hosts and hostesses of any requirements and restrictions in advance of get-togethers. Be alert to other people's capabilities—many homes are not wheelchair accessible, for example, and cannot be made so without considerable expense—and be willing to work with family, friends, and neighbors to find creative solutions.

- **Try not to take offense at perceived insensitivity.** People will ask questions, and most try to do so in a sensitive and courteous manner. But mistakes will be made, and you are in the best position to correct errors and provide accurate information in a respectful manner. Some people will be tactless, and you will have to deal with ignorance while protecting your child from thoughtless comments. Others—young children in particular—simply do not have the language and social skills to ask questions in the most thoughtful way. Try to remember that the insensitivity of others is most often the product of misguided goodwill, not cruelty or condescension.

- **Take breaks for yourself.** No one can function at peak level all the time, so give yourself regular breaks and attend to your own health. You'll probably find yourself better able to cope with the world at large when you have given yourself reasonable rest and recreation time.

Some Advice for Others

Good manners are often the best way to ease tensions and make everyone comfortable in situations that seem awkward. In your social interactions and as you teach your own children, it is helpful to remember that children with special needs are children first and foremost and they deserve your full respect.

- **Be sensitive when asking for information.** There's rarely a reason to ask pointed questions of a stranger or new acquaintance. Be guided by the parent, caregiver, and child; it's best to let them bring up the subject when they feel the time and place are appropriate.

- **Demonstrate respect.** When meeting children with disabilities, for example, greet them as you would any child, address them directly, and be sure to make steady eye contact. Avoid assuming that a disability implies other limitations. People with impaired sight, for instance, are probably not hearing impaired, so raising your voice to address them will only impede normal communication.

- **Do your own homework.** It's important that adults know what they are talking about, especially when explaining disabilities to children. If you have regular contact with an adult or child who has a disability or chronic illness, inform yourself about the condition. Get up-to-date information and don't rely on what you may have been told in the past. Your health-care provider may be a good source of both medical information and social guidance. Even with good information, you should always defer to the knowledge of those with special needs and their caregivers.

- **Do not identify or label people by their disability.** A person has a disability or chronic illness; he is not the condition. For example, if it is necessary to refer to a condition—and most of the time, it isn't—you would say, "Mark has diabetes" rather than "Mark is a diabetic." Be especially sensitive when discussing children with special needs with other children. Avoid comparisons. A remark that seems innocuous or even beneficial— "You're so lucky not to be disabled like James" or "James has such wonderful manners even though he is disabled"—can spark jealousy and resentment and set one child against another.

- **Help when you can.** But always be guided by the person with special needs or his caregivers, and do not insist. Use common sense. It's fine to hold the door for a person who uses a wheelchair or has a sight impairment, just as you would for anyone. On the other hand, it's insensitive to push the chair or take the person's arm unless your assistance is requested.

Helping Healthy Siblings

It's obvious that a disabled child requires a lot of time and attention, and the more severe the disability or illness, the more occupied the parent will be. Despite the best efforts of parents and caregivers, healthy siblings can often feel left out. Resentment and feelings of guilt or inadequacy are not uncommon. While no one can substitute for a primary caregiver, relatives and friends can help healthy siblings with extra love and attention. Consult with the parents, and ask about ways you might assist other children in the family.

- Does a sibling need a ride to activities?
- Could he benefit from regular playdates with your child (even though his parents are unable to reciprocate)?

- Could you include an older child in your family's shopping excursions and field trips?

- Can you step in when a parent cannot attend a school event, recital, or athletic competition?

- If you're close, are you available for just talking, listening, and enabling a healthy sibling to let off steam every now and then?

Adolescent siblings of a special-needs child may not be as open about their emotions as younger children, but they, too, need loving support from family and friends. Your offer to assist may not be accepted, but it shows support in a kind and considerate manner.

PART TWO

Learning the Basics:
One to Three Years

NOW'S THE TIME TO . . .

- Model values and consideration for others
- Begin to give choices
- Introduce sharing and cooperating
- Control aggression
- Promote correct speech
- Introduce basic telephone manners
- Begin teaching table manners
- Introduce basic rules of public behavior

FASTEN YOUR SEAT BELTS. THE roller-coaster ride of parenthood is about to enter one of its most exhilarating and challenging phases. Ages one to three aren't always easy; the terrible two's lie ahead as your child deals with new emotions and conflicting needs for independence and dependence. Yet this is an extraordinary time for parent and child, because there is nothing to match a toddler's energy, curiosity, and unrestrained joy in her widening world. Your child will also begin acquiring the basics of a lifetime of social skills—table manners,

greetings, polite requests and thank-you's, sharing and taking turns—
as the underpinnings of etiquette and good manners are laid, secured,
and reinforced.

Usually between a year and eighteen months, babies learn to walk
independently. When she takes her first wobbly and unsupported
steps, your baby becomes a toddler, literally acquiring a new perspective on her world. She will continue to acquire physical skills, growing
stronger and taller and gaining increased control of her motor skills.
Her boundless interest in exploration and experimentation will lead
her "into everything."

Understanding and use of language will expand enormously;
short-term memory will mature; and problem solving will become relatively sophisticated. She will begin to think symbolically, not needing
to see something in order to imagine it, and to engage more and more
often in imitative and imaginative play. She will be able to follow
fairly complex verbal instructions.

A toddler's growing physical and intellectual abilities set the stage
for genuine learning. Your example will remain your child's most
influential teacher, but as she approaches her third birthday, you will
begin formal instruction in the fundamentals of etiquette. The first
steps she takes into the world of good manners during toddlerhood
will eventually translate into the ability to handle all social situations
with confidence in herself and respect for the needs and feelings of
others.

CHAPTER 6

Establishing Your Values

DURING THE TODDLER YEARS, YOUR baby will begin thinking of himself as a separate being and asserting his individuality. It's not a smooth process. All parents have heard of the terrible two's—a period marked by frustration on all sides. Yet this difficult adjustment, which happens to all toddlers to some degree, is absolutely essential.

Your child's natural curiosity will shift into high gear, and he will probably never again be so open to learning. He is also becoming socialized—learning to deal routinely with others in ways that maximize his experiences and those of the people around him. You will continue to set limits and, sometime around three years, begin his formal etiquette education. But by your example, you will teach good manners and positive behaviors throughout his toddler years.

He will soak up your values, attitudes, private and social behaviors, use of language and nonverbal communication, interests, and likes and dislikes. The eighteenth-century English politician Edmund Burke once wrote, "Example is the school of mankind. . . ." For you and your child, school is now in session.

Conflicting Emotions

Between the first and second years, your toddler's attachment to you, his need for emotional security, and his fear of separation will be at their peak. He will experience a new range of emotions—from pride in his achievements to frustration at his failures to anger at the limitations you must impose. A toddler's newly independent spirit, dependence on his primary caregiver, fears of separation, emotional range, and still-immature verbal capabilities—all contribute to the behaviors character-istic of the terrible two's. It is critical to your toddler's long-term happiness and emotional security that you understand what is happen-ing.

Often lasting for six months to a year or longer, the terrible two's is a time when you may find yourself constantly confused. One minute your baby may scream to wear his socks *over* his shoes; the next minute he graces you with his most endearing smile. He has learned the word "no" and uses it even when he means "yes." Beneath the mood changes and stubbornness, your baby is struggling to understand himself, his world, and his place in it. Be assured that the terrible two's will end; meanwhile, you can blunt some of its effects with an abundance of love, tolerance, sensitivity, and consistent discipline. Your child loves you fiercely and is counting on you to guide and support him through this often chaotic period.

Not every minute with a two-year-old will be a battle. He can be unbelievably sweet. His joy in the world and his own accomplishments is infectious. If you pay attention, you will begin to see your everyday sur-roundings through his fresh, curious eyes—a place of wonder where every mud puddle is a kingdom of delight just begging to be explored.

Clarifying Your Values

THE VALUES YOU TEACH AND model now will be central to the teach-ing of manners and etiquette. It's worth taking a long, hard look at the values you want to pass on. When members of the same family define their values, their concepts can be contradictory. Parents and grandpar-ents often have differing ideas, and even spouses can disagree, leading to situations in which a child receives confusing and conflicting messages from the people he trusts most.

If you haven't done so, take time to define and clarify your basic values. Make a complete list, and be honest with yourself. Here are a few values you might consider, though your list will doubtless exclude some and include others:

Consideration and kindness	Good manners
Honesty and integrity	Honorable behavior
Self-discipline	Reliability and loyalty
Family	Good sportsmanship
Hard work	Leisure
Community service	Generosity
Religious beliefs	Respect for ethnic and cultural diversity

What's Most Important?

Once you have your list, decide which of your values are most important and rank them in order of priority. If you have a spouse or partner, he or she should also list and prioritize personal values. When you compare your thinking, you will probably agree in many areas, but you may discover conflicts. Resolving these differences doesn't mean you must give up your own values; rather, you will aim for comfortable compromises and respect for differences.

Teaching Right from Wrong

ALL MAJOR CULTURES AND RELIGIONS have their version of the Golden Rule—the injunction to treat others as you wish to be treated. This is also the core of good etiquette. Following the Golden Rule in adulthood requires a finely tuned understanding of other people and their needs. But children must begin with the fundamentals. And what is more basic than the difference between doing right and doing wrong?

A toddler doesn't have the intellectual capacity to draw moral and ethical distinctions. But after sixteen months or so, he *begins* to acquire the rudimentary ability to understand alternatives, anticipate outcomes, and choose different ways of doing things. Through repeated trial and error, he learns that if he stacks big blocks on small blocks, the tower he is building is likely to fall. He begins to anticipate the outcome by stacking the bigger blocks first—distinguishing the right way from the wrong way to do something and achieve his objective. He is at the start of a process that will—when he is much older—enable him to choose between right and wrong attitudes, motives, and actions.

The Golden Rule of Parenting

For the time being, your child's behavioral choices depend on you. He won't understand why you act in certain ways, but he will imitate what you do. His short-term memory is growing, so what he sees and hears will stay with him for hours or even days. His growing ability to think symbolically means that he understands more of what you say than you may expect.

Thus another Golden Rule comes to the forefront. It is the Golden Rule of Parenting: *Always behave in the way you want your child to behave.* It's crucial to remember that your actions speak louder than your words; if you act one way but tell your child to act another, he will imitate your behavior. A parent can talk about consideration for others, but if he is consistently rude to salespeople and swears at other drivers, his child will assume that rudeness and swearing are the right way to deal with people. A parent with poor manners cannot expect to rear a child with good manners.

Encouraging Empathy

EMPATHY IS THE CAPACITY TO understand how others feel, to be able to walk in someone else's shoes. Empathetic impulses seem to be innate—a one-year-old may try to comfort another child who is crying—but must be nurtured if empathy is to develop and mature.

When empathetic impulses are not encouraged, they can wither. A child who is abused or neglected loses trust in adults and has more difficulty learning to care about others. But there are less obvious ways of undermining a child's empathetic capabilities. Psychologists use the terms *bounding* and *bridging* to describe how children are taught to deal with differences among people. A bounded child is one who is only exposed to people like himself—the same race or religion, socioeconomic background, family, ethnic group. His empathy is confined to the people he knows; he learns to behave morally and ethically with his "own kind," but his moral sense may not extend beyond these boundaries. Bridging involves exposing a child to people of diverse backgrounds and characteristics. Children reared in a bridging environment are more likely to develop inclusive moral standards and behavior.

To promote the development of empathy, it's important to discuss feelings with your child. Every experience doesn't call for deep analysis, but your toddler needs the language to talk about emotions. You can help by identifying his feelings—happy, glad, sad, angry, confused, lonesome, bored, scared—and letting him know that you have the same feelings.

- **Encourage your toddler to see his behavior from the point of view of others.** If he pinches a playmate, talk to him after you've stopped the behavior. Express your concern that the other child feels hurt, and ask your child how he would feel if someone pinched him. Don't pinch him to illustrate your point.

- **Look for opportunities to discuss concern for others.** Books and stories can provide excellent lessons in empathy. When you recount the tale of "Goldilocks and the Three Bears," talk to

---

A Question for Peggy and Cindy

My in-laws are very involved grandparents and visit once or twice a week. Every time they come, they bring a little present for my daughter. I feel like I'm drowning in clutter. Would it be okay to ask them to stop?

Your in-laws clearly take pleasure in selecting these gifts, and your daughter enjoys receiving them, so why ruin everyone's fun and upset your in-laws? When they show up with gifts, be appreciative. Even if you don't like the gift, let your in-laws know how grateful you are for their thoughtfulness. Not only will this reaction maintain family harmony, but you'll also send the right message to your child, who needs to learn how to receive a gift graciously. To keep the flow of gifts under control, tell your in-laws that you're afraid your daughter expects gifts every time they arrive and suggest that they spread the gift giving out a bit. But again, make sure to let them know how much you appreciate their involvement with their grandchild.

your child about how he would feel if someone slept in his bed or ate his breakfast without asking. Would he be mad or sad? Toddlers are wrapped up in their own emotions and experiences, but parents can help them to relate to others by pointing out that others have feelings like their own.

- ***Praise your child's early empathetic reactions.*** Kind responses may be few during toddlerhood, but they do occur. If you have a cold and your two-year-old pats your hand and seems worried, thank him for his concern and tell him that his caring helps you feel better. Praising his gesture begins to establish the value of kindness.

- ***Model concern for others.*** If, for example, you and your toddler find a toy on the sidewalk outside a store, take it to the store manager and ask the manager to keep it in case the person who lost it returns. Then talk to your child about returning lost things. Discuss how the person who lost the toy probably feels. The toy may never be claimed, but you will have given your child a priceless demonstration of concern for others.

- ***Practice what you preach at home.*** Behaviors at home set the pattern for your child's relationships beyond the family. How you handle the normal conflicts and flare-ups of family life will have a powerful influence. Do family members belittle and insult one another? Can the adults in the house forgive others easily? Do adults control their voices and language when they are angry? Do family members regularly apologize for mistakes in judging others?

The Real Meaning of Discipline

DON'T LET THE WORD "DISCIPLINE" scare you. Your child has no way to know right from wrong behavior unless you make the difference clear, and words are not going to be enough. Effective discipline is a system of teaching that includes:

- Setting clear limits on behavior and enforcing the limits consistently

- Using appropriate methods to enforce the limits: distraction, substitution, time-outs, and removing the young child from dangerous or difficult situations

- Taking time to talk with the child to explain and reinforce lessons in behavior

- Rewarding the child with praise for positive behaviors

- Recognizing that a child's values can sometimes legitimately conflict with parental values and respecting these differences

- Being flexible enough to adapt, when feasible, to a child's natural need for control

- Tailoring restrictions and explanations to a child's developmental capabilities and level of understanding

- Consistently following through with responses and consequences

- Never punishing out of anger or demeaning the child for his behavior

- Never abusing a child physically or emotionally

Without consistent discipline, a toddler is denied the reference points for right and wrong. A two-year-old who has experienced lax or inconsistent discipline can become willful, thoughtless of others, and lacking in self-control. At the other extreme, excessively rigid discipline, especially when coupled with corporal punishment, can create a child who obeys out of fear and fails to internalize the concepts of right and wrong.

Discipline That Works

WHAT IS THE MOST EFFECTIVE way to discipline a toddler? There's no single answer, because each child is different and will respond differently. You will have to try various approaches and combinations of methods to see what works best.

Distraction and Substitution

If your child is doing something risky or troublesome, direct his attention to another area of interest or substitute a less hazardous

Whether to use physical punishment is one of the most contentious issues in any discussion of discipline. The American Academy of Pediatricians has cited the general ineffectiveness of spanking and warned about the long-term, negative outcomes. It seems that everyone should know, intuitively, that violence begets violence. But frustration can sometimes overwhelm parents. The old advice to "count to ten" (make it a hundred if you need the time to cool down) still works. Or you can just walk away from the situation. In any parent–child confrontation, the parent holds the ultimate power and must exercise it wisely.

The most effective and beneficial forms of discipline include giving a child consistent messages; anticipating behaviors and setting clear rules, expectations, and consequences; negotiating rules and consequences with school-age children and teens and being firm about nonnegotiable rules; increasing restrictions when needed; and applying rules with consistency and love.

Parents and professionals are divided on the appropriateness and effectiveness of the use of a controlled slap or spanking as a method of discipline. While slapping or spanking a child may have an immediate effect, it simply does not work in the long run. In addition, the act of slapping or spanking is demeaning and humiliating—the antithesis of what you are teaching.

Hitting a child repeatedly with the hands or with an object such as a belt or a stick or hitting hard enough, even once, to leave a bruise or mark constitutes child abuse and is a reportable offense. Discipline at this level often represents an adult's loss of control. It is important to note that although not reportable, repeated and abusive verbal correction (including screaming, cursing, and using demeaning and degrading language) can scar a child just as deeply as abusive physical punishments.

Parents who are having difficulty with discipline should work with their pediatrician or consult with a social worker or other qualified professional to develop an effective plan for discipline.

object. Tell him "no" and explain why, but don't make a big issue of minor infractions. You want your child to develop a sense of proportion in regard to his and others' behavior.

Removal from the Situation

Removing your child from situations where he is in jeopardy is essential, and there is no need to waste precious time with explanations. If your child is heading for the edge of the pool, grab him immediately; don't stop to explain or argue. Act just as quickly if your child is endangering another person. If he smacks a child in his playgroup, even a firm "no" is not enough. Remove your child at once. Removal can also mean taking something away, which will often lead to crying and protests. Substituting something else may help, but the older the child, the less likely he is to be distracted.

Time-outs

Time-outs are used to defuse a difficult situation and give a child a few minutes to calm down. Set your child in a quiet place without distractions and tell him to remain there. Time-outs shouldn't be protracted; the recommended length is one minute for each year of a child's age. Depending on your toddler's temperament, time-outs may not always work, but they will contribute to his eventual mastery of self-control. Follow a time-out with some discussion of what happened and why you stopped the behavior.

Reinforcing Good Behavior

Consistent, positive reinforcement teaches a child what it means to do right. Parents are usually quick to stop naughty and dangerous behaviors, yet may be slow to praise positive actions. Be on the lookout for behaviors to praise. Use your toddler's good behavior to begin explaining concepts such as "kind" and "thoughtful" and "courteous." If your child puts some of his toys away without being asked or tries to comfort another child who is crying, acknowledge the action and tell your toddler why his behavior was good.

Following Through

Effective discipline requires follow-through. Explain why the behavior is wrong in language your child can understand and in a context to which he can relate. With toddlers, it's also important to pick your battles. There are situations when you can give in without compromising discipline. If your two-year-old demands to wear one purple sock and one yellow sock, let him; mismatched socks are really a matter of personal taste, not an issue of right and wrong.

Managing Tantrums

IT'S CRITICAL TO UNDERSTAND THAT toddlers' tantrums are not simply selfish, attention-seeking displays. Though often precipitated by something as minor as being denied a particular item in the grocery store, tantrums are the product of built-up frustration and anger. The causes are myriad: A toddler doesn't yet have the physical capabilities to accomplish much of what he wants to do. He lacks the self-control to keep powerful emotions in check and doesn't have the verbal skills to express his feelings. His behavior is often restricted by his parents, but he doesn't understand the reasons for limits. When the pressures overwhelm him, he blows like a small volcano. Child psychologists agree that toddlers cannot control their tantrums and that the outpouring of pent-up rage is frightening for them.

Virtually all toddlers will have tantrums, some more frequently than others. Tantrums take a variety of forms. A child may scream wildly. Some run around; others fall on the floor, kicking and thrashing. Some children hold their breath until they turn ashen, and a few may even pass out from breath holding. Since tantrums can be disturbing, parents should warn other caretakers of what may occur. (For more advice about managing tantrums, see "Tantrums in Public," page 121.)

Think of a toddler's tantrum as a speeding car without brakes: You can't stop it, but you can steer its course to avoid a major collision.

- Stay calm and prevent your toddler from hurting himself or anyone else.

- If he tolerates being touched, cradle him gently in your arms and soothe him until the anger dissolves.

- If he won't be touched, stand back, watch closely, and step in only to stop him from doing anything—flinging himself against walls or furniture, for example, or throwing things—that can cause physical harm to himself or others.

- Don't try to argue or reason with him during a tantrum. It's pointless and will only increase your own frustration and fear.

Toddlers feel anxiety and stress, especially when they begin spending more time away from their parents. They often become attached to items that they associate with their caregivers—a blanket, favorite toy, or item of clothing. Comfort activities can include thumb-sucking, using pacifiers, hair twisting, ear pulling, and rhythmic noises and motions. Keep in mind that the behavior is normal and:

- *Respect your child's feelings.* Most children outgrow their blankies, teddies, and pacifiers at around age four. After that age, you can consider weaning your child from the habit; your health-care provider can give suggestions.

- *Keep comfort items clean.* Wash and dry items when your child is asleep. Or let her help with the washing; she'll see that you aren't taking the object away. Your child may accept two identical items; she can have one while you clean the other.

- *Make convenient substitutions.* If your one-year-old shows a preference for a large blanket, you may be able to cut the blanket down to a manageable size. But tread lightly. If your child is deeply attached to an object, you could add to her anxiety by altering or removing it.

- *Remember that comfort items and habits are related to your child's sense of security.* If your child's attachment seems extreme, ask yourself what kind of pressures she is under. If there is no obvious stress or the behavior seems obsessive, consult your physician or health-care provider.

A toddler's attachment can be worrisome in social situations. Most adults ignore the activity or are amused, but some will make disparaging comments when they see an older toddler sucking her thumb or dragging a blanket. The best advice is to ignore thoughtless remarks. Do explain your child's behavior to relatives and close friends.

Don't show amusement if the child's antics look funny. Laughing at an angry child may encourage future tantrums if he thinks his behavior gets positive attention.

- Depending on your child's temperament, ignoring the tantrum may be the best course. Be watchful, but appear to go about your business.

- When the storm passes, you may want to try a brief time-out or simply leave him to be quiet for a while. Then let the incident go: no lectures or punishments. If your child wants reassurance, embrace him in loving arms.

- Don't condemn your child for the behavior. Be tactful and considerate. He isn't "bad" or a "little monster" because he had a tantrum. He's a frustrated child.

Early Decision Making

ALLOWING YOUR CHILD TO MAKE some decisions on his own is a good way to promote thinking skills and teach mannerly behavior. You can begin by offering clear-cut choices whenever feasible. If you ask your toddler an open-ended question such as, "What do you want to wear to playgroup today?" he may be totally befuddled or come up with something preposterous. Instead, give him two reasonable options—his red shirt or green shirt—so that he can make a choice that suits him and you.

Offering choices affirms to your child that you value his opinions and want his involvement in at least some of the decisions that affect him.

- **Be certain that you can make good on the choice.** If he often makes choices only to be told you can't fulfill them, he will naturally be disappointed and may lose trust in you or come to distrust his own decision making.

- **Don't give choices when you can't control the outcome.** For instance, an expectant parent should not ask a child whether he would like a baby brother or baby sister. A youngster must learn that there are some things no one can control. He needs to realize that he can control his own reactions even when he can't control the situation itself.

- **Don't overwhelm your child with choices.** If you turn every little activity into a choice, he will probably feel overwhelmed. Too many choices given too early may promote indecision rather than thoughtful decision making.

- **Give your child opportunities to make some wrong decisions.** Use your common sense about the circumstances, but there are times when a bad choice can be very instructive. When your two-year-old insists on wearing a heavy sweater for a trip to the park on a warm day, don't fight about it. He'll soon enough complain about his discomfort. Change him into cooler clothes and talk about how people dress for the weather (a good first lesson about appropriate dress for all occasions). Even if he refuses to back down, he may remember the uncomfortable experience and learn not to repeat it.

- **Avoid "I told you so."** A child who is frequently subjected to "I-told-you-so" comments is likely to feel belittled, and his self-confidence can suffer. Do talk about and explain specific wrong choices. Toddlers are literal in their understanding, so choose your words carefully. A parent may say that a choice was "dumb" or "stupid," but the child will hear that *he* is dumb or stupid.

CHAPTER 7

Respecting Others

BY DEMONSTRATING COOPERATION AND GENUINE respect for others in your own relationships, you are preparing your child for later lessons in the essentials of civility, courtesy, and consideration. Between one and three years, your youngster's awareness of and reactions to others will grow more sophisticated. She still sees everything from her own point of view, but she is increasingly aware of how other people affect her and how she can affect them.

Welcoming a New Baby

WHEN A NEW BABY ARRIVES, your toddler may seem to take the newcomer in stride or even to ignore the new brother or sister at first. But a new sibling, especially when the baby becomes mobile, is inevitably something of a threat to a young child.

A new baby demands your care just at the time when your toddler most craves your attention. It is very common for toddlers to regress to babyish behavior—asking for a bottle or diapers, crying to be held—soon after the arrival of a new baby. The toddler, being a literal thinker, tries to reclaim the top spot in your heart by imitating the baby. Her regressive behavior is the result of her love for and dependence on you, not defiance.

Helping a Toddler Cope

Your toddler cannot explain uncomfortable feelings like anger, resentment, fear, and sadness. So she acts them out. It is a parent's job to recognize the signs and respond without encouraging regression or other attention-seeking behaviors. There is much you can do to help your toddler cope with a new baby.

- *Don't overreact to regressive behavior.* When your toddler asks for a bottle or deliberately wets her pants, she is really seeking your attention. If you become angry, she will read your reaction as attention. Give her the bottle or clean up the mess; then calmly tell her how much you prefer her "grown-up" behavior.

- *Find compromises you can both live with.* If your toddler wants to be breast-fed, she probably needs cuddling. Let her sit close beside you as you feed the baby; then give her some lap time when the baby is finished and back in the crib.

- *Include your toddler in your baby's care.* Give your toddler a role to play when you bathe, diaper, and dress the baby. By allowing your toddler to participate, you are giving positive attention, teaching her what it means to care for another person, and encouraging bonding between your children. There are several caveats, however:

  - Don't force your toddler to participate, and don't show disappointment if she isn't interested.

  - Make it clear that the toddler is never to pick up, carry, feed, change, bathe, or perform any tasks for the baby unless you are present to supervise. *Never leave your toddler alone with the baby.*

  - Never give a young child responsibilities she can't handle. For example, don't expect a toddler to feed her little brother. She can't handle a messy, wiggling baby, and she may feel that she has failed you.

- **Talk to your toddler about her feelings.** Children need to be reassured that feelings like sadness and unhappiness are normal. Avoid any comments she can interpret as negative criticism of herself or the baby. Let her know that you understand how she feels and that you sympathize.

- **Make time to be alone with your toddler.** You can plan special activities, but this isn't essential. Just having your undivided attention for a half-hour or so each day will gladden a toddler's heart.

- **Stop aggressive behavior immediately and firmly.** Stay calm. Tell the older child in simple, straightforward language that hitting, slapping, smacking, pinching, or in any way hurting the baby, or anyone else, is never acceptable. Be prepared to repeat the lesson as often as needed, but keep in mind that the toddler who pokes her baby sibling may be acting out of normal curiosity and not hostility.

Toddlers and Older Siblings

TODDLERS INVOLVED IN CONFLICTS WITH older siblings are not as helpless as you might expect and may even be the aggressors. You will probably feel that you must be the fair arbiter in every quarrel. But it may be best, depending on the situation, to give your children the opportunity to work out their problems on their own.

Always stop any physical aggression and be clear that fighting is not allowed. Parents are inclined to assume that an older child is at fault, but younger children can be quite adept at provoking their older siblings. If you haven't witnessed the conflict, you will do well to question the circumstantial evidence and withhold judgment until you have some testimony. With their growing ability to imagine, what toddlers imagine to be true *is* true in their minds. This imaginative ability can be one of the delights of early childhood, but it also makes toddlers highly unreliable when it comes to getting the facts.

Resolving Conflicts

· Showing respect for each child's age, experience, and individuality is critical. Your older child deserves to be heard and then evaluated fairly. Assuming he is normally truthful, honor his record and believe his account. The older child needs your commiseration; the toddler may need a brief time-out to soothe her emotions followed by a clear, firm explanation of why the aggressive behavior is unacceptable and what the future consequences will be.

Sometimes you may feel that you need the wisdom of Solomon (not to mention the patience of Buddha) to sort out sibling conflicts, but don't give up. You are teaching your children important lessons in conflict resolution. How you help your children to settle their disagreements will exemplify some of the most fundamental principles of moral and mannerly behavior:

- Honesty and truth telling
- Balancing self-respect with respect for the rights of others
- Self-control
- Compromise and negotiation
- Reasoned rather than emotional problem solving
- Peaceful rather than violent resolutions

Playing with Peers

USUALLY, IT'S NOT UNTIL A child has turned two or three that she begins to show any interest in playing *with* children of a similar age. A one- or two-year-old is still on the verge of grasping intellectually that she is an independent person; she can't care much about other children until she establishes her own individuality. However, during the toddler years, your youngster will learn a lot of the basics of cooperation, sharing, and getting along.

It's normal for young toddlers to ignore one another and go about their own interests. Your child may engage in parallel play—side-by-side activity in which toddlers share the same space but do not interact. She may also imitate or mirror another toddler's activity. This parallel and imitative play will eventually become more cooperative.

Aggressive behavior is common among young toddlers, but it's unlikely your child is being a bully when he hits or bites another child. He's probably curious and wants to see what the child will do—just as he explores a new toy. Stop the aggression quickly and firmly, and comfort the aggrieved party. Then explain to both children that hitting, poking, punching, scratching, biting, and the like are wrong because they cause pain to another person. Avoid casting children in the roles of victim and victimizer. And stay calm. If you overreact, you tend to lose the opportunity to teach correct behavior. Worse, the little hitter or biter may get the impression that aggression is a good way to get adult attention.

Introducing Sharing

Sharing is one of the grounding principles of good manners, so begin your child's lessons now. Whether your toddler is naturally shy or outgoing, be sensitive to her feelings and avoid pushing her into social behavior that is uncomfortable for her. Toddlers may interact sporadically, and you can praise this behavior, but don't expect a few minutes of sharing between two-year-olds to become a pattern anytime soon.

A good place to start is by demonstrating and encouraging turn taking. Introduce the concept and model taking turns with other family members. ("When Daddy finishes reading the magazine, I'll have my turn.") Use simple activities including:

- *Playing turn-taking games.* Stacking blocks with your child will give her practice at taking turns: She stacks a block, then you, and so forth. She'll discover that sharing is fun.

- *Using a cooking timer to set limits on activities.* This is a good tactic to use with siblings. Your toddler can have an item in dispute until the timer rings or buzzes, and then her brother gets the toy until the timer buzzes again. It won't always work but is worth a try.

- *Taking turns in your playgroup.* Pass out snacks to one child at a time rather than letting them all grab at once. Teach toddlers how to line up for turns on the slide or swing. While it's not productive to force toddlers to cooperate, repeated turn-taking experiences teach that they don't have to be first in order to get what they want.

Playgroup Etiquette

Exposure to peers can promote early socialization. Toddlers in day care or a regular playgroup sometimes begin to interact with their peers and even form something akin to friendships as early as the end of their second year, but don't worry if your toddler remains uninterested in anyone but herself until she is three or older. Think of exposure to other children as the preamble to real peer interaction. At the same time, remember that toddlers who are not routinely around peers catch up quickly when they enter nursery school or kindergarten.

If you participate in a playgroup, the etiquette recommendations discussed in Part One (see "Playgroups and Other Children," page 19) still apply, but adult members of the playgroup will want to revisit some questions, including:

- **Discipline.** Parents should discuss how to discipline and when it's appropriate to discipline children other than their own. Quick action is necessary to stop aggressive behavior. You'll be more comfortable letting other parents handle a problem if you have all discussed the issues of setting limits and discipline and agreed on procedures.

- **Scheduling.** Schedules change as toddlers need fewer hours of sleep during the day. As nap routines change, you may need to adjust the hours of your gatherings. If your child's nap pattern is out of sync with the majority of the playgroup, it may become necessary to take a break from the group for a while or find a group that meets at a better time for you.

- **Introducing new participants.** The makeup of playgroups is rarely static, and the adults must decide how to bring in new members. Be sure that new parents understand your rules and expectations, and take the time to answer their questions. If you join an established group, be certain that you are willing to accept its standards and rules.

- **Supervision.** As they grow, toddlers become increasingly adept at entertaining themselves, but they still cannot be left unsupervised. Maintain a ratio of one adult at minimum for every three or four children, and be sure that all parents take their turns watching the children.

Playdate Etiquette

Playdates are fun and also offer socializing opportunities for children who aren't in day care or playgroups. Once the toddlers feel comfortable, one parent can mind them while the other gets a much-needed hour or two of free time. Just be sure to establish the rules with the other parent or parents in advance.

- *Set clear starting and ending times and adhere to them.* When you leave your little one, always return on time. If you must arrive early, return late, or cancel the playdate, let the other parent know as soon as you can.

- *Be clear about whether the playdate includes the parent.* When you first get toddlers together, it's advisable for both parents to stay with the children. This allows the visiting youngster to get used to new people and surroundings. As the relationship grows, children can be left with one parent for longer periods. If you live some distance apart, you or the other parent may want to stay during the playdate for convenience, so be prepared to welcome the parent for the duration of a visit. When you leave your toddler with another parent, always provide a phone number or numbers where you can be reached.

- *Consult about feeding and other care and health issues.* What kinds of snacks are acceptable? Is your little guest allergic to anything? If you have a house pet, tell the other parent. Children may be allergic to or especially fearful of animals, so you may have to keep Rover outside during the playdate.

  If a child is on medication or has special health needs, parents should not expect another parent to be nurse. Never leave your child with anyone who is not fully qualified for and agreeable to the responsibility. If your child is ill—with or without a fever—you should always cancel the playdate as soon as possible.

- *Provide all the necessary supplies when your child is the guest,* including diapers, wipe-ups, and extra clothing.

- **Have plenty of toys and activities on hand when you host a playdate.** Since young toddlers won't play together, you should be prepared to keep each child entertained individually. Older toddlers become quite possessive, so a well-stocked toy chest may help prevent battles.

- **Keep it casual.** A playdate is a socializing opportunity for toddlers, not an excuse for parents to practice their formal entertaining skills. The objective is to accustom youngsters to the company of other children and to establish and model the basics of everyday interactions.

- **Allow the toddlers to set the pace.** On a first visit, toddlers may do nothing but cling to their parents or whine to leave. Don't despair. It may take several playdates for the children to feel comfortable. You can plan activities, but if they aren't interested, don't push. Look for activities, such as reading a storybook or building with blocks, that you can do with both children. Sharing an experience with you is an effective way to introduce toddlers to the mechanics of sharing with peers.

A Question for Peggy and Cindy ◂◂

My two-and-a-half-year-old son has a weekly playdate with his friend Stephen. But I've begun to dread get-togethers at my house because Stephen is prone to scattering bins of toys on the floor and intentionally spilling his milk. When his mother comes to get him, she doesn't say anything to him about the mess, nor does she offer to clean up. Is it okay to say something to her?

When Stephen's mother arrives, engage her in the cleanup by saying, "If you have a few minutes, I'd like to have the boys toss the toys back in the box. It won't take long." Children at this age won't show the initiative in picking up, and they'll only attend to it for a few minutes, but they can take part in the process. Stephen's mother may even pitch in and help. You can also start the cleanup a few minutes before she arrives. When you speak with her, be careful not to criticize her son or imply that this is a discipline issue she's neglected. Putting away is simply the routine expectation at your house.

◂◂

- **Prepare older children.** If you have older children, give them notice that their younger sibling is going to have a visitor and be clear about their role in the event. A child age four or older can often play very well with toddlers, but parents shouldn't expect an older sibling to babysit. Even if an older child is present, *never leave the toddlers unsupervised by an adult.*

- **Reciprocate.** The best thanks you can give to someone who hosts a playdate is to issue a similar invitation for the earliest convenient time.

Dealing with Adults

A CHILD'S CONTACTS WITH ADULTS increase throughout the toddler years. There are grandparents and relatives, babysitters, child-care workers, family friends, and neighbors. There are the health-care providers whom she sees regularly but infrequently and adults who pop in and out of her day—mail carriers, delivery people, supermarket clerks, bus drivers, pharmacists, and repair persons.

How your child reacts to other adults will be governed in part by her emotional development and also by the example you set. An outgoing toddler may happily approach other adults. A shyer child may hang back, ducking her head or hiding behind you when a stranger is introduced. Young toddlers may go through a phase of *stranger suspicion* and fear any adults other than their primary caregivers. Or your toddler may simply balk at being talked to or touched by people she doesn't know well. A toddler's reactions to adults are unpredictable and not always easy to regulate.

Don't be embarrassed by your toddler's "manners" with new people. Chances are your child has a perfectly logical reason, in her own mind, for her reaction. You can, however, encourage your toddler's sociability and take the tension out of difficult situations.

- **Prepare and explain.** Whenever possible, prepare adults for your toddler's standoffish behavior, especially grandparents and others who have a close relationship. Adults should greet the child quietly, acknowledge her presence, and then visit with you until your toddler warms to them. If your child is willing, take

Mannerly Role-Playing Is Fun

Toddlers love to play at grown-up behavior with parents. You can make use of your child's interest in play-acting to share good times and teach etiquette. Role-playing allows you to demonstrate appropriate etiquette for a wealth of situations, to introduce concepts such as sharing and taking turns, and to promote imitation of mannerly behaviors.

A pretend tea party lets your toddler act out proper table manners—setting a table with toy dishes and utensils, sharing, and conversing with you, his dolls, and other inanimate "guests." You can initiate role-playing games that exemplify good meeting and greeting habits, with your little one playing the child's role and then taking the part of an adult meeting a child. Role reversal like this encourages your toddler to put himself in another's position and experience another person's feelings in a rudimentary way. Keep it fun, and the learning will come naturally.

---

her to the door when someone you know arrives. Don't push the child forward; just let her see you welcome your visitor.

When you meet an adult without advance notice—running into an old friend while shopping, for example—quietly explain that your child is in a phase of being fearful or anxious around other adults. Most people won't take your child's behavior personally. But it's a good idea not to make such explanations within your child's hearing; she may think that she is doing something bad or wrong.

- **Follow your child's cues.** If she runs behind you or cries when someone tries to greet or touch her, don't force her forward. Adults should know better than to approach or touch a child they don't know well, but some can't restrain their impulse to kiss, pat, tickle, or pick up a cute youngster. You can't change the adult's behavior, but you should always protect your child from unwanted physical contact.

- **Always demonstrate the correct manners for meeting and greeting.** Even if your toddler is whimpering and clinging to you, she's still watching and learning. Show your good manners

whenever greeting another adult. You may want to keep a meeting short if you're in a public place, but take the time for a
friendly greeting, a few words, and a pleasant good-bye. Introduce your child, but keep it brief and don't expect your little one
to respond. If the other adult is inclined to chat, you can politely
excuse yourself without laying the blame on your child. ("I'm
sorry to run off, but it's almost Corinne's nap time, and we still
have a couple of errands.")

- *Set clear limits for a toddler who is too open to strangers.*
  Some children love new people and have no sense of propriety or
  fear. In addition to the possible hazards of approaching
  unknown people (see "Stranger Danger," page 122), your toddler may not always be welcomed. Begin teaching her not to frat-
  ernize with other adults unless a parent is with her. In social and
  professional situations when children are included, it is impolite
  to ask others to entertain your youngster or to leave your child
  with an accommodating adult for longer than a few minutes.

The Groundwork for Courtesy

Some children are naturally gregarious and outgoing; others are not.
But all children can learn to be courteous and to show respect for adults.
During the toddler years, the following ideas will help you lay the
groundwork for good manners:

- *Introduce the language and rituals of meeting and greeting.*
  The process usually begins around age one with "hi" and "bye"
  and waving. By the time your toddler approaches three, she will
  be naming some people and perhaps saying "hello" and "good-
  bye." Once your child becomes relatively comfortable in encounters with new people, you can encourage eye contact and even
  introduce handshaking.

- *Model consideration and respect and explain to your toddler
  what you are doing and why.* For instance, when you hold a
  door open for someone, tell your child exactly why you do so.
  ("The lady was carrying lots of packages. It would be hard for
  her to open the door. It feels nice to be helpful.") Be sure to use
  your best manners within the family circle. You want your child

Relying on Friends

With many parents living far away from their families, a few good friends can be a godsend. But friendships need careful tending, and the following ideas will help you nurture and maintain friendships that are meaningful to you and your child:

- **Understand and accept diverse child-rearing values and methods.** You don't have to agree with your friend on everything, but common ground on key issues such as discipline, eating, and sleep schedules will make everyone more comfortable. Be realistic: As long as a friend's home is child-safe and clean, her casual housekeeping methods are of little consequence. Besides, children need to be exposed to diversity if they are to become tolerant, considerate, and open-minded adults.

- **Talk openly and calmly about any problems that arise.** If your friend, who knows that you restrict your child's sugar intake, serves candy and soda pop during a playdate, don't speak from raw emotion. Calm down and honestly evaluate the problem. Then find a quiet time to discuss the problem when children aren't around. Don't let your resentment simmer until the friendship evaporates.

- **Model respect for friends.** Always speak of your friends with respect, and never involve your child in disagreements. Express your gratitude to friends for favors and kindnesses. Your child is learning about human relationships by observing you.

- **Be a giver as well as a taker.** Except in a real emergency, don't expect a friend to watch your child without being asked in advance. Supply whatever your child needs and reimburse expenses. Give your friend a break when you can and volunteer to mind her child. If a friend is imposing on you excessively, let her know how important the friendship is to you but that your time is limited. Work it out together. And remember to receive criticism in the same spirit.

- **Value the friendship for what it is.** Parents can often form strong bonds based solely on their mutual concern for their children. A friendship that develops between parents may expand to other areas, or it may not. Either way, it should be valued and respected.

to see that good behavior and consideration for others are natural and consistent—not something to turn on and off like a faucet.

- **Expose your child to the company of adults.** A toddler needs to see you interacting with a variety of people. Over time, let your child get to know all the people who are part of your daily life. Tell her who the people are and what role they play in her life. By introducing your child to the adults in her world and encouraging respect, you help her learn that she is not the center of the universe—a basic principle of courteous behavior.

- **Avoid negative or stereotyped characterizations of others.** Obviously, you should never use hateful terms such as racial, ethnic, and religious slurs. But it can be easy to slip into negative remarks without realizing it. If parents consistently refer to a neighbor as "fat, old Mr. Wilson," their child is likely to do the same. Even playful epithets—as when adults call one another by childhood names such as "Stinky" or "Smarty-pants"—can convey negative impressions. Characterizations that seem harmless to adults may frighten toddlers away from perfectly fine adults and promote negative stereotypes that the child then applies generally. (If a parent conveys the message that there is something odd about Mr. Wilson, who is "old and fat," what is the child to think about Grandpapa, who is also gray-haired and a bit on the heavy side?)

- **Avoid criticizing or labeling your child for reticent or standoffish behavior.** Be empathetic. Your child isn't necessarily scared, rude, bad-tempered, or babyish because she doesn't want to be pawed. By respecting your child's feelings now, you support her emotional security and prepare her for considerate meeting and greeting behavior later on.

Respect for Property

RESPECT FOR PROPERTY IS AN extension of respect for self and others. Young toddlers, however, have no real concept of property, although the typical two-year-old says "mine" almost as frequently as "no." Initially, the toddler applies "mine" and "my" to just about everything—*my*

When your child advances to nursery school or kindergarten, the move is welcomed by everyone. But you may want to change your child-care arrangement for less felicitous reasons. It isn't easy to leave a day-care service or to let a nanny or babysitter go because of a serious problem, and these suggestions may help:

- **Give notice.** You probably want to remove your child from a troubled situation immediately, but whatever your reasons for the change, you should inform the provider and honor any contractual obligations.

- **Be honest, but avoid accusations.** The provider needs to know about problems with the actual care of your child—lack of attention, unsanitary conditions, unqualified or abusive workers, and the like. Be calm and clear when you explain. It usually helps to document your experiences and observations so that you can keep the discussion on an objective plane. Most professional child-care providers want to know about problems in order to correct them.

- **Be concerned about other children.** You have a moral obligation to protect other children from harm. If the problem poses a threat to other children, contact the appropriate local and state authorities immediately. Give them your documentation—facts, not rumors and gossip. Ask to be informed about the actions they take. If you feel that nothing is being done, take your concerns to a higher authority.

- **Be tactful if the problem doesn't involve serious issues such as unsafe conditions or negligence.** Your child may be unhappy in a day-care program that doesn't suit his temperament, or you may prefer a different approach to child minding. These kinds of problems are not the provider's fault. It's enough to explain that you have found a more convenient arrangement. Be sure to thank the provider for the services you have received.

- **Be firm but considerate if you have to fire an in-home worker.** Presumably you have given warning if the problem is not threatening to your child's safety and well-being. If the issue is a clash of personalities or methods, there's no need for anger and recriminations. Keep the discussion on a professional level. Do it privately—not in front of your child. Offer to provide a reference if you feel comfortable doing so.

- **Evaluate your experience.** Ask yourself the difficult questions: Were you clear about your expectations? Did you investigate the provider thoroughly in advance? Did you let a problem grow before taking action? By evaluating a failed arrangement—and being honest about your role—you will be better prepared to make a satisfactory choice the next time.

----

dollie, *my* bathtub, *my* grocery store—and means it literally. Toward the end of her second year, she begins to understand that other people have possessions ("my dress" versus "Mommy's dress"). As she approaches her third birthday, she will probably have a fairly well-developed concept of ownership, but respect for property is closely related to sharing—and most children aren't ready for sharing until age three or older.

Parent of toddlers have to walk a thin line when teaching respect for property. You want your child to know that she does not own everything while remaining sensitive to her developmental capabilities.

- **Continue to set limits.** While setting and enforcing limits, it's important not to restrict too much or overdo "don't touch." Do make absolutely sure that her environment is full of safe objects and playthings.

- **Watch for physical hazards.** A toddler driven by curiosity knows no bounds and has little sense of personal danger. Protect your child first, and then your possessions. Keep your home and surroundings child-safe, reinforce the concept of off-limits for unsafe and private areas, and teach and enforce restrictions consistently. Be cognizant of her growth and improving physical capabilities. Things that were once beyond her reach, like the stove top and doorknobs, are now accessible. Your health-care provider and child-rearing manuals will provide comprehensive safety information and advice.

- **Protect your home.** A toddler can sometimes seem like a small wrecking crew. Things play an important role in her imaginative life, and when she is off on a make-believe adventure, your house and its contents become props for her play.

If your child draws on walls and furniture, what do you do? You want to encourage creativity, but not at the cost of repainting and expensive repairs. A few approaches you can use to save your surface include:

- *Teach your child to associate artwork with paper, and keep plenty on hand*—the bigger the better.

- *Set up an art area in the kitchen or other uncarpeted space that is easy to clean.* Provide a sturdy child-sized table and chairs. If a project is particularly messy, spread a drop cloth on the floor. You might install a large chalkboard on the wall, but avoid easels that can collapse and cut or pinch little fingers. When the weather permits, take the artwork outside.

- *Always supervise painting, pasting, and the use of pens, pencils, and scissors.* Keep art materials locked away when not in use. Purchase only nontoxic, water-based, washable paints, colored pens, pastes, and play clays.

- *Include your toddler in the cleanup.* Let him wipe his table and help put supplies away. Praise his creations *and* his cleaning. Cleanup and picking-up rituals promote cooperation and help him understand that cleaning is the necessary follow-up to making messes.

If your toddler does scribble on the wallpaper or furniture, try not to get upset. Explain clearly that he is never to write on walls or furniture; then get him to participate in the cleaning. If he marks on the walls in someone else's home, offer to clean up or to reimburse cleaning expenses.

---◄◄

Since a toddler's movements cannot be restricted in the same way as an infant's, you will probably be making more areas available to your child. But most of the recommendations in Part One still apply (see "Respecting Property," page 26). Protect or store valuables, keep off-limits areas latched, encourage "putting-away" routines, and carefully guard the possessions and privacy of older siblings.

Choosing Toys and Activities

TODDLERS LEARN BY PLAYING, AND at this imaginative age they can make practically anything into a toy. When you purchase toys or others ask for gift suggestions for your child, keep these fundamentals in mind. All toys should be safe and:

- **Developmentally appropriate.** Select toys in keeping with a toddler's abilities. Pay attention to the manufacturer's age range recommendations and consult your child-rearing guides for recommendations.

- **Interesting.** A good toy can be used in more than one way. A shape-sorting box, for instance, can become a little table, part of a building project, and a seat for a stuffed toy. Be guided by what attracts your child's interest. If she likes to watch Mom and Dad do repairs, a set of toy tools may be just the thing.

- **Challenging.** Look for toys that encourage intellectual development. Beginner puzzles with two or three pieces are fun for young toddlers, promote hand-eye coordination, and encourage problem solving. Once your child masters the simplest puzzles, move on to more difficult versions. Picture books illustrated with bright, realistic images have high toddler appeal. Electronic and computer toys, however, offer few creative challenges at this stage.

Tasks for Toddlers

IT WILL BE YEARS BEFORE you can trust your child to take out the garbage or wash the dishes. But it's not too soon to introduce the concept of personal responsibility. (Start now, and she will be a most welcome houseguest in the future.) Use your toddler's natural imitative impulse to encourage good housekeeping habits. Let your child help you with daily chores. She can lend a hand when you do the laundry—sorting colors and tossing dirty clothes in the washer. With supervision, an older toddler can help remove dishes from the dishwasher. Let her wad up your junk mail and throw it into the wastebasket. When she is old enough, she can help you make up her bed. Under your watchful eye, she can pick up leaves and pull weeds in the garden.

Safety Concerns

One of the most significant demonstrations of respect for your child is the provision of safe playthings. Do not buy toys with small pieces that can be detached and swallowed. (A choke tube, available at most toy stores, will let you check the size of objects. Anything you can insert in the tube is too small.) Avoid items with hinges, springs, and gears that can pinch or cut, long strings and ribbons that may cause strangulation, and any sharp or rough edges, points, or projections. Secure battery compartments with heavy tape. Avoid balls and toys made from sponge-like material; toddlers may bite them and can choke on the pieces. Very loud items may cause hearing damage. Inspect and clean toys routinely and discard any cracked or broken items. Check with your child's physician or health-care provider for more safety information.

Her interest in helping will be sporadic, and she isn't ready for chores. But she will begin to get the message that people are responsible for themselves and their things if you:

- **Set the example by maintaining reasonable order in your home** and letting your toddler see you picking up, putting away, straightening, and cleaning without complaint.

- **Involve the whole family.** Even if you are fortunate enough to have paid household help, your child needs to see that everyone in the family has responsibilities.

- **Talk about responsibility.** Tell your toddler how important it is to care for her own things and the possessions of others. Look for opportunities to discuss other people's rights and needs. ("Daddy hasn't read his newspaper yet. If we paint on it, he will be unhappy because he really enjoys reading the news.")

- **Always praise your child when she helps,** especially when she does something on her own such as picking up her clothes or putting toys away.

- **Make it easy and fun for your toddler to be responsible.** Put a low clothes hamper in her room. Give her a bookshelf and color-ful containers for her books and toys. Maintain a picking-up routine before bedtime. Sing while you and your child clean up; "Whistle While You Work" and other tunes add to a child's sense that chores are positive activities.

- **Be conscious of her limitations.** When she fails to put away her toys after you ask her to, be patient. Encourage her to complete the task by joining in and helping.

Protecting the Property of Others

WHEN YOU AND YOUR TODDLER are invited to visit the homes of relatives and friends, there are three main points of etiquette to consider:

- **Give your host or hostess advance warning.** Explain that your toddler is very active and tends to get "into everything." It would be rude to tell your host to rearrange his house, but if the person asks for suggestions, by all means give them. If he seems hesitant at the idea of hosting a toddler, you might consider getting a babysitter and visiting on your own or suggest having the get-together at your house instead.

- **Try to schedule visits when your child is rested and fed.** Keep your visits relatively short. Most hosts would rather you leave early than have everyone endure a tired toddler's "meltdown."

- **Watch your child's every move when you visit.** A new or different environment is full of attractions for a toddler, and her natural instinct will be to explore. Don't allow your child to wander, and anticipate accidents. Bringing your child's favorite toy or book may help if your host does not have items appropriate for child's play.

CHAPTER 8

Building Communication Skills

BETWEEN ONE AND THREE YEARS, your child is going to perform one of humankind's greatest feats: learning a language. At age one, he will have a very small speaking vocabulary though his mental dictionary will be somewhat larger. By age two, he may know several hundred words and have the ability to put together simple two-word sentences. When he turns three, his language vault may include as many as a thousand words, his sentences will be more complex, and he will be using some of the fundamentals of grammar. His language development is essential to all future social interactions and good manners.

Normal rates of acquisition and use of spoken language, however, vary dramatically, and a child's interest level is a key factor. Some children are just more interested in their burgeoning physical abilities and would rather be playing. Others develop an efficient "vocabulary" of sounds, gestures, and other nonverbal language. When caregivers are always quick to anticipate and satisfy a child's needs, the toddler may be slow at using words because he doesn't need to. Whatever the reasons, language development is not predictable and should not be forced on toddlers.

Encouraging Language Learning

EARLY ATTENTION AND ENCOURAGEMENT BY close caregivers promote a child's understanding, use, and appreciation of communication
skills. In fact, language acquisition helps with thinking and cognitive
development. Articulate, well-spoken, and learning-oriented adults are
more often than not the products of homes where language is valued.

- **Talk with your child.** He can't learn what he doesn't hear. Naming things and people is extremely important. Repetition is critical for building a child's vocabulary.

- **Be precise.** Most toddlers tend to generalize. For example, the
  family cat is a furry creature with four legs and a tail, so any animal that meets the general description will be a "cat" or "kitty."
  Some toddlers limit their labeling to specifics: "chair" may mean
  only the rocking chair in the child's room. With gentle correction and explanation, you can help your child distinguish
  between similar things. ("Yes, that does look like a car. But it's a
  truck. A truck is bigger than a car.") A child's understanding of
  general categories and specifics will become more exact with
  experience.

- **Be descriptive.** Use adjectives and adverbs to describe the people
  and things in your child's world. Vary your descriptions so that
  your child will hear that there are many ways to express a
  thought.

  - Describe things by color, shape, position, and direction.
    ("Use that big red napkin beside your plate to wipe your
    mouth, please.")

  - Use a variety of action verbs. ("We are driving to Grandma's
    house today. We'll probably visit for a while. Let's remember
    to thank her when we leave.")

  - Introduce words and terms that express time. ("It's time
    now to go to playgroup. We don't want to be late.")

  - Give your child the words to express feelings and needs and
    relate abstract terms to concrete situations. ("I was glad to

Reading Together

One of the best ways to build your toddler's communication skills and promote sharing is by reading together. Encourage participation by asking her
to point out objects in picture books; she may not be saying the words, but
she is learning their meanings. You'll soon move on to simple story and
rhyming books, including early etiquette books written for toddlers. Keep
reading sessions short, but extend reading time as your toddler's attention
span and interest increase. Cuddling up for a story is part of many nap
and bedtime rituals, but include some daytime reading so that your child
learns reading is an activity and not just a soother.

Don't rely on television to teach. Even the best children's programming
is like half of a conversation. There is no feedback with the TV set, so there
is no interaction. Some exposure may help reinforce a toddler's language
skills, but television is no substitute for talking and reading.

meet your friend Matt at day care. I know you feel happy
when you play with him.")

- **Model correct speech.** A young child needs to hear language
used correctly and politely—complete sentences, clear pronunciation, and proper grammar. Exposing your toddler to correct
speech is much more important than correcting his grammar.

Use respectful language. If parents pepper their speech with
slang and swear words, their toddler will imitate. An easy test is
to ask yourself, "If Will said this in front of his grandmother,
would I be embarrassed?"

- **Help with pronunciation.** Children regularly mispronounce
some words until they are six or older. You can help by correcting your toddler's errors without criticism. He may point to his
picture book and exclaim, "Helafump!" Give him a cheer and say,
"That's right. That's a picture of an *elephant*."

Reinforcing and Expanding the "Magic Words"

Saying "please" and "thank you" is so fundamental to good manners
that you will want to model these courtesies at all times. Say "please"

when you ask your child to give you something and "thank you" when he complies. Say "please" and "thank you" among the members of your family and to the people you deal with daily. When "please" and "thank you" and other verbal courtesies are natural to you, your toddler will soon want to imitate. Explain why these words are important—that when we want something or when someone does something nice and helpful for us, it's important to be nice in return. Experience will teach him that people usually respond positively when he uses "please" and "thank you."

If you want your children to address adults as "sir" and "ma'am," by all means introduce these terms now. Use of "sir" and "ma'am," which was once expected of all children, is now largely a matter of individual parental choice and local custom.

Your child will probably learn "please" sooner than "thank you" simply because "please" often gets him what he wants and "thank you" doesn't produce tangible results. But don't pressure your toddler to use courtesy remarks or criticize when he forgets. He should sense from your behavior that polite speech comes from genuine consideration for the feelings of other people. For now, the most effective teachers are your example and consistent encouragement.

The Importance of Listening

One of the essential elements of polite behavior is good listening, which is learned first through a parent's example. Parents should be their child's most attentive and appreciative audience. Listen closely and show your delight in his communication efforts. Just don't overdo it. Praise is an effective motivator when it is deserved.

It's not always easy to interpret a toddler's speech, so watch as well as listen, and follow your child's nonverbal cues. For example, if he says "grim ka" while pointing to his toy box, you can probably guess that he wants something from the box. Through trial and error, you establish that he wants a toy car. Now take a moment to say, "You want me to give you the car? Good talking!"

Toddlers will also attempt to say things that you simply cannot understand—frustrating for you and more so for your child. One of the causes of bad behavior in the terrible two's is a young child's inability to verbalize his thoughts. Sometimes you can guess his feelings and verbal-

After the first year, it's time for parents and caregivers to give up *parentese*—the exaggerated speech habits and terminology that work so well with infants. Continuing to talk to your toddler as if she were a baby robs her of the challenge presented by more advanced speech and can interfere with her ability to interact socially. A toddler learns language in a specific order—words first, then phrases, and finally sentences—but you are modeling all three elements. Though toddler speech can be adorable, you want to set the correct example. Her blanket will probably be her "blankie" for some time, but you should say "blanket." When talking with your child, keep your statements and questions relatively simple and speak clearly. If you are a naturally rapid speaker, be aware that your toddler may not get your meaning the first time around, so be ready and willing to repeat.

ize for him ("I took away the crayons and that makes you feel angry"), but don't be too quick to assume you know what's in his little head. Be careful about putting words in his mouth or you may increase his frustration.

What About Computers?

While there has been little comprehensive research into the long-term effects of early exposure to computers, there is some evidence that computer use under age three may encourage shorter attention spans, have negative impact on creative development, and possibly retard language and interpersonal skills including manners. Current best thinking is to wait until a child is at least three before introducing him to the computer. If you do expose your toddler to the PC, always sit with him, talk about what is happening, and limit sessions to fifteen minutes or so.

Vocal Control

IT TAKES YEARS FOR CHILDREN to master their voices. Making sounds is exciting, and many toddlers love to raise the volume as high as possible. A happy, shrieking child, however, is disruptive in many situations, from worship services to the grocery line. Some suggestions for encouraging voice control include:

Question Games

Even before children have the words to form answers, they enjoy playing question games. If your young toddler can shake her head, point, and say "no," you can hold up her cup and ask, "Is this your teddy bear?" She'll get a kick out of your mistake. Then you can supply the correct word for the object.

When her vocabulary and understanding are better, begin to elicit verbal responses. If she points to her cup, ask her, "What do you want?" and give her time to respond. If she knows the words for cup and juice, she may say them. If she doesn't, don't hold out on her. Give her the cup and say the words, adding "please" and "thank you" to the exchange. Question games are a good way to build vocabulary, engage your child in back-and-forth conversation, and encourage use of the "magic words."

- **Use diversion.** If your toddler is screaming for fun, try to redirect him by starting a song or sounds game. Ask him what a dog says. Start a round of "Row, Row, Row Your Boat" or put on his favorite CD of kid tunes and get him to sing along, or turn his high-energy yelling into a marching or running game. You can send an older toddler to a place where loud voices are permitted—his own room, the playroom, or outside.

- **Never try to outshout a toddler.** If you shout at him to stop shouting, he'll conclude that you are joining in the fun and be confused when you become stern or angry. Keeping your voice calm and low gives him the example to follow.

- **Demonstrate different volume levels.** Begin teaching your child to speak softly and to whisper, but be aware that whispering is not an easy skill for most young children. Show him the finger-to-lips signal for quiet. Read stories and recite rhymes in different levels and tones of voice. Use your voice to act out the different characters in your child's bedtime story: When the little mouse in a story whispers, read in a whisper. When a character is sad, read the words in a sad tone. Give your toddler the

When a Child Stutters

Toddlers are so new to spoken language that it's normal for them to stumble over their words. They may stutter when they are tired, excited, or feeling pressured. About a quarter of all toddlers repeat sounds and words. The best advice for parents is to listen attentively and not show impatience or concern by word, tone, or facial expression. Your natural impulse will be to interrupt and help your child complete her thought or to tell her to slow down and begin again. Instead, give her time to get it right. If she becomes frustrated, don't exacerbate the situation by becoming too solicitous. She needs to work this out for herself, and she will. Most early stuttering disappears on its own as a child's language skills develop. If the stuttering seems excessive or prolonged, you should discuss it with your pediatrician.

terms for different sounds, levels, and tones of voice—loud, soft, high, low, whisper, whine, and so on.

- **Introduce "big voice" and "little voice."** When your toddler is about a year and a half, you can put some limits on his noise making. Explain that there are places where he can be loud and places where he must be soft. Introduce the concepts of "big voice" and "little voice." Compliment him when he uses the right voice at the right time.

You will have an easier time teaching your toddler to modulate his voice if you let him be loud when appropriate and don't overdo the hushing and shushing. Some toddlers' voices are just powerful or carry far. What to these children is a normal volume may be disturbing to others. Be sensitive and recognize efforts to speak softly. Above all, avoid making a toddler feel self-conscious; otherwise, he may start avoiding speech, and language development can be slowed. Take heart; with gentle teaching and encouragement, he will learn to control his volume and even to project that strong voice to great effect.

Telephone Manners

INFANTS SEEM TO HAVE A special affinity for toy telephones, so it's probable your toddler has been playing with one for some time. In toddlerhood, the toy becomes a teaching tool, enabling you to introduce the basics of telephone manners, polite conversation, and taking turns.

By age eighteen months or so, your toddler will be getting the idea that a telephone is for talking. When he observes you on the phone, he wants to imitate. This is a good time to begin drawing a distinction between his toy and the real thing. Unless you want your phone sets constantly off the hook, make the real phone off-limits except when you are using it with your toddler.

Use the toy version to introduce good telephone manners. You can hold make-believe conversations, accustom your child to answering with a cheery "hello," and practice talking by turns. Make a game of sitting back-to-back when playing telephone; this will help your toddler begin to understand that it is used for talking to someone he cannot see.

Managing Interruptions

Toddlers are by nature jealous of anything that comes between them and their primary caregivers. When you pick up the receiver and dial a number or answer the phone's ring, your child will fly to your side and demand your attention. He may cling and cuddle, whine, or cry. When he has the verbal skills, he may command in his bossiest tone that you hang up. He might beg for food or start banging toys.

In the preschool years, you can begin to enforce telephone rules, but during the toddler years, parents are wise to be adaptive. There are many techniques for controlling interruptions—special toys to distract your child when you're on the phone, setting a timer and ending the call when the timer goes off, keeping your child close to you while you talk—and some may work occasionally. But none of these approaches are foolproof, and most children soon see through your efforts. When dealing with toddlers and telephones, you should:

- **Schedule long calls for times when your child is not around—** during naps or after he has gone to bed.

- **Make appointments for business calls.** Parents who do business on the home phone need to protect their professional reputations by setting up phone appointments just as they would office meetings. Schedule calls during nap times. If your child awakens and interrupts, arrange a time to call back and end the call as quickly as possible.

- **Keep calls brief when your toddler is with you.** Distractions may keep your child at bay for a few minutes.

- **Limit calls during times when other activities are underway.** If you are playing with or reading to your child or having a family meal, a ringing phone is an annoying distraction. If you repeatedly jump up to answer the phone, he may think you value the phone more than his company. Use your answering machine to manage calls. Most calls can wait until you have the time and solitude to return them.

- **Let your spouse or partner tend to your toddler when you are on the phone.** If a child is secure that he has one parent's attention, he may be less inclined to interrupt the other's phone conversation. If your spouse or partner receives a call, be courteous and take over the child-minding duties.

- **Avoid giving a toddler advance notice when you are about to make a call.** He may begin his antics before you can get the dial tone.

- **Stay calm.** If you become angry or visibly frustrated when he interrupts, your child may think that he has succeeded in regaining the spotlight and repeat his behavior whenever the phone rings.

- **Avoid subjecting innocent bystanders to your phone battles.** Unless a call is urgent, cut it short if your toddler is whining and begging for attention. It is rude—even if you excuse yourself—to turn away from the person on the other end of the line in order to speak to your child (or anyone else). Most callers are sympathetic when they hear a child in the background and would prefer to speak with you at a better time.

A child's first real telephone conversations, when you hold the receiver to her ear so that she can hear grandparents or other relatives, will probably be one-sided—no matter how well she chatters into her toy phone. The real thing is very strange to a child, like magic, and she may find it scary or weird to hear a voice without a face. If you put the phone to her ear and she pushes it aside or backs away, don't force the issue.

It's a good idea to limit these first attempts to people who know your child well and will speak softly and naturally even when she doesn't respond. It can be quite disconcerting for people who don't know your child or the ways of children to find themselves speaking into a void or hearing cries of protest at the other end of the phone line.

◄◄

Answering the Phone

Your child will be five, six, or possibly older before you can entrust him to answer your phone on his own. This is not a job for toddlers. They do not have the ability to carry on a coherent phone conversation. They can't take messages and often hang up in midcall or won't hang up when the call is ended.

Use these years for early modeling of telephone manners. Role-playing games are helpful teachers, but your real-world example will be your child's best guide.

- *Begin and end all your calls with gracious hello's and good-bye's.*

- *Be attentive to and respectful of all callers.* Don't make silly faces or gestures indicating to your child that you are bored or intolerant of the caller.

- *Always give your name at the beginning of your calls,* even when phoning a close friend or relative.

- *Speak clearly and in moderate tones.*

- *Write down phone messages and ask the caller to repeat any information you didn't understand.* Someday you will be the beneficiary of this close attention when your child is taking messages for you.

- **When you can, tell your child what your call was about when you finish.** If you spoke with the plumber, your child will be interested to know that "Mr. Craig is coming to fix the bathroom sink." You won't discuss every call with your child, but simple explanations will show him that the phone is used for important matters.

First Thank-You Notes

TODDLERS DON'T WRITE THANK-YOU NOTES, but they can contribute to the notes you write for them. If Aunt Ethel sends your child a birthday present, you may be tempted to fall back on a phone call to express appreciation. But it's well worth taking the extra time to write a note. Tell your child what you are doing and why—that writing a letter is how you say "thank you."

If your little one enjoys using crayons or finger paints, you can suggest he create a picture for Aunt Ethel. It may be scribbles, but the activity will promote your toddler's sense of involvement, and his effort is sure to please the recipient. An older toddler can make marks at the end of your letter as a signature and put the stamp on the envelope. With a little assistance, even a one-year-old can drop the note in the mailbox or hand it to your letter carrier.

Try to write thank-you notes as soon as possible after an event or receipt of a gift. A toddler's memory is very short, so you'll want to involve him before he forgets the reason for writing. It's good manners in any case to respond promptly and a good lesson in courtesy for your child.

Times to Write

When do you write toddler thank-you notes? For gifts, certainly. You will also include your toddler in the thank-you when she accompanies you on a weekend stay at a friend's home. Whenever someone does something especially thoughtful for your child—a neighbor might repair your child's broken wagon—you have an excellent opportunity to involve your toddler in writing a brief note of appreciation. Thank-you notes aren't necessary for routine activities such as playdates and birthday parties.

Choosing a Name to Go By

Do you want to be Grandfather or Grampa? Grandmother or Grannie? Or do you prefer something more individual?

New parents often adopt the names by which they addressed their own grandparents, and they may start referring to you as Nana or Gramps. Or perhaps your toddler grandchild has christened you with one of her own words, and you've suddenly become Boppa, Mimi, Poppy, or something equally adorable. If you like the nickname you've been given, by all means stick with it. If not, don't hesitate to make your preference clear. Explain to the new parents that you are uncomfortable with your assigned name. Let your family know what name you prefer and ask for their help in establishing that name with your grandchild or step-grandchildren. The name you choose may work its way through your entire family, so pick something you can live with.

CHAPTER 9

Toddler Table Manners

_____ ◂┼

MEALTIME CAN BE VIEWED AS a microcosm of all group social inter-action. People of different ages and personalities gather for a common purpose, and beyond eating, each participant probably has something to discuss. There are expectations for polite behavior. The activity requires organizational and social skills if it is to be successfully completed. It may be a simple family meal, but look at it as preparation for life outside the home. If everyone does his part, the experience can be pleasant and fun as well as productive.

First Steps

MOST TODDLERS ARE NOT READY to begin learning the higher skills of dining until they approach their third birthdays, but they will absorb a good deal about what is expected when the family sits down to a meal. A toddler's primary accomplishment will be the use of a spoon to feed herself—a messy process but fundamental to all table manners.

Parents should use this time to establish and reinforce the behavior basics. You'll want to continue observing and reinforcing the mealtime rituals discussed in Chapter 4. If you haven't yet begun, it's time to introduce your toddler to the meaning of mealtime. Children need to understand that the primary purpose of dining is the consumption of food. Whether your toddler is eating separately or dining with the family, the focus of the experience should be the meal. When you see that your toddler has eaten her fill and is ready to do something else or when she simply doesn't want to eat, end the meal for her.

Parents worry constantly about how much their toddler is eating. But if a parent tries to force a toddler to eat, every meal may be turned into a power struggle. Food can quickly become an issue of control between parents and toddlers, setting the stage for later eating problems and even eating disorders.

Using a Bib and Napkin

Until your child gains the ability to feed herself, her eating style will be primitive. But consistent use of a bib sends the message that food is designed to go into the mouth, not onto faces, hands, clothes, or the immediate surroundings. Begin each meal with a clean bib, using it to wipe your little one's face occasionally during the meal, and encourage imitation by using your own table napkin. Be sure to remove the bib as soon as your toddler finishes her meal. As she grows, you can give her a napkin at each meal and show her how to use it, though you'll probably continue using a bib as well. You are establishing the link between neatness and dining in a routine, casual way; just don't expect spic-and-span behavior anytime soon.

The High Chair

For their safety and everyone else's peace of mind, toddlers need to learn how to *sit* at the table. Set clear limits: no standing in or climbing out of high chairs and a minimum of wiggling and squirming. Position the high chair next to an adult who can supervise, and place breakable table items beyond the child's reach. It's best to reserve the high chair for eating only, so your child will learn that mealtime is different from playtime. If you establish the basics of sitting at the table during the high chair phase, your child may adjust more quickly to the use of a booster seat (usually around age two to two and a half) and eventually a chair.

"Let's Wash Your Hands"

Following a washing ritual helps your child to associate cleanliness with eating, which is both a health essential and a fundamental of considerate dining behavior. Wash your child's hands before meals, and clean his hands and face after the meal is completed. Wiping your toddler's hands with a damp cloth before every meal will lead to washing hands at the sink and teaching the older toddler to use soap and to rinse and dry hands thoroughly.

Handling Utensils

Your young toddler will be attempting to feed herself with a spoon, and though she probably won't gain control of a utensil until she is three or older, you'll want to encourage her efforts and clean up the aftermath. At this stage, proper hand position is not important. Promote use of a spoon by setting her place at the table and handing her the spoon. Praise her when she succeeds at getting food from plate to mouth, but don't criticize misses and spills. If she reverts to using her fingers, don't stop her; she may be willing to try the spoon again once she has eaten a bit, and she'll soon learn that eating foods such as applesauce, mashed potatoes, and oatmeal is infinitely easier with a spoon.

The use of a spoon is a difficult skill to learn, and your child needs lots of time and reinforcement, as well as your good example. Toddlers are usually ready to try a fork by the time they are three, but knives should not be introduced until later.

Behavior at the Table

SOCIALLY ACCEPTABLE BEHAVIOR REFLECTS AN individual's consideration for the comfort and pleasure of others. A toddler, however, has no real concept of needs beyond her own, and the pleasure of other people is not yet of much concern to her. But you can bring these seemingly irreconcilable viewpoints together at the family table. Your toddler can acquire the social graces only if she is exposed to them regularly.

- **Provide the example and expect considerate mealtime behavior from other family members, including older children and adolescents.** Everyone should use good manners—napkins in laps, elbows off the table, chewing with mouths closed, no talking while chewing, eating with the correct utensils held in the correct way, and taking reasonable portions. If you have older children, you will prompt them to eat politely, and your toddler will observe and learn from these lessons. Toddlers and older children will benefit if you establish clear standards and follow the rules yourself. Among the basics are:

  - No interrupting when another person is speaking.
  - Taking turns speaking. Everyone deserves a chance to talk.
  - No yelling, shouting, teasing, or insulting remarks.
  - Moderating voices. Keep the volume down.
  - No roughhousing at the table.

- **Start with an empty table and set it correctly.** Start with a clean, clear table and set it with plates, dinnerware, and napkins. Your table setting doesn't have to be elaborate to be gracious. Older toddlers and preschoolers can be given age-appropriate tasks. Allow your toddler to put napkins and place mats on the table. Don't force, but do take advantage of her desire to imitate and begin familiarizing her with basic table settings. (See "Setting the Family Table," page 110.)

- **Maintain a low-stress environment at meals by minimizing distractions.** Background music is fine, but turn off the TV. Use the answering machine or designate one person to answer the phone and take messages. (Establishing and enforcing firm telephone rules early will reduce mealtime frustration when your children reach adolescence.) Toys, books and magazines, games, handheld computers, portable listening devices, cell phones, and so on should not be allowed at the table during meals. When older children are excused from the table, they should go to a separate area. It is much easier to feed a toddler who isn't watching her siblings playing close by.

- **Establish beginning and ending rituals.** A family meal should have a clear start. Saying grace serves this purpose for many fam-

Use family mealtimes for productive conversation, not for airing family disputes and grievances or gossiping about others. Parents must set the tone. Discuss the day's happenings. Encourage your children to participate by asking them specific questions and paying attention to their responses. (Comments and questions such as "Tell us about the fireman game you played" and "What book did you read at the library?" show that you are aware of your child's activities and interested in what he has to say.) Take the opportunity to reward good behavior by praising your child publicly. ("Simon drew a great picture today. I put it on the fridge for everyone to see.") Include your toddler in conversation by looking at him and speaking to him directly.

---

ilies. Some families have the very nice custom of thanking the person who has prepared the food before beginning the meal. An important starting point for older children is spreading napkins in their laps. If the meal is served at the table, wait until everyone is seated to serve. If it is served buffet style or individually from the kitchen, it's acceptable to begin eating when you sit down; the idea is to eat while the food is hot. If you want your children to master the virtue of punctuality, be prepared to start meals on time.

The most common meal-ending ritual involves teaching children to ask to be excused when they finish eating. It's unrealistic to require young children to sit still after their meal is completed. Older children will be taught to place their knives and forks on their plates and fold their napkins or to remove their plates and utensils from the table before being excused. Older toddlers can take their bowls and cups to the kitchen. Whatever your family customs, clearly defined expectations will make meals more pleasant for everyone, and the good manners will pay off when your children begin dining in other people's homes and elsewhere.

- **Discourage gross or disruptive behaviors by your toddler and other children.** Sometimes adults are tempted to laugh when children deliberately burp, belch, hiccup, blow bubbles in their

Toddlers are notoriously finicky and erratic eaters. Some can barely wait to escape the table, so they gulp down whatever is set before them; others are as slow as molasses, particularly when they begin to feed themselves. All children will balk at eating if they aren't hungry.

At this age, it's okay to indulge your toddler's eating eccentricities, within reason. But you'll want to continue offering a variety of foods, introducing new flavors and textures often. If he doesn't like his foods "mixed up" or refuses to eat foods when they are "touching" on his plate, then use a divided plate or serve his portions in separate bowls. The extra washing up is minimal. Giving food choices may help an active youngster become more interested in mealtime; your toddler may be more inclined to eat his breakfast cereal if you allow him to choose bananas or berries for a topping. If your child is a slow eater, be considerate and don't rush him. As long as he is really eating (not just playing with his food), allow him to proceed at his own speed; stay with him and talk to him until he is finished.

---

milk, and so on. Don't. Make it clear that the behavior is not acceptable and should not be repeated, then continue the meal.

- **Include guests at your table on occasion.** It is good for children to experience informal gatherings when someone else is welcomed into the family circle without a lot of fuss and bother. The willingness to share daily bread with outsiders is one of the true hallmarks of civilized behavior.

Setting the Family Table

PROBABLY THE BIGGEST MISCONCEPTION ABOUT setting a table is that the process is too elaborate and complicated for everyday living. Not so. The purpose of a well-set table is practicality. The objective is to see that each place setting includes all the utensils the diner will need. The organization of table settings lets you look at the table and quickly see if anything is missing.

The basic family place setting comprises a plate, knife, fork, teaspoon, drinking glass, napkin, and place mat or tablecloth. The fork is placed to the left of the plate; the knife (next to the plate with cutting side toward the plate) and spoon are laid to the right. Folded napkins can be placed on the empty plates or to the left of the forks. Glasses and coffee cups are set above the knife. Depending on the meal, other items can be included: butter plates and butter knives, salad plates, soup bowls and soupspoons. Butter plates are placed above the fork, and salad plates to the left of the fork. Salad forks are seldom necessary for a family meal.

Provide your toddler with at least a plate or bowl, a spoon, and a bib. When she has progressed from high chair to booster seat, give her a place mat and a napkin.

Serving Meals

Even a simple family meal can be served attractively. Food can be put onto plates in the kitchen or at a side table and then brought to the table—not a bad idea when your children are small and apt to drop heavy serving dishes. If food is served at the table, it should be put in serving dishes, not cooking pots or commercial containers. Milk, water, and other drinks should be served in pitchers if poured at the table.

A family meal will usually include a main course, dessert, and possibly soup to start. You should remove dishes between courses; scraping and stacking dirty dishes at the table is messy and unappetizing.

Going Out and About

FOR ALL THEIR CHARMS AND delights, toddlers are never predictable, and their unpredictability makes every out-and-about venture a challenge. You may be tempted, after a recent tantrum in the shopping center, not to take your toddler anywhere. But toddlers really do need to get out in the world and to see new people and places, and it is vital that your toddler see you using good manners in a variety of settings.

Car Travel

FEW TODDLERS LIKE TO BE confined, and in their second year, they often begin to fight the use of a car seat. Diversion and distraction may help; however, physical discipline is likely to escalate the battle, and the child's resistance can turn into a full-fledged tantrum.

If your child is a car-seat rebel, the first rule for caregivers is never to give in. Do not allow your child, even once, to ride in an adult's lap or sit alone, with or without a seat belt. Your child's life and safety are at stake. Besides, surrendering the car-seat issue to your toddler may raise his expectations that he can win again the next time.

Some things you can do to promote good conduct in the car are:

- **Check the car seat for comfort.** Your toddler may be resisting because he has outgrown the seat, the strap is too tight, or a crack in the plastic seat cover is scratching him.

- **Leave plenty of time for buckling up.** Be realistic. If your toddler resists using the car seat, don't increase your own frustration with fear of getting a late start.

- **Lower the stress of departures.** Put everything in the car, including comfort items and soft toys, before you strap your toddler in. Never leave a toddler alone in the car while you go back for a forgotten item. Heat or cool the interior before taking him to the car.

- **Focus on the destination, not the ride.** When getting your toddler ready to go out, talk with him about where you're going, who will be there, what you will do, and what fun you will have. Announcements like "I don't want any arguments about your car seat" will prime the pump for resistance. As you strap him in, engage him with conversation and questions about what is going to happen.

- **Employ distraction.** It's easier to get your toddler seated and strapped in quickly if you are talking about something that interests him. Point out the red bird in the bush near the car; ask your child to make silly noises or clap his hands. Put on his favorite tape or CD. Sometimes a child needs a graceful way to avoid a struggle, and a diversion can do the trick.

- **Follow a consistent ritual once your toddler is safely strapped in.** Even if he continues to protest, follow the safety drill and say the steps aloud in a calm, authoritative voice. "Everyone is buckled in. All doors are locked. Hands are inside the car. Start the engine. Look carefully in all directions. Go." As your child learns to join in the ritual, he may forget about his car seat aversion.

- **Never expect anyone other than a parent or primary caregiver to buckle up your toddler** unless the person is fully prepared for any difficulties. Sometimes toddlers are beautifully behaved with other people, but don't assume that others will have the patience or skills to handle a struggle. Your child's safety is your responsibility.

- **Clearly establish the rules of in-car behavior.** Your toddler
  must stay seated with seatbelt on, and keep hands to himself.
  "Little voice" only. No playing with locks, automatic window
  buttons, and door handles. You should be prepared to repeat the
  rules like a drill sergeant for years to come.

Private Occasions

THE RULE FOR PRIVATE GATHERINGS is the same for toddlers as for
infants—if your child is not *explicitly* included in the invitation, he is *not*
invited. Never assume that it's okay for your child to join you, and don't
put your host on the spot by asking to bring a child. An invitation must
come from the host, so don't ask or hint for one.

If your child is included, prepare for any eventuality and bring everything you may need. It's nice to introduce your child to social situations
with family and friends, but remember that a toddler's sociability is erratic.
He may be happy for a time, then suddenly become cranky, cry when other
adults approach him, and demand your full attention. Hard as it may be to
leave a pleasant gathering, it's usually preferable to depart early if your child
has become overly tired or overly stimulated and will not settle down.

When You Entertain

If you are entertaining at home and your child will be present, prepare him in advance. On the day of the event, you can tell him that the
family is having a party. Tell him who will be coming, but don't overwhelm him with details. Be sure your child is well rested. Feed him
before your guests arrive. If you are hosting a sit-down meal, you may
want to include your child, and his table behavior will probably be more
sociable if he isn't ravenous.

Since your time will be occupied with meeting and serving guests,
your child may feel excluded from your attention. A good solution is to
hire his favorite babysitter or arrange for his nanny to help. If your child
has someone caring for him, you will feel freer to be a gracious host. Do
include your child in some of the festivities. Ask him if he would like to
be with you as you greet new arrivals. Let him sit on your lap when you
chat with guests, so he can see how adults behave in social situations. Be
guided by your guests' reactions and your child's interest; you can't force
a toddler to be friendly.

Guidelines for behavior in the car apply as well to airplane travel and other forms of transportation. Whenever you use public transport—commuter trains, buses, subways, ferries, and the like—hold your child securely at all times. Her safety is your first concern, but you also want to be considerate of other passengers. Include some diversionary toys or books in your tote bag, and never let your toddler run around or approach other travelers. Try to keep her seated, not standing. If available, a window seat will give her an entertaining observation post for the ride. A seat near an exit will enable you, your child, and your equipment to disembark with the least inconvenience to others.

If your child begins to act up, don't ignore the problem. Most people are understanding when toddlers disturb the peace, but parents or caregivers who make no attempt to calm a crying or rowdy child are simply inconsiderate. Immediately stop disturbing behavior such as kicking the back of a seat or leaning over another passenger's seat. If your child is hungry or tired, relieve her discomfort as best you can. (It's a good idea to keep crackers and juice in your bag for such times.) Try distractions or soothing talk. Whatever you do, don't ignore your child or the comfort of your fellow travelers.

Who's Minding the Child?

WHETHER YOU ARE ATTENDING A gathering or entertaining at home, always know where your toddler is and who is with him. If other toddlers are present, don't expect them to entertain one another. If older children are included, never expect an older child to mind toddlers. A teenager who is experienced at babysitting might be drafted to help out, but it's inconsiderate to ask a teen guest to be responsible for the duration of the event. Be sure to arrange your child-minding in advance of the event.

- Spouses and partners can alternate watching their child. Just don't become too involved in the adult fun and forget to relieve your partner.

- At a family gathering, a grandparent or other responsible relative can probably be recruited to watch your toddler for a time. In some families, the child care is rotated among all the adults.

I'm thirty-seven, my husband is forty-eight, and we have a two-year-old who everyone assumes is our granddaughter. How can we correct people without causing anyone undue embarrassment?

It's best to respond as soon as possible since it will only become more difficult to correct the misunderstanding as the conversation continues, and it could confuse your daughter if people don't refer to you as her mother. Just say, "You know, Ellie is actually our daughter." If you take the right tone, people shouldn't react defensively. If they seem embarrassed, assure them that it's a common mistake and doesn't bother you. You can also head off misunderstandings by always introducing your child with "This is our daughter, Ellie"—making your relationship clear from the start.

This relieves any one person of sole responsibility and is a wonderful way for youngsters to get to know the members of their extended family.

- When several families with young children are invited to an event, parents can plan in advance to rotate child care. Each parent will watch a group of little ones for a designated amount of time. Keep the child-to-adult ratio low: One adult should be responsible for no more than three or four youngsters.

Follow-up after the event can be beneficial for your child. Talk about the party after you leave or the following day. Encourage your child's social self-confidence by praising his good behavior. ("You were very good to sit still at dinner.") Pass along compliments. ("Your Aunt Lucia said that she really enjoyed playing with you.") You can play out a few make-believe situations, with your child alternating the roles of host and guest; this will prepare him for later lessons in courtesy and thoughtfulness when he entertains others.

About Birthday Parties

FROM A TODDLER'S PERSPECTIVE, SECOND and third birthday celebrations need not be much fancier than his first birthday party. The motto for successful toddler birthdays is still "simple and short." Family gatherings with birthday cake and ice cream will satisfy toddlers, but if you plan a party with other youngsters, these suggestions will be helpful:

- *Keep the guest list short.* For a two-year-old, adults are still the preferred guests. A peer or two may add to the fun, but don't invite a toddler army. Three-years-olds are usually ready for more guests of their own age; three or four children, including your child, will make it a real party. You can send written invitations, but phone calls to the parents are equally correct.

- *Time it right.* Pick a time when your youngster and other toddler guests are most likely to be rested and well fed. Early afternoon is often a good time because party food won't interfere with children's normal morning and evening meal schedules. Limit the length of the party to a reasonable hour or ninety minutes.

- *Keep safety in mind.* Even if your toddler is more physically advanced than others, prepare your home or select an outside party setting with the capabilities of the least adept child in mind. Confine the party to a safe area; lock and block off places (bathrooms, bedrooms, stairways, outside exits, and so forth) where curious toddlers shouldn't go.

- *Invite parents, too.* Constant adult supervision is essential for two- and three-year-olds, so it's probably wise to include the parents of toddlers in your guest list and also to have a designated adult or teen helper available.

- *Go easy on decorating.* Simple decorations featuring favorite story or cartoon characters, paper streamers, and Mylar balloons will delight two-year-olds. Third birthday parties can be more elaborate, and your toddler will enjoy helping you select decorations. Use only flame-proof items, do not use latex or rubber balloons, and avoid favors such as noisemakers that are easily broken or have small or sharp pieces.

- *Serve safe foods.* Ice cream, cupcakes, juice, and safe finger foods make a tasty menu. But don't serve candies, nuts, grapes,

Fun Party Games

Well-planned, *appropriate* activities are essential to all successful entertaining. Games are lots of fun at toddler parties, as long as there's no competition. Toddlers are notoriously sore losers, so it's best to avoid winners and prizes. London Bridge, Farmer in the Dell, modified Musical Chairs (everyone gets a seat), singing and dancing to recorded music, and creative projects (if you can manage the mess) are good for two-year-olds. For a third birthday party, you can add games and activities that are age-appropriate. Many three-year-olds are not ready for clowns and magicians, but you might include a skilled storyteller. Make time for free play and have plenty of toys available for everyone. A short videotape may be entertaining when youngsters are winding down near the end of the gathering.

---

popcorn, hot dogs, and other foods that can cause choking accidents or allergic reactions.

- **Expect squabbles between toddlers and be ready to intervene.** Conflicts may not occur, and you can breathe a sigh of relief. But two- and three-year-olds are not yet ready to be gracious. You should encourage your child to say "thank you" for gifts and "good-bye" when his guests depart, but don't make an issue of it. He may be too pooped to manage even a wave when the party's over.

- **Keep present opening low-key.** A toddler's sense of ownership and property rights is very tentative, so you may want to skip present opening or consider whisking gifts away immediately after they are opened. Perhaps you can supply a present that all the children can share or gifts for everyone to open. For a full-fledged unwrapping, limit gift opening to the packages brought by young guests; save presents from family and other adults for after the party.

- **Write thank-you notes** for any gift opened when the giver is not present, and include your child in the process. (See "First Thank-You Notes," page 103.)

Out in Public

EVEN ROUTINE TRIPS TO THE grocery store and the gas station present learning opportunities for your youngster as he begins to grasp that certain behaviors are expected in public places. All outings will require your eagle-eyed supervision. For as long as he will tolerate confinement, your toddler can ride in a stroller. But if he demands to walk, you must keep a firm grip on him, so teach him to hold your hand at all times. For safety and consideration of others, you will now set limits on behavior in public places: Walk, don't run. Use your quiet voice. Keep your hands to yourself (let him carry a toy or comfort item). Should your youngster become upset or rowdy, you must be prepared to leave public places and events immediately.

At the Supermarket

The market or grocery store is not the place to turn a toddler loose. For his safety and the safety of other shoppers, keep your little one in the seat of the grocery cart the entire time. The older he gets, the less likely he is to be cooperative, so it's smart to limit the duration of your shopping excursions. No matter how much you are tempted, don't fall into the habit of bribing your child to behave by buying the things he demands in a store. He will soon figure out that unruly behavior brings rewards—and you'll face a long struggle to undo this damaging message.

Dining Out

Restaurant visits should be limited to places that cater to young children. Your toddler will enjoy the bright environment and the sight of other youngsters, and he can practice his dining-out manners, limited as they are. If you use the drive-through services of fast-food restaurants, save take-out meals until you reach home unless there is another adult supervising. Allowing a toddler to eat in the car is messy, offers the opportunity for throwing food, and may present a choking hazard.

It's best to save upscale dining with your child until much later. There is nothing as likely to ruin a pleasant and expensive adult night out—for yourself and other diners—as a whining, crying, or loud and boisterous toddler. If you aren't sure of a restaurant's policies about young children, call in advance and ask. Investigate your locality: There may be midrange restaurants that serve excellent food and welcome families with young children.

At Religious or Secular Services

Religious services and solemn secular occasions, including weddings, funerals, and christenings during regular worship services, are generally not appropriate for toddlers. If nursery care isn't available and you are determined to take your child, sit near the back, preferably by an aisle, so that you can make a quick exit the instant your child grows restless. You can supply items to occupy your child's attention—a favorite doll or storybook, for instance—but be sure they are not distractions for others. A toddler rattling the pages of a book, crooning to his teddy bear, or scrambling under the pews to retrieve a dropped toy can sound like a herd of elephants during a service.

At Outdoor Events

Outdoor places, from parks to public concerts, may provide more scope for your toddler's good spirits. Always supervise your child closely. Check the environment carefully for safety hazards (the metal pull-tab in the grass, the glass shard in the sandbox). Pack all the supplies you might need. At outdoor events, try to find seating near the edge of the crowd so you can exit early if necessary. Be clear about the rules: no running, climbing, or shouting when around other people.

Child-Friendly Places and Activities

Places and activities designed for children offer perfect opportunities to teach out-and-about manners while having a good time. Parents can maximize their toddler's exposure to other people and new experiences without great expenditures of money and effort. There may be a children's museum, aquarium, or petting zoo in your area. Local, state, and national parks frequently plan events for families. Local schools host fairs, rummage sales, and performances at which little children are expected. Instead of fighting the crowds at a professional sports event, take your toddler to a high school football game or a local horse show or rodeo. The children's department at the library is always a good place to visit, especially on storytelling and puppet-show days. Your town may host holiday parades, ethnic appreciation activities, and special events such as the annual Fourth of July fireworks display.

Even at family-oriented events, parents should be sensitive to and respectful of their child's unique temperament. Don't expect your child to enjoy every new experience, and don't force participation if he is shy or unwilling. If the fireworks display frightens your two-year-old, for example, watch the next year's celebration on television. He will probably be intrigued by the visual excitement and adjust to the loud noises. You can try the real thing again when he is four.

Tantrums in Public

SOONER OR LATER, ALMOST EVERY parent must deal with a toddler who has a temper fit in a public place. Tantrums are much easier to handle at home than in a store (see "Managing Tantrums," page 70), but even in public, your first concern is your child's welfare. You can ease the situation if you:

- *Plan out-and-about excursions carefully.* Children are more prone to tantrums when they are tired, hungry, overexcited, or bored.

- *Try distraction if you see an outburst brewing.* Don't use bribery, but if, for example, you are in a mall store, suggest going outside to see the fountain or something else interesting. A change of scene can sometimes evaporate a child's anger.

- *Don't give in.* If you let your toddler have the piece of candy he is screaming for, he'll get the message that tantrums earn rewards, and he may begin throwing tantrums for attention.

- *Leave.* Pick up your child gently (no arm pulling or dragging) and make a quick departure. If you must abandon your shopping cart, do so. Most stores will hold your items until you can return and pay for them.

- *Find a quiet place*—your car, a rest area or rest room, or home if you can safely get there—and ride out the storm following the advice in "Managing Tantrums," page 70.

- *Be considerate of others by removing your child from the center of activity.* A sensible parent knows that she cannot control a toddler's tantrum, but she can control her own reactions. When

When out shopping, we often see parents struggling with their tantrum-throwing children. It's hard to watch, especially when the parent is very angry or hitting the child. When is it right for a bystander to intervene?

While you might offer to help if you know the parent well—perhaps by distracting the child or carrying packages while the parent manages the child—it's generally best not to involve yourself when the parent is a stranger. The parent is likely to misinterpret your concern as interference, increasing his or her anger and frustration. But if the parent is hitting or you believe that the child is in danger, immediately find someone in authority and report what is happening. Store managers and security personnel are usually trained to handle such situations. If the parent–child conflict does not appear to be dangerous, you can observe discreetly to be sure it doesn't escalate, but do not make comments or offer advice. A parent who appears to be angry may actually be trying to restrain the child from hurting herself or to get the child to a safe place. By stepping in too quickly, outsiders may thwart a reasonable parent's efforts and prolong a child's tantrum.

◄┼

you see a parent fighting with or yelling at a screaming child in public, ask yourself what is really more embarrassing: the child's behavior (difficult but normal) or the parent's excessive response?

Stranger Danger

CRIME STATISTICS SHOW THAT MOST child kidnappings involve adults who are related to or known by the family, but there are other people who harm children—and you don't want to take chances. However, being overly protective can lead your child to develop a genuine fear of or even paranoia about all adults. A child who fears adults may not seek help when he is in need.

A toddler doesn't understand an abstract concept like "stranger." He may grasp that a stranger is someone he has never seen before, but what about people he has seen—the man who sits in the park, the woman who walks past the day-care center? Predators rarely conform to stereotypes, so there's no way for you or your child to spot a dangerous person by his or her appearance.

The Best Defense

Your best defense against stranger danger is constant supervision of your toddler. Outside your home, never let your child out of your sight. Hold your child's hand at all times. Never leave him unattended in a stroller, grocery cart, or car. And don't leave toddlers alone outside your house, even in a fenced yard or play area.

Set clear limits for children, and begin now to teach the rules about dealing with strangers. Instruct your toddler not to talk to any unfamiliar person unless you are present. Calmly and tactfully introduce your older toddler to the following basic rules of personal safety. He won't understand fully now, but it pays to begin this part of his education early.

- Never talk to someone he doesn't know, even if the person knows his name, unless a parent or caregiver has said it is okay or has introduced this person.

- Never answer a stranger's questions.

- Never approach a car unless accompanied by a parent or caregiver.

- Never accept candy, toys, or other items from a stranger without a parent's permission.

- Never go anywhere with a stranger.

- Never leave the yard or a play area without a parent's permission.

- Never open the door to your house to anyone unless accompanied by a parent or caregiver.

- Always tell a parent or caregiver if approached, spoken to, or touched by a stranger or unfamiliar person.

Try Role-Playing

A child who is learning meeting-and-greeting manners may be confused by a seemingly kindly stranger. Role-playing is a good method to begin teaching the difference between normal social situations and dangerous ones. Pretend, for example, that a stranger asks your child for help finding a lost puppy. Concentrate on what the child is to do, and assure him that it's right to ignore this person and to run to you or the grown-up in charge. (When your child is older, you can explain that an unfamiliar adult with good intentions would never ask a child for help.)

There may be times when your toddler screams or runs away from a friend or relative he knows. Don't criticize him for "bad manners" or belittle his reaction. You should praise his caution, and then assure him that the person is really a friend. Explain the situation to your friend or relative as soon as possible. Then reintroduce your child to the person at the earliest opportunity and in a relaxed atmosphere.

New Family Etiquette Issues

THE VARIETY AND PROLIFERATION OF so-called "nontraditional" families means that there really is not a norm in society today. Etiquette is adaptive, and new family forms raise new questions. Some of the most common issues of appropriate manners and respect include the following.

Changing Surnames

Divorce, remarriage, adoption, and blended families frequently raise name problems that may be easier for adults to resolve than for children. When, for example, a mother resumes her maiden name after a divorce, young children are often confused and older children and teens may be resentful. In blended families, stepsiblings with different surnames may feel less inclined to accept one another. It's vital to talk seriously with children about naming issues. A name is part of a person's identity, and even a young child becomes attached to her name. Changing a child's surname or your own may add to her sense of loss and abandonment after a divorce or death of a spouse. A child may worry that she is being disloyal to the parent whose name is being changed. Older children and teens really must be consulted if a name change is contemplated, and their wishes should be respected above your own. Before changing a child's name, a parent should inform others who will be affected, particularly grandparents and family members whose surname will be dropped.

Relationships and Introductions

You can avoid confusion and embarrassment by clarifying your family relationships for people who deal regularly with you and your child, including playgroup participants, child-care workers and babysitters, teachers, school officials, coaches, and health-care providers. It's not fair to expect a child to explain that Mommy has a different name because she and Daddy got divorced and she married again. (Kids will do this among themselves, but telling authority figures is another matter.) Keep explanations between adults, and don't subject your child to the same story again and again. If another child asks about a relationship, explain honestly and simply. ("Jane has her father's name. But I became Mrs. Blackburn when I married Mr. Blackburn.")

In most social encounters, introduce your child as your child—or grandchild or niece or nephew—and don't load introductions with extra information. But first and always, be sensitive to the child's concerns. A stepchild who is close to a biological parent may resent being introduced as a stepparent's daughter or son. If a child is not related to you, you might explain briefly ("This is Robbie Dickerson, our foster child. We're so glad that he's staying with our family for a while.") and be sure the introduction is positive.

Think carefully about how you want to be introduced; then teach your child the form that is most comfortable for you both. ("This is my stepfather, Tim Harris." Or "This is my mom's partner, Sue Sims.")

When you meet parents or caregivers and children whose relationship isn't clear, don't ask. You might inquire when you know the parents better, but don't ask the child. Be sensitive when meeting parents and children who appear physically unrelated. Restrain your curiosity. Questions such as "Is this *your* child?" and "Are *all* these children yours?" are rude and especially thoughtless of the feelings of youngsters. In all likelihood, adults will explain when they are ready.

Invitations and Announcements

Birth and adoption announcements are discussed in Chapter 1. Except in an adoption announcement, the fact of adoption is not mentioned in invitations or announcements. In more formal invitations when parents entertain for unadopted stepchildren, the relationships are included in a format such as:

Mr. and Mrs. Michael Carlton
invite you to celebrate
the Sweet Sixteenth birthday
of her daughter
Mary Kay Frazier

When parents who have different surnames (including divorced parents) entertain, the form will be a variation on this example:

Christine MacDonald and Joseph Rubin
request the pleasure of your company

at a graduation dinner
honoring their son
Joseph Thomas Rubin
(or Joseph Thomas MacDonald-Rubin)

Teaching Respect

Whether built around two parents, one parent, stepparents, adoptive parents, same-sex parents, grandparents or extended family, or foster parents, every family deserves respect. It's important to teach children that families come in all sizes and configurations; the basis of family is mutual love and caring, not a specific arrangement. Children—lacking experience and strong self-control—can be cruel to other youngsters whom they perceive as "different." So don't let negative feelings and biases you may have affect your child or her interactions with others. In word and deed, model respect for all loving families.

The Age of Discovery: Three Through Five Years

N O W ' S   T H E   T I M E   T O . . .

- Focus on developing values and encouraging empathy

- Introduce the concept of honesty

- Teach respect for self and the rights of others

- Teach and encourage sharing

- Introduce sportsmanship

- Build communication skills

- Practice greetings and introductions

- Teach basic telephone manners

- Teach basic table manners

AT THREE, YOUR CHILD KNOWS that he is a separate being, and now—during the preschool years—he will begin to understand that other people have feelings and needs just like his. He will learn and start to use many of the basics of good manners. He'll interact with peers and develop his first friendships. His responses will sometimes be genuinely empathetic, as his emotional development becomes entwined with others.

Your child is embarking on a great voyage of discovery, and the prize is learning who he is. He will begin to think, act, and speak in new ways—using language as his chief means of communicating with you and others. As his memory matures, he will begin to grasp the concept of future time. This insight, which enables him to anticipate and to wait, is essential to self-control and delayed gratification.

Your child's unique personality is forming. Until now, his innate temperament has governed his reactions, but during these years you will see a range of distinct traits, qualities, and preferences emerge. Is he direct or reticent? Is he softhearted? Is he bold? Is he eager to follow directions, or does he challenge commands?

Physically, he'll lose that adorable, chubby baby face and body as he grows taller, stronger, and more coordinated. He will become increasingly capable of taking care of himself—eating, dressing, and grooming with growing skill. With much help and encouragement on your part, he'll learn the essentials of toilet training.

In countless ways, your child is readying himself to take on the world outside his family with competence and confidence. Near the close of this period, he will probably enter kindergarten—the first big step toward formal education—and he will begin to put into practice what he is learning about cooperation, consideration, and good manners.

CHAPTER 11

Learning About Values

—◄←

DURING YOUR CHILD'S PRESCHOOL YEARS, the groundwork for etiquette education that you laid during infancy and toddlerhood will start to pay off. You'll focus on teaching standards of etiquette and encouraging socialization. As your child realizes that you and others have expectations of her, she will discover that good manners help her get along.

Values are the basis of all good manners. While children will eventually come under the influence of institutions, media, and associates that parents cannot easily control, the family is the primary teacher of morals and values. If your child is taught honesty, integrity, self-control, self-respect, respect and consideration for the rights and feelings of others, generosity, loyalty, and cooperation, then there's every reason to believe that she will cling to these values in adulthood.

Four Vital Steps

DURING THE PRESCHOOL YEARS, MANNERS are a critical component of moral education, because good manners express positive values, especially in relation to others. As you introduce your child to values, you'll want to:

- *Model moral, ethical, and mannerly behavior every day.* Your preschool child wants to be like you; she takes her behavioral cues from what she sees you do. Consistency is vital, so good manners must be routine at home and among family members. Parents should closely watch what they say. A child will soon pick up the inconsistency of a parent who is polite to neighbors but regularly makes disparaging remarks behind their backs.

- *Talk about values in concrete terms.* Use simple, direct language your child can understand. ("It's good to be quiet when someone else is speaking." "It's wrong to hit anyone when you're angry.") Books and storytelling will be helpful as you teach concepts like kindness and caring for other people's feelings. When you read "Cinderella," for example, talk about how sad Cinderella is because her sisters are mean to her. Be on the lookout for real-world examples of positive values. Point it out when someone does something helpful or thoughtful, and talk about how such kindness makes you feel.

- *Establish basic standards of behavior.* Your child needs to know what you expect of her, so set guidelines for her behavior, including good manners. If you do not want her to interrupt when others are talking (a particularly hard lesson for voluble preschoolers), you have to explain that interrupting makes other people feel frustrated or angry. Let her know that your standards apply to everyone in the family and that she isn't being singled out.

    Between ages three and five, your child will begin to know that other people expect certain behaviors of her. Her comprehension is not sophisticated, but she has a need to please and will begin to realize that others respond positively when she behaves politely. Saying "please" and "thank you," for instance, is likely to earn smiles and compliments. A preschooler's desire to please is self-centered, but it's also a good starting point; you want your child to find pleasure in doing right.

It's important for parents to understand why a child sometimes does "bad" things and then discipline accordingly. A preschooler's basic interests are still egocentric. Given a choice between something he wants and your values, he will usually choose what he wants. If your three-year-old grabs a playmate's toy, correct him and use the incident to teach consideration and sound etiquette principles.

- Tell him clearly that the behavior is unacceptable. ("It's not okay to take a friend's toy without asking.")

- Encourage him to see the other person's point of view. ("How do you think Tommy felt when you just took his toy?")

- Help him to put things right and prompt mannerly behavior. ("Now, please give Tommy the toy and tell him that you're sorry. When you apologize, Tommy will feel better.")

- Give him alternate solutions, and encourage patience. ("Let's ask Tommy if you can have the toy when he's finished. While you're waiting, you can play with the blocks.")

Feelings of empathy are usually sporadic before at least age five, and *conscience* is not fully formed until adolescence. But long before he develops his own inner voice, your child will internalize your values and standards and learn to regulate his behavior based on how you discipline.

◂┼

- ***Reinforce your child's good behavior with praise.*** Your preschooler will do good deeds, and you should praise her. This requires paying attention to what she does. If she sits quietly in her car seat for the entire ride to Grandmother's, tell her what she did right and how pleased you are. Share the news with Grandmother, who will reinforce the lesson with some extra praise. Don't overdo the hurrahs, but stay alert for opportunities to promote your child's good actions and feelings. Positive reinforcement is the most effective and enduring form of discipline.

"Why?" is a preschooler's favorite question, and sooner or later, he'll ask why you keep insisting on good manners. It's a valid question, and you'll want to supply an answer he can comprehend.

Go for the obvious: Good manners make people feel good. When he makes other people feel good, he'll feel happy. When you talk about manners and politeness, use illustrations from his experience. ("I saw you smile when Mr. Rodriguez said hello and shook your hand. Mr. Rodriguez was polite to you, and that made you feel nice.") Concrete examples help to encourage empathy and to define kindness and consideration. Children generally want to be liked, so tell your child that people like people who are polite.

Your child also needs to learn the meaning of words like "rude" and "impolite." Explain that doing something rude or thoughtless makes people feel bad. Instead of criticizing people your child knows, find instances of bad manners in stories. Make up examples that appeal to your child's imagination. ("What if your teddy bear talked so much that you never got to say a word? Would you feel mad?") Give him reasons to use good manners. ("If you talk with food in your mouth, it looks icky. Also I can't understand your words.")

Empathy and Fairness

THE PRINCIPLES OF ETIQUETTE ARE grounded in empathy and fairness. The remarkable capacity to feel what others are feeling seems to be present in every human being, but empathy must be tended carefully. Three- to five-year-olds are not naturally considerate, because consideration isn't really possible until a child is able to *identify* with other people. At three, a child's comprehension that others have feelings is just beginning to develop. By five she is better able to grasp that people, including peers, feel, want, and need in the same ways as she does. As she approaches school age, she can, in fact, "feel" someone else's pain and offer comfort that is not totally self-centered.

Despite their developing feelings of empathy, preschoolers are still not inclined to share and take turns without prompting. A youngster's

The nature of a child's aggressive behavior usually changes during the pre-school years. When a three-year-old is angry or frustrated, he may lash out with hands, feet, or teeth. As he grows older, aggressive behavior becomes more verbal. Teasing and threatening words are likely to replace physical blows, and children by five or six become adept at name-calling and insults.

In a verbal conflict between preschoolers, caregivers are best advised not to take sides. Step in, calm tempers (time-outs at opposite ends of the room might work), and then talk with the children about why they shouldn't call names. Be clear that verbal insults are no more acceptable than physical aggression.

If you see that a child is really disturbed by being insulted, respect his feelings and don't compound his self-doubts by dismissing his worries. Explain that when people are angry or feeling bad, they sometimes say things they don't mean. Be sympathetic, but avoid overcompensating. Don't soothe a child by telling him that he's "the best little boy in the world" or by heaping criticism on another child. Extreme comments strike false notes with children and may harm their trust in you.

---

preschool years are a period for acquiring a healthy humility as the child moves from believing that she is the center of all attention to compre-hending her place in a world of individuals like herself. This awareness is essential for both self-respect and respect for others.

Fairness and Sharing

When a three-year-old demands fairness, she means getting her own way. But between four and five, she begins to associate fairness with sharing, and she has to find reasons to get more than her share. Her jus-tifications—"I get the biggest piece of cake because I'm older"—can be annoying for parents. As she approaches six, she'll begin to define fair-ness as absolute equality. The preschooler's progression from "I get what I want" to "I have to have a reason to get what I want" to "everybody gets the same" indicates important progress in the development of empathy and awareness of the needs of others.

Honesty and Reality

HONESTY IS A BASIC PRINCIPLE of etiquette, and preschoolers are ready to begin learning the meaning of honesty. Without intending to be dishonest or deceptive, all young children tell untruths. Preschoolers still live largely in a world of fantasy and magic. Their play is highly imaginative, and their creative minds don't click off when the games end. They do not yet know what truth is because what they can imagine is often as real to them as what they actually experience. They will tell tall tales and falsehoods for a number of reasons.

- *Fantasies are exciting and fun.* Children enjoy entertaining themselves and others with make-believe adventures.

- *Fantasies reflect something children would like to be able to do or have.* A three-year-old gives a detailed account of how she flew like a bird to day care. A four-year-old only child convinces everyone at preschool that she has a big brother in high school. This kind of imaginary wish fulfillment helps a preschooler cope with the world; in her fantasies she has the power to control what she cannot in real life.

- *They want to please.* A young preschooler doesn't want you to be upset, so she may make up a story that she believes will please you. "I ate all my supper," she might say proudly, although the evidence of a half-full plate is in front of her.

- *They want to avoid punishment.* As children begin to separate truth from fantasy, lying to escape consequences becomes more common. Parents should be careful that they aren't punishing too much or too harshly, thereby pushing the child to be dishonest.

- *They want to have or do something that isn't allowed.* Your child might beg to drink soda pop by telling you that a playmate "always gets soda."

A parent who says that his preschooler never lies is not paying attention or is in denial. By trying out lies, a child learns about honesty through trial and error. She tells a whopper, caregivers show disapproval,

An older preschooler is likely to face conflicts between honesty and other values. A typical example involves telling on a friend. A child may be genuinely torn between telling the truth about a situation—his buddy threw rocks at the cat—and protecting a friend from punishment. The child wants to be truthful, but he doesn't want to tattle. Some youngsters will even take the blame for something they didn't do. Try getting at the problem by asking leading, nonaccusing questions. ("The cat hid in the pantry while you and Jeremy were playing. Do you know what made her afraid?") Recognize the seriousness of your youngster's dilemma. He is caught between two positive values: truthfulness and loyalty. Offer assurances that his difficulty is real and that adults also face such situations. Explain that he won't be tattling if he tells you what happened. If he's still reluctant, let the matter drop for the time being. You can discuss it later in another context—perhaps a story in which a character faces a similar dilemma.

and she eventually learns that her caregivers value honesty. She begins to distinguish between truth and fiction. When she internalizes the difference, she is constructing that inner voice of conscience that will guide her behavior when she is much older.

Encourage Truth Telling

It's your job to help your youngster sort out reality and fantasy by recognizing her untruths and pointing them out to her. Ask the right questions. Straightforward questions about what happened allow her to explain in her own words. Give her time to tell the truth, and don't put words in her mouth. Stay calm and as objective as possible, and don't frighten her with the threat of punishment.

A three- or four-year-old is likely to lay blame on outsiders, including objects and imaginary friends. If she tries to hang a mischievous action on a real person, tell her firmly and immediately that you know she isn't telling the truth. ("Your brother is at school, so he couldn't have broken the vase.") If she blames her doll or imaginary friend, be clear that you know the truth without undermining her imagination. Make the point that blaming the doll is your child's fantasy—not yours—and that she will take the consequences. Your child will more easily learn to distinguish between truths and untruths if she understands that you can't be hoodwinked.

Rewarding Truthfulness

Parents should recognize honesty and reward it when possible. When your preschooler has done her best to tell the truth, don't press for every detail; she may resort to making up details just to satisfy you. Instead, tell her that you're glad she told the truth. Introduce the idea that other people expect honesty and that telling the truth is the right thing to do.

When she is truthful without prompting, show her how much you value her honesty. You want her to talk to you about things that may not be comfortable for her. If she informs you that she didn't share with a playmate in day care, tell her how much you appreciate her honesty. She is giving you a chance to talk about values and feelings. Don't let the moment slip by.

Modeling Honesty

Have you ever told a caller that someone was at the door in order to get off the phone or taken a "sick day" from work because you wanted a day off? Small lies can become an unconscious habit, and fundamentally good and honest people may be surprised at how often they use white lies out of a strained sense of politeness or for personal convenience. A child is incapable of understanding the subtle distinctions between little fibs and bald-faced lies. Hearing a parent tell falsehoods may confuse your child and upset her budding understanding of truth and reality.

It is wrong to engage a child as a coconspirator in dishonesty. What may seem like a tiny fib to an adult can be very harmful to a child. A parent might ask a child to deliver a false excuse or cover-up—saying to a caller that "Mommy can't come to the phone. She's not here," when Mommy is available, or telling the nursery school director that "We're late because the clock is broken," when the parent simply overslept.

Involving a child in indirect dishonesties and omissions can be just as harmful as blatant falsehoods. "Don't tell Mr. Marshall that Daddy got a new job" or "Don't tell your cousin about our visit to Grannie's house" may not seem like lying. But the parent who expects a child to keep too many little secrets is encouraging the child to be secretive and deceptive. At the same time, you want your child to understand that there are such things as "good" secrets, such as planning a birthday surprise for someone and not revealing the contents of Christmas gifts. If she's figured out that *you* are Santa Claus or the Tooth Fairy, urge her not to spoil the fantasy by sharing her discovery. Her friends will learn the truth in their own time.

Promoting Respect

RESPECT FOR SELF IS INTIMATELY related to respect for others. In the preschool years, children begin to connect with people in new ways and to care about others not as people who exist to serve them but as people like themselves. It's the start of a remarkable transition—from being the center of the universe to one of billions of stars and planets.

By respecting themselves, parents and caregivers teach children self-respect. Parents teach respect for others by setting limits—knock before entering, don't interrupt, and so on. When parents consistently demonstrate the link between respect and behavior, their child begins to think, "That's how I want to act and be treated."

Parents should also show respect for their preschooler's growing skills and self-sufficiency, letting the child do more for himself and resolve his own difficulties, within reason. In hundreds of subtle ways, parents encourage a child's self-control and self-respect, which are essential to respectful, considerate, and well-mannered behavior.

A Delicate Mix

In order to rear a respectful child, caregivers must strive for a delicate mix of teaching and restricting. Expectations and consequences should be clearly spelled out and firmly enforced. Praise for respectful behaviors should be generous. You'll continue to intervene in situations your child can't handle, but more and more, you can allow your child to work out his problems. As your child progresses through the preschool years, your role will shift. From the ever-present guardian and protector, you will become more mentor, guide, and ever-dependable mediator.

Sibling Relations

RELATIONS BETWEEN A PRESCHOOLER AND his sibling or siblings go up and down like a yo-yo. One minute, a preschooler and his older brother or sister are playing and giggling like best friends; the next minute they are at one another's throats. Or your preschooler seems to be handling the presence of a new baby with grace, until he demands his own bottle.

Despite the unpredictability of sibling relationships, don't underestimate the influence of siblings on a preschooler's development. Older siblings model and encourage social behavior and provide gender-role examples. Sibling interactions also help children learn to handle aggression and disagreements. A parent's role in sibling conflicts is to respect each child's unique temperament and personality, stop physical fighting, and give children the chance to settle their differences in their own way.

Interactions among siblings are often confusing. On one hand, a preschooler's empathetic responses extend to brothers and sisters. A preschooler may take an active and affectionate interest in his infant or toddler sibling or hero-worship his school-age sibling. On the other hand, sibling rivalry will be a factor, along with other sources of conflict. Children at differing developmental stages get on one another's nerves. An imitative sibling is flattering to an older child, but when the younger child attaches himself like glue, he can be extremely irritating. A four- or five-year-old is becoming interested in fairness and may be incensed when he perceives that a sibling is being treated "better" than he is. Ownership and privacy issues frequently arise. Teasing and taunting often lead to fights and tears.

Encouraging Sibling Civility

At times, you may despair of your children ever behaving civilly to one another. But the following ideas may ease the emotional stress of being referee in sibling squabbles:

A three-year-old will probably react much like a toddler to a new brother or sister. Regression is common, and you must be on constant alert for aggressive or excessively physical actions. Four- and five-year-olds are generally more temperate. Their emotional bonds with their parents are firmly established. However, it's still important to pay close attention.

Parents may be tempted to make a preschooler responsible for a new sibling to some degree. But even a mature five-year-old is not ready to be a babysitter. She can assist with more tasks than a toddler can, but expecting too much of her may foster resentment. Be flexible with an older child; let her help when she's interested, but don't force participation.

- **Avoid comparisons.** Remarks of the "Why can't you be nice like your big sister?" variety imply favoritism and may stifle individuality. Help your children understand that they are not in competition for your love and attention, and also discourage them from making comparisons among themselves.

- **Give siblings the opportunity to settle their disputes.** You want your children to develop their own problem-solving and conflict-management skills. When they argue, wait and see what happens before intervening. They may be able to come to some resolution on their own. Even if the fight ends when your children storm off to their separate rooms, take comfort in the fact that they haven't allowed the conflict to come to blows.

- **Don't take sides or cast blame unless you are absolutely certain who initiated the trouble.** There's a good chance you will miss the behaviors—a whispered remark, jogging an elbow, flipping a sibling's hair—that start quarrels.

- **Focus on resolution when you have to intervene.** Refuse to listen to either side's tale of woe. Calm the children down and enforce a time-out if necessary. Then work with your children to resolve the situation. Make it clear that the argument is over and it is time to move on.

- **Protect possessions and enforce limits.** Conflicts often arise when one child takes or damages another's property or invades another's sacred space. If your preschooler takes his big

Potential Dangers

Never allow sibling conflicts to compromise safety. Quick action is essential to protect your children and others, especially in a vehicle or a public place. If your children are engaged in a free-for-all in the backseat of the car, pull off the road and stop the car in a safe spot. Turn off the engine and inform your little battlers that you won't proceed until the fighting ends. Stay calm and stop any physical aggression. Don't get involved in their argument, but don't drive off until order is fully restored. It's much better to be late to your destination than to endanger anyone by driving while distracted.

In public places, sibling squabbles are at best annoying and at worst dangerous for innocent bystanders. Even nonphysical fighting consumes a child's attention. In a crowded mall or a confined space such as a bus or subway car, she may trip and fall or cause an accident to someone else. Stop the fighting immediately. If necessary, remove the children from the situation; you may have to retreat to a quiet location, leave a public conveyance, or go home. Be clear that public arguing and fighting will not be tolerated and that you are in control.

---

brother's things without asking or messes up his sister's room when she is at school, you must treat the infraction seriously. Three-year-olds may not be clear about the meaning of "mine" and "yours," so go over the rules about respect for property. An older preschooler may need stricter discipline. Clarify house rules and the consequences for violating them, then follow up consistently when the rules are broken again. (See "Respect for Property," page 86.)

Playing with Peers

AROUND AGE THREE, YOUR CHILD will become more sociable with children his own age. By around four, peers begin to engage in genuine interactive play and may form friendships. Peer play also brings a new level of fussing and feuding. Even children in day care or playgroups may have difficulty with aspects of peer interaction. But learning to get along—to be cooperative and treat other children with respect—is a key step forward in becoming a mannerly person.

The etiquette of peer play will be easier for some preschoolers than others. Children must adapt to others in order to play together. How well they adapt will depend on individual temperament and personality and also the guidance provided by parents and other adults.

The Importance of Sharing

Learning to share is central to developing good play behaviors. Sharing isn't instinctual, but during the preschool years, most children start to realize that there are reasons for and benefits from sharing and taking turns.

- Sharing is an avenue to making friends and being liked by other children.

- Sharing and turn taking make it easier to play happily with others.

- Sharing and turn taking make it possible to participate in games and involve others in imaginary play.

- Sharing and turn taking are expected and encouraged by parents, teachers, and other key caregivers.

Good manners promote sharing and cooperation. A preschooler who demands, "Give me your truck" of a peer is likely to be ignored or told to get lost. But if he says, "Could I please play with your truck?" there's a possibility he may receive what he asks for. When preschoolers are reared in households where politeness is the norm, they are often more open to politeness among their peers. They have observed and experienced the positive reactions that "please," "thank you," and "you're welcome" bring at home. They don't know exactly why, but courtesy seems to produce pleasing results.

Even children who haven't had much early exposure to politeness can learn fairly quickly when they enter preschool and kindergarten. They will usually pick up the manners of peers and teachers in order to become part of the group.

Fun Toys and Play

As soon as your child can tell you her likes and interests, toy selection becomes easier. Ask yourself if the item will support a child's love of fantasy and creative play. Consider toys that will help reinforce good manners and social interaction—a dollhouse or activity center, toy dishes and utensils, puppets for role-playing games. Since preschoolers love imitating domestic routines, supply toy implements such as brooms and sweepers, irons and ironing boards, workbenches, wheelbarrows, and garden tools. Because imagination is so much a part of the preschooler's play, parents can create dress-up and prop boxes with items from the family's closets. Old hats, shoes, scarves, ties, and clothing can be magically transformed into the costumes of a child's favorite characters.

Cooperating with Adults

WHEN YOUR CHILD ENTERS NURSERY school or kindergarten, he must be prepared to cooperate with adults and to do as he is told. You must be perfectly clear about the role of caretakers—that they are in charge—and set out your expectations and standards for your child.

- **Respond to all adult caretakers including teachers, teacher's aides, and sitters.** A preschooler must understand that when parents or primary caregivers are not around, he is to mind the adults in charge without complaint or argument. Encourage cooperation by expressing respect for and confidence in his teachers and caretakers. If you have a problem with a preschool teacher, don't talk about it to your child beyond seeking basic information. A child is not going to respect a teacher or babysitter whom his parents have belittled.

- **Show respect for caretakers by being polite, listening to what they say, following directions, and not interrupting when an adult is speaking.** A simple way to instill respect is to teach your child his caretakers' names and titles. Generally, a preschooler should learn to address adults by "Mrs.," Miss," "Ms.," or "Mr." He will forget at times and may call adults "Mommy" and "Daddy" when he can't remember their names. Be patient, but set the standard of polite address.

- **Trust caretakers to provide help when asked.** You don't want your child so awed by or shy of teachers and other authority figures that he is afraid to request assistance. Encourage his comfort with adults in charge by complimenting and praising the adults. ("Mrs. Jackson is such a nice person. She really enjoys taking care of you.") When your child complains about a teacher, listen to what he says and try to explain. ("Mrs. Jackson tells you to be quiet during story time so that all the children can hear the story.") Suggest solutions. ("Wait until the story is over. Then ask Mrs. Jackson your question.") Stay in touch with teachers and caretakers so that you can follow your child's progress and work with them when problems arise.

Coping with Peer Problems

GETTING ALONG WITH PEERS IS hardly trouble-free for preschoolers, who are still torn between self-centeredness and concern for others and are inclined to react emotionally. Problems and conflicts often occur during play, and older preschoolers will begin developing methods to deal with their difficulties without adult help. But parents must be ready to intervene when teasing and aggression are taken too far. Problem behaviors range from merely irritating to hurtful, and responsible adults must draw the line.

Boastfulness

Listen to children at play and you'll hear lots of bragging: "I'm the strongest"; "I've got the best new toy"; "My dress is prettier than yours." Preschoolers do a lot of comparing among themselves, and claiming superiority is one way a child builds self-esteem. Caregivers find such talk discomforting, but the most effective cure is often the reaction of playmates. Children are very good at turning deaf ears to the boasting of peers, and when the boasts fail to get a positive reaction, the behavior is likely to fade away.

If your child seems excessively boastful, talk with him about it. Explain what boasting is and how claims to superiority can annoy other

No Favorites

Even though they may see more of a grandchild who lives nearby, it is important for grandparents to show affection to all their grandchildren. Establish regular communication and acknowledge special days with calls and gifts; make the effort to see your grandchildren whenever possible. In blended families, you'll want to give equal attention to your own grandchildren and your step-grandchildren. When sibling conflicts arise, it's better not to take sides, but you may be able to help an older grandchild express her frustrations and find positive solutions.

people. His self-confidence will probably benefit from some extra love and reassurance from you. But if he has been rejected by his peers because of his boasting, don't compound the problem by telling him that he really is the best or has the best things.

Bossiness

When your preschooler puts his hands on his hips, cocks his head, and loudly declares, "I want my snack this minute!" or "Don't dare touch my blocks!" he is asserting his independence. But is he being bossy? A preschooler's thoughts often run faster than his ability to form words; he hasn't yet learned to control his volume, pitch, and tone; and he is inclined to imitate the language he hears from caregivers, including commands and demands. For all these reasons, a preschooler is likely to speak in a brusque manner that strikes most adults as unpleasant bossiness.

He must learn to express his independence, but not at the expense of good manners. Modeling polite speech and mannerisms is always the best teacher. In addition, you'll want to:

- *Correct consistently by giving your child the polite language he needs.* When he demands, "Give me the airplane!" restate his request in an acceptable way—"Please, may I have the airplane, Harry?" Ask your child to repeat your words. You'll have to go through this exercise many times before he gets the message.

- *Prompt, prompt, and prompt again.* Encourage your child to be polite to playmates, but don't embarrass him in front of his peers. Forcing a preschooler to be polite can turn manners education into a power struggle.

- **Keep your own voice and mannerisms normal.** If a parent shouts, the child assumes that shouting is acceptable. Don't mimic his tone of voice or mannerisms as an object lesson. Parody goes straight over a preschooler's head, and mimicking a child in front of his peers is humiliating.

- **Be aware of the circumstances.** Children tend to be more tyrannical when they're tired, stressed, or frightened. During a playdate, for example, your child may suddenly command a playmate to "Go away" or "Don't touch my book." Chances are that the visit has gone on too long and it's time for a restful activity.

- **Stay calm when he's bossy or boastful around other people.** You may need to apologize to other adults, but don't demean or embarrass your child. ("Jeffrey is learning good manners, but sometimes he forgets." Not "Jeffrey can't seem to learn to be polite.")

Tattling on Playmates

It's hard to think of a more common preschool practice than telling on peers. Almost as soon as little ones get together, the outcries begin: "Robbie was mean to me!" "Becky poked Ari and made him cry!" Tattling generally annoys adults much more than children. Unless harmful activity is taking place, adults are best advised to stay aloof from the action. Preschoolers tend to tattle with burning passion, then forget the whole thing almost immediately.

At age five or so, preschoolers become increasingly intense about justice and fairness, and tattling tends to change tone. They see right and wrong in black and white, and their objective in telling on others is often to see that wrongs are addressed and equality is enforced. Their tattling may seem petty ("Walter took an extra turn on the swings"), but it is part of their growing moral awareness. By around age seven, children begin to understand that right and wrong are more complicated and also that their peers will ostracize tattlers, so the incidents of tattling usually decrease.

Adults can register their objection to tattling; often no more than a disapproving look is needed. But punishing a preschool tattler can confuse lessons about honesty and trustworthiness. Let your child know that truthfulness is valued and that telling on a friend may sometimes be necessary for a good cause, as when the friend is doing something dangerous or dishonest. (See "Honesty and Reality," page 136).

Teasing

It normally starts around age three. Children learn very quickly how to annoy others by teasing, and they enjoy getting a rise out of a sibling or playmate. Among preschoolers, lighthearted teasing can turn mean-spirited in an instant because youngsters don't have the internal controls to stop the teasing. You can help an older child understand the difference between playful teasing and the hurtful kind, but with a preschooler, you'll want to be very clear that teasing and name-calling are wrong and unacceptable.

How children react to being teased depends to a degree on individual temperament; some take it in stride, while others are extremely sensitive and easily hurt. Should your preschooler become a frequent victim of teasing, the best advice is to:

- *Be sympathetic, but also teach him how to ignore the teasing.* You can encourage your child to continue whatever he's doing or walk away when teasing begins. Some role-playing with your child can be very good training.

- *Discuss why children his age usually tease*—to be funny or to attract attention. Explain that teasers often don't mean what they say and just want to get a reaction.

- *Avoid approving of or encouraging a preschooler's instinct to respond in kind.* If you appear to accept teasing as a defense against being teased, you will undercut your own credibility when you talk to your child about the painful effects of teasing.

- *Help your child out of a difficult situation.* If the teasing is persistent and interferes with your child's life—he resists going to preschool or becomes especially tense or anxious—you have to step in. Talk with his teachers and ask for their help. If a playmate is the problem, you may have to speak with the parent. Be as sensitive and nonjudgmental as possible. If the teasing continues, you can discontinue visits and playdates for a while.

- **Be firm when teasing occurs between your own children.** Make it clear to siblings that hurtful teasing is not allowed, and spell out the consequences.

Discovering Diversity

IN THE PRESCHOOL YEARS, CHILDREN begin to notice that people are different and that differences are interesting. One of a preschooler's basic discoveries will be gender difference. By age five, preschoolers generally prefer to play with children of like gender and increasingly engage in gender-specific activities.

Sorting the world into male and female is just the beginning of his interest in differences. He will notice that people come in all sizes, shapes, and colors. He will be conscious of age and physical attributes and abilities. He'll want to know why people dress and speak in different ways. He'll be fascinated by certain occupations—firefighting, policing, teaching, nursing, zookeeping, and so on—and role-play interesting jobs in his imaginary games.

The discovery of differences is vital to the development of empathy and tolerance, and later to the ability to accept and appreciate human diversity. Even if you live in a fairly homogeneous community, you can use books, magazines, television, and videos to introduce your preschooler to the wider world. Remembering that your child is deeply engaged in the intellectual process of learning that he and others are separate and individual, you can do a great deal to teach and promote positive values and attitudes that will benefit your child throughout his life.

Uncomfortable Questions

Preschoolers are unerringly vocal and direct when they encounter someone or something new. They have no qualms about asking questions that polite adults would never voice: "Why does that lady walk with a stick?" "Why is that man so little?" "Why does that girl talk funny?" To a child, such questions are as normal as "Where does the sun go at night?" Parents are often more embarrassed by children's questions than is the person who is the object of a child's curiosity.

When your preschooler shouts out a question or remark that makes your blood run cold, remember that he is by nature curious and has no intention of causing hurt or embarrassment. These recommendations will help your child develop basic self-restraint and satisfy his inquisitive mind:

- **Work with him on the polite way to express his curiosity.** Teach him to ask questions and make remarks about others in a soft tone of voice. Encourage him to speak directly to you and not to point at strangers. Give him the correct manners without discouraging his interest.

- **Respect his questions and answer with timeliness.** If you are in a public place, you may not want to have a lengthy discussion. Just tell him, "That's a good question, and we'll talk about it when we finish shopping." Be sure to follow up as soon as you can. You don't want your child to think that differences are secretive or forbidden topics.

- **Provide accurate information.** You may have to do a little research to answer your child's questions. There are many good books for preschoolers that explain differences, so a trip to the library may be in order. It's also important to say you don't know when you don't. If you aren't sure of the answer, don't risk passing on erroneous or biased information.

- **Enlist help.** Don't be hesitant to seek information from people who know about differences. If your neighbor is physically handicapped, for example, he may welcome the opportunity to talk with you and your child. It can be a very positive experience for a child to learn directly from people of other races, religions, physical abilities, and so forth. These sorts of interaction encourage empathy by helping a child learn that the differences are far less important that the similarities among people.

  Be sensitive when you seek help. Explain your child's interest, and ask the person if he or she is willing to talk with your child. If the person agrees, make the circumstances comfortable for everyone. Tell your child that you are going to visit with Mr. Buckley down the street—not that Mr. Buckley wants to talk about why he is blind or walks with crutches.

- **Treat others with respect and don't use negative labels.** Even well-intentioned remarks can have negative effects. If you repeatedly refer to your neighbor as "poor, blind Mr. Buckley," your child will gather that there's something wrong, pitiable, or scary about the person because of his disability. Unless the information is relevant, parents and caregivers should avoid characterizing others by a difference. Never use negative or stereotyping labels. When descriptive labels are necessary, be sure they are positive or neutral ("the nice saleswoman at the toy store," "the boy who wears the Mets baseball cap," and so forth).

Introducing Good Sportsmanship

LEARNING TO SHARE AND TAKE turns are the foundations of fair play, but don't expect your child to earn any good sportsmanship medals quite yet. Preschoolers are highly competitive and have a hard time losing. Winning can be important to their burgeoning self-image and their need to feel superior. As they near age six, however, they will begin to grasp the value of teamwork, and fair play will become a meaningful concept.

Younger children are not usually ready for structured, organized, competitive sports, but they will benefit from sporting activities. Learning to swim, riding tricycles and then two-wheelers, and playing catch and other ball games help children improve their motor skills and coordination and build self-confidence. Be prepared for frustrations, don't push your child to master a skill he isn't ready for, and leave plenty of time for free play. Older preschoolers will engage in one-on-one competition with playmates and play games such as hide-and-seek and tag that teach the basics of winning and losing. You may want your five-year-old to take part in an organized sport like T-ball, but be sure that the activity is run by a qualified coach and that fun and physical activity are the goals, not competition.

Letting Children Win?

Parents often wonder if they should allow a child to win at games. The answer is yes and no. A child who always wins misses out on critical lessons about handling loss. Yet a child who consistently loses can become so dispirited that he ceases to try. A parent can strike a balance by winning sometimes and letting the child win at other times. Model courteous winning and losing behavior: Winners don't brag and crow or disparage their opponents. Losers don't sulk or cry foul play. Your child may not be very good at a game, but you can still compliment her fair play. Let her know that you enjoy playing with her, no matter who wins or loses.

Winning and Losing

Parents and caregivers can teach most effectively by modeling good sportsmanship and introducing the etiquette of winning and losing. A good method is by playing simple card and board games such as Old Maid, Go Fish, Candyland, and Chutes and Ladders. The objective of early games is to teach a child that he can have fun by cooperating with others and following rules. Since only a relative handful of children will grow up to be star athletes, the wise parent will help her child to find personal satisfaction in games and sports by encouraging individual capabilities and interests and teaching what it means to be a good sport.

The Road to Fair Play

It's common for preschoolers to change the rules in midplay or cheat when they see that they are losing. In his fantasy play, a preschooler is used to making up the rules as he goes along, so altering the rules of a game seems reasonable to him. Don't become upset, but do let him know that you know what he is up to. Tell him that changing the rules is okay as long as everyone agrees before the game begins, but that cheating isn't acceptable. You can also begin to teach the rudiments of strategy and encourage him to think about smart moves *within* the rules of play. Be clear that you value good sportsmanship and cooperation—not winning at all costs.

Modeling Sportsmanship in All Activities

Good sportsmanship isn't limited to games and sports. A parent who vents anger and insults his opponent when he loses a business contract or an election to the school board is as guilty of modeling bad sportsmanship as one who throws his racket and refuses to shake hands after losing a tennis match.

About Privacy

PRIVACY ISN'T A BURNING ISSUE for most children until around age six, but during the preschool years, you can begin teaching that people need times and places to be alone. Explain to your child that there is a difference between respecting privacy and keeping secrets. You'll also need to discuss behaviors that are not acceptable in public. Finally—and most important—it's time to teach your child about the sanctity of his own body; child-rearing guides and your physician and health-care providers can give invaluable assistance as you tackle the task of educating your preschooler about good touching/bad touching.

Private Behaviors

Preschoolers' interest in how their bodies function can translate into some very embarrassing public activities—from nose picking to genital touching to burping the ABC song. These behaviors are not bad in themselves, but they can annoy others. The best approach is not to make a major issue in public. If it is really obnoxious—shedding his clothes in a store, for example—stop the behavior and try to distract your child's attention to something else. Later, explain that the behavior is okay when no one is around but not appropriate in the presence of others, including you and the rest of the family. He can burp to his heart's content in the privacy of his room, but not at the family dinner table or on a visit to his grandparents.

Also, be alert to behaviors that may signal other problems. Excessive nose picking, head scratching, or scratching the genital area or rectum may indicate health problems. If you are concerned about any of these behaviors, call your doctor. Masturbation can be a part of normal self-exploration at this age; but if you believe it is excessive, you should consult with your health-care provider about it.

Private Places

A child of three or older needs some space to himself. A private place is a safe harbor for thinking, daydreaming, and playing independently as well as indulging in those private behaviors that are unacceptable elsewhere.

At home, you'll want to define and respect a child's private space. His bedroom or the part of the room he shares with a sibling is the most obvious spot, though children often adopt places like a closet or even the space beneath a table as their own. Outdoors, they may gravitate to a corner of the yard or under a bush when they want privacy. Make it clear to siblings that their spaces are off-limits without permission from one another but that you have access to private places when necessary. Respecting privacy doesn't mean abdicating parental authority.

Teach your child to knock on doors and request entry to closed rooms and other people's spaces, but be patient when he forgets. The best teacher now is your example, so honor his privacy and demonstrate your concern for the privacy rights of others.

Taking Care of Property

AFTER AGE FIVE AND CLOSER to six, your child will probably become quite conscious of other people's property rights and ready to defend a friend's things against any takers. Younger preschoolers, although still functioning on instinct, are beginning to learn the basics of self-control and consideration for others, and taking more direct control of their lives. Their new independence gives parents opportunities to introduce the concept of responsibility and to begin integrating the child in family routines.

Concerning Chores

Parents need to be realistic: Preschoolers, especially three- and four-year-olds, can learn to help but are not yet ready to take full responsibility for chores. The most effective approach is to set standards and help your child carry out specific tasks but not to punish or become angry when he doesn't meet expectations. Let him know that

Nature is on your side when it comes to teaching organization. Preschool children become fascinated with sorting and categorizing. They'll separate toys by type (action figures in this corner, stuffed animals in that) and group leaves, twigs, and rocks in separate piles. You can build on this natural interest to encourage taking care of and putting away possessions. There are many kinds of storage systems available for children, but don't overlook the obvious; empty shoe boxes and plastic food cartons are great for everything from baseball cards to doll clothes. Include your child in household organization: sorting forks and spoons, putting cans and boxes in the kitchen cupboard, separating and stacking magazines, dividing nonbreakable items for recycling, and so on.

Introducing organization won't automatically produce a neat child, but learning to organize while she is interested will help establish a pattern of respect for things—preparing her to be orderly at school and for peer interactions. By organizing her own things, she will notice when something is out of place or lost. As she comes to identify with others, she will begin to sense how peers, siblings, and caregivers feel about their possessions.

there are jobs that must be done in every family and that everyone has to participate.

- ***Begin with his own possessions and build on whatever "putting-away" rituals you have already established.*** He can drop his dirty clothes in the hamper, help put his clean clothes in his drawer, set his place at the table, and take his plate and utensils to the kitchen after every meal. He can put toys away and shelve his art supplies. Let him feed the family dog, cat, or goldfish and water plants under your supervision. Get your preschooler used to the idea that cleaning up and putting away are part of his normal activities.

- ***Give him the tools to make cleaning up and putting away easy:*** wastebaskets in his room and play area; sturdy drawers and shelves that are within reach; plastic storage containers; a low bar, hooks, and large plastic hangers in his closet; and a place in the garage to park his riding toys.

- *Involve him in your daily chores.* Let him assist when you pre-pare meals; he will enjoy stirring, pouring, and spreading. He can help you dust, sweep, and wipe up spills. His participation may slow you down a bit, but he is learning that tasks can be shared and that his environment doesn't magically clean and repair itself.

- *Put some fun in chores.* More often than not, he will forget his chores, and at some stages of development, he will be downright defiant. But you can encourage helping if you make it interesting and fun. Sing songs. Use chores such as sorting his socks to teach colors and numbers. Remind him gently when he fails to do something, but don't criticize him for being lazy or sloppy. Express your appreciation for his assistance, and give praise when he completes a task.

Being Careful

Preschool children can begin learning to be careful. Be understand-ing; some preschoolers are more awkward than others, and allowances must be made. Set limits and explain that these restrictions apply in your home and everywhere else:

- No running, stomping, or jumping indoors
- No jumping, climbing, or pulling on furniture
- No pulling or swinging on cords, curtains, tablecloths, and so on
- No slamming of doors and drawers
- No touching things that aren't yours without permission
- No playing with electronic equipment, power tools, and other dangerous and delicate items

During the preschool years, your child will take on more responsibil-ity for his own safety (by four or five, he probably understands not to put his finger in a light socket or touch a hot stove), but his self-control is tenuous, so remain vigilant. Discuss *why* there are rules—for safety, to protect property from damage, to respect other people by caring for their possessions. Don't wait until your child has broken something for a talk. Let him know that while accidents happen to everyone, he can avoid many accidents by being careful and following the rules.

Following Through

Not every incident is an accident, and children should know that there will be consequences for deliberate acts of destruction. Discuss the consequences for specific acts with your child. Ask what he thinks is a fair consequence for cracking your window with a rock or coloring in his brother's schoolbook. You may be surprised by his answer; preschoolers are often much harder on themselves than a parent would dream of being.

Encouraging Thriftiness

IT'S A GOOD IDEA TO start the savings habit as soon as possible. Around age five, a child can begin to understand the meaning of money and thriftiness and that it is impolite to constantly ask others for money and things that cost money. Begin with basics. Give your child a savings bank—kids love the clear plastic ones that enable them to see their money increase over time. Work out a plan by which your child

---

A Question for Peggy and Cindy

Several of my daughter's friends are now getting weekly allowances, and Nicki wants her own money. She just turned five. Is she too young?

Some parents prefer to wait until a child is older, but age five or six isn't too early to start an allowance. Begin with a small amount; a dollar is usually enough, and your child may prefer it in coins, which feel weightier and more important. It's generally recommended that parents not link allowance to chores because this gives a child mistaken ideas about the participatory nature of family responsibilities. Whatever you decide, try not to feel pressured by indulgent parents who give their children large allowances—a form of parental competition that can undermine a child's sense of values.

---

saves ten pennies of his allowance each week and can spend or save the rest as he likes—within reason. When he wants something more expensive than he can afford, explain that he has a choice. He can buy something less costly, or he can save his allowance until he has enough for the item. Learning to save for what he wants provides valuable, real-life experience in patience, self-control, and planning as well as the meaning of money.

CHAPTER 13

The Expanding World of Language

SPOKEN LANGUAGE DEVELOPMENT IS FAST and furious for preschoolers, although the timing varies considerably from one child to another. As their vocabulary expands, preschoolers often become fascinated with learning and using "big" words. They are also acquiring and using basic language structure and grammar and beginning to understand intonation.

Language acquisition affects how a child relates to the world as she becomes increasingly able to verbalize her thoughts, needs, and interests and to understand more complex instructions and explanations. Words give your child the ability to think symbolically—to form and shape ideas that are not inspired by the physical presence of an object or person. She begins to connect with you and others in her thoughts; she can listen to you describe an event at which she was not present and be interested because language draws her into the story.

As her comprehension grows, language becomes the primary means by which she learns mannerly behavior. A great deal of the etiquette she is learning involves vocal expression, both words and sound, and parents can now interweave manners education with their child's growing involvement with language and speech.

Conversing with Your Child

PARENTS SPEND A LOT OF time issuing commands, instructions, and corrections to their preschooler, but it's very important to be talking *with* her as well. Part of becoming socialized is learning that conversation requires give and take. Talking with a child about something as basic as what you both did during the day gives her experience in the natural flow and tone of conversation. Since she needs to learn listening as well as speaking skills, you will provide the model by listening attentively when she speaks.

Pleasant Chats

Converse in situations without too many distractions, so you and your child can be attentive. Look for relatively quiet times and places. Take your child on a walk; retire to a quiet spot in the garden or on the porch. You will talk often with your child while doing some activity, but there's no substitute for focused, one-on-one conversation. Keep conversations loose and pleasant.

Include your child in adult conversations whenever you can. She may not want to speak and will probably dash off as soon as she becomes bored. But she needs opportunities to observe the polite ways adults communicate with one another. At the dinner table and family gatherings, acknowledge your child by speaking directly to her and engaging her in the conversation at least some of the time. Avoid talking about any child as if she were not present.

The Basic Manners of Talk

PRESCHOOLERS ARE FAMOUSLY CHATTY. EVEN shy children can run on endlessly when talking to someone with whom they feel comfortable. At this age, children seem to be in love with the sound of their own voices, and in a way they are. Parents, however, need to introduce some manners into the talk stream by teaching and reinforcing these basic conversation manners:

- *Speak slowly and clearly.* You can begin gently correcting pronunciation and grammar with an older preschooler. Helping her slow her pace will do a lot for clarity. If your child is speaking too rapidly, gently prompt her to stop and take a breath. Wait a few seconds for her to collect her thoughts again and then let her finish.

- **Don't interrupt when someone else is speaking.** When your child breaks in on you, stop and address her directly. Remind her not to interrupt. Be firm and tell her that you will talk to her in a few moments. Then return to your conversation. Even if you end a conversation with another person fairly quickly, don't give your child the impression that you are giving in to her demands.

- **Take turns talking.** This lesson is truly hard for children, the loquacious ones especially. It will be a major part of your child's preschool and kindergarten education, but you can reinforce the message at home. Try playing talking games among family and with little guests. For example, ask your child and others a series of fun questions—What's your favorite toy? Your favorite story? A food you don't like eating?—letting each child answer in turn. To meet their demands for fairness, reverse the order of their responses occasionally.

Loud and Soft

Your child's mastery of loudness and softness is still some years away, so continue working with her on the distinction between "little voice" and "big voice." Since children often don't realize how loud they are, they need reminding to quiet down. Many parents find that nonverbal signals succeed at least some of the time. Work out two or three simple gestures—a tug at your ear means lower the volume, tapping the side of your nose indicates speaking up, and pointing at your watch or wrist signals that it's time to give someone else a chance to speak. Your preschooler will probably enjoy sharing this special signal system with you and other family members.

Reinforcing the "Magic Words"

IF YOU STICK WITH YOUR teaching, prompting, and modeling, "please" and "thank you" may become nearly habitual by the time your child reaches school age. Begin to teach that "please" and "thank you" are not limited to asking for and receiving objects. You can now add say-

Volume-Control Games

If a child persistently talks either too loudly or softly, he may need extra coaching. Appeal to his sense of fun and play voice games. Get a loud child to pretend he's a mouse or other animal he perceives as quiet; a normally soft-spoken preschooler can be encouraged to speak up by using his elephant or lion voice. Competitions for who can talk softest and still be understood or a period of "whisper only" can help children learn to modulate. It may help to identify certain "voices" with familiar situations; his "church voice" might be a whisper, while his "mealtime voice" is moderate in tone.

---

ing "thank you" to party hosts and whenever someone does something kind for her. "Please" takes on greater meaning as it is attached to routine situations: "May I be excused, please?" and "Please, may I go to the bathroom?" By your example, she will learn that "please" and "thank you" are everyday expressions that elicit positive responses.

Your child should also begin to say "yes, please" when accepting an offer and "no, thank you," when refusing. Learning when to say the latter is especially important; declining politely yet firmly will serve your child well now and later—when she's an adolescent, for example, and confronting peer pressure over difficult issues.

"You're Welcome" and "Excuse Me"

Add "you're welcome" to the list of polite phrases. "You're welcome" is the common-sense way to reply graciously to an expression of gratitude. When your child says "thank you," remember to respond with "you're welcome," and she will pick up the habit.

Explain to your child the many uses of "excuse me"—when leaving the table; after sneezing, burping, or making other body noises; when interrupting and entering someone's private space; after accidentally bumping into someone, and so on.

"I'm Sorry"

It's been said that "I'm sorry" is the most difficult phrase in the language. Adults and children are not so different when it comes to admitting and taking responsibility for errors, mistakes, and wrongdoing, but

Be sensible when teaching "I'm sorry." Some adults, through lack of self-confidence or out of sheer habit, tend to apologize for everything. They apologize for bothering a restaurant waiter when a meal is undercooked. They apologize for the weather when a sudden blizzard means canceling an appointment. A child exposed to such excesses is likely to draw the conclusion that he must be sorry for everything that happens or conversely that apologies are meaningless and he needn't make them. As a role model, make necessary apologies, but don't go overboard.

parents have to be consistent models and prompters. Apologize to your child if you make a mistake, and tell her the reason for the apology. ("I'm sorry that we were late to Albie's birthday party. I didn't understand the directions to his house.") Make amends if you can, but be reasonable and don't promise not to make a mistake again.

Prompt your child and give her the words she needs when she has to make an apology. ("Tell Chelsea that you are sorry you broke her toy.") Be direct and firm, but don't humiliate your child with a lengthy lecture.

Since your child will hear "I'm sorry" used in different contexts, she may be confused. Explain that people use "I'm sorry" when they feel sympathy for someone else ("I'm sorry you've lost your doll, Bonnie") and also when they express regret for something they have done ("I'm sorry for breaking your doll").

Meeting-and-Greeting Manners

THE TIME HAS ARRIVED TO teach more than "hi" and "bye." Preschoolers are ready to learn the proper ways to meet and depart and the basics of making introductions. Role-playing games can be very effective. Before parties and gatherings, act out with your child the courtesies that are expected—greeting her host or hostess before running off to play and saying "good-bye" and "thank you" before leaving. Role-playing and modeling will also help you to teach introduction manners, emphasizing these fundamentals:

- *Always introduce people who don't know each other.* Keep the formalities simple. ("This is Lisa." "Meet my teacher, Miss

Winters.") Explain that introductions bring people together and make them feel welcome and comfortable with others. Always introduce your child to people she hasn't met before. Including her in your meeting-and-greeting rituals teaches her to value these courtesies and understand that they are standards for behavior.

- **Respond politely when introduced to someone.** Children should learn to look directly at the new person and say "hello" when they are introduced. Preschoolers are often wary of strangers and may avert their eyes or turn away. You'll need to do lots of gentle prompting before your child is comfortable with greetings. Learning the basic ritual should make it easier for a shy or reluctant child; knowing what to do may boost a child's confidence when meeting someone new.

  You'll be lucky to get a tentative "hi" from a three-year-old, but with practice and encouragement a child approaching six should be responding to introductions with a direct look and a hearty "hello." Encourage her to add the person's name ("Hello, Mr. Sanders") to all her greetings.

- **Shake hands.** Some children will eagerly extend their right hands to a new person, but this courtesy can be difficult for younger or shy preschoolers. Enlist family and friends to help; a child will probably be delighted to shake a grandparent's hand or to stick out her hand when a familiar family friend drops by. You can also role-play and practice introduction manners using your child's dolls and stuffed animals. Hand shaking conveys welcome and trust, and practicing in safe, secure situations will help a child build trust and self-confidence.

- **Say "good-bye" when leaving.** Preschoolers may need prompting but are generally comfortable with this courtesy. Even if your child is squirming to leave, don't be tempted to make an end run around the parting courtesies. On the other hand, try not to turn leaving into a drawn-out process, and be considerate of your child's patience.

- **Use formal titles when addressing adults.** Teach that adults are to be addressed by their courtesy or professional titles—Miss, Ms., Mrs., Mr., Doctor, Reverend, Rabbi, and so forth—and last names unless and until the adult asks to be called by his first name. When introducing a child to an adult, give the correct form of address. ("Jane, this is my daughter, Rose. Rose, this is Mrs. Epstein.") Try to repeat the adult's name in conversation so that your child can make the identification. ("Mrs. Epstein has a son who is about your age.")

Unsavory Talk

IT'S OFTEN CALLED "BATHROOM TALK" or "potty talk" by adults and is as natural to older preschoolers as running and playing. Words for elimination and "rude" body functions will send preschoolers into fits of laughter. (At this age, children may also take up swear words, though swearing usually doesn't begin until the school years.) So what can you do about undesirable speech?

- **Don't react.** If your child dashes into your room, screams "Poop!" and collapses into a giggling heap, don't laugh or smile or become upset. Remind her that "poop" is a private word and you don't want to hear it unless she needs to go to the bathroom. Potty talk will usually lose its appeal when adults fail to respond. A parent who reacts with amusement, disapproval, or anger conveys the message that "naughty" words have power—encouraging rather than discouraging their use.

- **Relegate bathroom talk to the same realm as other private behaviors.** When she uses bathroom talk at home, you might take her to her room and tell her that she can rejoin the family when she's finished saying the words. With only herself to entertain, she'll move on to something more interesting pretty quickly. If she uses the words in public, tell her to stop and be clear about the consequences if she continues.

- **Give your child more sophisticated language.** Preschoolers like to learn big words, so you can introduce terms like "urination" and "bowel movement." If your child is still using infant language for genitals and other body parts, teach her the correct terminology and use the right words yourself. In addition to dis-

When it comes to good manners, parents are not the only role models. You will often be introduced to other children, and they will pay close attention to your behavior. Look at the child and include his or her name in your greeting. Offer your hand if you think the child is responsive, but if he doesn't take your cue, back off without comment. Talk with the adult, but find an opportunity to include the child if you can. And remember to express your pleasure at meeting the child when you part, even if he spent the entire time with his face buried against his parent's leg. "I'm very happy to have met you, Jimmy" models good manners and expresses your respect for the youngster.

couraging potty talk, teaching your child biologically correct language helps her understand and respect her body and its functions. Avoid labeling bathroom talk as "dirty" or "nasty" because a child can easily confuse the words with her own body and its functions.

A final idea is to direct your child's desire to amuse toward real humor. At three and four, she won't appreciate jokes, but she can learn funny rhymes and songs. Around five, she'll begin getting the humor in riddles and jokes of the "Knock, knock/Who's there?" kind based on wordplay and double meanings. She can memorize simple jokes and will probably repeat her favorites endlessly. Laugh at her jokes and share her good humor; your child will enjoy the positive responses that her bathroom talk doesn't garner.

Teaching Telephone Manners

FOR A THREE-YEAR-OLD, THERE'S STILL a lot of magic attached to the telephone. By five, your youngster will have a fairly realistic understanding of the phone as a means to communicate with people who are not actually present.

Toy telephones allow you to demonstrate phone etiquette, but remember that children who happily carry on make-believe conversations may still find the actual sound of phone voices to be strange and even a little scary. Look for opportunities to accustom your child to the real telephone—when grandparents or obliging friends call, for example. If a parent routinely phones home during the workday, let your youngster talk when possible, remembering that it may not be convenient to converse with a child when the adult is busy or in a professional setting. You and your child can talk using extension lines in your home, or call your home number from your cell phone and have a chat.

Rules of phone use in your household will change as your child matures, but your preschooler needs to begin learning now that the telephone is a tool, not a toy.

Answering and Placing Calls

Because preschoolers are just not ready to answer the phone, adults or older children should answer until your child is at least five or six. When your child seems prepared to answer on her own, an adult should supervise until you are confident of her answering skills. Even six-year-olds can become distracted in the time between answering the phone and summoning you. Restricting phone answering at this age also keeps your child from having to field unwanted calls—from wrong numbers to sales solicitations to obscene calls.

In general, preschoolers should not make calls without your permission and supervision. By five or so, your child may be capable of placing a call, but you cannot predict who will answer. An exception to the "no calls" rule involves teaching your child to use 911 and other emergency numbers. You may want to put 911 on your speed dial and teach her how to use it. Be clear that these are special and important numbers and that she is never to use them unless something bad happens and help is needed.

Don't expect other adults to speak with your child unless you are certain the adult is willing. Young children may talk a blue streak, or they may become shy and unresponsive. If the adult on the other end is not used to the ways of children, three or four minutes of trying to make sense of your child's chatter or silence can be very uncomfortable.

Supervise all calls and be prepared to take over your child's conversation when necessary. You may have to intercede or call back and apologize if your preschooler suddenly decides to hang up.

MODELING CELL PHONE MANNERS

When using cell phones and beepers in your child's presence, always model consideration for others. Turn off your cell phone or beeper in public places and at social gatherings. When you use a cell phone in public, find a secluded spot and keep conversations short. For safety's sake, don't use a cell or car phone while driving. By monitoring your own phone use, you will teach your child that cell phones are means of communication—not playthings.

Time for Praise

Reinforce good telephone manners with praise. When your child gives a proper greeting, speaks clearly, or listens attentively, tell her what she has done well. Pass on compliments and be specific. ("Mrs. Chang said that she enjoyed talking with you about your new day-care teacher.") If your preschooler does something unmannerly on the phone—banging the receiver or yelling, for instance—don't make a big issue of it. Talk with her about the proper etiquette and practice with some extra role-playing.

Stick to the Fundamentals

When she's older, your child will learn to distinguish different types of calls and callers, summon others to the phone, and take messages. For now, a few fundamentals will start her on the road to considerate phone use.

- **Greetings.** Teach your child that whenever she takes the phone from you, she is to begin with a simple, clear greeting: "Hello, this is Justine." She'll forget to say hello when she's excited or anxious to talk, so repeat the lesson and emphasize how important it is to say her name when she greets a caller, even to her grandparents and best pals.

- **Volume and speed.** Preschoolers often begin speaking normally, then escalate in loudness or drop off to barely audible whispering. Encourage your youngster to use her "little voice." Teach her to hold the phone receiver so that her voice isn't muffled or distant. You might use simple hand signals to indicate when her voice is too strong or too soft. Practice speaking at a normal pace with your child.

- **Duration.** Once they become used to the telephone, many preschoolers like to stay on the line for a long time. You don't want to interrupt your child in midthought, but when you hear the conversation winding down or your child repeating herself, signal her or tell her that it's time to say good-bye.

- **Closing.** Children must learn to end every phone call with a polite "good-bye." Teach her never to hang up or give the receiver to you unless she has said "good-bye" to the caller, and remind her that "good-bye" is as important as "hello."

- **Hanging up.** Putting the phone back in its cradle or on its hook should be considered the real end of a call. Show your youngster how to put up the receiver or switch off a cell phone. It's a good idea to designate a location for your home phone, whether on a cord or cordless, and return it to that place when calls are ended.

Handling Interruptions

The suggestions for controlling interruptions in Part Two (see "Telephone Manners," page 100) continue to be effective with young preschoolers, but sooner or later, you will have to spell out some rules.

Delaying long calls until your child is sleeping is still a good strategy, but by age four or five, preschoolers have often given up daytime naps, and your chances are narrowed, causing special difficulties if you do business from home. You may be able to head off interruptions by taking calls in your office or at your work desk and providing special play items (felt markers and computer paper, an old ledger book or business magazines for cutting and drawing, props for playing "business" or "store") for the times when you are using the phone.

Other Off-Limits Behaviors

In addition to the general rule about keeping a phone in its place, tell your child not to press the keys, pull the cord, or touch the phone when someone is using it. Children soon learn that pushing phone buttons can end your calls and pulling on the cord will drive you to distraction. Make it clear that this kind of behavior is unacceptable.

There are times when your preschooler can legitimately interrupt your phone conversations, so explain these situations clearly. If someone is knocking at the door or the bathtub is running over or another child has been hurt, you need to know immediately. Your child will doubtless get it wrong and interrupt you for reasons that are not urgent. He may even exploit this loophole and interrupt for attention. But when he does judge the situation correctly, reinforce his behavior with praise. If he consistently interrupts for attention-getting only, it's time for him to hear the story of "The Boy Who Cried 'Wolf.'"

A child should also learn that she must not pick up, listen in, or talk into an extension when someone is using the phone. Explain to your child how the phones in your house work. Show her that when you are using one phone, the voices can be heard on an extension. Make it clear that no one is to pick up an extension when another phone is in use. She won't feel so limited if she knows that this rule applies to everyone in the family.

Communicating in Writing

WRITTEN COMMUNICATIONS FOR PRESCHOOL CHILDREN are few, but you'll want to continue exposing your child to the etiquette of the written word. Thank-you notes are basic, but you'll also encourage interest in letter writing for other purposes and for the pure pleasure of sending and receiving mail.

When you write letters, your child will be interested in what you are doing and why. If you write a letter of complaint or thanks to a company, for example, explain the purpose to your preschooler. ("The man who fixed the dishwasher did such a good job that I'm writing his boss to compliment the repairman." Or "I want to tell the phone company that I'm unhappy with their service. I'm writing this letter to ask for their help.") If she wonders why you don't just call, tell her that letters last longer than phone calls and that people can read letters again and again. She may even understand that taking the time to write a letter shows special respect for the person to whom you are writing.

You will continue to write thank-you notes for your preschooler in response to gifts and special events. But you should include him in the process. Read him the notes you write and receive from others, so he can begin to sense the form and content of written expressions of gratitude. You may want to purchase some inexpensive notepaper for your child to scribble his own "notes" for inclusion in your mailings.

Offering Encouragement

Your older preschooler is probably experimenting with writing the alphabet and numbers. Promote her efforts and interest by complimenting her work and displaying it on the refrigerator or bulletin board. Ask her to "write" to grandparents and other relatives (even those who live nearby); letters can include family photos and pictures she has cut from magazines as well as her drawings. Make preparing and mailing letters a fun activity. If the recipients of her letters reply, your child will experience the thrill of receiving as well as sending. Involve her as you prepare holiday and special occasion cards, and encourage her to make special cards for the birthdays of family members.

Other People's Mail

Preschoolers must learn to respect the privacy of mail. Tell your youngster what the address on letters comprises, and explain that letters and packages are to be opened only by the person whose name appears in the address. Until she can read names, make it clear she is not to open anything until you or another caregiver goes through the mail first. When a letter or invitation does arrive for her, *be sure that she opens it herself.* You might let your preschooler open letters addressed to "Householder" or "Resident," but inspect all unsolicited mail and flyers first for appropriateness. You can make a ritual of getting the mail and sorting letters by addressee. Designate a place or container where unopened mail is to be kept. Your preschooler may be interested in saving stamps, so teach her to ask politely after recipients open their letters. Learning to ask will help your child understand that mail is private property.

Teaching Mealtime Manners

DURING YOUR CHILD'S PRESCHOOL YEARS, you can build his repository of table etiquette incrementally. Behaviors such as hand washing and sitting still in a chair are essential from the outset. Others— learning to eat with mouth closed and how to use utensils, for example—will be acquired and improved on as he gains physical skills and becomes accustomed to your mealtime expectations.

Although you will be teaching the basics, don't underestimate the continued importance of modeling. It's much easier to teach table etiquette to a preschooler if everyone else at the table is minding their dining P's and Q's. Older siblings may even be more mannerly when they know they are setting an example for little ones.

Mealtime Basics

THE FAMILY TABLE IS STILL the best place to teach and model table manners, so families should have meals together at least several times a week. Formality isn't necessary; routine exposure, clear expectations, and consistent, loving guidance from caregivers will enable a child to learn politeness in various dining situations. Even if you are picnicking in the backyard or grabbing a quick lunch at the local mall food court, it's important for your child to learn and practice these basics:

- **Wash hands and face.** Washing hands is a must before your child eats anything. Face washing is more a matter of aesthetics, but important if your child's face is very grimy. At three, he'll still need help with hand and face washing. By five, he will probably be able to accomplish the job on his own. Still, he will require frequent reminders, and you'll want to inspect hands before every meal and snack time. If he has done a poor job, insist that he wash again.

- **Stay seated—and no wiggling.** Your child will progress from high chair to booster seat around age three and perhaps to a chair by age five. When he can get down from his seat with ease, it's time to set limits. The minute your child has had enough to eat, he will become bored and wiggly. Teach your preschooler to remain seated while eating—keeping all four chair legs on the floor at all times—and then ask to be excused when he is finished. If you enjoy sitting at the table and chatting before dessert, your child can have his dessert early or return to the table for the final course.

- **Use a napkin.** Even if they continue to wear a bib, all preschool children can learn to use a napkin. Show your child how to put his napkin in his lap, use it to wipe his mouth and hands—without scrubbing—and place it on the table as part of your "being excused" ritual. You can work on the niceties (seeing that the dirtiest parts of the napkin aren't on display and placing it to the left of the plate) as his skills improve.

- **Everyone begins eating at the same time.** It's best not to seat a preschooler until you are ready to serve the meal. You can, however, teach him to ask, "May I begin, please," if a meal is delayed. If your family says grace together, teach your child to wait until the prayer or message of thanks is complete.

- **Say "please" when asking for items on the table.** Teach your child to ask for what he wants and always to include a "please." Demonstrate the correct form—"Will you please pass the salt,

Youngsters love to shake out a napkin with great flourish, and you can probably tolerate this theatricality until your child gets accustomed to the correct manners. Teach your child to unfold the napkin (roughly in half) and place it on her lap. If she needs to tuck her napkin into her waistband or under her legs, that's fine for now. Large cloth napkins are easier to keep in place than flimsy paper. Ask her to tell you if her napkin slips to the floor. You can retrieve it or excuse her to get down from her chair.

Isaac?"—and be sure to say "thank you." Include your child in passing dishes and items that aren't too heavy or awkward to handle. Reaching or stretching over other diners is not allowed.

- **Eat with utensils, not fingers.** Most children are beginning to master a spoon by age three and will add a fork within the next two years. By five or six, they will usually be able to hold these utensils correctly and may be using a knife as a spreader. Don't worry too much about hand position. The important lessons at this stage are to use utensils and not fingers and to bring the food to the mouth, not the mouth to the plate.

At the End of a Meal

Once a child has eaten his fill, he can be off his chair and out of the room in a blink. But he needs to learn to end a meal politely by asking to be excused. For a three-year-old, "Excuse me, Mommy" is adequate. When he learns to ask permission, teach him to say, "May I be excused, please?" If he forgets, you can call him back to the table to make his request. Do this in a lighthearted manner. He just needs reminding.

It's very nice to include a thank-you to the person who prepared the meal. Explain that people like to be complimented on their work, just as your child likes being told when he does something thoughtful. Practice thank-you's routinely at home, and your preschooler will become a welcome guest at everybody's table.

Learning to Help

A young child will gain a better understanding of the importance of mealtimes if he is actively involved. A three-year-old can lay out place

Your child will discover that it's correct to use fingers to eat certain foods—sandwiches, fried chicken, corn on the cob, pizza, rolls, crackers, cookies, raw veggies, cheese, pretzels, and so on—and that other foods require utensils. Serving child-friendly foods will help your preschooler learn to use her spoon and fork. (Green beans and broccoli can be scooped or speared. Thicker soups are easier to eat with a spoon than broths.) Give her a plate with a high rim so that food doesn't slide off. Serve small portions so that there's room on the plate to maneuver a spoon or fork. When she begins using an open-topped cup or tumbler, fill it only a third to half full to aid drinking without spills.

mats and napkins. Put his napkin and place setting in a drawer or cabinet he can reach, and let him set his place for each meal. Depending on agility and interest, four- and five-year-olds may be able to set the entire table and help with serving.

Cleaning up is usually easy to include in your mealtime routine. A preschooler can take his cup and plate to the kitchen, help wipe the table, put dirty linens in the laundry basket, throw away used paper napkins, or dry plastic items with a towel. If you recycle, he can put unbreakable items in the correct bins—a good sorting exercise. If he gets bored or grumbles, ask him to finish just what he is doing, then thank him and let him go on to more interesting activities.

Engaging a preschooler in table setting and clearing encourages his sense of responsibility to and identification with others in the family. Even if you are fortunate enough to have paid household help, it's wise to include your preschooler in some aspect of the process in order to build his respect for the people who care for him and for the nature of work itself.

Respecting Food Preferences

YOU WANT YOUR CHILD TO become an adventurous eater when he grows up so that he can enjoy diverse dining experiences. In the preschool years, the best you can do is offer your normal family fare and encourage him to give everything a try. Preschoolers are usually big eaters but are not experimental. They may go through eccentric

Preschoolers learn dining etiquette over the course of thousands of meals, so concentrate on adding and teaching new skills gradually. By the time your child turns six, she should have all these fundamentals under control most of the time:

Starting the Meal

- Arrive at the table with clean hands and face.

- Place napkin on lap.

- Start eating when everyone else does or when given permission.

Sitting

- Stay seated; use good posture.

- Keep elbows off the table while eating.

Eating

- Chew with mouth closed.

- Don't talk with food in the mouth.

- Don't make bad comments about the food.

- Ask for food and say "please"—no reaching.

- Use utensils as able. (You should shorten the list of finger foods you serve.)

Talking and Noise

- Make some pleasant mealtime conversation.

- Don't interrupt when others are talking.

- Don't make rude or disturbing noises (burping, snorting, singing, etc.).

Ending the Meal

- Ask to be excused when finished.

- Thank the person who prepared the meal.

- Offer to help clear the table.

When your child makes mistakes, quietly remind her of what to do. Be sensitive to her feelings, and whatever you do, don't show your amusement at deliberate displays of bad table manners. She may take your smiles as approval.

phases—demanding rice at every meal or green vegetables only. Continue to offer a healthy variety of foods, and he'll accept the family fare when he's ready. If he really hates a particular food or foods, discuss it with your pediatrician in case your child's reaction signals an allergy.

Preschoolers are quick to speak up when they perceive a food as "yucky" or "gross." Explain to your child that the food is delicious to other people. Tell him that the person who cooks works hard to prepare foods for everyone to enjoy. Let your child know that you respect his preferences and don't expect him to eat something he doesn't want. But also help him to understand that disparaging comments are hurtful and not acceptable. Give him a polite way out by teaching him to say "No, thank you" when offered a food he doesn't like.

Out-and-About Behavior

_____ ⤙

IN THE PRESCHOOL YEARS, GETTING your child out and about is a wonderful way to build on her curiosity, promote her communications skills, and teach good manners. Up to now, she has accompanied you on shopping trips and to some public and private events. She may be in a playgroup or day care and is probably familiar with local parks and playgrounds. It's time to expand her horizons, feed her new desire to know how and why, and encourage her socialization.

Public Places and Activities

PARENTS SHOULD BE OPEN TO their child's interests, seek out suitable activities, and plan field trips whenever possible. If your four-year-old loves to help in the garden, take her along to the nursery or plant store. If she enjoys books about trains, schedule a short train ride if you can. Your preschooler is curious about everything you do, so when convenient and appropriate, take her to your workplace and introduce her to your colleagues. Recruit obliging family members and friends: Uncle Simon, who works for an auto dealership, might give your young car enthusiast a tour of the showroom.

Preschoolers become increasingly aware of what is happening in the out-side world and are influenced by what they see advertised on television. But don't be pressured into taking your preschooler somewhere that he's not ready for. He may beg to go to the gigantic theme park he saw on TV, but have more fun at the neighborhood school carnival where he isn't too small for the rides. You can substitute reasonable, interesting, and usually less costly choices—a trip to see the elephants at the zoo instead of the monster truck rally.

No new experience is ordinary to a preschooler. Her world is full of firsts—first movie in a theater, first ride on a pony, first visit to a farm or museum, first trip on an airplane. Even if she's been to some of these places before, her memory now allows her to hold onto experiences and make them her own. There are some guidelines that will help make every-day and special out-and-about occasions more satisfying for you, your child, and other people.

Selecting Activities
Look for activities suited to your child's age and personality. Check your local newspaper and Internet city guides for announcements of events and activities that are planned with children in mind. Look beyond the obvious; it's good to cater to your child's interests whenever possible, but you'll also want to expose her to new people and places.

Try to keep the activity brief and focused. Although a preschooler's attention span is growing longer, it is still limited, so look for activities that last an hour or maybe two. A preschooler who has sat enraptured through story hour at the library is likely to turn grumpy if you run another hour's worth of errands afterward. Out-and-about occasions should be fun for children, not a test of their endurance. Whatever the activity, be prepared to leave early if your preschooler becomes tired or cranky at a public event and threatens to disturb others.

Good Manners Reminders
Your child will be increasingly able to transfer the good manners she is learning at home to the outside world. But it's still a good idea to

remind her of these rules of behavior every time you are about to enter a public place:

- Walk; speak softly; keep hands to yourself.
- Always be quiet at the parent or caregiver's instruction.
- No begging or whining for items if the caregiver has said no.
- No touching anything without permission.
- Stay with the caregiver at all times.
- Remember "please" and "thank you."

Preparing for New Experiences

Children deserve advance warning when they are going to encounter a new situation and new expectations. If you take your preschooler to a movie, for example, take time to prepare her. Tell her that she will stay seated and be quiet during the movie. She should whisper to you if she wants to go to the rest room. If you face a wait in a ticket line, let her know ahead of time and be prepared to keep her entertained.

When you begin taking your child to performances, religious services, and other events with row seating—on airplanes, trains, and public transport as well—you will add these to your list of good out-and-about manners:

- Stay seated at all times. (She can sit on your lap to get a better view.)
- No turning around to look at or talk to the person behind you.
- Keep hands and feet to yourself. No kicking, scuffing, pulling, or scratching on the seat in front of you.

Lost and Found

By age four, your child needs to learn what to do if separated from you in a public place. Assure her that if you are separated, you haven't left her alone on purpose and that you will find her as quickly as you can. Some people advise telling a child to stand still and wait to be found, but this can be dangerous if she is caught in a crowd. Show her instead how to find a safe place—next to a counter or some other

Charting the Territory

In places you visit regularly, show your child the sales desks and customer service locations and tell him that the people who work there want to help children who become lost. In an unfamiliar place, point out the manager's office, ticket booth, security guards, police officers, and the like. Instruct your child not to leave a store or other place if he is lost. He should learn to find the nearest person in charge and tell that person that he is lost. It's important that your child knows his full name. Reunions are quicker if authorities can page "the parents of Christopher Martin" rather than "the parents of a little boy in a green sweater."

sheltered area—and remain there until you or a person in authority finds her.

You can use books and age-appropriate videotapes to introduce the concept of helpful authority figures—uniformed police and security personnel, managers and salespeople in stores, adults in charge of ticket collection and cash registers, playground supervisors, and so on. Preview instructional tapes and books to be sure they are suitable and not frightening; stories of the awful things that can happen to lost children will only make a child more terrified if she does lose sight of you. When she knows the steps to follow to find help, she's less likely to panic or, worse, become the prey of strangers.

Disciplining in Public

WHEN YOUR CHILD THROWS A tantrum, barges into a stranger, or misbehaves in any way in public, you have to remain calm and in control. Emotional responses will not cure the problem, so count to ten before disciplining.

Most public misbehavior is merely offensive and can be dealt with quickly. Tell your child to stop whatever she's doing and inform her of the consequences if she continues. Save the lectures until later, when you are alone, and never resort to corporal punishment. Consider why your child misbehaved: Was the act deliberate, or was she tired, hungry, or overly excited? Ask yourself how you would discipline if the misbehavior had occurred at home. Too often, the presence of other people impels parents to overreact to a child's misdemeanors. Humiliating a child in public—yelling, name-calling, smacking—reflects on the parent rather than the child and can make the child resentful or fearful of the parent.

Occasionally, public misbehavior can result in physical harm to others or damage to property. A child may pull down a store display or cause an older person to fall. In such a situation, a parent's first responsibility is for the safety and well-being of the child and others. Discipline can wait.

- *Stop all dangerous or disruptive behavior instantly.* Words might work, but you may have to restrain your child by holding her securely. (See "Tantrums in Public," page 121.)

- *See that your child is unhurt.* If the incident involves others, check if anyone else is hurt and immediately seek help for injuries. Even if the other person says he is okay, don't assume that medical attention is unnecessary.

- *Notify the appropriate authority of any damage.* Provide your name, address, and phone number to the authorities. Always offer to pay for any breakage or damage to property.

- *Do not leave until you are sure that everyone is well and that any damage has been cleared away.* Do not leave hazards such as spills or broken glass unattended. The result could be harm to the next person who comes along.

When a serious accident occurs because of your child's behavior, in all likelihood she will feel guilty and need comforting, not blame. Hold her and tell her that you love her. Assure her that what happened was an accident (even when the precipitating behavior was deliberate) and you know she didn't mean to cause harm. When she seems receptive, talk about how accidents happen. Help her understand that she must follow your rules and that misbehaving can lead to unexpected consequences for others. If you do impose a consequence, be sure that it is for the misbehavior and not the ensuing accident.

Mobile Manners

PRESCHOOL-AGE CHILDREN WILL RIDE MORE frequently in other people's cars. They participate in car pools, accompany friends on outings, and travel with grandparents and relatives. Just as you have rules for the family vehicle, you'll want to be clear about your expectations when your child rides with others. Teach your child to:

- *Do as the driver instructs.* Children are sometimes better behaved with others than with their parents, but not always. Your child must respect whoever is driving and follow their instructions just as she minds you. She should also learn that different families may have different standards—some allow toys or eating in the car, but others do not—and she is always to do what the driver says.

- *Do not distract the driver.* When more than one child is in the car, preschoolers can get carried away. They have to be reminded to sit still, use "little voices," and not kick seats or throw objects.

- *Follow the safety rules.* Be certain to provide the correct equipment and see that it is properly installed whenever your child rides with someone else. You may have to have a polite discussion about safety if the driver isn't used to children. Be clear that your child must be strapped securely in her safety seat before any car ride.

- *Tell the driver if you feel sick.* Motion sickness is common among young children, so teach your child to tell the driver if she feels ill. Assure her that the driver wants to know. Give the driver advance warning, so he can be alert for the signs of impending car sickness.

School Bus Behavior

Kindergarten and some preschool programs bring a new experience for many children: daily rides in the school bus or school van. It is essential to prepare children well for the behaviors that make bus riding safe. Go over the rules and have pretend practice sessions. If your child has never ridden in a bus or van, you might take her for a city bus ride. Be

Car-Pool Consensus

Whenever you transport other children in your car, you'll want to make your rules clear to the children and their parents. Car-pool members should agree on the safety rules and passenger etiquette they will enforce. Some serious advance planning can prevent conflicts and confusions later on. Preschoolers love to test limits, so presenting a united front will help each parent to maintain order and discipline when at the wheel.

---

sure to instill respect for the school vehicle driver. Your child won't understand how very difficult a driver's job is, but she can learn that the driver deserves attention and considerate behavior from all passengers.

Be sure to consult with your child's school about their specific restrictions and guidelines. As you work with your child on the proper behavior, let her know that the rules are *rules* and you expect her to follow them even though you won't be with her.

- **Walk—never run—to and from the bus.**

- **Stand well back from the curb or roadside when waiting for the bus.** Wait until the bus comes to a full stop and the doors open before approaching the bus.

- **If you drop something near or under the bus, don't pick it up.** Tell the driver what has happened and follow his instructions to retrieve the item.

- **Take a seat and stay seated for the entire ride.** If there is a seat belt, buckle up. Don't stand up until the vehicle has reached its destination and comes to a stop.

- **No yelling, throwing, horseplay, or any behavior that can distract the driver.** Use "little voices" always.

- **No eating or drinking on the bus.** (Parents can help by not sending a child off with that last piece of breakfast toast or container of juice.)

- **Hold backpack, lunchbox, books, coat, and other items in your lap.** Never put any objects in the aisle or on the floor where they may trip someone.

- **When getting off the bus, stand away from the bus doors until the driver opens them.**

- **Walk away from the bus when preparing to cross in front of it**— far enough in front so that the child can see the driver. (If the child can't see the driver, the driver can't see the child.) Watch the driver and cross only when he signals that it is safe. Look both ways before and while crossing the street and always walk. If the driver honks the horn, children in the process of crossing must stop instantly and follow the driver's instructions. *Never cross behind the bus.*

It's wise to have a responsible adult or older sibling wait for the bus with a preschool or kindergarten child and meet the bus when it returns. If a number of children wait at the same stop, you may be able to rotate bus-stop duty with other parents. When an older sibling accompanies your little one on the bus, be sure that the older child understands his responsibility. Make it very clear to the younger sibling that her big sister or brother is in charge.

Party Manners

THE PRESCHOOL YEARS LAUNCH THE golden age of birthday parties, school parties, holiday parties—and learning party manners. Good behavior at preschool social gatherings may seem like an oxymoron, but parents can guide their child through the basic courtesies. Even if you aren't staying at the party, accompany your child to the door and remain with her while she greets the hosts. Come in when you pick up your child, and don't let her leave without saying a polite "good-bye" and "thank you for inviting me."

When you give a children's party, these suggestions will make the event more fun for the children and easier on you:

- **Keep the guest list to a reasonable number.** The general recommendation is one young guest for each year of your child's age plus one.

- **Don't issue invitations at day care or preschool unless all the children are included.** Prevent hurt feelings by mailing invitations or calling parents.

- **Have plenty of adult help on hand.** Even as they approach six, children need lots of watchful supervision.

- **Expect your young host or hostess to greet guests, say "thank-you" for gifts, and say "good-bye" to everyone.**

- **Plan activities.** Preschoolers enjoy games and creative projects. Plan activities—singing and dancing games, for example—in which everyone is a winner. Be flexible, however; a successful pre-school party usually requires a balance of free play and organized activity.

AN UNINVITED GUEST

If an uninvited guest shows up at a party—perhaps an older sibling—be gracious and include the child without comment. To prevent an older child from dominating play, you might draft him as your helper—setting and clearing the party table, pouring juice, and organizing art supplies. Before your next party, you will probably have to tell the older child's parents that the guest list is limited. ("We certainly enjoyed seeing Mitch last year, but this year we want to keep the party just for the young ones.") Be polite but also perfectly clear.

Working It Out, Parent-to-Parent

IN OUR LOOSELY KNIT SOCIETY, parents often do not know the parents of their child's friends. Your child may have playdates with children from day care or preschool. He'll go to other people's homes for parties. Neighborhood youngsters may flow in and out of one another's houses as they play together. After he enters elementary school, there will be sleepovers and social gatherings at which you are not expected to be present. These kinds of contact raise important issues for parents who have, at best, a nodding acquaintance. You don't want to restrict your child's social life unnecessarily, but neither do you want to throw caution to the wind.

The best approach is to become well acquainted with other parents before entrusting your child to their care or taking responsibility for their children. When you plan playdates, for instance, include the parent or caregiver. You and the other parent can get to know each other and your homes, talk over mutual concerns and interests, and develop trust. When you invite a young child you don't know to a party, invite the parent; the inclusion itself is a confidence builder. When a youngster visits without a parent, talk to the parent in advance about your plans, particularly if you want to take the children somewhere other than your home. Something as innocent as going to a movie can be problematic if the child's parents do not approve.

Parents need to be open to different lifestyles. Just because another parent is lax about housekeeping or less punctual than you doesn't mean she is irresponsible. Should you be doubtful about a single parent or same-sex couple, try getting to know the individuals before making any blanket assumptions about their child-minding capabilities. Prejudices are often based on ignorance of diversity and tend to evaporate when adults interact one-on-one. Conversely, if your own lifestyle is somewhat unconventional, be understanding of other parents' misgivings and provide assurances. There are some people who won't give up their biases, and that's a shame. But keep in mind that your objective is your child's happiness, not defending yourself or converting other parents to your values.

When to Ask Questions

It does not violate etiquette to ask about important issues of safety and supervision. Do other parents keep guns in their house? Do they have pets you consider dangerous? Is their outdoor play area fenced off from busy traffic? Is their swimming pool or workshop secured? Who will actually supervise the children? Are older children or teen babysitters ever left in charge? You are not obligated to leave your child in any environment that makes you uneasy.

Finally, don't put your child in the position of choosing between your restrictions and those in another household. For instance, if you don't allow television watching and your neighbor does, try to come to a workable compromise between the adults. Your neighbor might agree to keep the TV off when your child is present, and you would not send your child to play when your neighbor's child's favorite program is on. Parents simply have to take full responsibility for these kinds of decisions and compromises. Never make negative comments about another parent's lifestyle, beliefs, and customs, or encourage a child to bend or break another parent's rules and restrictions.

If you must limit or refuse visits to another child's home, your child will need an explanation. Keep it simple and honest. ("The Butlers' home is very pretty but not as safe as we want for you." Or, "Rick's parents can't be at home in the afternoon, and we think Rick's big sister is too young to be in charge.") Continue to welcome your child's friend into your home.

PART FOUR

The Socialization Years:
Six Through Ten Years

NOW'S THE TIME TO . . .

- Continue to teach and model moral values

- Model and encourage acts of kindness

- Introduce common-sense problem solving

- Reinforce honest behaviors

- Stress good manners at school

- Teach and model respect for teachers and all adults

- Teach and reinforce skills needed for friendship

- Stress good sportsmanship

- Teach the manners of effective communication

- Expand and reinforce table etiquette and out-and-about manners

THE ELEMENTARY SCHOOL YEARS ARE often romanticized as golden days filled with innocent fun and endless adventure. Children grow taller, stronger, and increasingly agile. Their brains grow, too, enabling them to learn and communicate in more sophisticated ways, retain and use complex information, and employ reason to solve real-life problems. As concrete thinkers, they are receptive to learning the rules and guidelines of etiquette and polite social interaction, and your teaching of social skills will accelerate.

As your child progresses through elementary school, your oversight will become more subtle. The nature of discipline will change as you begin to reason with your child and appeal to her developing awareness of others. During these years, her circle of role models will enlarge to include teachers and coaches, and peers will become her companions of choice. She will learn to adapt her behavior and manners in order to be liked by others and form friendships. Through her daily interactions with others, she will develop a more realistic image of who she is—her identity as a social being.

As idyllic as the early school years may seem, the process of socialization is full of potholes. Your child will discover, among other things, that *you* are not perfect; you make mistakes and don't know everything. But you remain her primary model, and when she needs comfort, yours is the shoulder she will lean on. When she feels confused and helpless, you will be there to provide clarity and guidance. Your child will need all your love and support as she begins to grapple with the complicated expectations, rules, and rewards of society at large.

CHAPTER 16

Instilling Values and Ethics

YOUR CHILD HAS PROBABLY BEGUN to grasp the basic moral and behavioral precepts you've been teaching, and it's time to firm up these fundamentals and add new concepts that will shape his moral, ethical, and social attitudes and behaviors.

During the elementary school years, he will have many more opportunities to try out his new skills and test his ability to adapt to the needs of others. He will regularly deal with more adults, especially authority figures, and new institutions. He will be expected to follow school rules that are often different from those at home. His peer group will expand, and friends will become a major factor in his life.

As your child's interactions with others intensify, you must share influence over and responsibility for him, but you remain his rock and his primary teacher and role model. In a sense, society is now serving as your teacher's aide. Society as a whole shares your basic goals for your child and all children—that they grow into decent, honest, thoughtful, dependable, cooperative, and productive adults capable of taking on the responsibilities of citizen, worker, neighbor, leader, friend, parent, and teacher of future generations.

Kindness in Action

CHILDREN NEED TO SEE PARENTS and caregivers exerting themselves for others in order to understand that altruism and kindness are not passive virtues but active qualities. The little things mean a lot. Set a good example through your daily actions—saying "thank you" to the bank teller and the grocery clerk, holding the door for the person entering behind you, or running an errand for a friend who is ill. Everyday life is filled with examples of good manners, so point out and acknowledge acts of kindness and courtesy by others. Let your words show that *all people deserve respect*. Be on guard against unintentionally pejorative or condescending comments. Remarks such as "I don't understand why that man can't get a job" or "I'd hate to have to spend my life in a wheelchair" may seem benign but can create the impression in a child's mind that poverty and disability are character flaws.

Encourage your child to engage in selfless acts. Perhaps he will donate some of his toys or books to a holiday gift drive or work as a junior helper in the nursery run by your place of worship. When you do volunteer work, take your child along occasionally so that he can observe how people interact while they help others. Letting him participate enables a child to make concrete connections between the idea of kindness and everyday practice. Don't force the issue; making a child give away a toy, for example, obscures the goal of self-motivated generosity and may encourage resentment against the people he is supposed to be helping.

Introducing Common Sense

COMMON SENSE IS REALLY A way to describe good problem-solving skills. It is the ability to apply what we already know to future behavior, and it often gets people successfully through new and difficult circumstances.

You can encourage your child's common sense once he has accumulated enough experiences and observations on which to base his decisions. A third- or fourth-grader has built a limited but important reservoir of experiences that he remembers and can draw on. He observes how adults react in a variety of circumstances and should be learning to recognize social cues and to size up a situation before he takes action. When he begins to put his knowledge and social skills together, he is exercising common sense. You can promote common-sense problem solving by:

- **Recognizing your child's use of common sense.** If, for instance, your son informs you that he stopped an argument at school by telling the combatants a funny joke and getting them to laugh, congratulate him on his common-sense solution.

- **Generalizing from specific incidents.** Talk with your child about how to apply his common sense in similar circumstances. Good humor, for example, is often a means to defuse difficult situations like an argument between schoolmates. Also discuss when a solution won't work—if his schoolmates are throwing punches, a joke will probably be ineffective—and other approaches such as finding a teacher to stop the confrontation.

- **Encouraging your child to work out problems by himself.** Intervene when a situation is dangerous or outside his experience, but don't be too quick to step into every dilemma. A too-ready-to-take-over parent can discourage a child's self-management and impede development of normal social skills.

- **Modeling common sense.** Let your child know how you think your way through situations, and point out when others use good common sense.

New Issues in Honesty

DURING THE ELEMENTARY SCHOOL YEARS, children begin to understand some of the subtleties involved in honesty and deception. Telling fibs is no longer a matter of pure imagination and fantasy. By age seven or eight, children will understand that lying is done deliberately in order to achieve an outcome they desire. School-age children tell lies for a number of reasons including:

- To avoid punishment or embarrassment
- To get their way

Sometimes children lie because they don't know the alternatives. Your usually honest child might fabricate a story to make herself more attractive to her peers—that her family is rich or her uncle is a famous singing star. Her falsehood is motivated by her natural desire to be popular, and she needs guidance as she deals with her need to be liked. Talk about appropriate ways to get along with others. Help her to understand that good manners and kindness are the right ways to make friends. Don't avoid the issue of lying, however. You want to be absolutely clear that telling false stories and boasting will not make and keep friendships.

- To aggrandize themselves and gain peer respect
- To cover up things they consider private or none of their parents' business

Young children can understand that lying brings immediate consequences—parents become upset or disappointed and respond negatively. By age nine or so, children also begin to grasp that dishonesty has unintended and long-range effects. A child who lies to friends to be "cool" discovers that his friends no longer trust him and that he is left out of their activities. Learning these lessons can be painful, but sooner or later, most children will realize that they risk a lot when they tell lies. Even though lies may not always be detected, their developing conscience makes them uncomfortable when they are untruthful.

Dealing with Lying

Lying is fairly common among elementary school–age children and not a huge issue unless a child begins to lie habitually in a variety of circumstances. Eventually, as part of their moral development, children will see that honesty is a matter of choice and personal responsibility.

What should a parent or caregiver do when he catches a school-age child in a lie? First, *stay calm*: A parent who overreacts may only confirm a child's belief that dishonesty is the best way to avoid unpleasant consequences.

- ***Find out why your child has lied.*** Give him the opportunity to explain. Don't grill him, but do get the facts. Children sometimes lie to cover up accidental or unavoidable behavior or to protect someone else. If consequences are to be just and meaningful, you must know what your child did and why he lied about it.

- **Be sure your child understands how much you value truthfulness.** When he admits to the lie, tell him that you appreciate his honesty. Also be clear that telling lies is separate from the behavior that precipitated the lie. If he stole a candy bar from the drugstore and then lied about his action, he must understand that (1) stealing is wrong and (2) lying is wrong.

- **Impose appropriate consequences.** Children need help sorting through the complexities of their actions. Parents should draw clear distinctions and then discipline for each misbehavior independently. Sometimes the original misbehavior is more serious than the lie (as in stealing the candy bar) and requires the stronger consequence. At this age, children benefit if parents impose separate penalties for the original behavior and the lying.

- **Believe your child unless you have good reasons to suspect lying.** Assuming routinely that a child is telling falsehoods can become a self-fulfilling prophecy. A child's story may seem unbelievable, but don't assume it is a lie unless you are certain.

- **Explain the difference between tact and lying.** By thinking about the feelings of others, your child will learn that he can be both truthful and tactful. Discuss ways to save hurt feelings without being brutally honest. Thinking requires practice, so you might play out scenarios your child can relate to. What should he say if a friend gets a new haircut and your child thinks it looks dumb? To blurt out, "It's dumb," will make his friend feel unhappy. Instead, your child might say, "I bet short hair is really cool in the summer." (Most youngsters benefit from specific examples of what to say in varying situations.)

Fibs for Safety

Parents often begin leaving nine-year-olds alone at home for short periods of time, and many children return to an empty house after school. This requires parents to impose some restrictions that, at bottom, involve deception. The child is instructed to tell phone callers that

Mommy or Daddy is busy and can't come to the phone. Or he is told not to answer the doorbell. Parents need to be very precise about safety situations that call for deception and to explain that these situations are rare and special.

If a Child Steals

FEW CHILDHOOD MISDEEDS ARE AS devastating to parents as stealing. Yet it may not be as bad as you think. Elementary school–age children know that it is wrong to take what isn't theirs, but they are still creatures of impulse, and stealing may be a one-time occurrence. From adults' reactions and his own feelings of guilt, a child learns that stealing is not desirable, and he doesn't want to repeat it.

If you discover that your child has stolen something, confront the issue calmly and let your child explain. He may deny his behavior, and you will have to persist. Or he may confess immediately. When you get the story, stay focused on the behavior. Don't call the child a "thief" or humiliate him. But be very clear that stealing is never right and that you will not excuse it for any reason.

Making Restitution

Discipline should include return of or restitution for the stolen item and a direct apology to the injured party. Even though your child may feel embarrassment, it is critical that he take personal responsibility for his actions and take part in the restitution.

Repeated incidents of theft can hide deeper problems. Talk with your child's physician or health-care provider, who can recommend courses of action including counseling.

Concerning Cheating

IN THE PRIMARY SCHOOL YEARS, cheating tends to be minimal; children learn in a cooperative environment, and learning basic skills is emphasized over grading. They become interested in following rules and playing fairly. But it is important to lay a strong foundation for integrity now in order to help youngsters resist the pressures to cheat that build in middle school.

To lie is to *deliberately* tell an untruth or create a false impression. But people make honest mistakes. They get facts wrong, misunderstand or misinterpret what they see and hear, rely on faulty memories, and tend to exaggerate details. Untruths and false impressions are passed along without actual lies being told. A friend isn't a liar because she forgot a promise. And no one is a liar simply because of ethnicity or occupation, religion or politics. Children who hear adults regularly accusing others of lying can easily become confused and distrustful. To instill respect for truth, be sparing with the word "liar."

◄←

- *Be sure your child understands what cheating is.* Children in the early grades develop a strong sense of justice, so this is the perfect age to explain cheating and discuss why it is wrong. Cheating involves deception and fraud. It is a kind of theft by trickery and sneakiness. Be sure your youngster understands that cheating is not victimless and that often the cheater is hurt because other people learn not to trust him.

- *Discuss cheating in ways that are relevant to your child's experience.* Your child is now a concrete thinker, so use examples. Perhaps he labored over a school project; ask him how he would feel if a classmate presented it to the teacher as her own. Explain that using someone else's work is cheating, and that it hurts other people because their work has been stolen.

- *Model moral behavior.* If parents cheat, their children are much more likely to cheat. Adults may be unconscious of the ways they cheat. Did you keep the five-dollar bill you received in change when you should have gotten a dollar? When a child sees that his parent regards even minor cheating as acceptable, his own attitude becomes distorted.

- *Focus on the importance of learning.* Parents whose overriding interest is high grades may be setting up their children for cheating and other devious behaviors. Grades are not always the best measure of a child's learning. If your fifth-grader scored below expectations on a natural science test but can explain the differences between sleet, hail, and snow and has built his own rain gauge, which is the better measure of his knowledge? To encourage real learning, talk often with your child about school and other activities.

- Ask specific questions that signal your interest: "What instrument do you want to play in the rhythm band?" rather than "How was school today?"

- Be alert to your child's enthusiasms and difficulties. Don't be frustrated when your child has interests and talents that diverge from yours.

- Help your child make connections between what he is learning and other aspects of his life. If he's a sports fan, for instance, following the statistics in the newspaper will encourage him to relate math studies to the real world. Children who understand that school serves real-world goals are likely to apply themselves to learning.

- **Treat cheating seriously.** Letting a child get away with cheating or assuming that it won't happen again sends the message that cheating is tolerable. When a teacher or coach catches your child cheating, don't become defensive. It's vital that parents not assume that their child is the victim of unfair accusations.

Borrowing and Trading

MOST ELEMENTARY SCHOOL CHILDREN HAVE a fairly good understanding of personal property and are not as likely as preschoolers to take things without asking. But they often borrow and swap to get something they want. You may discover that your son's new bike is missing because a friend "borrowed" it or that your daughter "traded" her old doll for an expensive pair of party shoes.

There's nothing inherently dishonest about borrowing and trading, but children don't know how to value possessions and are simply not equipped to negotiate fair deals. Some children will lend or trade expensive items in order to keep a friendship, and some are just generous to a fault. Children don't necessarily comprehend that "borrow-

Doing homework for a child is not only cheating but also deprives her of the opportunity to learn, practice, and refine skills. The early school years are a good time to work out your approach to helping with schoolwork, team sports, and other activities. Be available, but wait to be asked for assistance. Think of positive ways to help: having supplies on hand, toning down household noise at homework time, providing a comfortable and well-lighted study space, teaching organizational skills, giving encouragement when a task seems overwhelming, and recognizing when your child has done her best even though she hasn't completed a task.

ing" implies "returning." Parents should encourage generosity and sharing, but children need help to develop common-sense attitudes about giving and taking.

- **Set restrictions on borrowing and swapping.** This usually means that you allow no lending, borrowing, trading, or swapping without a parent's permission. In addition to limiting the number of things that disappear from your house, this restriction gives your child protection against pressure from other children. He's not being selfish; he just can't lend or swap anything unless you agree.

- **Work on developing negotiating skills.** Suppose your third-grader's big sister wants to borrow his marker pens for a few days. Your younger child may lend the pens out of the goodness of his heart, but you can provide a lesson for both children by helping them negotiate an agreement. Give-and-take is required to satisfy each child. Big sister may borrow the pens but must agree to return them at the end of three days. Help your children reach verbal agreements and have them repeat the terms in their own words. Correct any misunderstandings; then suggest a polite handshake to seal the bargain. You'll also want to see that the agreement is carried out and be prepared for some renegotiation if necessary. Guiding children through a process like this is an excellent practical demonstration of the fine art of negotiation.

My eight-year-old son lent his new baseball glove to his friend Seth. But it's
been a week, and Seth hasn't returned the glove. Now his mother claims
that the glove was a gift. My son needs his glove for Little League, and I
can't afford to buy another new one right now.

First, be open to the idea that Seth may truly believe your son gave him the
glove. Eight-year-olds are not too clear about the difference between borrowing
and giving, and your son may have unintentionally created the impression that
the glove was a present. Try again to explain the problem to Seth's mom, but
don't say anything that implies her son has lied or stolen the glove. If you don't
get the response you want, you'll probably have to be content with an object
lesson. Don't criticize Seth or his mother to your child. Make sure your son
understands that he is not to lend or give things away—or borrow from others—
without your permission. He may have to play with his old glove for a while, but
it will be a good reminder of the importance of thinking before acting. If something like this happens again, get in touch with the other parent as soon as you
know about the "borrowing." Waiting days or weeks for the item to be returned
just adds to the impression that it was a gift.

The Value of Tradition

SCHOOL-AGE CHILDREN ARE SURPRISINGLY INTERESTED in tradition. Learning about and honoring family traditions gives them a
sense of who they are and their place in the grand scheme of things.
Traditions provide order and organization in daily life and give children things to anticipate with pleasure. Whether it's a kiss from Mom
and Dad before bedtime or the annual family Kwanza celebration, traditions and rituals give children and adults a sense of stability and
belonging. Traditions also help children integrate into the larger
worlds of community and nation and offer wonderful teaching opportunities. What a wealth of family and national history you can impart
when you take your child to see his grandfather march in the Veteran's
Day parade!

Passing Down Memories

Grandparents and great-grandparents possess one of the greatest gifts an adult can give a child—a storehouse of memories, knowledge, and family history. Elementary school–age children are eager to know who they are and where they came from, so be alert to their interests and open to their questions. Children are curious about their parents' lives, and who better than you to recount their mom's first job or their dad's summer on a cattle ranch. (Be careful not to embarrass the parents.) Share family photos and mementos. Show family treasures that have been passed down to you. Take your grandchildren to places that have significance to your family. If you don't have frequent opportunities to visit, you can always write letters or send tape recordings in which you relate bits of family history and lore. Every memory you share is a gift beyond price.

Tradition and Manners

Respect for traditions plays an important role in manners education. It may be easier for a child to sit still at a wedding if he has a sense of what weddings are, what will happen during the service, and how other guests will behave. Good manners have meaning when presented in context, and understanding traditions enables a child to transfer his notions of good behavior in one situation to similar situations.

School-age children want reasons, and they often enjoy hearing about the origin of mannerly customs that, on their face, seem arbitrary. A child who has difficulty remembering to shake hands when introduced may be more attentive if he knows that handshaking comes from the time when knights carried swords. An open hand showed that the knight was not armed. When the child shakes hands, he is showing—just as knights of old once did—that he is a friend.

Help your child appreciate diversity by introducing him to different traditions. Attending an ethnic fair, going to a worship service outside your religion, reading about other cultures and practices, visiting historic sites—there are many opportunities to expose your child to the tapestry of customs that comprise his national culture. He will learn that traditional forms of etiquette vary from culture to culture but that virtually all cultures base their etiquette on consideration for and getting along with others.

The Importance of Respect

BETWEEN AGES SIX AND TEN, your child will grow increasingly aware of herself in relation to other people. In the latter years of elementary school, she will be better able to show consideration for others based on her observation that the way to *get* respect and kindness is to *show* respect and kindness. Her maturing sense of empathy should make it easier for her to learn mannerly behavior. Relationships with peers are vital in the process, but you are still her moral linchpin. When she isn't sure what to do, she'll look to you for guidance and limits.

The school-age child begins to internalize concepts and behaviors such as sharing and taking turns. Not only does she now understand the basic distinctions between right and wrong, but she can also comprehend that other people have ideas and lifestyles different from hers and that she must be accommodating if she wants to get along.

As this understanding dawns, it often leads to a period of selfishness, and around age seven or eight, a child can be quite adept at "using" others. She may ask to play with the peer who has the best toys or newest video games, and she can be amazingly open about motives. This stage is a necessary transition between total self-involvement and real concern for others, and it will pass as her conscience grows. In the meantime, a parent should continue to teach and demonstrate attitudes and behaviors that are genuinely empathetic, including good manners.

The Privacy Question

YOUR SIX- OR SEVEN-YEAR-OLD NEVER complained before about sharing a room with a sibling or bathing and dressing when a parent was in the room. Now she's demanding her own room and flipping the lock on the bathroom door. She may increasingly enjoy being alone and have private places and items like a diary or a locked box that only she can open. During the elementary school years, children develop a real need for privacy and an equally genuine sense of personal modesty. As children become more aware of their own bodies and the differences between the sexes, parents need to be sensitive to their feelings.

Since she now values her own privacy, she can appreciate that others do, too. As you establish clear rules and guidelines for privacy, be sure to model these rules and good manners in your home:

- *Always knock.* Knock and ask to come in when entering your child's room and other private places, and expect her to return the courtesy. As your child learns the knock-before-entering requirement, you can explain the more complicated rules of knocking. Whether to a bathroom or someone's office, a closed door indicates a desire for privacy. Knocking is the polite way to interrupt.

- *Give your child some private space.* If you have more than one child and can't provide separate bedrooms, organize shared space so that each child has clearly defined areas. Separate closets and chests are helpful. Be sure that children clearly understand what is common space and what is off-limits to them.

- *Establish bathroom privacy rules.* A child should know not to open a closed bathroom door without knocking and being told to enter. Clearly instruct her never to use other people's toothbrushes, bath products, or toiletries. (It's still important to keep prescription and over-the-counter medicines out of reach.)

Privacy is a basic human need, but it also carries obligations. A six-year-old can learn to tidy the sink, lower the toilet seat, and hang up towels when he uses the bathroom by himself. A seven-year-old can understand that dressing and undressing in private also requires hanging up clean clothes and putting dirty items in the hamper at home and storing personal items neatly when on a sleepover. Curious eight-year-olds should be expected not to open drawers or cabinets in other people's homes or go into schoolmates' backpacks and cubbies.

━◄━

- ***Don't go into a child's private things.*** Don't open a child's mail unless you believe that the contents are unsuitable. In general, don't give away or discard a child's toys or clothing without consulting her. And don't show a child's things—that lovely drawing or amazing science project—to others without the child's permission.

- ***Be clear about situations when you can and will enter your child's space without permission.*** If you suspect unhealthy conditions—from chemistry set spills to moldy sandwiches under the bed—or your child has done something irritating to others, like leaving a radio playing at full blast, you have a right to remedy the problem. You and other caregivers always have the right and duty to intrude if you suspect any dangerous or destructive activity.

- ***Apply privacy broadly.*** Children should learn that respecting privacy includes not interrupting or listening in when another person is on the telephone, not eavesdropping on conversations, not reading someone else's mail or computer files, and so on.

- ***Say you're sorry.*** Apologize immediately if you unwittingly violate your child's privacy. Teach your child to say "I'm sorry" or "excuse me" and to leave a private situation quickly. If it's necessary to interrupt someone's privacy, your child can say, "Excuse me, but ..." and explain. ("Excuse me, Mommy, but someone is at the door.") Teach your child that it's also important not to become angry or rude when someone accidentally interrupts her privacy.

The New World of School

AROUND AGE SIX, CHILDREN REACH one of modern life's major milestones—the first grade. To this point, home and parents have been the primary socializing influences in a child's life. Now school assumes a nearly equal share in the process.

What a child learns in school will profoundly affect her adult life. The foremost objective of schooling is to acquire intellectual knowledge and skills, but the school experience is integral to social, emotional, and moral development. Over the next twelve years, your child will become increasingly independent and self-regulating. She will learn how to get along with others and form peer relationships, when and how to accept outside authority and when and how to assert herself, how to cope with unfamiliar social situations and expectations, and how to deal with rejection and failure as well as success. She has a long distance to travel, and the road isn't always smooth. But loving, supportive, and sensitive caregivers can do much to help her through the rough stretches.

Respect for Teachers

Directly and indirectly, you will be teaching your child manners and attitudes that will affect her relationships with teachers throughout her school years. Though your child may have problems with a few teachers along the way, in the main, teachers sincerely want students to do well and will go the extra mile to help youngsters learn and make the necessary adjustments to school life. But teachers are more likely to respond to children who are well mannered and respectful. The manners of elementary school behavior are really the basics of most group situations your child will encounter throughout life.

- **Pay attention.** Teaching and encouraging your child to be attentive, listen to instructions, and focus on assigned tasks will translate into better performance in the classroom and other learning situations. Much of your child's school time will be spent mastering study skills, and you can help by promoting these skills at home.

- **Do as the teacher says.** Your child should understand that in school, the teacher and his or her assistants are in charge. Even

Teachers want students to ask questions and contribute to class discussion, but not at the expense of classroom order. Children who have been taught to take turns and not to interrupt others may have a fairly easy time, but reinforcement at home is important. Naturally outgoing children may need to have turn-taking manners emphasized; shy children may require encouragement to speak up. Work with your child on the polite way to get attention in class: raise hand, wait to be recognized by the teacher, and use "little voice" to ask questions and make statements. Be sure your child understands not to interrupt or talk over other children and not to wave his arms or call out to be recognized. Role-playing at home can prepare young children to behave appropriately in class.

---

children with preschool and kindergarten experience may have difficulty adjusting to the more structured environment of elementary school, and some children have trouble adapting to differing teaching styles. You can help your child adjust by talking about the importance of minding the teacher. Let your child know that you expect her to follow instructions at school just as she does at home.

- *Address teachers politely.* By age six, a child should be able to remember and use the names and proper titles for teachers and other adults in their lives. Addressing teachers, teaching assistants, and other school officials by their correct names and titles is polite and respectful. In some schools, teachers are called by their first names, but if you aren't sure of the school's or teacher's policy, teach your child to use the more formal terms of address. Children should not address an adult by first name unless and until the adult invites the casual usage.

    As soon as possible, find out the name of your child's teacher and introduce your child to the name in conversation. Becoming familiar with a teacher's preferred form of address can boost a child's self-confidence and ease her adjustment to her classroom.

    If your child speaks of a teacher in a joking or pejorative manner, don't let the remark pass. Correct your child's language and be clear that insulting words are not acceptable, even in jest.

- **Stay seated and ask permission to get up.** Children who are constantly moving around the classroom can drive teachers and other youngsters crazy. Whenever lessons are being presented, during reading time, and anytime the teacher instructs students to stay seated, your child must do so. Discuss with your child how getting up and wandering interrupts the teacher and distracts classmates. When your child has a real need—going to the bathroom is the most common—tell her to raise her hand and ask permission or follow classroom protocol. (Shy or especially modest children may need encouragement to ask for bathroom privileges or to speak up when they feel sick. If your child has difficulty expressing her needs, alert teachers to the issue.)

- **Line up according to the teacher's instructions.** Lining up and proper behavior in line are extensions of lessons in turn taking and sharing. Teachers try to be fair, rotating positions in line alphabetically, for example. But to children in the early grades, what is fair over time is often irrelevant. Help your child understand that her place in line is not important—somebody must be first and someone has to be last, but these positions rarely reflect any preferential treatment by a teacher.

  Be clear that in line, your child is to follow the teacher's instructions and be quiet and thoughtful of others—no pushing, shoving, or breaking in, and no changing places or holding places for others unless the teacher says to do so. Use everyday situations (lines at the grocery store, bank, and movie theater) to point out examples of well-mannered and rude behavior.

- **Put things away and clean up.** Six-year-olds should already know to put away toys and clean up their messes, but most will require reminding at school and reinforcement at home. Let your child know that you expect her to help with classroom cleanup. Talk about all the things her teacher has to do and ask her to think of ways she can help. Be specific: throwing papers in the wastebasket, putting back toys and books after playtime, wiping up spilled paints and picking up dropped materials, keeping her desk neat, hanging up coats and hats, and so on. Introducing regular chores at home will help your child learn that some tasks must be done routinely. Sooner or later, your child will understand that being neat and tidy also makes her own life more comfortable.

- **Don't make unnecessary noise.** Making noise on the play-ground is a healthy outlet for schoolchildren. Noisiness during lesson and reading time isn't. Children must learn that noisiness is more than vocal. Dropping books, rattling pages, banging

---

A Question for Peggy and Cindy

My third-grade son tells me that his teacher gets mad at his mistakes and says he is "messy." I know Mike isn't always organized, but now he begs to stay home from school at least a couple of times every week. My wife wants to have a showdown with the teacher, but I think that will just make things worse.

You need to find out what's going on, so try to get more information from your son. What kinds of mistakes make the teacher mad? When does the teacher say that he is messy? By calmly focusing on facts, you may discover that some prob-lems are due to your child's perceptions. (It's common for nine-years-olds to have exaggerated feelings of being treated unfairly by adults.)

Then schedule a meeting with Mike's teacher. Think seriously about your goal for the meeting, which should be to work with the teacher to improve your son's school experience. At the meeting, state your concerns clearly, but don't be confrontational or defensive. (If your spouse is very angry, it may be best to attend the meeting on your own.) Listen carefully and try to keep an open mind. If the teacher explains that "messy" means Mike's school papers are usually crumpled and torn and that his mistakes are often caused by not following instructions, ask about ways that you and the teacher can cooperate to help your son. One meeting probably won't produce the results you want, so arrange a convenient plan for keeping in touch with the teacher. It's a good idea to follow up the meeting with a note of thanks. In your note, confirm any specific commit-ments you've made (that you will check homework assignments, for instance). Finally, be sure to talk with your child and explain that you and his teacher are working together for his benefit.

desks, ripping open Velcro fasteners, tapping pencils and pens, sharpening pencils, crushing drink cartons, and even yanking tissues out of a box are some of the ways children make noises to entertain themselves and disturb others. Body noises—fake coughing, sneezing, and nose blowing, hand noises, joint popping, flatulence, finger snapping, and foot tapping—will probably get laughs from peers but earn few points from teachers. (See "Private Behaviors," page 154.) If your child has an unconscious habit such as constant humming, finger drumming, thumb sucking, or foot shaking, begin working with her to break the habit. Be sensitive: Annoying habits may be stress-related or comfort behaviors, and nagging or punishing can aggravate the problem. Children often modify habits when they become aware of the action or as the result of negative peer reactions. Consult your health-care provider before taking any drastic measures to break comfort habits.

A Parent's Responsibilities

IN THE PRIMARY AND MIDDLE school years, children are heavily dependent on their parents to set behavioral standards, handle logistics, and make the day-to-day business of school as comfortable as possible. A child's success will reflect parental involvement to a great extent, and often seemingly small things—like seeing that your child gets to school on time and has the right supplies—will make big differences in a youngster's feelings about and performance in school.

Meeting Teachers

Establish a sound relationship with your child's teacher—a collegial relationship based on mutual concern for your child. Open lines of communication by meeting the teacher as early as possible in the school year. Attend all regular parent–teacher conferences or schedule makeup meetings. When you make appointments, consider the teacher's convenience and be punctual. Unless there's an emergency, it's impolite to expect time with a teacher without prior arrangement—at least twenty-four hours. Teachers are generally available in the hours before or after school. Most will arrange phone conferences when parents cannot meet at these times. Some teachers give out their home phone numbers, but parents should not abuse this privilege. (There is nothing so annoying as late-evening calls requesting assignments for a child who didn't pay attention in class.)

Be prepared to discuss behavioral issues as well as academic performance and be open to the teacher's insights. Whatever problems your child may be having—and all children will have some problems in school—your best ally is almost always the teacher.

Realistic Expectations

Your child's teacher may have twenty or more children in her or his charge and is constantly struggling to balance fairness and individualized attention. Expecting special treatment for your child puts an unfair burden on teachers and may cause peer problems for your child. When there are unique issues—a physical or emotional problem, learning disability, restrictions on physical activity or diet, required medications, and so forth—you must consult with the school as soon as possible. School authorities and teachers will do everything possible to accommodate your child's needs. Be cautious about asking for favors: When a child has a special interest or aptitude, tell the teacher, but don't expect her to devote a disproportionate amount of time to a single child.

The Importance of Punctuality

Teaching children about punctuality is an important life lesson, so be sure to get your child to school on time every day. Late arrivals disrupt classrooms, break the attention of other youngsters, create problems for teachers, and often embarrass the tardy child. Know the attendance and late arrival policies of your child's school. If she rides a school bus, be sure she is at the bus stop or designated waiting place before the bus's scheduled arrival. If you take your child to school, plan to arrive at least ten minutes before the start of the school day.

If your child must be absent, follow your school's notification policy. Truancy is not a major problem in elementary school, but you may head off future problems if your child knows that you will consistently contact the school about absences.

PRESENTS FOR THE TEACHER

It's very nice for a child to give a present to his teacher at appropriate times. Check with your child's school about policies regarding gifts for teachers. Try to involve your child in the selection of the gift. Most gift and card shops offer a wide selection of teacher-oriented items. In addition to the usual scarf or tie, you might consider other options such as:

- A book, a desk accessory, or an item related to the teacher's hobby.

- A homemade gift—a box of your lemon squares and a card created by your child can be enjoyed as much as costly store-bought gifts.

- A book for the school library given in the teacher's name—a gift that keeps giving for many years. Talk with the school librarian about choices.

- A donation to a worthy cause in the teacher's name. Your child's teacher may have a favorite cause, or you can contribute to any established and noncontroversial group. Donations to political organizations and campaigns are inappropriate.

- Group gifts are increasingly popular, with several parents pooling funds. But be sensitive to varying family budgets.

Before- and After-School Care Courtesies

If your child is in a morning or afternoon care program, abide by the program's regulations, particularly drop-off and pick-up times. If you are likely to have problems picking up your child in the afternoon, have a backup plan—a grandparent, friend, or babysitter who can get your child. Always tell the adults in charge of the program who is authorized to pick up your child. If your child will be absent, follow procedures. Let the school or program director know about any anticipated absences.

Other Parental Responsibilities

A child who arrives at school every day with books and materials in order, lunch money or ticket at hand or lunchbox packed, and homework done is learning behaviors and attitudes that will earn the appreciation of all teachers. Involve your child in the everyday preparation, so she will learn to organize herself. Since mornings can be chaotic, many parents find it best to prepare the night before—selecting and laying out clothes,

Is your child getting too much homework? Many teachers assign roughly ten minutes of nightly homework for each year a child is in school. Some assignments will be more time-consuming, especially in the higher grades, and some courses require more intensive study. But if your third-grader is routinely spending two hours a night on homework, there's a problem.

Before talking to your child's teacher, observe and evaluate your child's homework habits and environment for a few days. If there's a TV on or a younger child playing video games in the study area, a change of setting is probably necessary. Your child may be ignoring homework in favor of something productive, such as reading, and might need work on his time management skills. If you think that the amount or difficulty of the work is really the problem, arrange to talk with your child's teacher. She or he wants to know when students are having trouble and can work with you and your child to find solutions. Homework is a fact of life, and primary school is the perfect time to help your child establish his priorities and understand his responsibilities.

checking that the child has the necessary work materials, seeing that homework assignments have been completed or attempted, and packing schoolbags. When advance preparation is a matter of routine, it won't take much time, yet it will establish lifelong habits of organization.

Be considerate and label all your child's clothing and possessions. Do not expect teachers to keep up with each student's precious possessions. Your child should keep her toys and "treasures" at home unless they are requested for special activities. The wise parent will lay down restrictions from the very first day. Once the restrictions are clear, make sure your child understands that anything she does take to school is her responsibility. It's also a good idea not to immediately replace any item that is lost or damaged; children can only learn personal responsibility if their actions have consequences.

Respect for All School Personnel

MOST YOUNGSTERS HAVE A HEALTHY respect for school administrators. But day to day, children deal with teaching assistants, school sec-

When making a life change—taking a new job, moving to a new house, marrying, becoming a single parent—don't forget to notify your child's school of the alteration. School officials must know how to contact you *at all times*. Your current home and work addresses, phone numbers, and work schedules should be on file. If you change your name or use a different name at work, inform the school. Notify the school of any changes for people you have authorized to be contacted in emergencies, including your child's doctor. Should there be a custodial or other legal issue in your family, the school must know who is authorized to remove your child from school. Legally and morally, schools are obligated to protect children in their care, but they cannot always act in a child's best interest when parents fail to be responsible.

---

retaries, nurses, librarians, counselors, lunchroom attendants, custodians, security staff, school bus drivers, and crossing guards. Each of these adults is in some way responsible for your child's health, safety, and academic performance. It is vital that children respect, trust, and obey all school officials and staff members. If the custodian tells a child not to run across a just-washed floor or the bus driver asks for quiet, your youngster should respond just as promptly and politely as if the principal gave the direction.

Young children pick up on the hierarchy in school and may think that some adults aren't as important as others. Talk with your child about the jobs adults do and why those jobs matter. Relate the work of school personnel to her experience; if her chores include helping in the kitchen or taking out the trash, for example, she may better appreciate the work involved in cooking meals or handling garbage disposal for 200 people every day.

Setting a Good Example

Let your child know that "please" and "thank you" are expected at all times, and demonstrate good manners in your dealings with school staff. Setting a good example also means avoiding disparaging remarks. Keep criticisms of school management and policies between adults. Avoid blanket characterizations such as "all the public schools are failing" and unkind remarks about individuals. Even a one-time, offhanded comment can implant a strong negative impression in a child's mind. Most school workers will try to be helpful, but be considerate and don't expect staff to drop what they are doing to take on a task for a parent or student.

The Power of Peers

THROUGH DAILY INTERACTION WITH CHILDREN her own age, your child will learn what it takes to be liked by others, what behaviors are acceptable and unacceptable, how to work cooperatively, how to consider the feelings and opinions of others and to use negotiation and compromise to settle conflicts. A child's sense of her identity will be strongly influenced by her peers. Through friendships, her empathetic skills will grow.

Parents frequently have problems with peer relationships even at this early stage. When a child suddenly uses bad language or is unmannerly, a parent may blame peers. Be very cautious about criticizing and blaming, however. Friendships are both necessary and meaningful to youngsters. Childhood friendships tend to be shifting, and today's best friend may be quickly replaced by another. But primary school–age children are developing values of loyalty, honor, and trustworthiness. Their bonds with other children can be very strong. Caught between a parent and a friend, the child will not automatically choose the parent's side as she once did. Even if a new playmate is not the one you might select, it's very important to respect your child's choices and show respect and courtesy to her friends.

Bad Influences

Negative peer pressure does exist, and your child needs your support to resist bad influences. But parents must distinguish between differences and genuinely negative influences. Think about your own friendships. Do you accept and enjoy your friends' differences, or do you expect conformity?

Respecting your child's choice of friends doesn't require you to ignore rude or aggressive behavior. If you are seriously concerned about a peer relationship, you can try to redirect your child's interest by expanding her peer group. Encourage her to join an organized sports team, take art classes, participate in a reading group at the library, or join a scouting group. The "bad influence" will probably be less attractive as your child's circle of potential friends widens.

Good Manners Make Friends

Being liked is important to all children, but few children are naturally blessed with the social skills to make friends. *Social competence is learned,* just like reading and arithmetic. A child's ability to get along with others is directly linked to the bonds she has formed with her parents. A child who feels loved and supported by the most important adults in her life, experiences consistent and caring discipline, and has her parents' model of the fundamental values of kindness, respect, honesty, and courtesy will have a big head start on her own social relationships.

Social Essentials

STUDIES OF CHILDREN AND THEIR interactions show that there are specific characteristics that contribute to a child's social know-how. It's an interesting list, since the elements included here are no different from the instincts and abilities that socially successful adults display:

- The impulse to trust others and approach social situations in a cooperative spirit
- The ability to regulate one's emotions and deal with negative feelings including anger, frustration, and fearfulness
- Awareness of social cues and the ability to evaluate other people's expressions and emotions correctly
- The ability to initiate social contacts and enter into groups effectively
- The capacity to deal with conflicts without aggression and to negotiate solutions to problems

Nobody can get it right all the time. But mastery of fundamental social skills, including good manners, enables people to more easily and effectively deal with various situations and to recover from their own social blunders. What your child learns on the playground will someday translate into gracious behavior and meaningful relationships in all areas of life.

Influencing Behavior with Peers

As your child moves through the school years, you will continue to influence her socialization by:

- **Encouraging polite behavior.** Children sometimes think that good manners only matter around adults. Far from it. Good manners are an almost sure-fire way to establish positive relationships with other children. It's important to teach and reinforce the message that good manners are for everyone, regardless of age.

  Be specific and illustrate your points with examples your child can understand. Start dialogues with questions that tap into her growing empathy: "How do you think the new boy felt when no one asked him to play at recess?" "Would you enjoy eating with someone who throws food?" Children need to understand that their behavior and manners affect how other people feel about them. Gently prompt your child to say "please," "thank you," and "you're welcome" to her buddies, and to introduce her friends to you and to other friends. Stress the importance of making apologies to peers when she is in the wrong and of paying polite compliments when she can. Always set the example in your own peer interactions and with other children.

  Keeping communication lines open is a must, so your child will feel comfortable telling you about problems with peers. Some parents fall into the trap of assuming that their child is always right or their child is always wrong. It's hard to be totally objective about your own child. Try to avoid blaming, and keep your focus on problem solving. Your child will gain essential life lessons as you help her to understand troubling situations and to learn that there are usually several ways to resolve a problem with others.

- **Emphasizing sharing and turn taking.** Children develop and hone their sharing skills during the school years—aided by their growing empathy and supported by the teaching and modeling of adults. Before they begin to master the dynamics of give-and-take, there will be tears and even fights. Until sharing comes to her naturally, be sure your child knows that you expect her to share and take turns. Help her understand that sharing involves more than playthings—that letting other people talk, listening to their ideas and opinions, finding compromises when peers want to do something that she doesn't want to do, giving other children time to be with a teacher, and so forth are acts of sharing.

- **Teaching about social cues.** For most children, the shift from preschool to elementary school marks a change from self-centered activity to group activity. Children must learn to read social cues—the verbal and nonverbal signals people use to communicate their feelings and wishes. It's a process rather than a quickly learned skill, but children who have been encouraged to express emotions may be more sensitive than others.

  By first grade, most children can recognize obvious signals: Tears mean pain or hurt feelings, a frown signals some kind of unhappiness, a parent's harsh tone indicates displeasure. Through repeated social interactions, they acquire more sophisticated understanding and eventually can distinguish among, for instance, a worried frown, an angry frown, and a "just thinking" frown. Parents can help the process along by encouraging their child to interpret a range of social cues. If an adult smiles wanly when you see him, you might explain later that "Mr. Jarvis seemed a little sad today. He smiled, so I'm sure he was glad to see us, but it wasn't his usual big smile. Maybe he's worried about something." It's not appropriate to speculate about Mr. Jarvis's worries. Your child benefits from the knowledge that someone's expression can reveal complex feelings and motivations.

  Role-playing and games can help your child begin to pick up on social cues. You might get a six- or seven-year-old to try different facial expressions in a mirror. How does she look when she's excited, afraid, grumpy, lonely, curious, annoyed? Talk about gestures, posture, tone of voice, and "personal space." (Even children can feel uncomfortable when someone stands too close or wags a finger in their faces.)

Parents, be warned. A natural division between the sexes usually appears sometime in the first grade, and by the third grade, most boys stick with boys and most girls with girls. There may be some crossover—a third-grade boy will tolerate his fifth-grade sister and vice versa, but barely. The normal preference for same-sex playmates will continue until adolescence. So don't expect your school-age daughter to enjoy playing with your best friend's son, even though they got along beautifully as preschoolers. Until children become interested in the opposite sex again, it's best not to try to force interaction between boys and girls. Of course, if your child strikes up a friendship across gender lines, welcome it.

◂┼

Dealing with Bullying

DURING THE ELEMENTARY SCHOOL YEARS, children's quarrels are primarily verbal. A bully, however, is a child who makes an effort to intimidate, both verbally and physically. There are specific characteristics of bullying that differ from the usual playground squabbles:

- A bully tends to be consistent; threats and physical aggression are recurrent and predictable.
- A bully usually picks out a vulnerable victim and limits his or her aggression to that child.
- A bully is usually not well liked by other children, even those who are not his or her targets.

It is very difficult for parents to admit that their child is a bully. But bullying is often symptomatic of deeper problems. The sooner parents recognize that their child is bullying, the quicker the child can be helped to overcome the behavior and address the underlying cause.

Since bullying normally happens when parents are not around, parents often learn about it from other parents, caretakers, or teachers. Don't be defensive and don't blame the messenger. Talk with your child about the bullying, tell him it is not acceptable, and establish consequences if the behavior occurs again. Supervise your child's activities closely to prevent any more incidents. Your concern is your child's well-being and the safety of other children, so your best move is to consult immediately with school officials and your pediatrician or other health care provider who can evaluate the situation and make informed recommendations. (For more about bullying and teasing, see "School Problems," page 346.)

If Your Child Is a Victim

If your child is the target of a bully, you have to step in. It's irresponsible for any parent or caregiver to expect a young victim to defend herself. Contrary to popular thinking, most bullies are not physical cowards. Some bullies suffer from low self-esteem, but recent studies indicate that many bullies have high, exaggerated self-esteem and won't back down in the face of physical retaliation by a victim. Encouraging a child to fight back may increase the likelihood that the young victim will be bullied further—as can direct intervention by a parent. You should take action quickly, but do not confront the bully yourself. Instead:

- Inform authorities if the bullying occurs in school or a child-care program and get assurances that your child will be protected. Let the authorities deal with the parents of the bully. If the bullying isn't stopped, you may have to go to a higher level.

- If your child is being bullied on the school bus or on the walk to and from school, you should seriously consider taking your youngster to school and picking her up until the situation is resolved.

- If the bullying occurs during playdates or neighborhood play, you must get your child away from the bully. Unpleasant as it may be, you should also inform the parents of the bullying child. Removing your child from the situation only means that the bully will move on to a new victim.

If you suspect that a child who is bullying others is himself the victim of bullying or more serious abuse at home, you have a responsibility to report, even when your child is not a victim. Rather than going to the parents, present your concerns in confidence to a teacher or school principal. If you don't know whom to speak with, ask your child's pediatrician for guidance. The authorities will probably be able to protect your anonymity, unless the problem becomes a legal matter.

Teaching Joining-In Skills

SINCE SCHOOL-AGE CHILDREN TEND TO play in groups, the ability to join in is essential to peer relationships. Most children have difficulty entering an established group. Failure to enter is fairly common even for outgoing children and shouldn't be regarded as failure to be liked. There are lots of benign reasons why a group may reject a newcomer. An organized team may not need additional members. A group may not want to stop their activity in order to accommodate a newcomer, or they may not realize that a lone child wants to participate. Older children often form cliques and limit members to a select group, and some groups are simply less friendly than others.

There are steps that every child can take to enter groups, but children should know that they won't always be successful.

- **Stand back for a while and observe the group.** See what schoolmates are doing and evaluate the situation. Is it an organized game or casual play with children drifting in and out? A child should observe openly, not giving the appearance of sneaking or eavesdropping, so the group can get used to her presence. Although no interaction seems to be happening, children in groups tend to be alert to outsiders, and they need a little time to size up a newcomer.

- **Show interest in the group.** If the ball goes out of bounds, the child might retrieve it and then make a remark about the game when she gives the ball back. If she knows someone in the group, she can say hello. If a cluster of kids are talking about some common interest, she may be able to add a comment ("I really liked that movie, too"), be of help ("I have an extra pencil if you need one"), or ask a relevant question ("Do we all get to see the fifth grade play?").

- **Try not to interrupt.** A child who interrupts peers will be perceived as pushy. A child who is too loud, demands to join, or is critical or mocking of the group is almost sure to be rejected.

- **Ask to join in.** This requires subtlety and understanding of social cues, but school-age children are rarely subtle. The point is to be flexible and adaptive. If the group doesn't need more players, the child might volunteer to keep score or to take someone's place when another player is needed. Offering to help or share assures the group that the child's approach is positive. Even if she isn't included, she has shown interest and may be invited to participate the next time.
- **Deal with rejection.** Children need lots of parental support if they are to understand that rejection by a group is frequent and normal. Explain how groups work and encourage joining-in skills. Never be disdainful of the group. Rarely should a parent tell a child that a group is snobby, unimportant, and not worth her efforts. She believes differently and will be inclined not to trust the parent's advice.

The Meaning of Tolerance

In school, children will encounter more and more people who are different from them. Ethnic and cultural differences are obvious, but just as important at this age are differences in capabilities, lifestyle, and attitudes. Your child is learning through experience that not everyone thinks as she does and that her peers have different opinions. To acquire the art of getting along, she needs to learn tolerance, and your teaching and example are essential.

For the best of motives, parents may try to ignore differences and teach that everyone is the same. But children know otherwise. A shy child knows that she is different from the gregarious children. The athletically gifted child knows that he is different from children who can't catch a fly ball or score a goal. Physically abled children know they are different from the disabled. It's important for parents to respond forthrightly to children's questions and concerns about differences. Be specific and factual. For example, when a child asks why Naomi has red hair or Henry has big feet, explain that certain physical characteristics are inherited from parents and ancestors; use her own appearance as an example—she has brown eyes because her parents have brown eyes. If you don't know the answer, do some research and find out rather than giving an offhanded reply that may instill prejudices.

Parents should be alert to budding intolerance. Children pick up a lot of wrong information from peers and the media, and they also tend to generalize from a specific individual to a group. If your child suddenly declares that he hates all people of a certain race, nationality, or religion, you want to get to the bottom of his remark. Be sensitive, but ask why he feels that way. There's a good chance he or a friend has had some conflict with another child and he is generalizing his anger. Instead of criticizing, use the incident to talk seriously about judging other people. Explain that it's impossible to like or dislike people whom we don't know. You want him to learn to form his attitudes toward others based on their individual actions and behaviors.

Encouraging Good Sportsmanship

COMPETITION IS IMPORTANT TO ELEMENTARY school–age children, and the drive to win can be very strong. They love games, from Old Maid and Chinese checkers to organized T-ball, baseball, and soccer. Part of the process of developing their sense of personal identity is comparing themselves to other children and gauging their own strengths and weaknesses through competition.

School-age children also want to learn the rules of games and to play fairly. (Just watch how quickly a group will reject a child who bends the rules or cheats.) But they need adult guidance. Children should understand that it's fun to win, but not at all costs. They also need help to deal with losing. It seems so basic—a good sport is gracious in both victory and defeat—but the national obsession with winning and the material rewards of being Number One make it harder than ever for parents to promote good sportsmanship.

As you teach the following principles, keep in mind that good sportsmanship is a quality of moral, ethical, and, yes, highly successful people:

- **Follow the rules.** Talk to your child about the meaning of winning fairly. For victory to have meaning, the rules must be the same for everyone. When you play games with your child, go over the rules before beginning and ask if there is any part of the rules she doesn't understand.

- **Don't argue with referees and judges.** Teach your child that in organized sports and other kinds of contests, referees and judges do not take sides. Their job is to see that competitors follow the rules, to enforce rules that are broken, and often to decide who wins or loses based on what the players do. If your daughter loses the spelling bee, for instance, it is because she spelled the word incorrectly and not because the judge was wrong. Referees and judges do make errors, but your child should understand that these instances are the exceptions. If your child feels that she or her team has been unfairly treated, show her how to protest effectively: Stay calm, stick to the facts, present her case as clearly as she can, make no personal comments, give the judge or ref some time to consider the case, and then accept the final decision and stop complaining. This is a lot to expect, even of a fourth- or fifth-grader, but if you model the process, she will begin to imitate.

- **Be considerate of other players.** This includes sharing equipment and not walking away with the ball when the child is mad or upset. It means being cautious of other people's safety. Many sports accidents can be prevented if children learn to watch out for others and not to push, pull, shove, run into, and physically tease other players. Consideration also includes not boasting and showing off. Children really dislike boasting (though they tend to do it themselves), especially when one team member claims credit for a cooperative effort. Likewise, children should learn not to berate other players for mistakes. Saying "thank you" and paying compliments to teammates build team spirit and cohesion.

- **Win or lose, do it with grace.** Whenever you watch televised competitions or attend sporting events with your child, don't fail to point out the positive role models. Tell your child exactly why this or that player is a good sport, and try to avoid professional sports in which bad sportsmanship is exalted for entertainment. Set out clear guidelines and let your child know that you expect thoughtful and courteous behavior whatever the outcome of the games she plays.

- Winners are happy but never gloating or boastful. The first rule is to thank the loser for a good game. It's good form to compliment the opposition. ("You played really great defense.") Never make remarks such as "Your team might have won if you didn't have that lousy pitcher." Coaches and parents can set the example by showing some humility and thanking the coaches on the other side. If your child's team scores a major win, such as taking first place in a local play-off, plan a postgame celebration like a pizza party and be sure the children know to contain their self-congratulations until they are on their own.

- Losers shouldn't pout, sulk, or complain. Smile, congratulate the winner, and be complimentary. Never blame others on your team for a loss. Coaches and parents should not encourage poor losing behavior by voicing their own complaints. Don't replay the game move by move, and don't try to cheer up a losing team with grandiose promises of victory next time. Children know when they have been out-played and their performance wasn't up to par. Adults help most by focusing on ways to improve and strengthen winning skills.

The Overzealous Parent

Normally polite and pleasant parents can turn beastly when their children engage in competitive activities. The problem, say psychologists, is often that parents project their fears of failure onto their children and that modern society supports "winning is everything" thinking. Sadly, overzealous parents generally do more harm than good, embarrassing young players and sapping all the fun out of competitions.

You can't do much to control other parents, but keep the following recommendations in mind when you are on the sidelines:

- **Leave the coaching to the coach.** Shouting negative comments and instructions at the adult in charge will confuse your child. (Which adult is she supposed to listen to—you or the coach?)

Backsliding is fairly common among elementary school–age children and may increase as they approach middle school. Children in the early school years are learning and doing so much at such a rapid pace that they can feel overwhelmed. In all likelihood, a backsliding child has not forgotten his good manners; he's just put them on the back burner as he deals with more pressing issues.

Parents and caregivers need patience and good humor when dealing with typical backsliding. Don't panic or become angry. Continue to reinforce mannerly behavior and correct gently, but pull back on new rules and expectations for a while. Unless the behavior is downright rude or unkind, don't make too much of it. Do recognize and praise what the child is doing right. If the backsliding persists or grows worse, parents should look closely at their child's life. Is he having difficulty at school? Is he over-scheduled, with little free time on his own and with you? Is he responding to peer attitudes that it is "cool" to be rude? In most cases, backsliding will stop after a time, and your mannerly child will return.

◄‑

Aggressive sideline coaching sets a bad example for all children, undermines their confidence, and can actually harm performance.

- *Don't criticize referees and judges.* You will disagree with a referee's calls on occasion, but keep the criticism to yourself. Even if you think a referee was completely off base, don't convey your hostile feelings to your child. You can discuss a decision with your child, but stick to the action itself ("I don't think the ref saw Randy touch home plate") and never indulge in personal insults.

- *Compliment the opposition.* If the other team is playing particularly well, remark on their skills. Showing your appreciation for other children is not a betrayal of your own youngster, but it is an essential of good sportsmanship and good manners.

- *Stay clear of tantrum-throwing parents.* You can't reason with a furious parent. But if you know the person, you may want to speak with him about the behavior at another, calmer time. If a parent is throwing things or seems physically threatening, get the authorities immediately; don't take on an out-of-control spectator by yourself. Explain the situation to your child as best you can—"Mr. Tompkins forgot his good manners when he was yelling at the coach"—and be sure your child knows that you don't approve of the behavior.

Oral and Written Communication

LANGUAGE GIVES YOUR CHILD THE tools to express his feelings verbally and helps him make friends, settle conflicts, and debate issues internally as well as externally. His understanding and use of language will grow by leaps and bounds between ages six and ten. His thought processes will change to handle increasingly complex ideas, and his vocabulary and understanding of sentence formation will reflect his thinking.

The nature of your communications with your child will change accordingly. His memory and attention span are developing rapidly, and he is learning methods to keep information firmly in his mind. He uses language to aid memory, and he can describe his experiences and memories with greater detail and accuracy. He is also learning to think generally and not to relate everything to his experience.

Reasoning Begins

Your child is beginning to link separate pieces of information in a logical and systematic fashion—building the basic skills for inductive and deductive reasoning. (Aunt Felice is sick. Aunt Felice likes roses. So let's send Aunt Felice a bouquet of roses to help her feel better.) You can begin to reason with him now, in large part because he has the words to reason with, and you'll probably find yourself giving fewer commands with each passing year.

Elementary school–age youngsters are concrete thinkers; they want to know what, how, and why. They can follow complicated instructions, but they want the reasons for doing something one way and not another. Abstractions are beyond them as yet, but they are sponges for specific knowledge and language.

Not that all communication is suddenly easy. Children normally become somewhat argumentative, and between ages eight and ten they often seem ready to contradict everything you and others say. This phase may remind you of the "no" years of toddlerhood, but now your young-ster is ready to prove you wrong on every point. In fact, your child has the ability to think about problems in more than one way, and he can be abrupt as he takes time to marshal his thoughts and arrive at acceptable conclusions. Weathering this phase requires a great deal of parental patience, tongue-biting, and good humor.

More "Magic Words"

BY FIRST GRADE, "PLEASE" AND "thank you" should be firmly established in your child's everyday vocabulary. He may also be comfort-able with "you're welcome" and other courtesies discussed in Part Three ("Reinforcing the 'Magic Words,'" page 162). Over the next few years, you will make it clear that you expect him to use the basic terms of cour-tesy without exception. You'll also add more mannerly terms and expres-sions, including:

- "Excuse me" and "Pardon me" after committing a social faux pas (burping at the table or bumping into someone) and on those occasions when it is necessary to interrupt
- "Hello, how are you?" and "I'm fine, thanks. How are you?" for greetings
- "May I . . . ?" and "Please, may I . . . ?" to request permission ("May" is preferable to "can.")

- "Thank you, but . . ." to turn down an offer or request ("Thank you, Mrs. Bentley, but I've already had dinner" or "Thank you, Pablo, but I can't play right now.")

By age seven, children should be expected to make requests rather than demands. The child who constantly says "give me" and "let me" and "get me" will have difficulty making friends. Children as well as adults have little liking for bossy language.

Variations on the Courteous

Begin teaching your child that there are different ways to express similar ideas. "Thank you for coming to my party, Lucy" and "I'm so glad you could come to my party, Lucy" express the same sentiment. Learning to vary the language of common courtesy enables a child to keep his remarks fresh and believable. A child of ten who says "thank you for coming" to ten party guests in a row soon sounds (and feels) like a robot, and the thought tends to lose its meaning. Variety is not only the spice of life; it is also the stuff of sincerity. Older children can learn words such as "grateful" and "appreciate" to say what they feel in a personal way.

The Art of Conversation

SINCE YOUR CHILD IS AWAY from you so often now, it may seem that your time together is taken up with essential tasks. But don't forget the importance of conversation. By age nine, a child should have many of the language and listening skills to carry on a complete conversation. He should be able to sit for ten or fifteen minutes and talk pleasantly with most adults as well as other children. Conversation involves many of the skills and manners your child has been learning all along: self-control, consideration for others, and taking turns. By teaching and demonstrating the following basic guidelines now, you will be providing your child with the blueprint for a lifetime of successful interactions:

- *Look directly at the person who is speaking.* Lack of eye contact is one of the most frequent complaints that older people make about children and young people. Children should be instructed that it is rude to look away when someone is speaking to them. If your child has trouble looking others in the eye, try telling him to look at the spot midway between a person's eyebrows. When he is comfortable focusing on this point, he can more easily shift his gaze to the eyes.

- **Pay attention to what the person is saying and respond appropriately.** Conversation has a natural back-and-forth rhythm, which people learn through years of practice. Competent conversationalists are *listeners* as well as speakers. The real art is being interested in what another person has to say and not thinking only about what the listener will say when his turn comes. Good listeners usually have good role models—caregivers who take the time to listen closely and respond based on what they have heard.

- **Don't interrupt.** Let the person who is speaking finish her thought before saying anything. Encourage your child to regard conversation as sharing with others.

- **Speak clearly and slowly when it is your turn.** Parents may not notice when their child speaks very softly or at a rapid-fire pace because they are used to it, so be observant. When your child speaks to others, do they have trouble following his conversation? Do others often ask your child to repeat what he said, to speak up or slow down? Remembering that primary school–age children do not have complete vocal control, work on clarity, pacing, and modulation. When your child is speaking to others, gentle prompting and hand signals may help, but be sensitive and avoid embarrassing him.

- **Welcome newcomers into the conversation.** If another person approaches a conversation in progress, the speaker and listeners should acknowledge her with smiles and maybe nods but should wait until the speaker finishes to extend greetings and make introductions. Children should be taught how to enter a conversation—approach quietly, smile, listen, and wait to be spoken to. Include your child when you have social conversations with other adults; he will learn a lot about the subtleties of group interaction from your example.

A Listening Exercise

Through attentive listening, people hear the words and pick up on critical nonverbal cues that signal the meaning of words. A parent can help a child develop listening skills with a simple game. Say a sentence or ask a question in a variety of tones, emphasize different words in the sentence, and have the child guess what each version of the sentence really means. What is the difference between "We are going shopping **today**" (emphasis on time), "We are going **shopping** today" (emphasis on the activity), and "**We** are going shopping today" (emphasis on the participants)? The same sentence can be made as a statement of fact, a question, or a command, depending on tone of voice.

Add physical gestures and facial expressions to the exercise. Saying "We are going shopping today" with a smile indicates a positive attitude; a frown indicates the reverse. Some children are very sensitive to tone and emphasis in speech, but most need explanations, examples, and plenty of practice in order to understand the myriad complexities of everyday conversation.

- **End conversations pleasantly.** This is not an easy skill, but you can start by telling your child never to walk away from a conversation without some courteous remark. ("I have to go, but I had a really good time talking with you.") Your example of polite leave-taking manners will be a powerful teacher.

A Matter of Timing

A good conversationalist knows when *not* to converse. School-age children are much more sensitive than preschoolers are, but they haven't yet developed a real sense of timing. If your child is just dying to tell his teacher about his new bike, his focus will be on *his* news, and he's likely to interrupt whatever the teacher is doing.

Help your child learn when conversation is appropriate by clearly explaining when it *isn't*. It only takes a few seconds to explain why you can't talk at the moment. Remember that your child is a concrete thinker and wants reasons. Tell him what you are doing and why you need to concentrate. ("I'm working on our taxes. It's very important that I don't make any mistakes adding up all these numbers.") Assure him that you are interested in what he has to say, and, if possible, give him a time when you can listen to him. ("I want to hear all about your ball game. I should be finished in about ten minutes; then we can talk.") Don't go on to another task until you have had that talk. Parents can help their children understand the meaning of "right time and right place," but it takes willingness to explain situations and to repeat the lessons until they become ingrained.

Why Language Matters

CHILDREN MUST UNDERSTAND THAT EVERY language has rules and that the rules exist so that people can understand one another both in speech and in writing. Explain that you can't understand your child's meaning when he says, "I don't want no spinach." (If it's "no spinach" he

---

A Question for Peggy and Cindy ◄◄

My daughter and her friends are always whispering to one another. I don't want to horn in on their secrets, but I think whispering is rude, and I'm afraid my daughter will become a gossip.

The whispering bug bites during the elementary school years, and it's not sexist to say that girls are more vulnerable. Sharing secrets is one way children communicate and play. It is a normal phase and can linger into early adolescence. You won't be able to eliminate the whispered secrets, but you can be firm that whispering and telling secrets are not acceptable when other people are present. Whenever your daughter and her friends begin buzzing behind their hands, tell them to stop immediately. You are right not to ask about their secrets, but do explain that whispering excludes other people, causes hurt feelings, and shows disrespect. Make the point that well-mannered grown-ups rarely whisper and know to share secrets in private. Teach that whispering is a very quiet form of communication used when people don't want to disturb others (in a hospital, place of worship, or during a movie or a performance). As for gossiping—that is another developmental phase. In middle school, your child and her male and female peers will have complex and efficient grapevines.

◄◄

does not want, then he wants some spinach, doesn't he? He may be fascinated when you explain the double negative.)

Your child is beginning to care what others think of him, so you can discuss how language influences other people's impressions. You want him to dress well and mind his manners around others. Doesn't his speech deserve the same attention? Fairly or unfairly, others will judge a person's intelligence and education by his language.

Correcting Grammar and Pronunciation

The time has come to be more attuned to grammar and pronunciation. Correcting is necessary at this age, and most children do not resent it as long as correction is done with care and sensitivity.

School-age youngsters want to learn the right way to do things, and they cannot learn unless they are taught. Though spoken language tends to be more casual than written language, don't let your child slip into bad language habits. Listen for poor speech habits and correct them with gentle prompting. You don't have to be a language cop, but you do want to consistently correct errors when you hear them.

Poor grammar and pronunciation are widespread in the media. When you watch TV or videos or listen to the radio with your child, point out commonplace errors and give your child the correct language. If you hear a broadcaster say that "the team had ran onto the field," or a pop star proclaim that "this be good," tell your child what is wrong with the usage.

Encouraging Reading

Study after study has shown the correlation between reading and the development of language skills, so continue to emphasize books and reading. You can probably read to your child for several years to come. Give him subscriptions to age-appropriate magazines and introduce him to the newspaper. When he begins to read independently, you may want to read some of his books and discuss the contents with him—an excellent introduction to serious conversation. Don't push him to read what doesn't appeal to him, but do offer suggestions. Keep up the library habit; by the time your child reaches third or fourth grade, you can introduce him to the adult library and even begin showing him how to research information.

Every home should be equipped with a good dictionary so parents can teach their child how to use this fundamental language tool. Show her that the dictionary includes not only spellings and meanings but also guides to pronouncing words. You can give your youngster an illustrated children's dictionary, but she should be somewhat familiar with an adult version by the fourth or fifth grade.

◄←

Undesirable Talk

YOUR CHILD'S GROWING VOCABULARY IS going to include some words you *don't* want to hear. The "potty talk" of the preschool years tends to fade as children become more concerned about their privacy, but swear words become attractive long before youngsters have any idea what they mean. Children pick up the traditional "dirty words" from peers, the media, and all too often at home. (Before blaming the world for a child's first four-letter words, parents should examine their own speech.) Young children generally use this language because the words shock adults and add to a "cool" image among their peers.

Parents naturally want to stop such language in its tracks, but don't feed the fire by overreacting. When your child says something unacceptable, tell him immediately and firmly that the word or phrase is not to be used under any circumstances. You can explain without going into graphic details that the word is offensive. Using it is an act of disrespect to others, and most people have a poor opinion of anyone who uses foul language. Spell out specific consequences for swearing, and be prepared to follow through. But remain a bit flexible when your child comes home with new terms. Since he often won't grasp the meaning of each new word, you'll have to repeat your calm, firm lecture more than once.

Dealing with Slang

Use of slang usually begins in elementary school and escalates through middle and high school. It is one way children bond with one another and show their independence from adults. There's no reason why children can't use inoffensive slang among themselves, but you can curb it at home and around other adults. Tell your child, for example, that he is not to use the current slang greeting with anyone but his friends. Frame your discussions as a matter of consideration for others and speaking in a way that can be understood. Stop him from using any slang that is truly offensive, remembering that young children probably don't understand the meaning of slang they hear from teens and on television. Don't adopt the slang of the moment in your own speech; children tend to regard adults who use "kid talk" as silly and may resent an adult who tries to adopt their special language.

Dealing with Back Talk

Back talk is common among children of elementary school age and older. They are trying to think for themselves and have a strong sense of what is fair and unfair. But they lack the verbal and social skills to express their feelings with grace, especially when angry or frustrated. You won't accept back talk and sassing, but you do want your child to learn effective ways to disagree. Sometimes a parent simply has to lay down the law with no discussion, but there are also plenty of chances to talk about unacceptable behavior and to negotiate problems. You must control these kinds of conversations because children often want to argue their points endlessly. By your model, show your child how to express strong feelings with respect, keep a discussion focused on the primary issue, and end the discussion without storming off. You will also be demonstrating the language and attitudes that enable people to disagree—and to lose an argument—without hard feelings. Learning these important life skills isn't easy for a child, so regard your teaching as a cumulative process of many years' duration.

On the Telephone

THIS MAY BE THE BEST age for your child to master good phone manners. Six- to ten-year-olds take great pride in learning new skills and are often quick learners. They can make their own calls, answer the phone, and take messages for others. For school-age children, using the telephone retains some of its magic while also representing grown-up responsibility. Now is also the time to teach that using the phone is a privilege and not a right and that privileges will be expanded as they grow older.

Safe Phone Answering

Experts advise that children not give their names when they answer the phone. Unscrupulous or malicious callers can use a name to gain a child's confidence. Manners aside, children should be taught to hang up immediately if a caller says something bad or discomforting, then to tell a caregiver what happened and get an adult to answer if the phone rings again.

A child should not indicate to a caller that she is at home alone. Because your child's instinct is to say, "Mommy's not here," you must work out just what she is to say and practice it. Teach her to say something like "Mom is busy right now" or "Daddy asked me to take a message" whenever a stranger calls and asks for parents or anyone else in the household. There's an element of fibbing here, so discuss the reason for not telling the exact truth. Your child can understand that there are a few people who do not have her best interests in mind.

Also teach her to use the answering machine. When the phone rings, she can let the machine take the call and pick up only if she knows the caller. Answering machine messages should never indicate that you aren't at home.

Answering the Phone

By age six or seven, your child is probably ready to answer the phone for the family. The manners of polite answering are extremely important because the behaviors your child learns now will stay with him for life. With practice and some supervision until he is comfortable with the routine, your child can learn the following manners and earn his stripes as phone-answering expert without major difficulty.

- **Answer with a clear "hello."** People have differing phone-answering routines, from saying "Good morning" to the rather formal "You've reached the Montgomery residence." But a simple, pleasant "hello" is really all that's necessary. Polite callers will respond with a greeting and their name and then ask for the person they want to speak to.

- **Speak clearly in a normal tone.** Practice helps. When you speak with your child on the phone, let him know when his voice is too loud or he's speaking too quickly. Compliment him when he speaks correctly.

- **Be polite if the call is for someone else.** When a caller asks to speak to someone else in the house, a child's impulse is to drop the phone or yell at the top of his lungs. Instruct him in the following steps:

    - Say "Just a minute, please" or "Please wait, and I'll get my brother for you" to the caller. (Saying "I'll see if Dad is home yet" may indicate that the child is alone.) You may want your child to ask who is calling ("Who is calling, please?" or "May I ask who's calling, please?" instead of "Who's this?") if the caller fails to identify herself, but don't expect a child to screen your calls and give false excuses.

    - Lay the receiver down gently. Dropping, tossing, or banging the receiver makes a terrible racket at the caller's end of the line.

    - Go quickly to summon the person being called. Don't stop to do anything on the way. Be sure your child knows not to shout, even if if he covers the receiver with his hand.

- **Take messages for others.** Some first-graders and most second-graders can learn to write a simple message. Begin with the caller's name and phone number. The spelling of names may be odd, but writing something down will help your child remember who called when he passes the message on. Teach older children to repeat names, phone numbers, and messages back to callers and to correct any mistakes. If your child can't take a written message, he can get the caller's name and write it down later. Or, with your permission, he can give the caller a reasonable time to call again. ("Dad's under the car right now changing the oil. He'll be finished in about fifteen minutes if you'd like to call back.") Treat message taking as important family business. Keep paper and pencils near the phones. Your local business supply store has phone message pads that children like to use. Have a place at home where messages are placed—a small basket or bulletin board works well—so that your child's efforts aren't lost.

- **Be patient and polite when someone calls a wrong number.** The polite response is "You have the wrong number." Give the caller a moment to apologize (or not) and then hang up. Children must be cautioned not to engage in conversation with anyone who dials a wrong number or asks for an unknown person. This is a common ploy for obscene callers and others who use the phone to manipulate children.

Placing Calls

Your child is no doubt anxious to make calls and should be ready for some unsupervised phone use by first or second grade. This doesn't mean allowing unlimited access; children as young as eight and nine can become phone hogs if their use isn't controlled. Don't worry—you aren't invading your child's privacy or stifling his social life if you expect him to tell you when he is going to place a call and to whom. Parents who relinquish control over the phone are often in for some rude surprises, including sky-high long-distance bills.

Be sure your child knows how to use your phone. Explain phone mechanics, including speed dial, redial, and speaker functions, and the

---

A Question for Peggy and Cindy

My son is nine, and he's begging for a cell phone for his next birthday. Some of his friends have cell phones, and I don't want him to feel left out.

This is one of those issues to which our grandmothers would have responded, "If everyone else jumps off the cliff, would you?" There's no questioning the convenience of cellular phones, but bad cell phone manners are rampant. Businesses, government bodies, schools, and other institutions are imposing increasingly tough restrictions on cell phone use or banning them outright.

Until your child is old enough to have a practical reason for a cell phone—when he starts driving on his own or has a job with limited phone access—there is really no need to give in to pressure. Explain to your child that cell phones are helpful in emergencies but are not for chatting with his friends and that using cell phones is costly. (Even if you have a rate based on a set number of hours, children and teens can quickly exceed the limits.) It's unlikely that many of his friends have their own cell phones, so don't worry that your son will be left out of a trend.

---

difference between local and long-distance calls. Introduce him to the phone book and practice looking up numbers. He may enjoy receiving an address book and learning how to record the numbers of family members and good friends.

Your child should have all the following courtesies down pat before he begins making unsupervised calls:

- Speak clearly. Say "hello" and state his *full* name when the phone is answered. Giving the full name is important so that the person answering can quickly identify the caller.

- Greet the person who answers if the person is known. ("Hi, Mrs. Swenson. How are you?")

- Ask politely for the person he wants to speak to. ("May I speak to Geneva, please?" Not "I want Geneva.")

- Say "thank you" when a person takes a message or summons someone else to the phone.

- Leave brief messages on answering machines and voice mail. Automated message services terrify some children into dead silence yet lead others into flights of verbosity. Practice by using your answering machine or a tape recorder, so your child can learn to respond with poise. Work with your child to develop a brief but complete basic message: "This is Terry Jenkins. Can James please call me at home tonight? My number is 555-1234. Thank you." Emphasize the need for clear speech and polite manners because a real person will hear the message sooner or later.

Ending Calls Politely

A polite "good-bye" is fundamental when ending a call, but children do not know how to draw a phone conversation to a close. Except in emergencies, some brief pleasantry is needed if the person on the other end is not to feel curtly cut off. A child might say to a peer, "I'm glad you can come over tomorrow. I'll see you then. Good-bye." To a family member, he might conclude, "It's been fun talking to you, Uncle Bill. I'll call you again soon. Good-bye." Then he should wait for the other person to respond with "good-bye" before hanging up.

When a child learns to wind down a phone conversation with a courtesy (not a question, which will only extend the conversation) and say

Of all the phone extras available today, call waiting probably causes the most annoyance. Too many people hear the beep or tone signaling an incoming call and immediately switch away from the conversation that is underway, cutting off the person on the other end of the line in midthought or even midsentence.

If you have call waiting, teach your child the polite way to handle the service and practice manipulating the telephone keys so as not to cut off callers. If the electronic signal is audible to both parties, your child can say, "There's call waiting. Please excuse me a moment. I'll be right back." If the signal is not audible to the person on the other end, your child can learn to wait briefly for a natural break in the conversation before taking the new call. If the new call is for him, he should quickly and politely explain to the new caller that he's already on the phone and will call back as soon as he can. Then he should return to the first call.

It's more likely the new call will be for you or someone else in the home. If your child can manage it, he should put the new caller on hold, tell his friend that he will call back, say "good-bye," and immediately tell you that you have a call. After you finish, be sure to let your child know that he can use the phone.

◄◄

"good-bye," there should be no need for obviously made-up excuses of the "Someone's at the door" variety. Also, it is rude to call someone and open with a remark such as "I only have five minutes to talk." When you or your child places a call, it is not up to the other person to accommodate your schedule.

Putting It in Writing

NOW THAT YOUR CHILD IS learning to write and to organize his thoughts into coherent statements, he can begin to put his new skills to good use. Thank-you notes are an obvious starting point, but parents should encourage general letter writing as well. Explain to your child that it is customary to thank others in writing for gifts, special occasions, and thoughtful acts. A warm thanks makes people feel good, knowing that their gift or action has been gratefully received and is being enjoyed.

Children need to learn how to plan what they will say and to *write by hand,* so don't fall back on impersonal preprinted note cards or computer-generated forms. Children's thank-you messages are generally brief but often stated with enthusiasm and great charm.

Stationery

Don't worry about fancy stationery at first. Let your child use his school paper and pencils for notes and letters. He'll enjoy writing more if he can also add his artwork to the page. Neatness counts, but don't worry too much about erasures and corrections until the fourth or fifth grade. You can help with spelling, but if "dear" is spelled "deer" by an eight-year-old, let it pass. You will have to address envelopes until your child's writing is legible, but explain the correct form for addresses and return addresses. He can fold and insert his letter, seal the envelope, and stamp it.

By fourth or fifth grade, your child will probably have control of his writing, and you can introduce real stationery. There are attractive ruled papers available for children, and your youngster may enjoy choosing his own design or personalizing plain stationery with rubber stamps or stickers. Giving him an address book can also encourage his interest in correspondence.

What to Say?

Children often complain that they don't know what to say in notes and letters, so be ready to assist. Ask your child what he would like to say. Suggest ideas and wording if he is really stuck. Begin teaching older children to write down some ideas before beginning a letter, perhaps even drafting important letters before they write the final version. Letters and notes can be learning opportunities as children develop the skills of expressing their feelings and thoughts in ways that are clear and intelligible to others.

Younger school-age children may be enthusiastic about writing their own thank you notes and letters; this kind of responsibility makes a six-year-old feel very grown up. Take advantage of this interest to teach the fundamentals of letter form: date, salutation, body, closing, and signature. Older children often balk at note writing, so parents have to insist and persist. Try not to nag. Appeal to his empathy. ("Uncle Luiz spent a lot of time finding the binoculars you wanted. A note from you will make him feel so happy.") Organize a place, time, and the materials for letter writing and sit down with your child while he writes. Once he gets the hang of it—and realizes that you will not let the matter slide—your child will probably choose to do his writing independently, but you still need to check that thank-you notes are completed and mailed.

Thank-You Note Specifics

When are thank-you notes expected? In general, notes for gifts are written when the gift is opened outside the giver's presence and the giver isn't available to be thanked face-to-face, though thank-you notes are always welcomed. A gift sent by mail or delivery service requires an immediate acknowledgment. (If your child is just learning to write, he can call the sender and follow up with a note.) When birthday or special-event gifts are opened after the event, notes are required even if the gift giver attended the party. Notes of thanks for gifts of money should include some indication of how the money will be used. ("Thank you for the birthday check. I have been saving for a new catcher's mitt, and now I can buy it.")

Thank-you notes aren't necessary for playdates and routine playtime at a friend's house, sleepovers, or small, inexpensive gifts. But notes should be written after lengthier visits and for special kindnesses and intangible courtesies. Should a friend of the family take your child to the circus or a coach spend extra time helping your child individually, these thoughtful acts call for written expressions of appreciation.

Closings vary depending on the child's relationship to the recipient. "Love" is correct for family members and close friends. "Yours truly" works just fine for others. "Your friend" is a pleasant closing for a child's letter to a peer or adult acquaintance, especially if he thinks that "Love" is too mushy.

In general, thank-you notes should be sent within two weeks, though there may be situations (your child is ill, for instance) when more time is required: it's better late than never to write.

First thank-you notes are usually no more than a sentence in length. As your child matures, his notes will grow in length and content. All

FUN WITH POSTCARDS

Postcards are a fun way to encourage writing other than thank-you's. The messages are necessarily brief, so even six- and seven-year-olds can write cards with your assistance. Remember to pack the address book and stamps and purchase postcards when you travel, and let your child select the cards she wants to send. Plan a little time for writing; in fact, card writing is an entertaining way to keep children occupied while waiting for restaurant meals. Since the social skills of writing to others are encouraged by the receipt of letters, try to send your child a letter or cards whenever you travel without her.

notes should refer to the specific gift or courtesy; notes by older children should also include some personal references for the recipient. These samples illustrate what is generally age-appropriate for young note writers.

A basic note from a first-grader:

Dear Grandpa,
Thank you for the great new fishing rod.
Love,
Joey

A basic note from a second- or third-grader:

Dear Grandpa,
The new fishing rod is just what I wanted. I can't wait to go fishing with you next summer. Thank you very much.
Love,
Joey

A more sophisticated note from a fifth-grader or sixth-grader:

January 19, 2002
Dear Grandpa,
     Thank you for the new fishing rod. It was one of my best birthday presents. I can't wait till I see you next summer, so we can

go fishing together. With my new rod, maybe I can catch as many fish as you do!

I'm working hard in school this year. My favorite subject is science, and guess what? We're going to learn about fish in the spring.

Thanks again for the great present. I can't wait to see you and Grandma in June.

Love,

Joey

CHAPTER 19

Improving Table Manners

OVER THE NEXT FEW YEARS, you'll be adding new rules of polite table behavior and reinforcing familiar ones. Don't be afraid of the word "rules." Elementary-school children become enamored of rules and enjoy learning and following instructions. When parents also take the time to talk about the importance of good table manners—and all etiquette—children at this age are usually more receptive to rules. The key is to combine concrete, relevant reasons for the behaviors you expect with clear instruction and consistent reminders and prompting. Remember, your child's acquisition of mealtime manners is incremental; she can't be expected to learn them all at once.

Fine-Tuning Basic Skills

SINCE SCHOOL-AGE CHILDREN SPEND INCREASING amounts of their time in the company of others, parents are now concerned with their child's behavior when she is on her own. She needs to learn that the following skills and manners—together with the etiquette basics already discussed in Chapter 14—are intended for both home and abroad. The rules are the tools that will eventually give your child the self-confidence to handle all sorts of new social situations with aplomb.

Handling Utensils

It's time to begin teaching your child the correct way to hold forks and spoons and how to use a knife and fork when cutting. At school, first-graders are learning the correct grip for pencils, and the hand position for forks and spoons is much the same; you can gauge your child's readiness for fork training by observing how she holds pencils and pens. Your child will sensibly opt for a spoon to scoop up tricky foods like peas, but you should encourage use of a fork.

Using a knife is problematic for young children, so you will still be cutting steak for your child for a few years, but show her the correct way to hold a knife and fork when cutting and encourage her to try on her own. Carrots, green beans, boiled potatoes, and other solid foods provide practice, but be prepared for the occasional flying vegetable.

Posture at the Table

Teach your child to sit up, eat with one hand, and keep her free hand in her lap. But both hands are employed for cutting meat, using a napkin, and passing serving dishes. Some youngsters take to these rules with ease, but for most, it's tough. That free hand, arm, and elbow keep migrating to the tabletop, and your child will probably think hand-in-lap is a pointless rule. But hands, arms, and elbows on the table affect posture so that a youngster slumps forward and brings her face close to the plate. Slumping interferes with the motions of eating and encourages use of fingers to pick up or push foods onto a spoon or fork—an unappealing sight for other diners. If your child wants a more practical rationale, tell her that keeping her hand in her lap holds her napkin in place.

Taking Manageable Bites

A child's instinct is to take in the maximum amount of food in the minimum number of bites. But safety and consideration for other diners dictate manageable bites. The safety concern is to prevent choking on overly large pieces of meat, vegetable, and fruits. As for consideration, no one enjoys eating opposite a diner who looks like a squirrel storing

The traditional American style of cutting and eating meat is to cut a bite with the knife held in the right hand, using the fork in the left hand to spear and stabilize the food. Then the knife is laid aside on the plate; the diner turns the fork over so that the prongs face up and switches the fork to the right or eating hand; and the bite is eaten at last. All this zigzagging seems quite a waste of time to children and many adults.

The classic Continental style—increasingly popular in the United States—is more direct. When the food has been cut, the diner lays the knife on the plate, as above, but does not switch the fork between hands. With the fork prongs turned downward, the food is lifted to the mouth using the left hand. Two steps are eliminated (turning the fork over and changing hands), and it is possible to cut the next bite without switching the fork yet again.

Either way is correct, and the choice is your preference. Showing your child both ways, however, will curtail comments of the "Hey, you're doing that wrong" kind when your child encounters someone using the other style.

---

nuts in its cheeks. Show your child exactly how large manageable bite sizes are. Tell her that a bite should never be so big that she can't chew it easily with her mouth closed. Be observant at the table. If you see that she has piled mashed potatoes onto her fork, direct her to put the food back on her plate and try again.

Eating Soup

Spooning soup from the inside to the outside of the bowl has a simple, common-sense purpose. Guiding a soupspoon from the tableside edge of the bowl or cup and lifting it at the far side reduces the chance of spilling soup onto the table or into the lap. Generations of children have learned the soupspoon rule with the help of a verse: "My ship (the spoon) goes out to sea empty and comes back full." Show your child how to dip the spoon into the bowl and then right the spoon to a horizontal position before bringing it to her mouth. Children generally master this skill quickly and take pride in their accomplishment. You can include a soupspoon in your child's place setting, although little mouths are often more comfortable with teaspoons.

Now that your child will be having one or two meals at school, the requirements may be somewhat different from home. Eating, for instance, takes precedence over conversation when a large number of children must be fed in short shifts. Often, children begin eating without waiting for others to be seated and may leave the table without being excused. Ideally, your child will be under the supervision of a teacher, although this isn't always the case. Overworked staff may not be alert to minor breaches of etiquette, but you can set out expectations for lunchroom behavior and explain why some rules are different from those at home. In addition to the manners discussed in this chapter and others, your child should learn these fundamental do's and don'ts of mealtime at school:

- Do follow the directions of the adult in charge at all times.

- Don't push, shove, or engage in rough play of any kind in lunch lines.

- Do hold food trays with two hands, and do not touch another person's tray. Your child can practice with a tray at home.

- Do sit down and eat as quietly as possible.

- Don't ask for someone else's food. Some young children find it difficult to refuse the request of a peer and may give away most of a meal.

- Don't make comments about other children's meals or eating styles. If a classmate follows a special diet or brings lunch from home while others buy theirs, this is no excuse for rude or teasing remarks.

- Do leave the table as clean as possible and dispose of trays, napkins, drink cartons, and so forth as instructed. To prevent accidents, report any spills or messes to an adult.

At Meal's End

Another easy rule for children to learn (if not always remember) is to put their utensils on the plate when they finish eating. Explain to your child that laying the fork and knife on the plate is like a signal or code. It tells whoever is serving the meal that she has eaten her fill and is ready for the next course or to be excused. The exact positioning of utensils (angled on the side of the plate with knife blade pointing inward) is not as important now as getting dirty utensils off the table. Show your child the right placement, but be happy if she puts her knife and fork onto the plate.

About Beverages

From infancy on, children love to play with the liquids they consume—swishing juice in their mouths, blowing bubbles in their milk, spitting water to see how far it will go. They tend to drink in great gulps. They have drinking contests and delight in the loud noises they can make with liquids. Yet this fun play is unacceptable at the family table and in all dining situations. Children need clear instruction. The basic requirements of polite drinking are:

- Take no more than one or two small swallows at a time and drink slowly.

- Swallow the liquid immediately—no swishing, sloshing, gurgling, or gargling.

- Chew and swallow food before taking a drink—no "washing down."

- When a glass or cup is full to the brim, do not tip the container to drink. Take small, silent sips at the rim of the glass until enough liquid is consumed to allow careful drinking.

- When eating soup, put the spoon in the mouth—no slurping or sucking.

- Do not upend or lick at a glass to get the last drop.

To help your youngster learn drinking etiquette, serve her beverages in easy-to-handle containers. She is ready for a real glass but not a large or tall tumbler and probably not stemmed glassware. She must learn to control a glass with one hand, so a fruit-juice size is perfect. Fill the glass no more than two-thirds full; let her refill her glass from a small pitcher kept on the table. It's best not to allow straws at the table as they encourage noise making and spilling. Reserve straws for milk shakes, sodas, and sick-day drinks. There will be lots of accidental spills before your child perfects her skills, so have her help clean up. If she hates to wipe up spilled milk and juice, she may be more careful.

When your child makes annoying noises with drinks, tell her to stop. Explain that the noises are unpleasant to hear and make it difficult for everyone else to enjoy the meal. You can be a little lax in casual, outdoor, non-dining situations. If your child is less than polite when drinking juice with her playmates in the backyard, let it go.

Dining Out

INCREASINGLY YOUR CHILD WILL HAVE meals away from home, and you won't always be there to supervise. She'll probably be included in more restaurant occasions, not all of the fast-food kind. In addition to teaching good table manners, you can help your child enjoy dining out by encouraging social skills that build confidence and enable her to handle new situations.

Rituals and Routines

Your child needs preparation for the variety of dining customs that other people have. You can discuss the many meal-starting routines she may encounter when eating out: bowing heads and saying grace, holding hands when saying grace, observing a moment of silence, waiting until all diners have been seated or served, waiting until the head of the household begins eating or tells others to begin, passing all serving dishes around the table and taking portions before anyone starts, and so on.

Your child should understand that dining customs vary from family to family, and there's really no right or wrong involved. What is right is to respect other people's rituals and follow their lead. If your child will be eating with a family whose customs are familiar to you, prepare her by telling her what will be expected and practicing at home if possible. The safest method for a child to follow when she isn't prepared for a new dining situation is to watch the adults and do as they do. ·

Review the etiquette basics before your child dines out. Remind her to take part in conversation but not to dominate table talk, to ask to be excused before leaving the table, and to thank the person who prepared the meal. Your child may routinely help clear the table in her own home, but when dining with others, she should ask first before removing her plate and utensils.

Trying New Foods

Children should learn to try some of everything without complaint. This is especially important when they eat at a friend's or relative's house. The obvious exceptions occur when a child has a food allergy or is taking medication that may be affected by eating some foods or when the food violates religious practices. When children have health problems related to foods and food additives or follow restricted diets, parents are obligated to inform anyone preparing meals for their youngsters. Don't expect a young child to explain graciously why she can't eat the foods her best friend's mom is serving.

Teach your child to eat at least one regular-sized bite of everything on her plate. (If you have been varying the meals you serve at home, this will be easier.) Explain that not trying foods may hurt the feelings of the person who cooked the meal. Your child can understand that most people go out of their way to please a guest, whether an adult or a child. If she tries something and doesn't like it, she can leave the remaining food on her plate and politely refuse second helpings with a simple "No, thank you." She should not attempt to hide food by spreading it around the plate or putting it in her napkin.

A Question for Peggy and Cindy

My son is seven and has good table manners at home, but when we eat at a restaurant or friend's house, he's a different child. He wiggles in his chair, talks too loudly, and gulps his food. I have to correct him constantly, which I know annoys everyone else. Should we just stop going out until he's older?

No. Your son needs the experience of dining out if he is to learn polite behavior. Like most seven-year-olds, he still has trouble with self-restraint, and his behavior probably reflects his excitement or nervousness in a novel environment. Correcting him in front of others can add to his tension because children are easily embarrassed. Try working out a nonverbal signal or two that will let him know when his behavior is out of bounds. Put a finger to your lips, for instance, when he needs to quiet down or slow down. After the event, you should talk with him about the behavior. Be tactful, but let him know that you expect him to use his "home" manners whenever he eats out.

Also teach your child polite replies to use when an adult tries to push her to eat something she doesn't like. Remarks such as "I know the zucchini is good, Mrs. Daniels, but I'm just too full for anything else" and "I don't really like carrots, Grandpop, but if I did, these would be the best" are always preferable to "I hate zucchini" or "Carrots are gross."

Restaurant Meals

Before going to a "nice" restaurant, remind your child what will happen: she will be given a menu, the waiter or waitress will take her order, and everyone will stay at the table until the meal is finished. If she needs something, she should ask an adult at the table who can signal a server. By observing adults, children learn the polite art of catching a server's attention. Since a young child is probably not used to waiting for meals, take materials such as a small drawing pad and colored pens to keep her entertained. (Be sure to put playthings away when the food arrives.) If you can sit beside her during the meal, she may feel more relaxed just knowing you are there to guide her.

CHAPTER 20

Learning About the World

⤙⤚

IT'S SAID THAT THE REAL test of manners education is how a child behaves when parents are *not* around. The time for testing has arrived. During the primary school years, your child will spend more hours away from you, and by around age nine or ten, he will engage in some activities without direct adult supervision. He may be allowed to walk to school, wait at the bus stop, and go to the local store for a soda. He and his friends may attend afternoon movies and youth theater performances (with parents dropping off and picking up). He is likely have the run of your neighborhood, disappearing for hours on end to ride bikes and play with his pals.

The degree of freedom children experience at this age varies depending on factors including the safety of the environment—children in large cities may have fewer opportunities for unsupervised play than those in rural and suburban areas—and parental comfort levels. But even at school and in organized extracurricular activities, your child will operate with growing independence.

Going Solo

MORE AND MORE OFTEN, IT will be your job to prepare your child for new situations and then watch as he goes off on his own. You'll worry, of course, but he needs reasonable opportunities to act independently if he is to become self-confident, self-reliant, and socially adroit. A few general suggestions can help make his first solo out-and-about ventures successful and enjoyable for everyone.

- *Talk about new situations in advance.* If your child is going on his first overnight visit to a friend's home, for example, discuss what will happen. Be clear that he is to mind his friend's parents just as he minds you. Review your manners expectations. Talk with the host parents, so you can prepare your youngster for any different or unusual circumstances he may encounter—visiting in a home with servants or where an invalid is present, for instance. (Also, inform the hosts of needs your child may have, even something as simple as sleeping with a nightlight on.) Your child may seem put out by your preparation, because he thinks he can handle anything. Be tactful and don't wait until the last minute to load him with instructions. Your efforts will enhance his social self-confidence.

- *Be sure your child is well equipped.* Does he have everything he needs for the Scout meeting, the class play, the sleepover? Getting organized should now become a mutual responsibility so that your child can eventually be fully responsible for himself and his belongings. Six-, seven-, and eight-year-olds need the active involvement of parents, though. Pack his overnight bag together; you are less likely to forget the necessities like toothbrush and clean underwear. Be sure that his soccer ball is in the car before you leave for the game. It's up to parents to think ahead, which often means seeing that a child has clean clothes and uniforms for specific activities. Teach organization by making written lists of items required for routine activities and special occasions and checking off items together before leaving home. Don't forget about money, which you still control. It's very embarrassing for a child to arrive at a movie or school fair only to find that he hasn't the funds to participate.

- **Reinforce safety rules.** More time on their own and with peers increases the chance that children will be confronted by dangerous people and situations. Use your common sense, and don't frighten your child. But do review the rules of personal safety (see "Stranger Danger," page 122). Explain to your child that well-meaning adults would never ask a child for help. If an adult or a teen he doesn't know asks for any kind of favor, such as assistance finding a lost kitten or directions to his school, he is to leave immediately and tell you or another responsible adult. (Child molesters often appeal to a youngster's instinctive desire to be helpful to adults.) Be sure he understands never to get into or near a car without your permission, and never to leave school or an activity with anyone other than you or someone you have specifically designated. If a person tells your child, "Your Dad is busy at work and asked me to pick you up" or "Your Mom has been in an accident and wants me to get you," the child should run away, find a teacher, coach, or other responsible adult, and tell what happened.

  Experts in child safety advise that parents focus on the positive things that children can do to protect themselves rather than horror stories of dire consequences. Knowing what to do boosts a child's confidence and makes him more alert to dangerous situations.

- **Clearly set times for dropping off and picking up.** Be absolutely clear about the exact spot where you will meet your child after an activity. If you are picking him up in a public place, choose a location that is protected from the elements and well lighted, away from heavy auto traffic, and where adults in authority are close by. Don't be late, but do tell your child what to do if you are delayed. Show him the location of public phones in places you frequent, make practice calls so he will know how to use the equipment, and be sure he has change to pay for a call if the need arises. Role-playing can prepare him for unforeseen circumstances. Imagine realistic situations and encourage your child to think of ways to handle difficulties. Even if you are never late, this kind of thinking will promote problem-solving skills and self-reliance. An inexpensive watch will improve your child's

Vital Information

For your child's safety, it's important that she knows which adults to turn to for help. Be positive when you point out law enforcement officers, security guards, store personnel, and trustworthy adults in your neighborhood. Be sure she understands that these people are ready and willing to assist her.

Your child should also learn the following information, which is needed if she ever becomes lost. The more precise her information, the better.

- Her full name and complete address including city, suburb or area, and state
- Parents' full names
- Home telephone number including area code
- Parents' work phone numbers
- Name and phone number of another responsible adult

When you travel with your child, be sure she knows where you are staying. Write down the address and phone number for her. If she's apt to lose bits of paper, you can pin or tape a small note inside her pocket. If your child travels alone, it is essential that she carry detailed information about who is to meet her and her final destination as well as all the phone numbers where you can be reached if necessary.

understanding of time and punctuality. First- or second-graders are usually ready for a watch, but make certain your child can read his timepiece. Don't give youngsters watches that beep, buzz, or chime; the noise is disturbing to others, especially in classrooms.

At Parties

AS YOUR CHILD GOES THROUGH elementary school, birthday parties continue at a fast pace, and other parties and social events begin, some associated with school and others just because someone wants to have a party. By second or third grade, most youngsters have learned how to handle themselves fairly well at parties. You will notice that the quality of their noise changes, tearful episodes diminish, and the nature of game playing is more cooperative. Older children tend to behave in a more civilized fashion than preschoolers because they have had numerous party experiences and also because of their growing understanding of the needs of others and their own desire for social acceptance.

Your job is not done, however. Parents rarely attend children's parties after first grade, but you should remind your child to greet his host and the host's parents or caregivers when he arrives and to say "thank you" and "good-bye" when he leaves. (The basics of party manners are discussed in Chapter 15.) A few more directions to add to his collection of party manners include:

- **Do join in.** This can be hard for shy children or those who do not know other guests well, but organized games give a child a point of entry. If a child cannot participate actively, he can still be an interested and friendly spectator.

- **Don't complain.** A child who asks for a soda instead of the punch being served or demands to play football when everyone else wants hide-and-seek will be resented by hosts and guests alike. Teach picky eaters to keep their complaints to themselves and to decline what is offered with a polite "No, thank you." To refuse food with a negative comment or to demand something that is not being served is rude.

- **Do be a good winner or loser.** Competitive games are appropriate for school-age partygoers, and children should understand that good sportsmanship applies in social situations as well as on the ball field. Children can be expected to congratulate a winner and never to tease a loser.

- **Do include others.** Parties are opportune times for inclusion, and children should know that it is polite and considerate to open their circles to others. This means introducing children to one another, not separating into tight little groups, and not engaging in exclusionary behaviors like whispering and teasing. If your child is hosting, he should take the lead in making introductions.

By age six, a child is usually ready to learn to make polite introductions. Keep it simple: making an introduction means trading names between people who do not know one another. Sometimes your child will introduce one person to another, sometimes she'll introduce one person to a group, and sometimes she will introduce herself. Whatever the combination, the requirements are not difficult.

- **Use names.** A six-year-old might introduce a friend by saying, "Wally, this is my mom," but she should soon learn to say, "Mom, this is Wally Adams. Wally, this in my mom, Mrs. Martinelli."

- **Pronounce names clearly.** No mumbling, whispering, or giggling when making introductions.

- **Use an adult's title and surname.** ("Dad, this is my troop leader, Dr. Winnett.") If the adult prefers to be called by his first name, he will say so.

- **Introduce each person in a group.** ("Everybody, this is Betsy. Betsy, this is Jimmy and Ashley and Jamal.")

- **Be friendly.** The person who makes an introduction sets the mood. Children should smile and use a friendly tone whenever they make introductions, no matter how grumpy they may feel.

When your child gets the basics under control, you can teach the correct order of introduction: child to adult, then adult to child. ("Grandpa, this is my friend Matt Perkins. Matt, this is my grandfather, Mr. Stallings.") Except for this show of respect for elders, wait until she's a good bit older to tackle the more complicated formalities. For now, compliment her when she remembers to make an introduction and prompt when she forgets.

◄+-

First Sleepovers

SLEEPOVERS AT THE HOMES OF friends—usually starting in first or second grade—are not exactly the same as staying with Grandmother. Most children enjoy sleepovers, but not all children and not at all times. Your first-grader, who happily trotted up the Joneses' front path at five in the afternoon, may be the desperate little voice on the phone at one A.M. begging to come home. Be ready to answer the call without recriminations. Until they become used to staying away from their parents and their own beds, youngsters can be unpredictable. Don't make too much of an early morning summons, but do encourage your child to try again when he's ready.

Sleepovers will probably become fairly regular from the third or fourth grade onward. In addition to the routine courtesies—minding the adults in charge, saying "please" and "thank you," minding table and car manners, and no indoor running or rough play—your child needs to learn some new points of etiquette to be a welcome guest.

On Arrival

Teach your child to greet the hosts when she arrives at their house. "Hosts" include your child's friend, the parents or caregivers, and anyone else in the household. Children tend to bound away to play the second they cross the threshold, so remind your child that greetings come first. Children should understand they are the guests of the whole family.

The second step is to take bags and other items to the assigned place, usually the hosting child's room. It is rude to drop clothing bags, sleeping bags, and playthings in the hallway or pile them up on a stairway. If no one tells a child where to leave his things, he can ask, "Where should I put my bags, Mrs. Jones?" or "Should I take my bag to Marty's room now?"

Going with the Flow

First sleepovers can be difficult if a child isn't prepared to follow unfamiliar routines. He will feel more comfortable knowing that you really want him to do what's customary in a host's home. Some children are easily confused or feel guilty if they do something away that they can't do at home—eating in front of the TV, for example, when you always have sit-down meals at the table. Reassure your child that it's okay to do as the Joneses do, and also tell him not to complain if the Jones house rules seem stricter than he is used to.

Neatness Counts

Children should always leave bathrooms tidy, hanging up towels and rinsing basins and tubs after use. Your child should make up his bed or roll his sleeping bag the next morning and pack his bag or suitcase. (Pack everything, including dirty clothes.) He must put away toys after play and throw away his trash.

Children also need reminding to wash their hands and faces, comb their hair, and make a neat appearance at all meals. Unless PJs, bathrobes, and slippers are normal attire at breakfast in the host's home, a child should dress for the day before a morning meal.

Basic Courtesies

Your child may be awake before anyone else, but he should not wander the house or go outside on his own. It is impolite to turn on the television, play music or video games, or make any disturbing noises until the hosts are up and about. If your child is an early bird, be sure he packs a book to read while he's waiting for others to rise. One clue is to listen for people stirring in the kitchen before venturing forth.

Offering to help is another courtesy. Hosts appreciate a young guest who volunteers to set the table or to turn down the television when adults enter a room. The point is to be considerate but not obsequious. If an adult doesn't need assistance, children shouldn't insist or ask why.

Stress the importance of saying "thank you" to caregivers and the hosting child when leaving. Youngsters are often exhausted after a sleepover, so you'll probably have to remind your child to make a gracious departure. If he forgets to thank his friend's parent or parents, accompany him back to the home and add your appreciation to his.

Post-Sleepover Etiquette

Good manners don't end after you've picked up your child. Check that he has returned home with all his belongings. If he has forgotten something, call the host parent and arrange to get the item as soon as possible.

Thank-you notes aren't necessary for most sleepovers, but if your child stays with another family for several days, a note and an appropriate gift (not too expensive) will be appreciated. If someone has helped you out by keeping your child at your request, the note and gift should come from you, although it will be nice if your child also writes a note.

Children need to learn that when they accept an invitation to visit, the polite response is to return the gesture at the earliest convenient

Talk to the Parents

Whether your child is the sleepover guest or host, talk with the parent on the other side of the invitation. Host parents should provide information about plans. If you want to take the children to a movie, for example, tell the other parent what film you intend to see and ask if it is acceptable. (Parental standards about suitable movies, videos, and television vary considerably, so don't be offended by a parent who restricts his child's viewing.) Taking children to worship services or religious events can be a thorny issue if you haven't cleared your plans in advance.

When your child is the guest, tell the host parent about any special concerns such as allergies and dietary restrictions, fear of pets, and the possibility of bedwetting, sleepwalking, or nightmares. Always provide the hosts with phone numbers where you can be reached.

Be clear about and observe arrival and departure times. Your child might call an hour before you are scheduled to collect her and ask to stay longer, but always speak to the host parent before extending a pick-up time. Listen carefully; if the parent sounds surprised or disconcerted, stick to the original time. If someone else will pick up your child, inform the host of who the person is and his or her relationship to the child.

---

time. Adults understand that reciprocating doesn't necessarily mean an exact exchange; you might enjoy a weekend at your best friends' cabin, then invite them to dinner a week later, and no one regards the exchange as unequal. Elementary-age children, however, want strict equality, so plan to host a reverse sleepover as soon as you can. It's not wise to frame the invitation as a social obligation or responsibility; your child should think of reciprocating as a nice thing to do for a friend—a way of following the Golden Rule.

Other Out-and-About Occasions

BY SECOND OR THIRD GRADE, your child should be able to manage most routine out-and-about activities with confidence and good manners. He will actually help in the grocery store and with other shopping.

He won't often want to hold your hand anymore, but he will know to stay close by if you make your expectations clear and set boundaries. (You must still be vigilant at all times, especially in crowded places.) Your child will probably be able to endure longer waits—at the doctor's and dentist's offices, for example—and to entertain himself as long as the waiting time isn't excessive.

His manners in the car and other vehicles are likely to be near perfect on many occasions. Elementary school–age youngsters are sticklers for rules and can become almost obsessive about safety. Don't be surprised if your child is the first to say "buckle up" and to remind you to keep your eyes on the road. But safety often takes a backseat to sociability when more than one child is riding with you, and you must be strict about noise levels and rambunctious behavior.

Depending on your child's temperament, interests, and self-control, you may be able to take your nine- or ten-year-old to "grown-up" restaurants and performances. Such special outings are worth a try, but be prepared to leave if your child becomes restless or complains. Choose events and activities that are age-appropriate; few nine-year-olds can handle a night at the symphony, but many are ready for an evening of live theater or a full afternoon at the ballpark. (Get aisle seating for easy bathroom breaks.) The more you expose your child to the ordinary and extraordinary experiences of his world, the more socially confident and adroit he will become.

In the Audience

In and outside school, your child will often be an audience member. Explain that good manners are important so that everyone can enjoy the event. You might add that movies, the circus, and the ice show are privileges; the rewards of these good audience manners will be more chances to attend fun events.

- **Sit up and be still.** Children are going to wriggle, but by emphasizing good posture, hands in lap, and staying in the seat, you can cut down on slumping, bouncing, kicking and pushing seat backs, turning around, monopolizing seat arms, poking seatmates, and other annoying behaviors. If your child has trouble seeing over the people in front, bring a booster cushion. A hint

Car Pooling

Car pooling is often the answer to the complexities of getting children to and from the myriad activities in which today's youngsters participate. But car pooling should be carefully planned and organized. Some questions to consider before jumping into a car pool include:

- Are all the parents responsible and reliable? Are they safe drivers, and are their cars safe?

- Are the parents ready to agree on and enforce a single set of riding rules for children? Are all members willing to share responsibility for discipline and support one another?

- Does the car-pool schedule suit your own schedule?

- Do you get along with the other parents? Do the children get along?

- Is there a backup plan for times when a driver is ill or has car trouble?

Car pools often work best when the adult members know each other well enough to anticipate problems. When there is a difficulty—such as a parent who is chronically late, has unsafe driving practices, or allows a teen driver to take his place without consulting other members—everyone must be prepared to deal with it quickly and to accept that hurt feelings are likely to result. When a car-pool arrangement suffers a breakdown, the relationships between members can be damaged. Think twice. If you are uncomfortable with an arrangement or feel uncertain of your ability to fulfill your commitment, you may want to sacrifice the convenience until a better time.

---

to parents of siblings: Sit between your youngsters at seated events to cut down on cutting up.

- **Stay quiet.** Be sure your child knows what is expected in different situations, and prompt as necessary. At the circus, it is fine to laugh when the clowns perform, but at big sister's music recital, it's unacceptable to talk when someone is playing an instrument. Clapping normally comes at the end of a performance or between acts. Learning when to be quiet and how to respond to different types of presentations is an important part of interpreting all sorts of social cues correctly.

- **Never address remarks to anyone who is performing.** Even if a child's best friend is on stage, he must never shout out, call the performer's name, or make direct comments. It's equally rude to point or laugh at a performer. If audience involvement is wanted, the performers will let the audience know when and what to do.

- **Whisper when requesting to go to the bathroom.** Be sure your child understands that this request should always be whispered when in public places.

- **If eating is permitted, do it quietly.** No slurping cold drinks or rattling candy boxes. No popping or smacking chewing gum— ever. Cellophane packaging should be opened and discarded quickly. Trash is thrown in refuse containers, not on the floor or ground.

The Over-Programmed Child

OVER-PROGRAMMING IS A CONTEMPORARY PHENOMENON that threatens to rob childhood of its joys and can stunt the growth of independence. For a wide variety of reasons, many parents feel compelled to fill every spare minute of their children's days with "productive" and organized extracurricular activity. The pattern may begin in preschool or earlier, but it is likely to expand in the elementary school years and continue through high school. Some young people enjoy all the extra classes and sports programs, but experts in child development and psychology are increasingly seeing the negative consequences of too much programming.

In the elementary school years, children are dealing with many changes in their lives and in their perceptions of themselves and others. They need time to disengage, think, dream, worry, and solve problems— to be children. Even very gregarious youngsters need time on their own as they form their identities and learn to function independently. As they grow older, children and teens experience growing pressure to perform well in school, and an overabundance of outside activities, no matter how enriching, can have negative effects on schoolwork, lead to burnout, and prompt resentment and rebellion.

A parent's responsibility is to help a child find balance in life, not to keep her constantly entertained. It is, quite simply, a question of respect for a child's individuality and consideration for her unique needs and interests.

Time to Slow Down?

If you are inclined to fill every day with planned activity, you may need to examine your lifestyle. Are you and everyone else in the household constantly frazzled and frantic? Is family life geared to your child's outside games and classes? Do you have time to spend with your spouse or partner, or are you too busy taking your children to their events? Does just doing nothing make you feel uncomfortable and unproductive?

Even if it's clear that your schedule is overloaded, you may have difficulty slowing the pace. One suggestion is to plan a do-nothing Saturday occasionally—no organized activities, no entertaining, no heavy-duty chores or cooking, no pressure. It may feel strange if you are used to living on the go, but give it a chance. There is a lot of wisdom in the old admonition to stop and smell the roses.

In general, special occasions will retain their special quality if not planned too frequently. School nights should very rarely be late nights for children; too many school nights out tire a child, interfere with her ability to perform efficiently in school, and may send the message that school is only a secondary concern. A really special weekend event every two months or so is a treat for a child to look forward to and to share with her family.

Observe and Discuss

Above all, be observant. Children often go along with a crowded schedule out of their desire to please parents, but there are cues and clues you can spot. Does your child seem tired, nervous, or unusually cranky? Is she having trouble sleeping? Is she behaving more aggressively at home or school? Have her school grades fallen below normal? Is she genuinely enthusiastic about her activities or only going through the motions? Be on the lookout for signs of too much stress and be ready to cut back on or drop activities. Discuss changes with your child and find out what she really wants to do. (She may love her music lessons but have little interest in the soccer team and French classes.) Most important, do not convey the impression that dropping an activity is a sign of failure. In fact, successful people are generally those who know their limits as well as their capabilities.

PART FIVE

The Bumpy Years: Eleven Through Fourteen Years

NOW'S THE TIME TO . . .

- Model values and discuss moral and ethical choices

- Clarify expectations and adjust discipline

- Model and encourage considerate treatment of others

- Support academic efforts and expect good sportsmanship

- Discuss early dating behavior

- Promote writing, conversation, and greeting skills

- Reinforce good table manners

- Teach appropriate party behavior

- Establish and enforce transportation rules

BETWEEN AGES ELEVEN AND FIFTEEN your child will be engaged in an amazing and often difficult process of change. During this period, which coincides roughly with the middle school years, he will leave childhood behind and enter adolescence. His body, mind, and emotions are growing and readying him for adulthood, and the changes he experiences can be welcome and painful at the same time.

These years can be tempestuous for children and parents, comparable in many ways to the highs and lows of toddlerhood. As your child struggles toward independence, it may sometimes seem that all notions of good manners and civility have been tossed aside. But have faith. With a clear-eyed understanding of the normal developmental imperatives of early adolescence, you will ride out the storms and guide your child into late adolescence.

Growth will be governed by the arrival of puberty. Children shoot up in height, and their bodies alter as nature readies them for reproduction. Physical changes triggered by hormones are accompanied by equally dramatic intellectual and emotional developments. You will see abstract thinking emerge as early as the seventh or eighth grade, when your child begins to recognize a variety of possibilities and to apply the basics of logic. Intellectually, he is no longer limited to what *is* but begins to explore the world of what *might be*. His new cognitive abilities will enable him to think and plan ahead. As you continue to teach and enhance the concepts of respect, courtesy, and consideration for others, his inner voice of conscience will increasingly confirm your teaching. The road may be bumpy, but the changes he and you must weather now will lead to the day when your child enters the world as a self-governing, compassionate, and mannerly adult.

Moral and Ethical Values

"TRANSITION" IS ONE OF THE words most frequently used to describe early adolescence—the psychological transition from the dependence of childhood to the relative independence of the later teen years; the physiological transition from child's body to the body of an adult capable of reproducing; the intellectual transition from concrete to abstract thinking; the moral transition from "me first" to "other people matter" thinking. By itself, each of these changes would be difficult. Together, they constitute one of the most challenging, explosive, and potentially traumatic phases in life.

Most children cannot successfully make these transitions alone, and your role as parent or primary caregiver is critical. Your child will begin to separate herself from you and home. She wants and may demand new freedoms, and you have to decide how to respond. When an eleven-year-old begins to treat home as an inconvenient pit stop or a thirteen-year-old screams that nobody understands her, it can be hard for parents to believe that they still have any influence. But your child is still years away from complete autonomy, and she needs your presence to complete her journey to self-reliance and social confidence.

Change for Everyone

PARENTS MUST ALSO MAKE A major transition. For the last decade, you have been in control, directly and through other caregivers and teachers. Now, you must adjust to your child's growing independence and adapt to her new thinking skills. You must be prepared to take a backseat to peers and outside social influences, yet know when and how to step in and counter negative influences. Most important, you should be ready to loosen the reins, trust your child to make decisions for herself, and allow her to take the consequences—pleasant and unpleasant.

Determining Priorities

By age eleven, your child has a pretty good understanding of your values and ethical standards. She has learned what is right and what is wrong in terms of her own behavior and established many of her own standards. She has learned the fundamentals of social etiquette and probably manages to be well mannered most of the time.

She is, in fact, ready for more freedom, and issues that were under your complete control just a year ago are suddenly up for grabs. Can she walk to the shopping center by herself? Can she ride to school with a teen who now has a driver's license? Can she pick out her own clothes and wear what she wants?

An adolescent's need to exercise control over her life will inevitably come into conflict with a parent's instinctive desire to protect and continue preparing her for responsible adulthood. If a parent is too controlling, an adolescent may rebel in dangerous and self-destructive ways. If a parent is too lax, an adolescent may face decisions and situations she cannot handle and come to resent her parent's apparent failure to care. Your challenge is to achieve the balance between strictness and laxity that fits your child's temperament, personality, and level of maturity. To find this balance, you will want to determine priorities and follow a strategy that probably helped everyone get through the terrible two's so many years ago—pick your battles.

What Matters?

Your child is going through what psychologists call *identity formation*—a process of deciding who she is, how she wants to be perceived by others,

Throughout most of human history, there was no concept of adolescence as a prolonged period. Our culture follows a different strategy: We extend the time of dependence well beyond the age when past generations were raising their own families and working as productive members of society. *Adolescence*—from the Latin for "to grow up"—is now a recognized stage in development, a decade or so of apprentice adulthood beginning around the onset of puberty. Children are expected to complete twelve to sixteen or more years of school before they achieve the full status and privileges of adulthood, and parents are legally and morally obligated to provide, at a minimum, material and financial support for most of this period.

◄◄-

and what she really values. Whether a child develops strong or weak personal moral and ethical standards at this time depends a great deal on the models in her life—parents chief among them. A parent who argues constantly about a child's choice of clothing and hairstyles or focuses obsessively on a child's material possessions may convey the message that superficial values are what really count. The better course is to concentrate on the higher values of respect for others, integrity, loyalty, self-sacrifice, and honesty—values that will stay with your child for life.

The Importance of Manners

Good manners should be high on your list of priorities because manners express in action the values we hold dear. Your child is now capable of thinking about manners on several levels. Good manners make other people feel good—the empathetic level. Behaving in mannerly ways makes her feel good and gets positive responses from others—the level of self-interest. Through peer relationships, she is learning that good manners promote social interaction and allow people to get along in their everyday encounters. As her solo out-and-about experiences increase, she will see that good manners help her navigate unfamiliar and sometimes challenging situations. She will begin to comprehend that her manners contribute to her image of herself and the way other people perceive and judge her. She may begin to sense that good manners have long-term benefits, helping her get into the schools she wants to attend and keep the jobs she likes.

Talk about manners with your child just as you would discuss other moral and ethical behavior. You may find that her interest rises to a fairly sophisticated level when manners are presented as part of abstract concepts such as civility, honor, and respect.

New Ways to Discipline

YOUNG ADOLESCENTS OFTEN SWING BACK and forth from childishness to behavior and responses so adult in nature that they catch you off-guard. You may feel as if you are dealing with many people in a single body. In a way, you are. Your child is trying on different roles for herself in the necessary process of forming her identity.

Disciplining a preteen and young teen is like a tightrope walk. You must be steady at all times, yet flexible enough to bend as the winds shift. Your goal is to respect your child's rapidly changing needs and capabilities while steering her along the straight path to maturity. She still wants you to provide a reliable framework of standards, rules, and expectations.

- *Be clear about your rules.* Young adolescents generally need fewer rules, but those you set should be crystal clear, and your child must understand the consequences of breaking them. If you are not firm, your child—with her growing ability to reason inductively and deductively—will catch every inconsistency. If you fail to follow through, she will regard your laxity as precedent setting.

- *Choose appropriate consequences.* Methods that work with younger children—time-outs, distraction, and so forth—are generally ineffective with preteens and teens. What often succeeds is the denial of privileges.

  - Teens value money and the freedom it brings, so parents might dock allowances and make adolescents use their own funds to replace or pay restitution for damage they cause.

  - Phone time and TV time are important to preteens and young teens, so limiting access to these pastimes can be useful.

Physically aggressive behavior may appear again in the middle school years. Hormones play a role, and some young teens become unpredictable, moody, and very quick-tempered. The fact that society exalts some forms of aggression—on the playing fields and in the media—may also contribute to a young person's aggressive behavior. The adolescent ego is fragile, and youngsters are subject to acute self-doubt and insecurity. Some boys and girls attempt to validate themselves by proving that they are stronger or tougher than anyone else.

If your preteen or young teen tends to lash out physically, he may well need more attention and reassurance from you. Some aggressive teens need more opportunities to make choices for themselves or more praise for their positive actions. Physical activity may provide an outlet and teach youngsters how to control aggressive impulses.

Be firm that hitting, fighting, and bullying are not allowed, but also work with your child to develop his self-restraint and find ways to resolve conflicts nonviolently. Parents should never respond to physical aggression with aggression. If it's clear that the aggressive behavior is serious—fights at school, school detentions or suspension, attraction to gangs—do not wait to seek help. Call on your health care provider and school counselors, psychologists, or teachers for advice and guidance.

- Grounding for serious rule breaking may be necessary, but parents should be careful not to overdo. When grounding an adolescent, a parent must keep the grounding period reasonable and be prepared to enforce the punishment by staying at home.

- Sending your adolescent to her room with limits on the use of telephone, TV, and computer can be helpful when a youngster needs to cool down.

Corporal punishment is not acceptable. Scolding an adolescent in public will inspire resentment. Consequences that punish other family members as well as the offending child (for example, canceling a family occasion) are unfair. Punishments

When you compliment or praise your child, do not attach conditions or undermine your positive remark with a negative one. Many adults assume that every compliment to a teen should include a lesson. A typical example: An eighth-grader pulls his C in math up to a B. His parent says, "That's a good start, son, but I know you can do better. I'd like to see an A on the next report." This kind of "damning with faint praise" can cut an adolescent to the core. The value of the compliment is likely to be lost, and the child may return to the original behavior out of resentment, spite, or the feeling that he can't please you, so why try. Fight the temptation to turn a compliment into an admonition to do better. Adolescents can use a fair amount of unconditional praise.

◄◄

---

are most likely to work when they are closely related to the child's misbehavior (restricting phone privileges for violating phone use rules), have been thought out and discussed with your adolescent, and are administered by an adult who is calm and in control.

The duration of a punishment is often less important than consistent enforcement. If you have determined appropriate consequences in advance and your child knows what they are, you are somewhat less likely to meet resistance.

- **Negotiate.** Your adolescent will question rules and restrictions that seem arbitrary or unsuitable for her age. If she wants to adjust or eliminate a rule, allow her to make her case and listen to her rationale with an open mind. Talk it over and explain your thinking. Whether or not you agree to a change, your willingness to negotiate shows respect for your child and her ideas. Some rules are not negotiable—especially those related to health and safety—but your child will appreciate your steadfastness in these areas if you are willing to bend, when appropriate, on other issues.

- **Emphasize personal responsibility.** Sometimes you can just sit back and let the natural consequences of your child's actions take their course. Say that she used up her allowance to buy something she wanted and has no money left to go out with her friends. You can sympathize, but don't try to fix the problem and don't give her reasons to excuse her mistakes or encourage her to think of herself as a victim when she fails to act responsibly.

- **Be generous with praise.** You remain your child's primary adult role model, and she cares deeply about your opinions. Look for opportunities to express positive reactions. If you catch her doing something nice for someone else—taking a piece of misdirected mail to a neighbor or holding a door for an elderly person—remark on it. Praise shouldn't be exaggerated or unwarranted; adolescents are very skeptical of false flattery. Genuine, deserved praise will work wonders.

- **Keep a rein on negative criticism.** When a parent is consistently negative, a child will eventually stop paying attention or even deliberately try to alienate the parent further. Negative criticism is most effective when it is specific and not personalized. ("Those clothes are okay for going out with your friends but inappropriate for church." Not "Those clothes make you look like a hoodlum.")

  If you don't like one of your adolescent's friends, keep it to yourself. If criticism is necessary, focus on specific incidents and not character. ("I was surprised to hear Janice gossiping about your teacher. I'm sure she doesn't want to be cruel." Not "Janice is a snippy little gossip.") Adolescents will often defend their friends with greater fervor than they defend themselves, so don't put their loyalties to the test.

Privacy Issues

AROUND AGE THIRTEEN, MAYBE EARLIER, young adolescents tend to become extremely sensitive about personal privacy. Often an obvious sign is an obsession with their bedrooms. The child comes home from school, goes straight to her room, and emerges only to get food. The only people welcomed in are her friends. She may tack a "do not disturb" or "keep out" sign on her bedroom door, and it's no joke.

For young teens, the bedroom is a space where they can physically and psychologically separate themselves from the family in a kind of practice leave-taking that anticipates the day when they will leave home behind. The desire for privacy reflects young adolescents' need to come to terms with the myriad changes they are undergoing. Their young bodies are altering in ways that are difficult to understand and accept, and they are often literally uncomfortable inside their own skins, especially around other people. Psychologically, they are dealing with the realization that they are people of many parts. They are also under a lot of pressure to conform to other people's expectations. It's far from easy to integrate all the aspects of personality into a comfortable whole, and teens need solitude to work on the monumental questions: "Who am I? What is my purpose? What do I want to be?"

How to Respond

Parents may feel hurt or infuriated by a child's leave-me-alone attitude. The temptation is to draw the child out and force her into family fellowship. Or, feeling rejected, a parent may reject in turn, abandoning attempts at communication beyond basic commands and instructions. Parents may also respond by violating a child's privacy—reading private writings, rifling through drawers, searching closets—in an attempt to find out what is going on with their young person.

By understanding that an adolescent's need for privacy is natural, parents will be less likely to take their child's privacy as a personal affront or to suspect wrongdoing. Yes, she is rejecting you, but in a way that is absolutely essential to her maturation. She is getting on with the business of growing up and learning to accept and eventually to like and trust herself. This is a process you can influence, but you can't do it for her. Keep in mind, too, that one of the hallmarks of a mature personality is the ability to be alone without loneliness and anxiety.

Working It Out Together

Respecting your child's privacy doesn't mean giving up your authority. You have rights and obligations that will override your child's privacy, and negotiation is often the best way to settle conflicts. You might agree that your teen can redecorate her bedroom any way she wants as long as she agrees to keep the room clean. Clarify exactly what you mean by *clean*. Dirty clothes in the hamper and washed at least once a week; dirty dishes and glasses returned to the kitchen every day; stereo and computer turned off at a specific time each night, and so on. In exchange, you agree not to enter her room or go through her possessions

A United Front

Consistent discipline can be difficult when parents are separated or divorced, but the last thing an adolescent needs is a stream of mixed messages from the people he loves. Whatever their feelings about one another, separated or divorced parents must reach agreement on disciplinary issues and communicate with one another when consequences have to be enforced. Even if a child will not be with another parent during a penalty period, that parent needs to know about the misbehavior. From embarrassment or fear of further consequences, youngsters may beg one parent not to tell the other about a problem. But parents must be careful not to allow their child to play them against each other. Such manipulation can become habitual and have serious repercussions on a child's later relationships. Put personal animosities aside and concentrate on your mutual concern—your child.

---

without permission, to make her things off-limits to siblings, and to not complain about messiness that isn't a health or safety hazard. She may argue about the details, but she will probably be more inclined to live up to her side of the bargain—and respect the privacy of other family members—because she knows that you trust her.

Encouraging Family Involvement

Family rituals can help keep your child engaged with others. When family meals, weekly worship services, family council meetings, and shared chores and hobbies are observed in a predictable fashion, adolescents are more likely to take part. If everyone routinely sits down to eat together, for instance, your child knows that meals are not planned to put her on the spot or make her feel self-conscious. (See "The Family Table," page 319.) Even when she's not enthusiastic, she will probably participate out of habit, presenting opportunities to communicate in nonthreatening settings.

Signs of Trouble

Too much solitude can indicate problems, and parents must be alert. An adolescent who demands private time but also spends hours with friends and on the phone and joins in activities at school is behaving

Communicating with your teen may seem like trying to open a tin can with your fingers—nearly impossible. Finding time within the harried and conflicting schedules of most modern families is difficult, and you are now dealing with a generally reticent adolescent who would rather sulk or throw a tantrum than talk about himself. So how do you keep the lines of communication open?

- **Pick your times.** Catch your teen in a good mood, not in the aftermath of an argument or emotional upheaval. Some parents find that later in the evening is a good time for reflective conversation. An adolescent who's tired but not exhausted is often open to personal talk.

- **Don't mix messages.** An adolescent who has just been ordered to take out the trash and clean his room is unlikely to be receptive if you suddenly switch gears and ask about his weekend plans.

- **Give your time.** When you start a conversation, stick it out. Nothing is so likely to shut down further communication as a parent who must go to work or keep an appointment just when the adolescent is beginning to express himself freely.

- **Talk about "big ideas."** Your adolescent is forming his ideas on lots of topics, so be open to conversations about larger issues—politics, the national economy, the environment, AIDS. He is making his first serious forays into deep intellectual waters. Respect his ideas and opinions. Correct mistakes in facts with sensitivity. ("I'm not sure about that. Maybe we can look it up" works much better than "You don't know what you're talking about.") You may find that talking about large issues leads naturally to discussion on the personal level.

━━

normally. A child who has few friends and little apparent interest in school or social interaction may be suffering from genuine loneliness. When loneliness and social isolation are prolonged, they can lead to depression and antisocial behaviors.

It can be difficult to distinguish loneliness and depression from the usual "teen angst." The intensely lonely adolescent is likely to betray her state of mind through an uncustomary and *persistent sadness* and by giving up even private activities (such as playing a musical instrument) that she once loved. Parents must take teenage depression seriously. Depression is a disabling condition that must be treated.

CHAPTER 22

Respect for Self and Others

EARLY ADOLESCENCE CAN BE TRYING but need not be conflict-ridden if parents respect their child and the changes he's going through. As your child is forming his identity, he also sees the imperfections of grown-ups. He must adjust his attitudes toward you and other key adults, leading to behaviors that appear to be disrespectful and ill mannered. In fact, though, he is striving for a higher level of respect for himself and others founded on realistic perceptions and expectations.

Parents face a critical choice here: to keep the blinders on and continue to treat the child as a "child" or to respect his growing maturity. You and your child are at a fork in the road, and one direction is more likely to lead to the trusting and loving relationship you want when your offspring reaches adulthood.

The Changing Child

THE PHYSIOLOGICAL CHANGES OF PUBERTY—beginning with a growth spurt that often finds sixth- and seventh-grade girls towering over the boys in their class—leave children worrying about what is happening, when it will happen, and how they compare to their peers. Puberty lasts between four and five years but can seem like an eternity to an adolescent and his parents. Some children seem to sail through, but for the vast majority, at least part of the time will be marked by uncertainty and self-doubt.

A Critical Time

Puberty is a period when intellectual development seems to switch into fast-forward mode, as preteens and early teens start to reason in adult-like ways and deal with abstractions. Your young adolescent is beginning to think about complexities of the world and to wonder about his role in it. He's trying to understand the deeper meanings of right and wrong and to make decisions based on *his* standards rather than the expectations of adults. This development means that he is willing and often eager to challenge you and put your rules and limits to the test.

For these reasons and others—most of which are beyond anyone's control—a child's self-image and self-esteem are likely to take a battering during early adolescence, requiring parents to be patient and respectful. No parent gets it right all the time, especially when confronted with an adolescent who seems to be the polar opposite of the sunny, cooperative child of the elementary school years.

Easing the Tensions

It's common to hear a parent describe his young adolescent as "thirteen going on thirty" or "fourteen going on forty." Such humorous remarks express a parent's frequent confusion and bewilderment. The son who was throwing a fit in his room just twenty minutes ago is now greeting guests with the grace of a seasoned diplomat. The daughter who said she would never speak to you again suddenly wants to have a serious discussion about the destruction of the rain forests. Often this type of quixotic shift is an adolescent's indirect way of saying, "I'm sorry about the way I behaved, Mom and Dad. Can we just forget it?"

Modeling respect is probably a lot more important than demanding a formal apology. An adolescent will often say that he is sorry sooner or later, if you allow him the opportunity to ease into it. He knows when he has been discourteous and may feel guilty or embarrassed. But in the boiling emotional cauldron of puberty, he may not always know why he

Young adolescents are under great pressure (from peers as well as adults) to perform and conform. Their moods change like quicksilver, the result of conflicts both internal and external. They need a release valve, and as often as not, that valve is you. While you must control aggressive, abusive, or consistently rude or hateful behavior, you can probably afford to be the scapegoat at times. An adult's ego is resilient compared to an adolescent's, and a loving parent knows better than to take every teen outburst personally. Be alert to the stresses in your child's life, be willing to take a little heat, let your adolescent know that you understand her feelings, and work at keeping a dialogue going.

---

behaves as he does, and he can be confused and frightened by his outbursts. Give him some leeway and then accept his apology or explanation, fumbling as it may be, without prolonging his misery.

The Influence of Peers

PARENTS CAN BE SURPRISED BY the degree to which their youngster shifts allegiance to peers during adolescence. Teens are basically conformists. Dressing like their friends, listening to the same music, and so on are their ways of bonding and of distinguishing themselves from the adults who still control them. They *want* to establish a generation gap and express their uniqueness.

Studies of adolescents reveal, however, that most young people respect their parents and hold them in high esteem. When parental support is firm and unwavering, adolescent conformity to peer standards tends to be at the fairly superficial level of clothing and hairstyles. Family standards, on the other hand, tend to hold sway in more fundamental areas including morals and ethics.

The Importance of Friends

Peer relationships are vital to healthy adolescent development. Friends provide support and fellowship, share interests and values, and appreciate qualities in one another that adults may not find so important or attractive. A preteen or teenager feels free to relax with his friends and be himself. Adolescent friendships may not survive into adulthood, but they establish many of the basic patterns of socialization and expectations for peer relationships throughout life.

The peer group is powerful, and young adolescents are more likely than elementary school–age children to go along with their peers. But don't assume that peer pressure is necessarily a bad thing. Friends can influence each other in positive ways and be highly critical of behaviors that the group regards as unacceptable, like smoking cigarettes, damaging property, cheating, stealing, and crude manners. A young adolescent who persistently violates peer codes risks ostracism, and the pressure to conform may be what is needed to keep him in line.

Cliques—small peer groups that often peak in importance in the middle school years, especially for girls—provide adolescents with a sense of security and solidarity. Some cliques are extremely tight, but most are fluid, and young people drift in and out. Wise parents will get to know their child's friends and keep an eye out for activities and behaviors that may signal problems. Watch and listen from a respectful distance and be prepared to intervene quickly if your child's clique steps over the line.

The Tough Talks

You know that your preteen or teen is talking with his peers about life issues including what an earlier generation succinctly summarized as "sex, drugs, and rock 'n' roll." Much of the information passed between peers is erroneous, and peer pressure is often built on these false underpinnings. A parent who has the facts and is willing to initiate conversations on sensitive topics can do much to counter negative peer influences. Whether the parent is effective can boil down to timing, attitude, and knowledge.

- *Know what you are talking about.* A young adolescent's data bank on subjects like substance abuse and sex may not be full, but he can often pick out your inaccuracies. The school nurse, your family physician or health-care provider, or a social worker are good sources of accurate information and up-to-date materials.

- *Don't assume that someone else is doing the job.* Many schools offer little or no sex education and only sporadic discussion of

It's a common lament among parents: When you have children, you begin to measure your own life by their birthdays. When a child enters puberty, parents may find themselves feeling a bit "elderly," and some decide it's time to be their child's best friend. But studies of adolescents indicate that preteens and teenager do not want parents to walk their walk and talk their talk. Adolescents really want loving guardians who continue to model mature behavior, make rules and expectations clear, and exercise their authority when necessary. Young people don't like to hurt their parents' feelings and may not speak up when a parent begins dressing too youthfully, using the current teen slang, or "hanging out with the kids" too often. But teens will feel embarrassed and resentful. Teens respect parents who work hard at understanding them and providing mature guidance and support—in other words, parents who act like parents.

◀◀

substance abuse. The basic responsibility to educate children falls squarely on parents, so be circumspect about outside sources of education and take the time to investigate the content of teaching programs.

- *Link behavior to your child's values.* Instead of focusing on long-range consequences, talk about what he values *now*—being liked and respected by others, being a good athlete, making good grades, having fun, staying healthy, earning more privileges, and so on—and help him see how reckless behaviors can undermine his values and goals.

- *Have lots of little talks.* Discussions about dangerous and self-destructive behaviors should be ongoing throughout the middle and high school years and are much easier to initiate if you don't try to address everything at once. Parents and young people alike are going to be embarrassed the first time they take on a tough subject, but it gets easier with practice. Start early and talk as frequently as you can. Focus your conversations, but let your child broaden the topic under discussion if he wants to.

- *Listen for your child's cues.* Often, young people want to talk to their parents about premarital sex, sex roles, substance abuse, drinking and driving, and other personal and social issues, but they may be uncomfortable asking direct questions. They will, however, give cues and signals. Parents should listen carefully and take the opportunities offered to start conversations. For example, instead of getting angry about an off-color joke or offensive music lyrics, ask your child what he thinks they mean. If you discover that he doesn't understand, you can explain what's being said and talk about why the material is offensive or hurtful.

- **Don't criticize your young teen's friends or use them as examples of bad behavior.** Your child will immediately go on the defensive and tune out whatever you have to say. An adolescent's loyalties may extend to adults, especially an absent parent. If your child does mention a name, he may be troubled by the actions of a friend or another adult. Listen objectively and then consider various options. When your child sees that you are looking at the problem in a responsible and caring manner, he may be more than happy to let you have control of a situation that is bothering him.

A Question for Peggy and Cindy

I have a dear friend who claims that she and her daughter talk about everything. But I've learned that my friend's daughter is hiding some potentially dangerous behavior. How can I tell my friend without hurting her feelings?

You must talk to your friend if her child is putting herself in jeopardy. It won't be easy, but think how you would feel if you failed to speak up and the child did get into serious trouble. Assuming that the danger is imminent, you have to address it as soon as possible. Keep the conversation on target, and don't criticize the mother. You may be tempted to handle the conversation over the phone, but a private face-to-face talk when the child isn't around will show your respect and concern for the mother. Your news will doubtless come as a shock, and it's impossible to predict how your friend will feel. Her reactions may range from anger to relief. Try to keep the conversation focused on your friend's child, and make it clear that you are ready to help if you can.

A Head Start on Dating

In the early years of middle school, children still tend to stick to friends of their own gender, but by the end of this period, contacts between the sexes will increase. Even parents who do a very good job of educating their adolescent about puberty may forget or hesitate to inform about what is happening on the other side of the fence. Boys need information about girls, and vice versa. From a practical standpoint, this information should help them to get along better and control the impulse to tease and taunt peers who suddenly look and act in unexpected ways. Learning to respect and value the opposite sex will soon be crucial to healthy interpersonal relationships including dating.

Near the end of the middle school years, boys and girls will be interacting fairly often. Kids come together in *crowds*—groups that are bound by some common interest or activity and may form when several cliques mingle. You'll probably hear your child talking about the "jocks," the "brains," the "rebels," and so on. Within their crowds, adolescents get to know young people of both sexes. Group dating often begins in middle school. When you drop your son and his friends at the movie theater or football game, you'll see that they are immediately joined by an equal number of girls. The youngsters may pair off within the group, but the group is the key unit for socialization at this age—though some middle schoolers may begin one-on-one dating. In any case, adolescents and their parents can get a head start on dating through open discussion of rules, manners, and expectations.

- **Age.** At what age can your teen begin one-on-one dating (often fifteen or sixteen), and what are the age limits on the people he or she can date? This latter consideration is important because young teens—most often girls but boys as well—can be flattered by and vulnerable to the attentions of older teens and young adults.

- **Curfews.** Parents determine curfews and must see that they are enforced. Your teen needs to know that you are serious and that violations will have consequences. There will be exceptions, but be clear that the occasional late curfew is not a precedent. A young teen may be more amenable if you link curfews to both age and behavior. Let him know that you will extend curfews as he grows older and if he proves himself to be responsible.

- **Dating manners.** Remind your child that manners are demonstrations of respect for others, including dates and their parents. In addition to the etiquette basics he has been learning for years, you should emphasize the importance of meeting a date at the door (not parking at the curb and honking), introducing and greeting parents politely, walking dates to the door at the end of the evening, and seeing that they are safely inside. While you are still chauffeuring, make sure that your child observes all these courtesies.

  Last-minute get-togethers are common among teens, but invitations should be issued as early as possible. If your child needs a date for the ninth-grade dance, for instance, he or she should call at least a week in advance. When your child receives an invitation, he should say "yes" or "no" promptly; a short delay is acceptable if he must check his plans with you, but he should reply within a maximum of twenty-four hours. Breaking dates may be necessary on occasion, but it is never permissible to break a date in order to take a better offer. Nor is it acceptable to ask several people simultaneously, hoping for at least one acceptance.

- **Money.** Middle schoolers probably won't face too many dating expenses, but even on group dates, they will worry about who should pay for what. A lot of money issues will be determined by local custom. In some communities and groups, "Dutch treat" is the rule, with boys and girls paying their own way. In others, the "boys pay" tradition is still observed. More commonly, the young person who issues the invitation—boy or girl—is expected to pay for reasonable expenses (movie tickets and refreshments, cab fare, and the like), and other costs are shared. When you are determining policies about "date money," talk with your child about the current practices in his age group. He needs to know what costs he is expected to bear and when you will supplement. It is also smart to discuss the issue with other parents and older teens to find out what is the standard.

Hygiene and Grooming

BODY CHANGES IN PUBERTY RAISE hygiene issues that your child hasn't dealt with before. Parents should include hygiene and grooming in discussions of other aspects of puberty. Some grooming issues will be questions of taste and style and open to negotiation, but basic hygiene is not up for argument. Good grooming and cleanliness are fundamentals of good etiquette and are a hallmark of the well-mannered person.

- **Body odor.** Daily bathing, clean clothing, and a mild deodorant should do the trick. Some adolescents may bathe or shower twice or more a day. If the behavior isn't obsessive, the extra showers won't be a problem, but you'll probably want to limit bathroom time. If your youngster is bath-averse or wants to wear the same dirt-encrusted clothes for days on end, you have to intervene.

- **Hair.** Clean comes first. Puberty brings changes in the skin's oil-producing glands, and hair tends to be oily for many adolescents, so shampooing may become a daily ritual.

- **Teeth.** Brushing and flossing are fundamental, and children with braces have to be extra attentive to dental care. Oddly, young people who are careful about every other aspect of appearance often neglect their teeth, so be ready to remind them to brush. Never neglect annual or semiannual dental visits.

- **Shaving.** This may begin during middle school. Young people need instruction in how to shave facial, underarm, and leg hair, what products to use, and how to treat cuts and skin problems.

- **Makeup.** Young teens often resort to heavy makeup to hide acne and other perceived imperfections, and parents have a hard time convincing them that less is best. You may be able to negotiate some trade-offs—nail polish on the weekends but not to school or mascara but not eyeliner. Be firm about cleanliness, and consult with your physician about skin treatments and makeup choices.

Be Careful with Scents

Perfumes, colognes, shaving lotions, scented bathing products—teens tend to splash them on with abandon. Young people must understand that heavy or mixed scents can be offensive to others and provoke allergic reactions. Your child may respond to the message that a single, understated scent is a mark of sophistication. Out of consideration for others, you should exercise authority over the scent levels at home, at school, and in public places including places of worship.

Respect Within the Family

AS YOUR ADOLESCENT PULLS AWAY from you, he may distance himself from other family members as well, begging off social gatherings and even behaving rudely or belligerently to family. Parents need to proceed with a balance of understanding and firmness. A teen may decide he'd rather be with friends than attend Grandmother's regular Sunday lunch. Instead of forcing him to go to Grandmother's or allowing him to opt out completely, a parent will achieve a better result through negotiation and compromise. Perhaps he can go to his grandmother's home every other week and call her at least once each week. Parents shouldn't make excuses for their teens, but you can help your young person learn to explain himself without hurting the feelings of others. In this example, the adolescent should talk with his grandmother about his plans, offering assurances that he values her gatherings but explaining that Sunday is the only time he can get together with his group outside school. Adolescents usually don't intend to hurt with their behavior and comments. But parents must be clear that relatives and close friends are always to be treated with respect and be firm about the consequences for rudeness.

With Siblings

Sibling conflicts can escalate if the siblings are relatively close in age but at different development and social levels. An eleven-year-old and a fourteen-year-old will be asserting their independence, but in different ways. The younger child may still be fairly happy-go-lucky; the older one may be more moody and argumentative. Both are likely to demand privacy, but the older child may be more aggressive in asserting his rights.

Little things often trigger sibling battles. The older adolescent begins spending an hour in the bathroom instead of the old ten minutes. The younger child teases his big sister about a pimple. Preteen and teen siblings may belittle one another's interests and friends. The one-upsmanship of competitiveness and comparing can start bitter quarrels. As much as possible, allow your children to work out their difficulties, but be firm that treating each other with respect remains your bottom line.

- *Every family member deserves respect.* Emphasize that each person in the family is an individual with his own strengths and weaknesses and must be respected and treated with courtesy.

- *Everyone must abide by house rules and schedules.* These include time in the bathroom, time on the phone, and doing assigned chores.

- *No hateful teasing is allowed.* Adolescents sometimes boost their self-confidence at the expense of others, and a sibling is an easy target. Youngsters must understand the difference between playful teasing and cruelty. Appeal to your children's better natures and also model respectful behavior by keeping your own teasing to a minimum.

- *Privileges and responsibilities increase.* Help younger teens understand that privileges are a function of age, experience, and the degree to which a person has exhibited responsible behavior. Use examples beyond the realm of sibling conflict—your child's favorite ballplayer, who spent years in the minors before making the big league, the company president who worked her way up from the factory floor. Be clear that privileges are not rights and also involve expanded responsibilities.

Grandparents and Older Relatives

Respect for elders is not the way of modern consumer culture, and young people are not often exposed to truly noble images of older and elderly people. Adolescents can be quick to stereotype based on physical appearance and can be misguided in their attitudes toward older people.

A Special Responsibility

Spying and tattling among siblings should not be condoned, but each person has a responsibility for the health and safety of other family members. Talk seriously with your children about the distinction between minor disagreements (who gets to watch what TV program) and major problems such as drug or alcohol use, sneaking out, shoplifting, gang membership, truancy, and the like. Reporting on a sibling who is putting herself or others in jeopardy is responsible behavior.

Parents should set the tone. If you show respect to the older members of your family, your child should follow suit. Language is crucial. A parent who makes blanket statements about "geezers" and "blue-hairs" is sending the message that age is the primary determinant of an individual's worth.

People now live longer and healthier lives, so young people are more likely to have active grandparents, great-grandparents, and other relatives. Contact with older relatives makes a great difference in an adolescent's attitude toward all older people (including teachers and employers), and parents should encourage these relationships. This is easy if family members live close by and back-and-forth visits are common. But with distant relatives or when family visits are infrequent, phone calls, letters, and e-mail have to substitute. Encourage your child to keep up regular contact and to regard the weekly phone call or letter as beneficial to *him*—not an act of charity to the older person. If you have conflicts with parents or in-laws, don't involve your children or expect them to take sides; parents simply have no right to poison the well of affection between grandparents and grandchildren. Help your young person understand how fortunate he is to have older relatives, and teach him that old age, like youth and adolescence, is just another part of life's cycle.

Teen Chores

CHORES ARE A WAY OF reminding adolescents that they don't live in a vacuum. If they want a smooth-running household, they have to take

When a serious or terminal illness strikes a family member, adolescents may hide their feelings, affecting a blasé and uncaring attitude. They may withdraw from the ill person. Don't be fooled by appearances. Preteens and teens will be frightened by the prospect of losing someone they love. They may feel guilt for past behaviors (fighting with a sibling, for example) and even for being healthy when a loved one is sick. They need to know what is going on, and that means explaining the family member's medical condition. Do not give your child false hopes when a condition is chronic or terminal. Young people can usually begin to deal with the truth when it is presented accurately and with sensitivity. But if kept in the dark, adolescents are likely to imagine all sorts of terrifying possibilities. Unless there are medical reasons such as fear of contagion, young people need opportunities to be with an ill or dying relative and to maintain contact through calls, cards, and letters. When a serious illness occurs inside the immediate family—striking a parent, primary caregiver, or sibling—adults will be focused on the ill person. But don't forget the children in the household. They need your love, attention, and even physical closeness more than ever.

◂╂

part. Doing chores shows consideration for others and also helps children to develop effective work habits and good visiting behavior. These suggestions should help to get the work done:

- *Show your teen how to do specific chores and be clear about your expectations.* Whenever you haven't fully explained how you want something done, your child will do it his way, and you lose the right to complain.

- *Be sure chores are appropriate for your child's age and abilities.* If your adolescent is going through a clumsy phase, don't expect him to dust your collection of fine porcelains.

- *Rotate chores among siblings to assure fairness.* Some chores are harder or more time-consuming than others, so why not alternate? To prevent arguments, post a written chore schedule and refer to it frequently.

- *Set reasonable schedules.* It's often possible to set timeframes—the lawn can be mowed on Friday or Saturday—rather than specific times. Be conscious of your child's schedule; a weekday packed with school activities is not the best choice for time-intensive chores.

- **Reward good work with praise and increased privileges.** While it's best not to link regular chores to allowances or payment (which can distort a young person's view of family responsibilities), you can give new privileges—increased phone time, for example—as a reward. When your child fails to do a chore, a suspension of privileges coupled with completion of the task will make the point that chores are not optional.

- **Provide opportunities for money making that are not related to routine chores.** Adolescents often want extra work to earn pocket money, so pay for jobs that aren't routine—cleaning the attic or raking the yard in spring and fall.

Caring About Others

ADOLESCENTS MAY NEED ENCOURAGEMENT TO interact with people outside their group. The middle school years are a great time to encourage concern for others by providing your child with opportunities to volunteer. School clubs, religious youth groups, Scouts, 4-H, and other interest-based organizations—there are numerous avenues by which a young person can participate in activities that take him into the wider world. Volunteer work taps into many adolescents' growing awareness of societal problems and questions of justice and fairness, allowing a young person to experience the difference that caring people who work together can make when they are ready to give of themselves.

- **Volunteering helps adolescents begin to understand the causes and consequences of the problems they see and worry about.** Helping at a homeless shelter or a home for the infirm elderly will give a young adolescent the opportunity to apply the Golden Rule, learn about issues that concern him, and use his critical thinking skills.

- **Volunteer work, like first jobs, promotes personal responsibility.** (See "Joining the Workforce," page 343.) But unlike a paid job, volunteering requires commitment without tangible incentives. Adult volunteers should provide role models of people who give without expecting material rewards.

- **Volunteering exposes young people to human diversity.** Young adolescents tend to pick friends who are very much like themselves in background, culture, and values, but you don't want your child to forget that the world is made up of countless people unlike himself. Working with a senior citizens' program can be beneficial for a child who has not had much contact with older people. Helping with your church day-care program may be just right for an only child or one who has had little experience with younger children.

- **Volunteerism encourages positive work habits and promotes key values** including empathy and compassion, generosity and selflessness, cooperation, respect for others, good manners and consideration, self-esteem, and pride in positive achievements.

Finally, a volunteer position keeps a youngster busy. As long as they know that their work is needed and appreciated, preteens and young teens are usually willing to take on almost any task. (Adults must be careful not to overestimate the capabilities of young volunteers.) But not every young adolescent is ready, and no one should be forced to volunteer.

CHAPTER 23

Skillful Communication

LEARNING TO WRITE AND SPEAK with competency is essential to the development of a well-mannered adult who can communicate with both grace and clarity. Because speaking, writing, and reading are inter-twined, learning in one area will improve the others. Literacy is achieved through the constant overlapping of these skills, and in the middle school years, writing becomes particularly important.

Children should have the mechanics of handwriting under control by the fifth or sixth grade. They can print clearly and have very likely made headway with cursive. They may even be learning intricate skills such as calligraphy. They understand that different types of writing follow different formats—letters, essays, test questions, diaries, invitations, thank-you notes, messages taped to the refrigerator, and so on. They may be using the computer for school assignments and e-mail. At home as well as in class, writing education will begin to shift from *how* to write to *what* to express and communicate.

Your Guiding Hand

YOUR CHILD NEEDS TO BELIEVE that you value language skills. When a parent downplays or belittles the importance of language education, he risks undermining a child's ability to communicate effectively and may hinder the development of capabilities essential for higher education, career advancement, professional reputation, and personal, social, and work relationships—in fact, for the success of just about every relationship and position his child will have throughout her life.

Correct Speech and Writing

Hopefully, you can leave it to your child's English teachers to explain the exact usage of the past perfect tense and the gerund form. Your primary role is to demonstrate respect for and concern about language. Correct your child's speech, but do so with great tact. Correction should never cause embarrassment, so avoid making an issue of minor language mistakes in front of other people. When you correct, do it quickly and offhandedly. If a child says, "Daddy drunk all the milk," a parent need only repeat the remark with emphasis on the correction—"Daddy *drank* all the milk"—and then continue with the conversation. Focusing on pronunciation at this age will contribute to your child's social skills. She will learn that it is a basic courtesy to say people's names and other proper nouns correctly. If your child corrects your speech, take it with good humor and thank her.

When your child asks you to look over homework or other written work, be attentive, point out mistakes, and encourage her to make corrections. This often means spotting grammar and spelling errors, but you can also tell your child when you think her meaning is unclear. Never write or rewrite work for your child, and don't look at her written work unless you are asked for help. This last injunction applies to all your child's writing. Letters, notes, journals, diaries, and so forth are private.

Don't forget praise. When your child relates a story in a particularly vivid way or writes a really effective thank-you note, tell her. Children who receive positive reactions for their verbal accomplishments are usually more open to correction.

Encouraging Reading and Writing

Your child is now (or soon will be) doing a great deal of reading for school. Still, she needs encouragement to read for her own pleasure and information. The example set by parents is vital.

Also encourage writing beyond schoolwork. Your adolescent may be interested in keeping a diary or journal as long as it doesn't become a chore. When you take a vacation, provide your child with a journal or scrapbook in which to keep souvenirs and record her impressions. Promote letter writing, and be sure she has the tools she needs (see "The Right Writing Materials," page 306). If you have a home computer, see that your child has her own personal files for letters and stories.

Invitations and Replies

MOST ADOLESCENT ENTERTAINING IS INFORMAL, so invitations are issued by phone or personal contact. But organized parties for birthdays, holidays, coming-of-age ceremonies (first communion, confirmation, bar mitzvah, *quinceañera*), and the like will require written invitations. Your child may receive her own invitations to formal occasions—a favorite teacher's wedding, a babysitter's college graduation—that require written replies. It's time for your child to learn the basic etiquette of written invitations and responses.

Issuing Invitations

The most effective way to teach invitation manners is to involve your child. She can share the responsibility of writing and addressing, and she will learn by doing that party planning requires organization and attention to details. Creative invitations set the mood for parties, and your child will enjoy choosing invitations or perhaps making her own. All invitations—written, phoned, or delivered electronically—must include these essentials:

- The name or names of the host and hostess
- The nature of the party or event
- The date, time, and location of the event
- Notation of any expected reply to written invitations

Purchased invitations normally include spaces for necessary information, and you can add an RSVP if you want replies. As you prepare invitations, keep the following guidelines in mind:

- **Give the host's full name.** There may be two Barbaras in your child's class, and it can be difficult for guests to determine which Barbara is hosting the party.

- **Be specific about the nature of the party.** If you are throwing a Halloween costume party, the invitation should clearly indicate that it will be a *costume* party. If you will drive the guests to another location during the party, include this information in order to alert parents about your plans.

- **Include the date of the event.** Mail can be delayed; e-mails may not be read immediately. Noting both day and date, as in "Wednesday, March 27," will avoid mix-ups and misunderstandings.

- **Be precise about time.** Invitations for young people's events should include starting and ending times. This is for the convenience of guests' parents, so they will know exactly when to drop off and pick up their youngsters.

- **Give directions if the location of the party is not well known to everyone.** Include the complete street address and area or suburb, and directions or a simple map. A phone number for the location is helpful in case a guest becomes lost.

- **Complete your RSVP** Include the party giver's name and phone number or address with an RSVP. You may not be acquainted with the parents of all your child's friends, so party invitees need to know how to contact you.

Invitations to most parties and special occasions should be issued well in advance. Two weeks' notice will give the families plenty of time to plan their schedules. Three or even four weeks is not too far ahead in a busy social season like the winter holidays or for a special occasion such as a bar mitzvah. (For more on timing of invitations, see "When to Invite," page 397.)

Should You Mention Gifts?

Invitations should not include references to gifts. Guests are expected to know when gifts are appropriate (birthdays, weddings, coming-of-age parties, and so forth) and to respond in their own way. Sometimes guests ask for ideas, and you can offer a suggestion or two. But remember that gifts are always the choice of the giver. Referring to gifts on an invitation also appears to emphasize gifts over the invitation itself. Do be clear about the nature of the event. If your child's birthday party has a holiday theme, for example, be sure that the invitation is clear ("A Valentine's Day Birthday Party"). Then leave gift selection to your guests.

If your child is inviting selected members of her class or team, don't distribute invitations at school or organized sports events. The likelihood of hurt feelings is just too great, and your child many suffer peer rejection because she has rejected others. Even if your child invites everyone, it's best not to hand out invitations at school or extracurricular activities. Teachers and coaches don't need the distraction, and party envelopes are too easily lost between school and home or forgotten in backpacks and sports bags. If you don't have a class or school directory, you can ask at the principal's office for addresses that can be released.

The E-Mail Question

E-mail is so fast and easy that it's tempting for invitations of all kinds. However, many people do not have home computers or are not regular users of the Internet. Some folks check their e-mail religiously, but others let it stack up. In addition, there is as yet no quick way to track down e-mail addresses. Mailing or phoning remains the best way to ensure that everyone receives your invitation. If you do issue invitations by e-mail, include an RSVP. Your Internet provider probably offers a receipt feature, but this doesn't mean the e-mail has been opened and read by the intended recipient.

Accepting and Regretting

Most invitations to your child can be answered by phone or in person, but some will require written replies, providing the chance to teach your adolescent how to write informal and formal response notes and reinforce the importance of promptness and polite language.

Whether formal or informal, a response to an invitation is short and to the point. The etiquette of regrets and acceptances requires no explanations; an invitee need not excuse an absence. A middle schooler can write a simple, informal note like the following examples:

October 6

Dear Krista,

I am really looking forward to attending your birthday party on October 19. Thank you so much for inviting me.

Patricia Lewis

June 20

Dear Bart,

I'm sorry that I won't be able to come to your beach party on the Fourth of July. My family is going to my grandparents' house that day. Thanks for asking me.

Chris Jeffers

If your child wants to use a closing courtesy, "Your friend" is always nice. She should sign her full name to prevent confusion.

Formal replies are sent for formal invitations. These are actually very easy to write because they follow the wording and form of the invitation. This example shows a traditional formal wedding and reception invitation and reply:

Mr. and Mrs. Edgar Allen Reece
request the honour of your presence
at the marriage of their daughter
Anne Lenore
to
Mr. William Kirk Hawthorne

Saturday, the eighteenth of May
two thousand and two
at four o'clock
Village Presbyterian Church
Springfield, Mississippi
And afterward at the reception
Oak Glen Manor
Locust Road
RSVP

Reply:

Miss Patricia Jane Lewis
accepts with pleasure
(Or: regrets that she is unable to accept)
Mr. and Mrs. Reece's
kind invitation for
Saturday, the eighteenth of May

Formal invitations are usually printed but may be handwritten. Replies are written by hand, preferably on plain or bordered notepaper. Less formal replies are also acceptable, but since your young adolescent is likely to receive relatively few formal invitations, use the opportunity to give her experience with the formal style.

Thank-You Notes

YOUR CHILD IS GAINING THE vocabulary and writing skills to compose her own thank-you notes, especially if she has had plenty of guidance from you in the past. There's no hard-and-fast rule about the length or contents of written thank-you's. Short is fine, so long as the necessary courtesies are observed. There are also times when your child may want to write a thank-you letter, such as when she writes to a close relative or friend. (The basics of written thank-you's are discussed in "Thank-You Note Specifics," page 244.) Whatever the length, however, a thank-you note should do the following.

RSVP (shorthand for the French phrase *repondez s'il vous plait,* or "please reply") on an invitation means that the recipient is obligated to respond whether he can or cannot attend. "Regrets only" requires a reply only if he cannot attend. In either case, the reply should be made as soon as possible, since the number of responses tells the host how many guests to plan for. The reply notation will be followed by the address or telephone number, indicating whether the host expects a written or phoned response. If an invitation doesn't include a reply request, the invitee is not expected to respond, though a note or call is polite if he is unable to attend.

To determine the exact number attending—as for a sit-down dinner— the use of RSVP gives the more accurate count. The RSVP notation also allows you to determine if any invitations have gone astray. "Regrets only" is less formal but might give you a fairly good estimate of your guests. You can include times to call with the phone number (555-1234, between 6 P.M. and 9 P.M.). If it will be difficult to take phone calls, put an address on the invitation. Very large events, such as conventions and banquets, often include a reply or "respond by" card, but these forms are unnecessary for most personal invitations.

The home computer offers another avenue for replies, and you can include your e-mail address, in addition to your telephone number, with your RSVP or "Regrets only" request. E-mail is an informal medium and is not suited for responding to formal invitations. Since not everyone is linked to the Internet, don't expect all responses to be electronic.

◄┼

- **Express gratitude for the specific gift or kindness.** To write merely "Thank you for the nice present" is not enough. The note should include direct and personal remarks: "Thank you so much for the video game. It's is my favorite, and I enjoy playing this new version a lot." Never indicate that you don't like, can't use, or plan to exchange a gift.

- **Refer to the intended use for gifts of money.** ("Thank you so much for the twenty-five-dollar check. I have my own college savings account now, and your gift will really help it grow.")

- **Include a personal reference to the gift giver.** ("Mom says that you like your job in England very much. Have you ever seen the

Queen?") Explain to your child how much people appreciate comments that show interest in them as individuals and not just as sources of gifts.

- **Include a little personal information.** Do this especially if the gift giver does not have regular personal contact with the writer. A big brother stationed overseas or a cousin away at college will enjoy knowing that a youngster is taking tap dancing lessons or has made the hockey team.

These guidelines point out the basic characteristics that distinguish a well-written thank-you note or letter from a perfunctory one: personality and genuine interest in others. Whatever the writer's level of sophistication, a good thank-you note is one that makes the reader smile.

Gentle Prods

The reality is that young teens are often not inclined to write thank-you notes, and they need prodding. This doesn't mean standing over them until the note is finished. A better approach is to emphasize the importance of expressing appreciation as soon as possible after the receipt of a gift or a kind act. Appeal to your child's empathy. How would she react if she devoted time, energy, and money to choosing just the right gift for a friend and then never got a thank-you? She will probably ask why she can't just call. Explain that phoning is appropriate in some situations, but because it is so easy, a phone call doesn't always convey a sense of effort and real caring. A person who receives a thank-you note knows that the writer truly values both the gift and the giver.

Don't hesitate to remind your child when notes need to be written. Tweaking her self-esteem may help. ("Aunt Pearl always talks about how courteous you are. You don't want to change her opinion, do you?") Your child may need help wording her note, so offer suggestions if she asks. She may want you to check a finished note, but do so only if requested. Be flexible—if your child has misspelled someone's name, the note should be corrected or rewritten, but if the penmanship is a little wobbly or the lines tend to run down the page, let it pass. Point out positive aspects of the note ("Mrs. Grunwald will be so interested to know about your piano lessons") and praise the completion of the effort.

Invest a little time and money to encourage gracious note and letter writing. Take your child to the stationery store and help him choose his own writing materials. By age eleven or twelve, he should be ready for unlined papers. Let him select attractively decorated notepaper for informal writing and a good-quality paper for formal notes and invitations. Stationery monogrammed or printed with your child's name is a way to emphasize the special and individualized nature of note and letter writing. Choose pens and inks. Explain why black or dark blue ink and white or cream paper are preferred for ease of reading.

At home, provide a desk drawer or sturdy box in which your child can store his pens, papers and envelopes, stamps, and personal letters. Be clear that this space is off-limits to other family members. In a very real way, this acquisition of writing materials constitutes a rite of passage. You are telling your child that he is ready for the adult tools and the adult responsibility of courteous correspondence. At a minimum, you will be heading off excuses of the I-can't-write-because-I-don't-have-anything-to-write-on variety.

Other Social Writing

Your middle schooler will probably have occasion to send birthday, congratulations, and get-well wishes, and handwritten notes and letters are always the most personal expression. The greeting card industry produces cards for every eventuality, and it is okay to send commercial cards, especially if the sender includes a personally written message. Parents should let their children make the card selection, but be prepared to veto inappropriate choices. Cards that appeal to an adolescent's sense of humor may not amuse some adults.

Holiday cards are normally sent by the entire family. Your child can add her friends' names to your list, write a brief personal message ("Have a happy Kwanza"), and sign these cards personally. If cards are exchanged at school or extracurricular activities—on Valentine's Day, for instance—children must have cards for every classmate or team member. (Leaving one child or several children out of this traditional ritual is one of the subtle cruelties of middle school.) Cards can be handmade or inexpensively purchased in bulk.

At the other extreme are sympathy notes. It is fairly unusual for a young adolescent to write a letter of condolence for a death, and your sympathy notes will usually include your entire family. But there may be times when a note from your child would be appropriate: A teacher might suffer bereavement or a close friend may lose a parent or grandparent. Writing these notes is difficult for people of every age, so give your child lots of help. Keep the message simple and sincere. There are no rules about what to say, but it's best not to dwell on the circumstances of the death. Talk with your child first and find out what she is feeling; then help her translate those feelings into words. A personal note as simple as this example from a seventh-grader to his teacher includes a personal remembrance that honors the deceased:

Dear Mrs. McBride,

I am so sorry about your loss. Mr. McBride was really nice to me when I met him at the school carnival. He helped me win the ring toss. I wish I could have known him better.

Yours truly,
Nicholas Steiner

Commercial sympathy cards are acceptable as long as a personal sentiment is added. But heartfelt, handwritten expressions, no matter what the wording, are always the better option.

Polite Conversation

YOUNG ADOLESCENTS SHOULD ALREADY KNOW the basics of polite conversation, although parents will continue to do a good deal of reminding and prompting. But despite your best efforts, your child will occasionally behave rudely. She may fail to look directly at an adult who is speaking to her or walk away from a conversation without excusing herself. She may not acknowledge greetings or make introductions. At times, she's likely to be argumentative, interrupt others to make her own points, or mumble hateful comments under her breath. None of these behaviors is acceptable, but they are all normal in early adolescence.

Don't panic. Your adolescent's solid foundation of considerate manners isn't crumbling away. When parents are sensitive and ready to adapt their disciplinary approaches, thoughtful and mannerly behavior will eventually triumph. Adolescents need and want boundaries, so you should continue teaching good manners, reinforcing the etiquette of social interaction, and making your expectations clear.

Nonverbal Language

As children acquire verbal sills, the nonverbal communication of infancy and toddlerhood becomes more of an adjunct to spoken words. But in early adolescence, young people often fall back on unspoken expressions to convey meaning.

A thirteen-year-old tells her mother, "Band practice starts in twenty minutes. We need to leave now"—a basically benign couple of sentences. But Mom sees her teen standing with hands on hips, tapping the floor with one foot, her head cocked to the side and lips pursed. Her tone of voice is sharp and impatient. If the parent delays at all, the teen is likely to groan and roll her eyes, turn on her heel, and storm out to the car, leaving a trail of mumbled comments in her wake.

There are a number of reasons for this kind of confrontational verbal and nonverbal language. It is part of identity formation, a kind of distancing by which the teen attempts to define her own psychological space and to test limits. Some experts theorize that habits such as eye rolling, head swiveling, and groaning are a crude mimicking of adult behaviors. Such displays are easier to deal with when a parent understands that they are normal and universal.

Since picking your battles wisely is key to successful discipline, it may be best to let the behavior go within the immediate family circle. Becoming angry about tone of voice or hair flipping can encourage more conflict. Interestingly, young people who seem to fill every word and gesture with contempt at home often do not let their poor manners show around others. Parents can be pleasantly surprised by laudatory comments on their adolescent's manners from teachers, coaches, and other parents.

The Fundamentals

You'll want to avoid public correcting and most prompting now, but talk with your adolescent about the following requirements of polite conversation and social interaction, and correct her in private when she goes astray:

- **Make eye contact.** Teens often look away from an adult speaker, possibly motivated by shyness or self-consciousness about personal appearance. They must be reminded how disconcerting it is to talk with anyone who is looking at the floor or off into the distance. Appeal to your child's self-image; tell her that people who can't deal eye-to-eye give the impression of being shifty, uncaring, and sometimes not very bright, as well as downright rude.

- **Never make whispered comments and jokes when other people are present.** Young teens love asides—whispered or laughing remarks, which are often snide cuts at someone else. Young people must be firmly told that such asides do not demonstrate superior knowledge or cleverness but are simply crass and hateful.

- **Silence electronic equipment.** Teenagers should offer to turn off the TV, video games, computer games, and loud music when others are present and trying to talk, making the offer whenever someone enters the room. Even if others say to continue the activity, the volume should be lowered so that people can converse comfortably. In rare instances—say, the last sixty seconds of the Super Bowl when the game is tied and one team has a fourth down and goal to go—it is all right to explain the situation and ask a new arrival to wait until there's a break in the action.

- **Remove headsets and ear pieces when speaking or being spoken to by anyone.** Lowering the volume on the portable radio or tape/CD player isn't sufficient. It is also impolite to lift one side of a headset and continue listening through the other.

- **Limit reading to appropriate circumstances.** Don't discourage your child's reading, but do point out that reading is discourteous when others are talking and socializing, at the table during meals, during any kind of instruction, during live performances, in worship services, and so on. Discuss situations when reading is acceptable—in the library, in study hall, on public transportation, while waiting alone in lines, and so forth.

- **Be quiet in movies and at plays, lectures, concerts, and performances of any kind.** Teens can laugh and clap when appropriate but should talk only during intermissions. No hooting, yelling, or talking back to the screen or performers unless audience participation is clearly encouraged.

During the preteen and early teenage years, bad language tends to become sex related. Young teens are very curious about sex and often express their interest through dirty jokes and double meanings.

There's not a lot you can do about crude language between peers, unless you catch them at it. But you should communicate your attitudes by modeling and through open discussion of sex and the physical and emotional changes your child is experiencing. Look for opportunities to initiate conversations. Television and movies may actually be useful tools here, if you watch with your child and discuss issues raised (dating, premarital sex, vulgarity, and so forth). If you hear your child or someone else using foul language, be clear that the language is unacceptable and explain why. Does your adolescent really know what the four-letter words and smutty jokes mean and why they offend others?

Some parents find that a penalty system—a quarter deposited in the cookie jar for every swear word or vulgarity uttered—helps to drive the point home, especially when the penalty applies to everyone in the household. Fairness and forbearance are important. A parent who punishes for language that he himself uses frequently is applying a double standard and can well be undermining the positive values he is trying to teach.

◄┼

Introductions and Greetings

ELEVEN- AND TWELVE-YEAR-OLDS ARE GENERALLY quick at memorization and learning to follow detailed instructions. This is an excellent time to polish their introduction manners (see "Making Introductions," page 260, for the basics) and begin working on the order of introduction. By eighth or ninth grade, your child should:

- **Use full names for introductions.** Your child needs to understand the importance of using full names when she introduces people and listening carefully when she is introduced. In a typical introduction—"Mr. Moreau, I'd like you to meet my cousin, Cecil Taylor. Cecil, this is my math teacher, Mr. Moreau"—the names are often said twice, and, if possible, an additional description is provided ("cousin—teacher"). This assists the people being introduced to recall names and pronounce them correctly. It's very important to use full names when family members, including parents and stepparents, have different last names. (Mark *White*, for example, will say, "I'd like to introduce my mother and stepfather, Mr. and Mrs. *Brown*.") Emphasize the importance of speaking names clearly—no mumbling, giggling, or chewing gum.

- **Use last names and courtesy titles to introduce adults.** If your child introduces a friend to an adult relative, she should say, "Uncle Jorge, this is my classmate, Veronica Sims. Veronica, this is my Uncle, Jorge Garcia." The friend can then respond, "Hello, Mr. Garcia." If the older person wishes to be called by his first name, it is up to him to say so—not the young person making the introduction.

  It may happen that a young person is introduced to an older person only by the first name. Since it is customary and courteous for a child to refrain from addressing an unknown adult so familiarly, the youngster can simply say, "Hello, it's very nice to meet you," and try to pick up the last name during conversation. If your child is accustomed to "sir" and "ma'am," these courtesies may ease the situation. "Hello, sir" or "How do you do, ma'am?" helps children slide gracefully past the problem of not knowing the correct surname and title.

  These days, some adults prefer that children put aside titles and use first names. As long as this is an adult's request for introductions, it is perfectly acceptable for the child to comply: "This is my uncle, Jack Smith. He wants us to call him Jack."

- **Introduce the younger person to the older person first, then vice versa.** As a mark of respect, younger people are traditionally introduced *to* older people and those of high rank or special position. An easy way to remember this is to say the name of the older or higher-ranked person first. ("Rabbi Cohen, this is my brother, Joseph. Joe, this is Rabbi Cohen.") Generally, adult family members also receive priority. ("Mom, I'd like you to meet Principal Skinner. Mr. Skinner, this is my mother, Mrs. Gentry.") When there is a question about adult rank, introduce the younger to the older. ("Grandmom, this is my volleyball coach, Miss Thomas. Miss Thomas, this is my grandmother, Mrs. Mueller."). Between peers, the order makes little difference.

These rules can be tough, especially in the pressure of an unfamiliar social setting, so don't make an issue if your child gets the order wrong in the beginning. The most important lesson is that introductions should be made, even if the correct order isn't always followed. A young person who knows the correct order may become flustered if she realizes she has made a mistake, so assure her that adults get it wrong, too. The best advice is to proceed with the introduction rather than trying to make a midcourse correction.

- **When being introduced, give the person making the introduction time to finish.** An introduction is a two-way street. Person A is introduced to person B; then person B is introduced to person A. Miss A and Mr. B should not speak until the introduction is completed. This is very important when three or more people are involved; if one person begins to chat before all the introductions are made, some in the group may be left out—a very uncomfortable feeling.

- **Start the conversation after making introductions.** The person who makes the introduction should get the ball rolling. Maybe the new acquaintances have some interest in common or there is a piece of information that others want to know. ("Leslie just moved here from Seattle, and she'll be in our class.")

- **Introduce herself.** This is hard for self-conscious adolescents but essential to the joining-in skills that lead to social acceptance and friendships. Self-introductions are generally casual and friendly. The young person should not interrupt anyone's conversation. Wait until a quiet moment and say something as simple as, "Hi, I'm Rita Williams." Then follow up with a remark or question that opens the door to conversation ("I just transferred here from Baxter Middle School"). If the situation seems awkward or conversation is difficult, the youngster should smile, make a pleasant parting remark ("It's been nice to meet you"), and move on. Socially adept young people learn to be aware of peers who are alone in a crowd and to introduce themselves.

Should a young person stand when greeting others or being introduced? Yes. Young people should rise for greetings and introductions unless they literally can't get up. (Your child has a plate, napkin, and utensils balanced on his lap, for example.) If engaged in conversation with someone, he should excuse himself for a moment, rise, and greet the person entering.

Children hosting a social event should always rise to meet and greet guests. Once an event is underway and everyone has been greeted politely, it's unnecessary to stand up every time someone enters the room.

Children and teens should always rise and offer their place to any older or encumbered person who enters a room or public conveyance (bus, subway) where seating is limited.

◄+

Introductions are a way of saying that we like people and want them to feel comfortable. There are practical considerations, too. The format of introductions gives people their best opportunity to hear and to remember names and allows people a few seconds to evaluate a stranger and think of something nice to say. The order of introduction is a demonstration of respect for elders and people of special rank or significance. Someday, when your child is dealing routinely with the pecking order of corporate or professional hierarchies, she will thank her lucky stars that you taught her to make polite introductions.

Greeting People

Your youngster should always acknowledge people she knows. In the car pool, she should greet the adult driver. She should smile and say "hello" to her bus driver, teachers, school personnel, neighbors, the mail carrier, the clerk at the convenience store, and so on. Greetings may be as casual as a smile and a nod or wave to an acquaintance sitting three rows away in the movie theater and a quick "hi" to a neighbor on the street. Every greeting does not require stopping to converse. In public places, self-conscious adolescents sometimes hesitate to greet others for fear of calling attention to themselves, but ignoring a person they know is more likely to be noticed and judged as unfriendly and unmannerly.

When visiting another young person's home, your child should greet the adult in charge on arrival. Parents are morally and legally responsible for everyone in their house or on their property and must know when your child is present. (When another youngster visits your home, your adolescent should always inform you or the responsible adult.) In many neighborhoods, children pop in and out of one another's houses with great freedom, but no matter how brief the visit, youngsters must always announce their presence to the adult in charge with a pleasant greeting.

On the Phone

HOWEVER RESERVED THEY MAY BE with adults, young adolescents have little difficulty conversing with their friends, and phone calls can go on for hours. To an eighth- or ninth-grader, the telephone symbolizes personal freedom much as a car does for a sixteen-year-old. The two main problems with this stream of chitchat are that uncontrolled phone use cuts into the time required for homework and other responsibilities and that other members of the family are frequently inconvenienced.

Time to Negotiate

Telephone use requires clear regulation. Determining the rules also gives parents a chance to engage their youngster in some serious problem solving. As soon as you realize that your child's telephone use is on the rise, start talking. You might begin by having the family, including younger and older siblings, discuss their phone needs. Make it clear that everyone deserves consideration when deciding phone rules. Talk about the relative importance of calls and state that there are times when some calls, or keeping the phone line open for calls, will take precedence. By participating in negotiations, making her points, and helping to formulate phone rules, your child may be more inclined to follow the rules and accept responsibility when she inconveniences others.

You may want to allow your child a day to think about her needs. Then sit down and start negotiating.

Determining Phone Time

Determine when your child can place calls. How long can calls last? Be precise. You might agree to half-hour conversations each night before homework time. You may think this means a single half-hour, but your child thinks it means a half-hour with each of her friends. If your child is at home alone after school, negotiate how much of that time can be spent on the phone. (Trust her to follow the rules, but check in as well. She may pay closer attention to the clock if she knows you will be calling.)

Generally, calls should be made no earlier than eight or nine o'clock in the morning and no later than nine or ten o'clock at night—even on weekends. If, however, your daughter's friend has a new baby sibling or there is an ill family member in the home, calling times should be modified. Also decide about different schedules for school nights, weekends, and holidays, and consider when exceptions may be made. If your child has already used her allotted school-night time and discovers that she needs to get a homework assignment, you might allow an extra ten or fifteen minutes, but she must ask permission before calling to prevent an exception from becoming a loophole.

You may want to exchange a privilege for a responsibility. If your twelve-year-old wants more phone time on Saturdays, she might get the extra time as long as she agrees to call her grandparents at least once a week.

Reinforcing the Basics

When negotiating phone privileges, don't forget to reinforce the fundamentals of courteous calling and answering. Your adolescent should understand that her phone privileges are directly related to the consideration she shows to others.

- **Review the basics of telephone manners.** (See "On the Telephone," page 237.)

- **Respect the privacy of others' calls.** Assure your child that you respect her privacy and will not interrupt unless you have to; make it clear that you expect the same consideration from her.

- **Reinforce the importance of courteous phone answering and calling others to the phone.** Stress that calls begin with a clear and pleasant "hello"—no mumbling or "funny" greetings. Remind your child how to summon someone else to the phone—no yelling and no dropping or slamming down the receiver.

- **Go over the manners of taking messages and using telephone technology.** Call waiting can be a helpful feature when you have an adolescent in the house, particularly if your child is often at home on her own. It's wise to set up call-waiting guidelines so that callers won't feel they're getting the brush-off. Establish rules about the use of answering machines. Generally, an answering machine should not be turned on or off without your knowledge and permission.

- **Be clear when your calls have priority.** Inform your child when you or other adults need to make or receive a call or to keep the line open for a call, and expect her compliance. This doesn't call for negotiation. But be considerate whenever you must put your needs first. If you will be using the phone all evening to call members of your volunteer committee, tell your child in the morning, so she can warn her friends not to call or expect calls.

- **Review the guidelines for interrupting.** Everyone in the family should interrupt phone calls infrequently and courteously. Many families ease the interruption problem by writing notes to the family member on the telephone.

A Question for Peggy and Cindy

My sons, ages twelve and fifteen, are begging for their own phone lines. It might cut down on the nightly fights about who gets to use the phone, but should I give in to the pressure?

Before making your decision, think carefully about your family's needs. How much time do your children spend on the phone? Is time the problem, or scheduling? If both boys are trying to make calls between six and eight o'clock, perhaps you need to allocate times that don't overlap. If one of your children likes to be on the Internet—tying up the phone line—you could get an extra line dedicated to computer use. If you already have a separate line, perhaps for business use, you might let your children use that line at night. You could consider a private line for your older son as a privilege of age and make him responsible for part of the bill. Should you decide to get separate lines for both sons, be clear that you aren't giving in to stop the fighting. Their lines will be your property and your responsibility, so be prepared to set and negotiate rules, especially regarding time spent on calls. Be firm from the start that any negative outcomes, such as a drop in grades or complaints from other parents about late-night calling, will result in immediate suspension of phoning privileges.

A cell phone seems like the answer to an adolescent's prayer—unfettered access to friends and an enhanced image among his peers. Your child will probably argue that *his* cell phone will be used for *your* convenience. (He can call you when he's offered a ride home from ball practice, so you don't have to drive. He can call when choir practice runs late, so you don't have to wait. Ad infinitum.) The truth is that few adolescents need cell phones before they begin driving. The cell phone encourages extended use because it is so convenient. Parents might resolve the cell phone dilemma, at least temporarily, by giving limited use of the family cell phone (during an after-school activity or on overnight camping trips, for instance). Be clear about the consequences of excessive or unmannerly use such as allowing phones to ring in inappropriate settings and talking too loudly and of endangering others by talking in a car when someone is driving.

- **Set clear rules about use of other people's telephones.** Your child must always ask permission before making calls from other people's phones, whether calls are local or long distance. If your child is likely to place a long-distance call from someone else's phone, provide her with a low-cost calling card.

    Teach youngsters not to use phones in places of business unless no public phone is available. When asking to use a business phone, a young person is more likely to get permission if she is polite and quickly explains the purpose of the call. ("Could I please use your telephone? My ride is an hour late, and I need to call home.") Calls on business phones should be kept short (a minute or two at most) and should never be used for chatting.

- **Establish penalties for misuse of the phone.** The most effective penalties are usually related to loss of phone privileges. Should your child call long distance or exceed the time allowed on a cell phone without getting your okay, then she must pay for the call out of her allowance. Adolescents readily understand this kind of eye-for-an-eye consequence. If you negotiate penalties, you may even find that your child is more severe on herself than you would be.

- **Include incentives.** Negotiate expansion of phone privileges based on clear criteria. Your child may be happier about current restrictions if she knows that her phone time will be increased next year. (Privileges tied to age may also ease tension between younger and older siblings.) Conduct is an issue; frequent violations of the rules, including rudeness, and falling grades at school may delay expanded privileges. Offering reasonable incentives helps a child learn that privileges are earned.

CHAPTER 24

Dining Manners

A **MIDDLE SCHOOLER'S MEALTIME ETIQUETTE** has an unpredictable quality. Your child may behave with exemplary grace at the dinner table one night and turn into a gulping, grabbing food forager the next night. There is a key fact that helps to explain the up-and-down nature of his mealtime manners: adolescents are always hungry. The biological changes they are going through demand a large and continuous supply of fuel for energy.

Yet even a ravenous middle schooler should be expected to observe the niceties of dining. You have laid down the fundamentals and some of the higher requirements of polite dining. Much of what you do now will involve refining your child's table manners and coping with the backsliding common to this age.

The Family Table

Getting the family together for shared meals is admittedly difficult but very important during the adolescent years—in large measure so that you can model and reinforce mealtime etiquette, which gets little attention in the school cafeteria or the local fast-food outlet. If you haven't yet established regular seated family meals, it's not too late. Carve out a little time for everyone to discuss and decide on at least one or two nights a week to eat together as a family. The choice of days is not nearly so important as making time to be with one another, and parents as well as children must be willing to keep the commitment.

Although your middle schooler will be dining away from home more often, the family table remains the best place to put good manners into practice, converse at a relatively leisurely pace, and see that your child is presented with a nutritious and well-balanced meal. (Eating together regularly also enables parents to observe their child's dietary and consumption habits and spot any potential problems.) Breakfast and lunch tend to be hurried, so evening meals are probably your best chance to affirm the basics and introduce new aspects of gracious dining.

Creating Opportunities

Family meals are fundamental, but you should look for opportunities to introduce your child to a variety of dining experiences. He's old enough now to be a good dinner companion in upscale situations, so the occasional luncheon or dinner at one of your area's finer restaurants may be in order. Because most of his previous dining out has probably been limited to fast-food and family-style restaurants, he may be impressed by the organization and effort involved in preparing and serving a gourmet meal. Point out the duties of the maitre d', waiters, sommelier, and so on. If you have the chance to compliment the chef in person, by all means include your child. If upscale dining isn't available where you live, there are probably midrange restaurants that offer adult-oriented dining but also welcome older children.

Perhaps your child's grandparents or other close relatives would treat him to lunch or dinner at a good restaurant—without you. Allowing your adolescent to be a well-mannered guest when you aren't around is important. He needs to understand that mannerly behavior is a *social* expectation that applies to every situation. Your child's business and social success as an adult may well depend, at least in part, on his ability to handle dining etiquette. (There's many an executive who has been left behind on the corporate ladder because of poor dining habits and lack of hosting skills.)

It's also a good idea to begin teaching your child the manners for different types of dining situations—formal buffets, informal buffets, coffees and teas—and what to do when something unexpected happens. (See "Table Traumas," page 325.)

Help your child make the connection between his manners and the impression he creates on others. Reinforce the idea that manners are a reflection of attitudes toward other people. To show respect for others, he should act respectfully and eat in a way that allows others to enjoy their meals and converse in comfort.

No More Children's Table

The children's table is a traditional solution to the problem of having small children eat comfortably when many adults are present. By early adolescence, your child is ready to "move up" to the adult table.

Young adolescents should dine with adults as (almost) grown members of the family. But the last thing they want is to be singled out, so when a young person does finally get his rightful place among the adults, do it without fanfare. Set a place for the adolescent and tell him that you are so pleased to welcome him to the adult table. You don't need to make a public announcement, but be attentive and look for opportunities to include the young person in the general conversation if he is shy or being ignored by his elders.

The Proper Setting

BY NOW, YOUR CHILD SHOULD be able to set a basic table with assurance but may not have much experience of more complicated or formal details. Young people are most likely to encounter the *informal* setting when dining at fine restaurants and attending parties and receptions where seated meals are served. If you haven't done so already, introduce more utensils and plates—at least to the level of the typical informal place setting—and explain their use.

- Salad fork, placed at the far left of the place setting, with the dinner fork to the left of the dinner plate
- Soupspoon at the far right of the place setting

To teach the higher arts of dining, you might encourage your child to host a luncheon or dinner party. Her guest list can include a few good friends—however many your dining room will accommodate—and she can help plan the menu. Make it a multicourse meal with hors d'oeuvres to start, and use the dinnerware and table linens. Your youngster should be fully involved in the details of preparation—shopping, cooking, cleaning, polishing silver, arranging flowers for the centerpiece, making place cards, setting the table, and so on—in order to experience the full range of responsibilities inherent in hosting. You, your spouse or partner, or another family member or friend can be kitchen and serving staff for the event, allowing your child to be the gracious hostess. Prepare her in advance for duties such as taking coats, making introductions, keeping conversation going, and overseeing food service. Most important, be available to offer advice when asked.

Since all youngsters can benefit from this kind of experience, you and other parents might want to propose a dinner or luncheon party for your child's class at school. Talk with the principal and teachers to be sure there are no liability problems or special burdens on school resources. Work with the teacher to involve all the children in the project. What is served will matter far less than the lessons in manners and the fun of carrying off their very own "banquet."

- Dessert spoon at the left of the soupspoon, next to the knife (or horizontally above the plate; see page 323)
- Salad plate to the left of the forks
- Butter plate and butter knife (laid across the plate) above the forks
- Coffee cup and saucer above and slightly to the right of the knife, with the coffee spoon resting on the right side of the saucer
- Wine glass or glasses (if the adults drink wine) above and slightly to the right of the dinner plate

Dinner plates are usually not included in the setting but brought to the table warm so that the food remains hot when served. The same applies to soup bowls whether the soup is brought from the kitchen or served at the table. Soup bowls are placed on a serving plate, which is removed with the bowl when the soup course is finished.

A dessert spoon is often included in the place setting. It is also correct to lay the dessert spoon with a dessert fork horizontally at the top of the place setting, above the dinner plate, or these two utensils may be brought to the table with the dessert plate. (Placement of dessert utensils above the plate involves one of those transoceanic quirks. American style is to lay the dessert spoon on top, with the handle of the spoon pointed to the right, and the dessert fork just below the spoon, with the handle pointed to the left. In the Continental style, both handles are to the right.)

Variations in Settings

The informal setting allows for a good deal of variation. You might not use butter plates or salad plates, although salad plates are a good idea if the food on the dinner plate includes gravy or sauces that will mix with salad dressing. You may not normally have a soup course, or you might serve coffee separately from the meal. The idea behind the rules of place setting is to create an attractive and workable environment in which each diner feels comfortable knowing which utensil and plate to use and when.

A Few Food Manners

THE FOLLOWING SUGGESTIONS ADDRESS FREQUENT "how-do-I-eat-it" questions from adolescents:

- Push food onto a fork with a small piece of bread crust or with the tip of a knife blade (knife held in the same position as when cutting) but never with fingers.

- Break bread or rolls into moderate pieces and butter the pieces before eating. Hold the piece of bread on the plate when buttering. Biscuits and muffins can be cut in half and buttered. Hot breads and toast can be buttered whole, but never lay a slice of bread in the palm of the hand to slather on toppings.

- Spoon soup from the inside rim to the outside rim. Your child probably learned this years ago but will need reminding when

Young children tend to wad up their used napkins and deposit them anywhere on the table. Preteens are ready for a bit more attention to the lowly napkin. After eating, the child should place her napkin on the table so that the messiest parts are hidden but should not refold it. Place it to the left side of the plate or in the center of the setting if the plate has been removed. When someone gets up from the table during a meal, the napkin can be laid on the table to the left of the plate (soiled parts out of sight) or on the chair until the person returns. These few seconds of attention mean that diners who remain at the table do not have to look at an unsightly mess.

---

he's really hungry. To get the last drop of soup, the bowl can be slightly tilted in the direction away from the diner; tilting the bowl toward the diner may result in stained shirts and laps. Never drink from a soup bowl, but if soup is served in a cup with a handle, it can be drunk (take a spoonful first to test the temperature) or eaten with a spoon. The spoon is laid on the saucer or plate underneath, not in the cup or bowl.

- Salad served on a dinner plate can be eaten with the dinner fork. But salad on a salad plate should be eaten with the salad fork if one is provided. If salad dressing is served on the side, pour or spoon on some of the dressing and then add more as you progress.

- When served with a meal, cheeses should be cut with a knife and eaten with a fork, not fingers.

- When confronted with a lemon wedge or slice for flavoring tea or other beverages, either drop the piece into the drink and then press it with a spoon to extract the juice or squeeze it directly over the drink. Shield your squeezing hand with your free hand to prevent squirting the juice at other diners. The wedge can then be dropped into the drink or placed on a plate.

- Ketchup for French fries and onion rings should be spooned or poured onto the plate, and the fries dipped individually. In others words, don't drown French fries in ketchup. French fries, usually considered a finger food, can also be eaten with a fork. A good rule of thumb: When French fries are served with finger foods like hamburgers, they may be eaten with the fingers. When served with knife-and-fork food such as steak or fish, use a fork for the fries.

- While most sandwiches are eaten with the fingers, open-faced sandwiches and sandwiches with gravy are cut with a knife and fork and eaten with the fork. Hamburgers, tacos, and tortillas are finger foods unless too large to handle comfortably, and bits that fall out should be eaten with a fork.

- Pizza can be cut with a knife and eaten with a fork, but most people prefer to use their fingers. Pizza wedges can be folded down the center and lifted to the mouth to prevent sauce and cheese from dripping over the edges.

- Other foods with stringy melted cheese like mozzarella should be carefully cut before being lifted to the mouth.

- Asian foods can be eaten with a knife and fork or chopsticks. When an Asian dish is served with a dipping sauce, each bite is dipped into the sauce dish; the sauce is not poured over the food on the plate.

- Taste foods before adding salt, pepper, and other seasonings and sauces. It is discourteous to the person who cooked the meal to season food before trying it.

Table Traumas

THINGS HAPPEN WHEN EATING THAT can be embarrassing, especially for self-conscious adolescents: the lettuce that gets caught on a tooth, the piece of meat that is impossible to chew, the soufflé that slips off the plate and onto the tablecloth. The etiquette is fairly simple: Handle the problem with as little fuss as possible and get on with the meal.

When the following things occur, teach your youngster by explaining what to do and emphasize the importance of discretion and consideration for others. A mannerly person never laughs at or draws attention to another person's table accident or difficulty.

There are three good options for spaghetti, linguine, fettuccine, and other long-stranded pastas.

- Cut the pasta into bite-sized portions and eat with a fork.
- Twirl several strands around the tines of a fork, using the edge of the plate to brace the fork.
- Use a fork and a dessert-size spoon, take several strands onto the fork, hold the tines of the fork against the bowl of the spoon, and rotate the fork until the strands are neatly compacted.

If a few strands escape, bite them and hope the bits fall onto the fork or plate. It's okay to suck short, dangling strands, but not to slurp. If a sauce is served on top of the pasta, gently mix it in with a fork and spoon before eating.

---◀◂

- ***Something in the food.*** What do you do when you bite into a piece of gristle or something hard that turns out to be bone or a little rock? What if you aren't sure what is in your mouth but you know that it is not food? You spit it out—discreetly and quietly. Work the unchewable or foreign matter onto your fork with your tongue, or put it on the edge of your plate. Never spit food into a napkin. If you see something before you eat it—a worm in the salad, a hair in the soup—remove it without comment, using a fork or spoon. In a restaurant, quietly tell a server about the problem and ask for a new portion.

    When dining in someone else's home, don't embarrass your host or hostess by making an issue of your find; leave it on the plate and go on with the meal. If the object is dangerous, such as a shard of glass or piece of metal, you must tell the host to prevent harm to anyone else.

- ***Food stuck on teeth or braces.*** If you can't dislodge it with your tongue, then excuse yourself, find the nearest bathroom, and remove the food bit. Don't use fingers, toothpicks, or floss at the table. For braces wearers, it helps to keep the proper orthodontic cleaning tools in a pocket or purse for these times.

If you see that a fellow diner has something in his teeth or on his face and isn't aware of it, be considerate and tell him. This is one of those times when a quick whisper ("There's something caught between your teeth") is called for. Once the person is alerted, let him handle the problem and don't refer to it again.

- **Sneezing, coughing, and nose blowing.** When the need to sneeze or cough strikes, there's usually not time to leave the table. Cover your mouth with a handkerchief, napkin, or your hand if nothing else is available and try to turn away from the food (and your fellow diner's face). If the sneezing or coughing continues, excuse yourself and return to the table when the bout is over. When others ask if you are okay, assure them that you are, but don't go into great detail.

  Nose blowing should never be done at the table. Excuse yourself, find the bathroom, and wash hands thoroughly before returning to the meal.

- **Food that is too hot.** When you eat something that is too hot or too spicy, a drink of water or cold beverage may stop the burning. If not, spit the item onto your fork as unobtrusively as possible and place it on the edge of your plate. Don't force yourself to eat a food that is simply too spicy. Eat whatever else is served and leave the spicy food on the plate without making a remark. (If the hostess notices, a young teen can politely explain that he just can't eat highly seasoned foods. It's nice to compliment the food: "The curry smells delicious, Mrs. Curtis, and I really wish I could eat it." Most hosts will understand and probably offer an alternative.)

  If an item tastes spoiled or "off," don't swallow it. Use your fork to remove the item and place it on your plate. If an entire dish or beverage seems spoiled, a diner should take the hostess aside and tell her. This can be difficult for a young teen, so your child should tell you discreetly if, for example, the milk is sour, and you can relay the message.

- **Table spills.** The gravy drips over the edge of the plate, the peas scatter, or the drink glass tips over. When spills occur, the diner should try to clean up as completely as possible. Solid items can be retrieved with a spoon or scraped up with a knife blade and

About Choking

Choking is not a minor embarrassment. It may be possible to dislodge a bit of food with a drink of water or a cough, but if the item is stuck and interferes with breathing, signal for help immediately. A person who is choking won't be able to speak, so stand up, grab someone—do whatever it takes to get attention. Try not to panic. Let yourself be helped by anyone who is performing first aid. If someone else is choking, act immediately by giving first aid if you know what to do or by summoning help. Don't wait even a second in hopes that the person can clear her own airway.

Since choking can happen to anyone at any time, it's a very good idea for all family members to learn the correct first aid procedures to use on adults, children, and infants. The Red Cross, YMCA, YWCA, and your local hospitals probably offer classes or can recommend qualified instructors.

---

put back on the plate. For stains on the tablecloth or place mat, dampen a corner of your napkin with water and dab at the spot. For large spills and liquids, help the host by getting a cloth or sponge and wiping up. If something is spilled on another diner—especially something hot—attend to the person first and worry about the table later.

Should a diner apologize for accidental spills? Yes, if the spill is obvious or may cause damage and if something is broken. But a certain amount of mess—bread crumbs, water and beverage drops—is normal. A good host or hostess doesn't expect tablecloths and napkins to be pristine at the end of a meal.

In a restaurant, attract the attention of a waiter or attendant and let restaurant personnel clean up any spills. In fast-food restaurants and school cafeterias, adolescents are likely to wipe up drink and food spills as best they can with paper napkins and deposit the mess with their trays. But if the spill is on the floor, they should always tell an adult what happened. Even a little liquid or food can cause serious falling accidents.

CHAPTER 25

Out on Their Own

————————————————————————◄◄—

YOU'VE BEEN PREPARING YOUR CHILD to go out into the world alone, and now she will begin to do just that—meeting friends at the mall and the movies and spending the hours she once spent with you in the company of peers. She may turn down offers to join you on occasions that you once enjoyed together, demand that she be allowed to shop for herself, and beg off family gatherings. Studies have found that children's self-esteem often takes a short-lived dive during early adolescence, but a parent's self-image can be affected as well in the face of what seems like constant rejection and distancing.

It's a bumpy ride, but hang on. Your remote adolescent will become the young adult who loves to shop with you and buys tickets so she can take you to the theater. In the meantime, you will adapt to your child's new sense of self-sufficiency and the changing nature of her academic and social life. But be careful not to abandon rule enforcement or manners education, even in public places.

Transportation Concerns

THE CAR WILL TAKE ON more significance with each passing year. While you may often feel like a hired chauffeur, you still control behavior in the car and have the right to expect adherence to your standards and etiquette guidelines. For everyone's safety and comfort, it's important to reinforce old rules and address new issues.

Safety First

This is a good time to review the importance of seat belts, safety rules, and thoughtful car manners. You may not be the one who will teach your child to drive, but you will be her primary model. If you apply makeup or make endless phone calls while driving, she's likely to do the same when she's behind the wheel.

Teens are often risk takers with little sense of their own mortality, and you may have to nag about seat belts and other vehicle-related safety devices such as helmets and padding for bike, skateboard, and scooter use and life vests for boating and water sports. But better to nag than take a chance on serious injury or death.

Noise in the Car

Reaffirm restrictions on noise; then negotiate with your teen about control of the radio, tape deck, and CD player. For example, she gets to listen to her music when you drive to and from activities or when her friends are riding with you, but you control the volume. If your youngster's favorite listening drives you wild, a portable player with a headset may be the answer for her; taped books are also worth a try on long drives.

Young people must learn not to turn on a radio, switch stations, or fiddle with anything on the dashboard, including temperature controls, without first checking with the driver. When you drive other young people, clearly state your ground rules about their use of cell phones, radios and headphones, handheld electronic games, and the volume of conversation. When the driver says to be quiet, everyone is to pipe down instantly without any argument.

Give your child a heads-up on driver education by talking about and explaining the legal and technical aspects of driving: why a speed limit is a limit and not a suggestion, what "right of way" means, when and how to pass another car, how to maneuver in snow and ice, and so on. All the driving rules that you follow by instinct are new and interesting to a young teen who is beginning to visualize himself behind the wheel.

You can begin discussing the issue of driving under the influence. Eleven- and twelve-year-olds may be very receptive to this topic. Their sense of justice and social rights and wrongs is strong, so raising the issue of driving under the influence may give you an easy introduction to the broader aspects of intoxicants and narcotics. Children often have the false impression that using drugs and alcohol is okay because it only affects the user. But the sometimes tragic consequences of driving under the influence are a practical and concrete illustration of the effects of this behavior on other people.

◄◄

In a Car with Others

Parents need to exercise judgment and carefully control who will be driving their preteens and young teens in cars. If an older sibling is now driving your younger child, the younger sibling must understand that in the car the big brother or sister has the same authority as you would. Every safety rule is to be observed, and good manners are expected. Have a serious discussion with both siblings before they begin riding together. Clarify your rules and set limits. (For example, the sibling who drives is not to take the younger one on side trips without your permission. The younger child is to be punctual and wait at the agreed-on location when she is being picked up.) Be firm about the consequences for disobedience.

When is a preteen or young teen allowed to ride with anyone other than a parent or sibling? You must be very careful, especially when your youngster wants to ride in a car driven by another teenager. By thirteen or fourteen, youngsters will usually prefer going to school and activities with an older teen. Before you agree, you must know who the teen driver is and talk to his parents. Find out if he is allowed to drive younger children and what restrictions his parents have set. As graciously as possible, inquire about the teen's driving experience and the kind of vehicle he drives. (You'll probably be more comfortable knowing your child is riding in the family sedan rather than a convertible two-seater.) Your child may be humiliated that you discussed driving arrangements with the other parent, but she will survive the embarrassment.

You probably know most of the adults who will drive your child. But it still pays to be cautious, especially since more and more chauffeuring will be at night. If you know that a parent tends to drink in the evening or suffers from a vision problem that might impair driving, you should politely but firmly turn down offers to give your child a ride. It may be necessary to alert other parents to a problem with an adult driver. These conversations are not pleasant. Stick to facts (an adult's DUI arrest or a history of accidents) and avoid letting the discussion devolve into rumors and gossip. Your goal is to protect the children by raising a red flag for parents.

On Public Transportation

In urban areas particularly, adolescents spend a lot of unaccompanied time on public transport. Alone or in groups, they make their way to and from school and their many activities. Young teens may be taking planes or trains for visits to relatives or to camp.

Make it clear to your youngster that considerate behavior is a responsibility that comes with being allowed to travel on her own and that you are trusting her to live up to your expectations. Loud talking, yelling, and loud music lead the list of behaviors to avoid on and around public conveyances, but also spell out these rules:

- *No pushing, shoving, or any aggressive behavior, even in fun.* The intent may be harmless, but the danger of rough play to themselves and bystanders—particularly in moving vehicles, in crowded areas, and near rail lines—is quite real.

- *Be polite to drivers, attendants, ticket takers, and all other transportation personnel.* Smart-alecky remarks can have serious consequences, including detention or even arrest.

- *Have tickets, bus passes, tokens, or exact change ready when boarding.* It is rude to delay other passengers by being unprepared.

When your child was young, you taught him never to talk to a stranger or approach a strange car. The rules will need reinforcement in the teen years. Young teens can be surprisingly naive, especially when an older person appeals to the teen's ego by asking for help or using flattery. Teens may also be open to strangers who masquerade as authority figures (a bright light on a dark car doesn't automatically mean that the person driving is a policeman).

Perhaps the best way to protect your child is to lay down the law: Never get in a car with someone you don't know well and never accept rides from anyone without the permission of a primary caregiver. Provide your child with information about the kinds of tricks and scams to be wary of. (Ask your health-care provider, local police department, and library for materials. Also check online. The Federal Bureau of Investigation at www.fbi.gov is just one government agency that provides accurate information and sound advice.) Drop your child off and pick him up on time whenever you transport him to and from any public place, and be sure other drivers are equally prompt. Know where your child is at all times, and keep in mind that boys and girls are equally vulnerable to molesters and other predatory adults.

- *Offer your seat.* A seat is generally offered to older people, pregnant women, parents with young children, and anyone who is disabled or encumbered with packages or other items. Teens don't have to get up when other seating is available but should be observant and never pretend not to see a person in need.

- *No public displays of affection.* Even with an eleven- or twelve-year-old, it's not too soon to talk about how couples should behave in public and to introduce the concept of decorum.

- *Get to the transportation stop on time.* If your child misses her bus or train or there is any kind of delay, she must call and inform you or another adult in charge. You can spare yourself many anxious moments if you see that your child has a stash of coins or a phone card in her backpack for emergency calls.

Reinforce warnings against speaking to strangers and accepting rides from anyone. If your adolescent doesn't spend much time in cars, the offer of a lift from a seemingly acceptable older teen or adult may be appealing. If someone approaches her in a waiting area, your child should move away quickly. If the person follows or persists, your child must go directly to a security guard or transport authority such as a ticket seller or gate attendant, report the problem, and ask for help. In this kind of situation, she should feel free to miss her bus or train in order to protect herself from a further encounter.

At School

IN SPITE OF HOURS AT the mall and in extracurricular programs, school will remain the focal point of your child's activities. The classroom comes first, but your preteen and young teen will have many more opportunities to become involved in school-based on-campus and off-campus functions. It's important that you stay involved, even if your child seems to resent your interest at times, and find a comfortable level that falls between being pushy at one extreme and passive at the other.

- *Support your child's interests.* If you expect your child to play soccer and she wants to go out for the school team, it's easy to be supportive. But if she hates soccer and opts for the chess club, you may have make more of an effort to convey your enthusiasm. Be genuinely open to what matters to her, praise her efforts, and learn from her. (It's amazing what a parent can gain from a young person who is engaged in an activity unfamiliar to the adult.) See that she has the necessary materials, equipment, and time to pursue her interest. Young people are often unpredictable as they flirt with different possibilities, so be patient and avoid making a major financial commitment in the beginning. It's most important to allow your child the freedom to try, and sometimes reject, new challenges.

- *Maintain contact with your child's teachers.* Parents and primary caregivers should attend all scheduled parent–teacher conferences, even when their children are not having problems. Be prepared to listen to what teachers have to say and ask about your child's social and behavioral development as well as her academic achievement. If you have concerns between conferences, call and make an appointment to meet with the teacher. Don't expect him to meet with you on the spur of the moment.

- **Find opportunities to help.** Parents can talk to their child's teacher or teachers and volunteer to work behind the scenes. Schools often have a hard time finding reliable parents to help with the less glamorous jobs—kitchen duty for the athletic banquet or cleanup after the school fair. Perhaps you have a special skill to contribute—legal advice, help with accounting or event planning, finding speakers for school programs. One of the secrets of excellent schools is the active involvement of parents in countless ways that children never see.

- **Be a chaperone for field trips and other school events.** When a number of parents participate, your child may be less likely to object to your involvement. School personnel determine the

A Question for Peggy and Cindy

The mother of a boy in my child's eighth-grade class calls at least once a month asking me to help with school projects. Last week, she wanted six dozen brownies for a bake sale. The month before, she asked me to organize a recycling campaign for the kids. I work full-time, but so far, I've said "yes." Now, I'm getting fed up and am looking for a polite way to say "no."

Some parents simply have more time for participating than others, and this mother may not realize that she is imposing on you. It's often difficult to find dependable volunteers, and since you have always said "yes" in the past, she probably regards you as a sure bet. Consider what you can reasonably take on, and then make your position clear. Try to catch this mother at a time when she is not in the midst of a project. Explain your situation politely, but be clear about what you can and cannot do and when. (If you have a regular slow period in your job, that might be a good time to accept a volunteer role.) If the mother is a good manager, she will be grateful for your help when she can get it. By clarifying the situation now, you will also be providing your own child with a valuable life lesson—how to say "no" graciously and firmly.

rules and guidelines for the activity. If you have problems, consult the person in charge.

- **Show up at events when parents are invited.** Whatever your child may say, she really wants to see your smiling face in the audience when she sings in the school choir or competes in the science fair. Your presence also signals to school personnel that you take an active interest in whatever affects your child (and may make teachers more inclined to approach you directly should a problem arise). Make the effort to get to as many activities as possible. Perhaps a grandparent, aunt or uncle, or close friend can take your place when you can't be on hand. If no one comes, your child will probably say it doesn't matter, but the disappointment is there and can be lasting.

Your youngster's performance is cause for pride but no excuse to whoop, whistle, and keep clapping when everyone else is ready for the event to continue. Considerate parents will applaud all the children in a special event, even competitors. They will not leave the minute their own child's part is done, no matter how boring the rest of the program may be. They should not stand and snap photos or roll the video camera when their child is on stage; popping flashbulbs and whirring cameras are a distraction to everyone, including young performers.

Party Time

IN EARLY ADOLESCENCE, CHILDREN MAY still prefer parties and get-togethers with their own gender. But it won't be long before boy–girl entertaining starts. Most partying, including birthdays, is casual— sodas, pizza, and lots of music. School parties also tend to be casual and often follow an activity such as a ball game, although your child's school may sponsor dress-up events such as an afternoon holiday dance.

Parents often wonder what their role in middle school parties should be. "Out of sight and out of mind" is what young people hope for, but parents are responsible and need to find ways to maintain control without being obtrusive. These suggestions will be helpful when your child entertains her peers in your home:

When Someone Is Disruptive

If a parent is behaving in a particularly obnoxious way at a school event, there's not much you can do beyond politely asking him to be seated or to use his cell phone after the performance. If an adult makes a remark that is critical of your child or other children, just grin and bear it. This kind of parent needs some serious manners education, but you will gain little by becoming defensive or verbally aggressive. Then stay clear of the thoughtless adult at the next event.

- *Participate in party planning and be clear about your expectations.* Your child will have her guest list, but you should work with her to determine the number of people invited, ages of invitees (it may be wise to not to mix junior and senior high students), party hours, menu, and decorations if any. (Follow your child's lead here; decorations that delight adults can seem ridiculous to young people.) You no longer have to plan party games, but you have a right to know what music or videos will be played. Set limits on where guests will be allowed and where entry is off-limits including bedrooms, siblings' rooms, home office, workrooms, swimming pool area, and so forth.

- *Review the basics of courteous hosting with your child.* Be sure she understands that it is her responsibility to greet and talk with all her guests, to make everyone feel welcome, and to encourage participation. She should introduce guests to you, and also introduce guests who do not know one another. Cleaning up after a party is part of every host's duties. Since a large party may be noisy, you and your child should inform neighbors of the day and hours of the event. Most people are understanding when they know what to expect.

- *Let your child handle the prominent hosting.* It's not necessary for parents to greet middle school–age guests at the door and take coats, although you should be somewhere nearby. Involve yourself in leave-taking to the extent of being certain that every child is safely where he should be—in the right car with the right parent. Use your good judgment and communicate with other parents in advance before allowing young guests to leave your home alone or in the company of other youngsters. Be ready to walk or drive a guest home when necessary.

- **Make your presence felt in a natural manner.** Serving food and cold drinks is a very good way to keep an eye out. You have a perfect right to walk through the party area and chat briefly with guests, but don't join in the fun unless you are invited. Keep oversight consistent but low-key.

- **Be available to help out, but allow the youngsters to handle problems that aren't serious.** If someone drops the bowl of onion dip, let your child and her guests clean it up. Give advice and assistance when asked. Step in if necessary (as when an argument threatens to become physical). And stay alert. This is an age of experimentation, so if you catch a whiff of cigarette or marijuana smoke, spot a beer can, or see the lights go out in the party room, take control immediately.

- **Set and enforce party ending times.** Since the young people are probably not watching the time, give them clear warning. ("It's quarter to ten. In fifteen minutes, the CD player shuts down.") It's often hard for a young host to play the spoilsport and declare a party over, so relieve your child of that responsibility.

Preteens and teens will often take advantage of a situation in which they sense that adults have surrendered control. A young party host may well find herself incapable of handling conflicts between what her friends want to do and what her parents expect. For everyone's sake, stay in the background but be ever vigilant.

Rituals and Celebrations

ELEVEN THROUGH FOURTEEN IS A time of passage, and for many young people this includes solemn religious rites. In the Catholic and Protestant traditions, children are confirmed. The bar mitzvah is celebrated for Jewish boys when they turn thirteen, although some Reform congregations have replaced the bar mitzvah with a confirmation-type service for boys and girls. In some Conservative and Reform congregations, the bat mitzvah is celebrated for girls who are thirteen or fourteen

Parents have a right to expect that their children will be safe in your care, so be prudent. Whenever you entertain preteens and teenagers in your home, make it an absolute rule never to serve alcohol or have alcoholic beverages available. This includes no open bar shelves or unlocked liquor cabinets. Remember that it is illegal for anyone to serve or provide alcohol to young people under the legal age of twenty-one. You can also be held criminally and civilly liable for any accident, injury, or illness that occurs as a result of alcohol consumed in your presence or on your property. If alcohol is served at a gathering for adults and young people—a summer barbecue, for example, or a bar mitzvah or wedding party—be certain that attendants and bartenders understand not to serve alcohol to minors and to inform you immediately if they see a young person drinking.

◄◄

and is the modern counterpart of the bar mitzvah, celebrating the young person's acceptance as an adult member of the congregation.

In all these traditions, the confirmation is a deeply religious service, coming after a period of instruction. Protestant confirmation is normally part of Sunday services. In the Catholic Church, the confirmation ceremony is held separately from the regular mass, with family and close friends in attendance. Services may be followed by church receptions attended by family, friends, and church officials and then luncheons at the home of the parents or relatives or at a restaurant. Parties are usually restrained in tone and limited to close family and friends. Gifts are not expected, but young people often receive Bibles engraved with their names, prayer books, gold crosses, and religious medallions to commemorate the occasion.

Bar mitzvah, bat mitzvah, and Reform confirmations, held as part of Saturday services, are both solemn and social. The service is often followed by a reception at the synagogue, which is open to all members of the congregation. A luncheon, dinner, or reception for invited guests is held later in the day. These invitation-only social events can be as simple or lavish as the family desires. The purpose is for friends of the family and the honored guest to joyfully celebrate the young person's passage. Gifts, which may be religious or secular, are expected and can be sent or taken to the party.

Whatever the faith, young people are expected to write their own thank-you notes for gifts they receive, and parents need to be certain that these notes—not calls or e-mails—are completed and mailed promptly.

Find Out What's Expected

When invited to services in another religious tradition, the first consideration is respect for the beliefs of others. Talking with others of that faith to find out exactly what is expected will increase your comfort. Perhaps your child can attend the service in the company of friends who belong to the faith. If she has someone to rely on for guidance, she will be more confident and can enjoy the experience of a religious celebration outside her own traditions.

In choosing what to wear, follow the customs of the congregation. Attire for the Christian and Jewish religious services is the customary "Saturday or Sunday best," although it's wise to check with the host parents about headwear. Out of respect, leave religious jewelry or symbols of a different faith at home. Whatever is worn to the service is appropriate for receptions and luncheons that follow immediately. Invitations to evening parties should specify if the event is formal.

Adolescents in Groups

MIDDLE SCHOOLERS ARE USUALLY WELL behaved at public events such as worship services and performances that they attend with adults. But manners tend to take a back seat when they are out and about with their peers. What adult has not been annoyed by the groups of giggling girls marching through the mall or the rowdy boys at the movies? Most of the time, their inconsiderate behavior is not deliberate. Young adolescents in groups quickly become oblivious to the world around them. Since you are unlikely to be there if your child happens to be in such a group, what can you do?

Clarify and Discuss

First, be clear about your expectations. Your child may sometimes forget her manners when she is with her friends, but she is more likely to behave if she knows your standards. Her conscience will tell her that cutting up at the movies feels wrong.

Discuss polite and impolite behaviors. If a group of teens delayed the checkout line when you were at the grocery store, talk about it later with your child. Chances are, she will agree that the behavior was inconsiderate, and verbalizing her ideas about how the teens should have behaved will help her firm up her own behavioral standards. She will also realize that her own behavior in public is being observed by others. Be careful not to use her friends as examples of bad behavior. Her loyalty to them is likely to override rational thinking.

Interaction with Peers

ENCOURAGE YOUR CHILD TO BE a role model for her peers. If she holds a door for an older person or says "thank you" to a salesperson, her friends will take note. Often a youngster can simply point out obnoxious public behavior among her friends (being too loud, blocking aisles and doorways, etc.), and everyone will stop when they realize what they are doing. Language matters when correcting others. A young person who tells friends to "shut up" is likely to be resented and ignored, but an inclusive comment such as "We need to be quiet" will often get results.

More difficult is saying "no" to peer pressure. Adolescents hate to go against the crowd, even when they feel uncomfortable with what the crowd is doing. Luckily, parents can come to the rescue without being present. Preteens and young teens will often accept "My mom will ground me for a month if I do that." Using Mom or Dad as an excuse lends weight to a child's refusal to participate in impolite, thoughtless, or dangerous behavior. You can afford to be the "bad guy" until your child is comfortable standing up for herself.

Summertime Activities

WHEN THE SCHOOL YEAR COMES to its close, it doesn't take long for the complaints to begin: "I'm bored." "There's nothing to do." Keeping a young person active during the summer helps to alleviate boredom, can improve school performance, and may prevent manners backsliding. Summer activities enable a child to meet new people and experience new environments while reinforcing lessons in cooperation, sharing, and consideration for others. The following ideas may help you find creative solutions to your adolescent's summertime doldrums:

- *Day camp or sleep-away camp.* Camp offers lots of opportunities to put good manners into practice: meeting and getting to know new people, sharing facilities, writing to family and friends, and being a good sport. Look for camping opportunities that support your child's interests, and check that camps are well supervised and promote values that you deem important. Be very careful about your child's readiness if you are considering a sleep-away camp.

- *Traveling and visiting.* Adolescents who balk at a family vacation or going to camp may be eager for a long visit with grandparents or other family members, especially if they live in interesting places. As much as possible, make the choice a family decision; your youngster will enjoy herself more when she feels some involvement in and responsibility for vacation plans. If she travels on her own, be sure to review manners expectations on public transportation and as a guest in someone else's home.

- *Classes.* This is a good time for learning new skills in ungraded classes that are less structured than school. Your child might want to try a new sport or join a computer or natural science class. Your local museum, college, or university may schedule art and photography classes and theater workshops. Most municipal park services offer summer learning opportunities. One or two such activities might be just right to keep your child from suffering summer boredom.

- *Summer jobs, paid or volunteer.* (See "Joining the Workforce" on page 343.)

- *Reading.* Summer is a great time for readers. You might introduce the classics if your child doesn't have a school reading list. Don't force reading or offer rewards. Do see that books, magazines, and newspapers are available.

- *Home projects.* This may be the summer to redecorate your child's bedroom, transform the garage into a recreation area, or redo the garden as a party spot. Engage your youngster in the planning, preparation, and hard work. A child who gripes about routine household chores may well be a tireless and cooperative

Graffiti attracts youngsters, and the need to add a name or comment to the wall writing of others or scratch something on a desk seems overwhelming for some. But there is never a good reason to deface public spaces. If you think your youngster is a budding graffiti artist, be firm that such vandalism is unacceptable, illegal, and can have severe consequences. And it is childish and immature—two labels your preteen or teen definitely does not want.

◄┼

companion when you share a project that she relates to and enjoys.

Joining the Workforce

IN THE MIDDLE SCHOOL YEARS, many children get the yen for a "real" job—in part to earn money but also because employment, unlike chores and paid work at home, carries adult responsibility. Young people are not legally eligible for regular employment until age sixteen, but there are lots of informal jobs—babysitting, paper routes, lawn mowing and garden care, dog walking and pet sitting, car washing, household help, tutoring—that will earn income.

Volunteer work offers many possibilities. Since it is unpaid, parents may want to offer a tangible reward—perhaps an increase in allowance or the gift of something the youngster would be saving to purchase. Be clear that this kind of compensation is special; volunteering itself is a gift to a worthy cause. (See "Caring About Others," page 295., for more volunteering ideas.)

First jobs will teach your child about personal responsibility, adaptation to the expectations of others, and the rewards of good performance including personal satisfaction. No matter how humble her job, she is beginning to form her work ethic and to shape the attitudes and behaviors that will govern her achievements in the adult workplace. When your child talks to you about getting a job, discuss all the following fundamentals. Be certain she understands that *keeping* a job depends on her good behavior.

- **Attendance and punctuality.** Show up on schedule and on time, and don't leave before the predetermined ending time without

Babysitting is regarded as the classic young person's job, but not all young teens are ready for or want to take on the responsibility. Unless a youngster has expressed real interest, parents should never volunteer their child for babysitting assignments. If he does want to be a sitter, it's very important to prepare him thoroughly.

Knowing what to do in emergencies is a must, so send your child to, at minimum, classes in first aid and CPR before he begins sitting. Many health-care facilities and service organizations offer special instruction for teen babysitters.

When your child begins caring for other children, it will boost his confidence to know that you are available if needed, so you may want to limit his early assignments to families in your neighborhood and times when you will be at home. Your young teen may phone you with a seemingly trivial question or request when he really wants some reassurance. Babysitting at night in a strange house with strange noises can be scary, so if your child calls home to chat with you at nine o'clock, be patient. He should also know never to invite friends over when he is babysitting unless he has the permission of his employers.

---

permission of the employer. If she has to miss a day or be late to her job, she must call her employer as soon as possible. She should give an employer advance notice of any scheduled absences (your family vacation, for example). Be clear that volunteer supervisors deserve the same consideration.

- **Good grooming and cleanliness.** It's hard to stay clean when mowing lawns or cleaning out garages, but an adolescent can at least show up with combed hair, clean hands and face, and clean work clothes.

- **Appropriate attire.** Whatever the job, employers expect employees to dress appropriately. Talk with your child about the meaning of "appropriate." If your adolescent is babysitting or working with a children's program, be sure she understands that she is a role model for younger children. Showing up in tight shorts and skimpy halter tops sets a poor example and is likely to end the possibility of further work assignments. Discuss the difference between self-expression in clothing and conservative dressing within the standards of the job and talk about setting her priorities. If she really wants to earn the money for that new CD player, she may have to give up the green hair.

- *Positive attitude.* A positive attitude includes being friendly and respectful to employers and co-workers and showing enthusiasm for the job, willingness to learn, and the ability to take constructive criticism. Explain to your child that her attitude and good manners reflect on the people she is working for.

- *Adherence to rules.* Your child may as well learn now that when she accepts a job, she is agreeing to follow the rules made by her employer. Discuss rules with her. Listen to her complaints and be supportive, but remind her that it is the employer's option to determine rules—not hers. By talking with your child about her job, you can also discover when an employer's rules really are arbitrary or onerous.

Overworking

Adolescents sometimes take on more work than they can handle, and responsible adults must make sure that the job isn't adversely affecting a child's academic or social life. Most middle schoolers won't have this problem, but it pays to be alert now and to reinforce the message that your adolescent's first work commitment is to school.

When Difficulties Arise

Your child may have difficulties on the job. A common example is when an employer imposes more responsibility than the child bargained for or expects unpaid favors such as staying overtime. Your child will need your help to resolve problems. She may have to renegotiate her work agreement, clarify the times she is available and types of work she can do, or even quit the job. Talk it out together, encourage your child to consider her options carefully, then back up her decision. Help her express herself to an employer clearly and courteously. If she must give up a job, it is not a failure so long as she has carefully considered other solutions and arrived at her decision reasonably.

School Problems

THE FIRST YEAR OF MIDDLE or junior high school—usually fifth or sixth grade—is a major turning point; youngsters move from group-oriented to individual learning and evaluation and from a nurturing relationship with one teacher to the more hectic and impersonal pace of multiple teachers. The move to high school requires another big leap as the child who has reached the top of the middle school ladder again finds himself back on the bottom rung. Virtually every student is going to have some problems at school. The road will be bumpier for some, but all parents need to be alert for problems before they get out of control. Working with school authorities will be more successful if you approach difficult situations with respect, good manners, and readiness to cooperate for the benefit of your child.

Conflicts with Teachers

In middle and high school, your child has perhaps a half-dozen or more teachers to contend with every day, plus part-time and substitute teachers, teaching assistants, coaches, librarians, and other adults. He is going to like some more than others and will respond to some teaching styles better than to others. He may have mixed feelings about some teachers. (For example, he loves and admires his football coach but can't stand the way the coach teaches math.) If he is having trouble in a class, he will be tempted to blame the teacher. While teachers do make mistakes, most conflicts with teachers are not as serious as your child may think. From professional self-interest as well altruism, teachers want their students to succeed and are usually willing to devote extra time to a young person who asks for help.

Your respect for your child's teachers will be more influential than you imagine. Make it clear that all teachers must be treated with courtesy. Help your child learn how to disagree and dispute without being contentious. Be firm that sarcasm, catty remarks, and insults are never called for. Emphasize the importance of getting assignments, following instructions, being prepared, and participating in class. You'll probably need to repeat lessons that go back to the kindergarten days—that getting along with teachers starts with a positive attitude and willingness to share and cooperate.

Keep in contact with teachers and school counselors. Inform them about situations such as divorce or a family illness that may affect your child's behavior and performance. Although you are your child's chief advocate with teachers and school authorities, these adults are your colleagues in the business of educating your child.

Homework

Whatever you think about the ultimate value of homework, it's a reality. There is sound evidence supporting the long-term benefits to self-discipline, skills mastery, and the development of effective study habits in particular. Problems generally arise when a child seems to have too much homework or the work is too difficult. Before complaining to the school, however, you should honestly evaluate your child's efforts and take a close look at the work in question. Does your child apply himself well? Does he focus on his assignments? Is he easily frustrated? Is he frequently distracted or prone to create distractions for himself? How well does he organize himself and his work? When he needs help, does he ask for assistance from his teachers?

Consider your own attitudes. Do you support the value of homework or convey the impression that it is a waste of time? Do you ever do or complete assignments for your child? Are you available to provide assistance when asked? It can help to talk with parents of other students in your child's class and find out if their children are overburdened. If you are sure the problem is not at home, schedule a meeting with the teacher, and let your child know about the meeting whether or not he will attend. Be prepared with samples and focus on your specific concerns. You are most likely to help your child when you and his teacher begin with mutual respect.

Cheating

The pressure to cheat normally begins in middle school and escalates through high school. Young people are tempted to cheat for a number of reasons, but parents must be sure that their children understand that all cheating is dishonest and unethical and will be treated seriously. Talk about specific forms of cheating and plagiarism and the difference between group study and using other people's work.

If you learn that your child is cheating, it is important to stay calm but react swiftly. Be clear that cheating is the real problem—not, as many young people today think, getting caught. Cheating may be a one-time indiscretion but can become a habit if not dealt with. Work closely with school officials. In addition to any disciplinary measures, you probably need to examine your child's life and attitudes. Is he under excessive pressure to achieve high grades? Does he lack motivation to succeed in school? Is he accepting the all-too-prevalent message that the ends justify the means?

Harassment

Bullying is intolerable, but it may be difficult to detect. In junior and senior high, bullying is often more subtle than flagrant physical abuse and can be practiced by students who seem unlikely to be bullies. In recent years, the extent of sexual harassment—from teasing and rumor-mongering to assault—has been well documented. Power is an issue with adolescents, and those who have it want to keep it. Bullies, relying on verbal assaults and threats of physical violence, can be ruthless.

Parents have an obligation to protect all children, and parents whose children are not being harassed may be most likely to hear about bullying. If you believe that bullying and harassment are taking place—whether or not your child is involved—report your suspicions to school authorities and be clear that you expect to be informed about their actions. Bullying is usually a sign of deeper psychological problems and can have serious, even tragic, consequences for the bullies, their targets, and innocent bystanders.

Truancy

Truancy is absence from school without a parent or guardian's knowledge. A child having problems at school usually doesn't want to be there. He may concoct excuses for repeated absences, or he may simply skip out. Parents often have no idea that their child is a truant until they receive a call from school authorities.

The one-time or occasional truant day may be a fairly benign act of independence. Habitual truancy and other attendance problems such as cutting classes may signal poor performance, school failure, or learning disabilities and can have serious legal implications for your entire family. Respond quickly and be ready to work closely with school officials (and social services and juvenile authorities if they are involved) to control the behavior and correct underlying problems.

On the Threshold:
Fifteen Through Eighteen Years

NOW'S THE TIME TO . . .

- Continue discussing and modeling moral and ethical choices

- Refine rules, expectations, and consequences

- Encourage personal responsibility

- Promote academic achievement

- Promote clear language and good communication manners

- Encourage entertaining and party etiquette

- Address one-on-one dating

- Teach interviewing skills

- Establish sound driving rules and etiquette

- Prepare for life after high school

YOUR HIGH SCHOOL DAUGHTER OR son is now on the threshold of independence. By fifteen, her conscience and most of her moral and ethical values are in place. The etiquette fundamentals required for most social interactions are established, and your child is almost, but not quite, ready to face the world on her own terms.

The high school years are marked by many milestones—chief among them, dating and maybe first love, jobs, driver's license, and possibly first car. Physically, teenagers will reach or come near adult stature in these years, and by high school graduation they will *look* like adults, albeit young and fresh-faced. Emotionally, they are still unsure of themselves in many new situations, but their self-confidence is growing and will, at times, display itself in assertive and even rebellious behavior. A high schooler's maturing intellectual skills lead her to new heights of contemplation. The good manners you have taught for so many years will now be put to use as she makes her own judgments about appropriate behavior in new and unpredictable situations.

Some teens rush toward adulthood, but for most, high school is a time of ambivalence. They want to make their own decisions and are quick to demand more freedoms, yet they still need your support, advice, and some hard rules. As a parent, your job is far from over, but it requires rethinking and retooling as the reins of parental control are loosened. There is still much for you to teach, including refinements of the manners and social behaviors that will ease your child's transition to adulthood.

Moral and Ethical Choices

THE HIGH SCHOOL STUDENT WILL face moral and ethical decisions that can affect his life in ways that are far-reaching. He is also thinking about his future, making plans, and probably struggling with the awareness that choices he makes today will have long-range consequences. His social conscience is developing, and he may become deeply concerned about politics, philosophy, religion, and aspects of social justice that are broader than the questions of fairness common in childhood. What he says to you about his concerns will not always reflect his thought processes, but his cognitive abilities now enable him to see that most problems are complicated, that moral and behavioral issues cannot be viewed in simple black-and-white terms, and that conventional standards may not necessarily be right.

He is grappling with shaping his uniquely individual identity. Who is he as a person? What does he stand for? What are his goals? What are his values? How should he judge himself and others? For the past fifteen or so years, your child has been immersed in your values and absorbing your beliefs through your teaching and example. What matters now is to recognize that he is making his own choices, to accept that his thinking will differ somewhat from yours, and to trust that his moral and ethical decision making is grounded in the principles and values you have given him.

Trusting Your Teen

DURING ADOLESCENCE, BOTH PARENTS AND teens are inclined to erect roadblocks that impede trusting relationships. But to become independent and responsible, teenagers need to be trusted. They will make mistakes, and their choices may sometimes appall you. There will be times when they violate your trust, and you will make your disappointment clear. Unless deceit and deception are habitual, however, a teen deserves trust. It's too easy to assume that the once bright and bubbly child who is now a moody or cynical teen is up to no good. We instinctively fear what we do not know, and parents often just don't know what their teens are thinking and doing. But the fact that your teen is not as open as you would like does not mean he is making poor choices or hiding something terrible. There are a number of ways parents can promote mutual trust, respect, and consideration—beginning with frequent and honest communication.

Keeping Communication Open

IT'S NOT ENOUGH NOW TO be available to talk. Parents need to take an active approach to communication with teens. Talk with them about whatever is going on in your world—the events of the day, what's happening in the stock market or national politics, sports news, family matters. Every conversation doesn't have to be deep or focused on your teenager. Including teens often in normal conversation and welcoming their contributions establish patterns that pay off when sensitive or difficult issues need to be addressed. By following the fundamental principles of good conversation and respect for others, you can do much to keep communication open on both sides.

Timing Is Important

During the high school years, your teen may be even busier than you. He is certain to be under a lot of pressure. So don't expect to talk with him only at your convenience. Pay attention to what is going on in his life and choose times for serious talks with care. The morning after a teen has been up late studying for a final exam is not the best time to initiate a conversation about his college applications.

If your teen usually has a free hour or two after school, it might be worth shuffling your work schedule occasionally to get home early and create opportunities to be together. You may also be able to include your teen, if he's interested, in some of your activities—the weekly golf game or fishing trip, for example—that encourage comradeship and conversation. He won't always be highly communicative, but he is listening to what you have to say, and he will know that you are open to him.

Never Be Dismissive

Teenagers are inexperienced and often unrealistic, but they have generational knowledge and insights that come from their experience of a world unlike the one in which their parents grew up. Dismissing a teen's ideas without a fair hearing by cutting him off, talking down to him,

---

A Question for Peggy and Cindy

Last night, our fifteen-year-old daughter, Michelle, told us that she'd been invited to go with her boyfriend and his parents to a beach resort for spring break. We told her "no," but before we could give her our reasons, she screamed "You just don't understand!" and ran to her room. Now, she won't speak to us. We may not know everything, but we understand a lot more than Michelle gives us credit for.

Yes, you probably do understand more than she realizes, but perhaps it is the *way* you reacted that caused the outburst. Saying "no" straight off the bat generally works with young children, but teens need to share in the decisions that are important to them. When an important decision must be made, everyone is more satisfied when give-and-take happens first and all sides show respect for the opinions of others. Michelle may be no happier with your final decision, but she is less likely to feel angry and misunderstood if she has participated in the process. And you will probably feel more confident about her decision-making abilities when you give her your time and the chance to express herself before you say "yes" or "no."

---

failing to listen or respond, or making light of what he says is sure to block communication and damage mutual trust. Teens need to be taken seriously. They are much more inclined to accept guidance and correction from adults who show them the basic courtesy of paying attention, encourage independent thinking, and honor their right to have ideas and opinions that you may not agree with. By listening to teens, parents may also find themselves learning a thing or two.

Don't Jump to Conclusions

When teens broach sensitive subjects, be careful not to assume ulterior motives. If your teen asks about contraceptives or the difference between marijuana and cocaine, you might infer from the question that he has engaged in or plans to try dangerous behavior. But more likely, he simply wants information and probably your attitudes as well. Answer questions to the best of your ability. You may want to ask why the particular subject interests your teen, but don't be accusatory or judgmental. You want him to feel comfortable coming to you with questions and problems, and he will continue to do so if he trusts you to trust him.

Admit Your Mistakes

Teens trust adults who can admit to mistakes and ignorance. If you don't know something, say so. Then ask for the time to get the information you need. You can't always solve problems or make decisions instantly, but your teen will benefit from your model of intellectual honesty and your effort to get the right answers before drawing conclusions.

Freedom Versus Discipline

THE PROCESS OF LETTING A teen explore his independence requires that parents reexamine their approach to discipline. In general, the fewer the rules, the better, but whatever rules you set will be easier to enforce if your teenager has a role in making them. Keep in mind that times have changed; although the fundamentals of decent and mannerly behavior alter little, your specific rules and expectations are likely to be somewhat different from those you encountered as a teen.

Hard rules for teens usually apply to behaviors of greatest significance: curfews, homework, school attendance, telephone use, household chores, dating, and driving. Another area that should be addressed involves reporting in—when and under what circumstances a teen is expected to check in with parents. No matter how much they protest, teens want rules in critical areas of their lives, and rules often protect teens from being pushed into behaviors they know are wrong for them. However, setting and enforcing rules now requires more finesse, tolerance, and willingness to accommodate than in the early and middle school years.

Rules and Expectations

These recommendations will help parents and their teens deal with rules and expectations with mutual respect:

- *Be prepared.* Parents sometimes make rules and decide on consequences in response to specific situations as they arise. Teenagers naturally resent this kind of after-the-fact discipline and may rebel. Anticipate problem areas and prepare yourself by thinking ahead.

- *Discuss and negotiate.* Involve your teenager in determining the rules. Be clear that you are ready to renegotiate rules in the future, based on the level of personal responsibility he has shown. Talk with him about appropriate consequences for violating rules. By negotiating from principles *and* open-mindedness, you set an example that will serve your teen for life.

- *Talk about principles.* Negotiation gives parents an excellent opportunity to explain and reinforce underlying principles. Let your teen know that you establish rules out of concern for him, not simply because you can.

- *Clarify what is not negotiable.* Your teen needs to know that certain behaviors are not up for negotiation. If he is caught using drugs or alcohol, damaging or destroying property, speeding or breaking other traffic laws, or cheating at school, for example, he must know that you will take immediate action and that the consequences are not open to debate.

- *Be clear about consequences and follow through.* As in the past, when consequences are necessary, they work most effectively when related closely to the misbehavior. Be sure that the

When you discuss rules with your teenager, bring up the subject of manners. While it's usually not necessary to make hard rules or set consequences for etiquette breaches, it's important that your teen know how much you value kind and courteous behavior to everyone at all times. Be clear that you trust her to be well mannered whether or not you are present. Promote her independent use of good manners by refraining now from correcting or prompting in front of others. She knows the difference between considerate and inconsiderate behavior, and her conscience will tell her when she has been rude or thoughtless. Encourage her to come to you with any etiquette questions or dilemmas.

---

consequences fit the situation and that you can actually carry through. Tempted as you may be to ground your teen for six weeks because he was two hours late returning the family car and caused you needless anxiety, grounding for a weekend is more effective and enforceable. Try to mete out any consequences as soon as possible after the misconduct, but not when you are angry. Sometimes, it's best to sleep on the problem before you deal with it.

- **Be flexible.** Parents should be willing to adapt rules as their teens grow older and demonstrate increased responsibility and trustworthiness. You may want to eliminate some rules entirely over time. Discuss with your teen the reason for relaxing or dropping a rule so that you don't appear to be letting something important slide. Make your expectations clear and explain that you have the option of reimposing restrictions if needed.

- **Praise good behavior.** If ever there's a time for positive reinforcement, it's now. Express your appreciation when your daughter remembers to call home and tell you she will be late for dinner. Say "thank you" when your son does the laundry or cleans his room without prompting. Teens frequently appear embarrassed by compliments and courtesies, so don't be put off when they brush aside your good words. Beneath the embarrassment, they are pleased by justifiable praise. Positive reinforcement is still the most successful form of discipline and a dependable confidence builder.

The Value of Education

INTELLECTUALLY YOUR TEEN CAN UNDERSTAND the importance of education to long-term success, but emotionally he will often care more about the here and now. Teens may also be convinced that they can make up later what they miss now.

Parents can do a great deal to help teenagers get the most from, and actually enjoy, their school experience. These suggestions will help:

- *Try to focus on effort rather than grades.* Most children and teens are likely to do better in school if parental expectations are realistic and praise is given for effort, perseverance, and attitude rather than a specific grade. By now, you should have a very good idea of your child's academic capabilities. Make it clear that you expect your child to do *his* best; avoid comparisons to high-achieving siblings, other students, or your own high school record. Pay attention to your teen's schoolwork. A low grade may come from lack of industry, or it might indicate that your teen hit an intellectual rough patch and is having difficulty with a basic concept.

- *Respect and support your teen's goals.* Most teens give some serious thought to what they want to do in life. Their goals may seem impractical, but the fact that the teen is setting long-range objectives is significant; your son may not become an astronaut, but his interest could lead to a career in medicine, engineering, or science. Even if your teen's goals change frequently or are poles apart from your desires, respect his thinking and encourage his interests.

- *Continue to relate school studies to your teen's values and goals.* Teenagers often don't see the relevance of what they are studying to their lives. You can now discuss the value of education with your teen in more abstract terms. Talk about the broader benefits of a well-rounded high school education—that it is the foundation of informed, critical thinking; prepares students to handle the unpredictability of life; and promotes respect for people whose talents and interests are different. Through the education process, a teen acquires and refines the

Because teens often increase nonacademic activities during high school, homework may get short shrift at a time when it, too, should be on the increase. It's a good idea to sit down together at the start of high school and clarify expectations and any rules you may want to impose. Be prepared to evaluate a teen's actual homework load. Check her school's handbook or stated policies about homework to find out what is expected. Encourage your teen to seek help from teachers. Discuss the immediate and the long-term benefits of homework, not least of which are preparation for independent, self-motivated work and development of effective study habits and time management skills—characteristics that are essential to success in higher education and getting ahead in any career. (For more about homework, see "School Problems," page 346.)

◂◂

---

skills needed to think for himself, make reasoned judgments, and be open to change.

- **Be alert for signs of excessive pressure.** A teen under too much pressure will often choose study over friends and social activities and may become unreasonably upset about a low grade. On the other hand, he may lose interest in academics and cease making any effort. Overachieving and underachieving are often flip sides of the same coin. Talk to school counselors or a family physician if your teen shows any signs of undue stress.

- **Protest if your child is receiving unusual academic treatment or special concessions.** The classic example is the student athlete who is placed in unchallenging classes for easy passes and given "tutoring" that amounts to having others do the work. Stereotyping—girls are not "science-minded" and boys don't need art education, students from low-income families should be steered to technical-vocational training, students of different ethnic backgrounds will perform differently, and so on—may deny teens access to a full education. There may be a genuine need—a diagnosed learning disability, for example—for special treatment in some situations, but parents should insist that all students be given every opportunity to live up to their individual capabilities.

After students have received their college acceptances or lined up post-graduation employment, senioritis is likely to strike. Senioritis is often characterized by loss of interest in school, below-standard grades, some rebelliousness, and emotional swings that vacillate between elation and moodiness or contemplation. Seniors may not feel ready for the independence that high school graduation implies. Many will soon leave home and friends, and these breaks can be very difficult. A teen may want to pack as much fun as possible into the final days or months of high school and possibly to experiment with behaviors she has thus far resisted.

Parents can often help by staying focused on practical considerations. Remind your teen that she needs to complete her courses and maintain acceptable grades in order to graduate. Step in if a teen engages in dangerous or destructive behavior, but also recognize that senioritis is a normal response to a life change that's often as bitter as it is sweet. Listen when your teen expresses her feelings and fears, sympathize with her ambivalence, and provide advice when asked.

The Truth About Cheating

CHEATING AND THE TEMPTATION TO cheat generally peak during high school. Studies show a disturbing tendency among today's young people to regard cheating as acceptable. Teens often have the impression that cheating is not so bad because no one is endangered. They could not be more wrong. Cheating is any calculated action to gain an unfair advantage at the expense of someone else, and a parent shouldn't soft-pedal when discussing it with a child.

When teens crib from another student's paper, sneak answers into a test, copy or purchase essays and term papers, copy from outside sources and claim the work as their own, and submit projects that they did not create, they are stealing. In sports and games, if teens deliberately break rules, use nonregulation equipment, take illegal performance-enhancing substances, sabotage a competitor, or manipulate or influence scorekeeping, they are stealing victory from those who honor fair play. Lying on a college or job application, exaggerating on a resume, making up excuses to delay an exam, feigning a disability to get more time on standardized tests—these common forms of cheating rob decision makers of the ability to make fair judgments. Facilitating someone else's cheating (doing someone else's assignment, for instance) is no less fraudulent.

Plagiarism is a form of cheating that involves copying words or organizational patterns from another source and using the material without crediting the original source. In high school, plagiarism is most likely to occur in written work, including mathematics, but can also be found in speeches, computer programming, art, and music. Young people must understand that to copy even a sentence or key phrases from someone else's work and not cite the source is plagiarism; changing a word here or there does not make the work original.

If Your Teen Cheats

Whatever excuse a teen may have for cheating, parents must treat the transgression seriously. You'll want to hear your teen's explanation, but don't be tempted to excuse the behavior or show relief that it was *only* cheating and not something worse.

- **Get the evidence.** Consult closely with teachers, coaches, and school authorities. Be realistic and accept the facts.

- **Don't expect special treatment.** Even when the evidence is clear, parents may be inclined to lobby school officials for a mild consequence or none at all. Don't expect the school to bend its policies for your child. Do, however, discuss what consequences are most likely to be effective with your teen.

- **Accept that your teen must take the consequences.** The outcome can be traumatic if the teacher or school fails the teenager for an entire course or suspends or expels students who cheat. It can be very hard to accept severe consequences, but what is really at stake is not a failure to graduate with the class. It is whether or not your child will become a person of honor and integrity.

- **Give your child the chance to redeem himself.** A teen needs a fair chance to repair the damage and to realize that the unhappiness he has caused is not worth the minor advantage cheating may bring. Give him time to absorb the gravity of his action and the consequences. Be open if he wants to talk; try to raise discussion to the level of personal integrity and respect for others rather than rehashing the specific incident. Guard against becoming overly distrustful; your teen must understand that he did wrong, but he also needs opportunities to make amends and demonstrates his trustworthiness.

Demonstrating Respect Every Day

SINCE QUESTIONING OF CONVENTIONAL WISDOM and adult standards is normal for teens, parents may find many of their cherished values and beliefs challenged on a daily basis. Often the questioning is not so much a problem as the *way* teens express themselves and how parents respond. Etiquette precepts and skills can often ease confrontations between teens and their parents.

While developing the cognitive skills of fact finding, logical reasoning, thinking ahead, and effective problem solving, teens tend to present their thinking with little or no social polish and cannot draw the line between making an argument and being argumentative. As a result, high schoolers are often perceived as brash, opinionated, self-important, and disrespectful even when they are making very good sense. Teens can also suffer from lack of self-confidence or confusion about complex issues, so they may become silent as sphinxes around parents and other adults. In some cases, teens may be so fearful of conflict that they put on a cheerful facade and refuse to be drawn into any substantive discussion.

Such behaviors are typical and vary in intensity depending on a teen's individual temperament. It is just as natural for parents to feel themselves constantly put upon and put down. But parents who respond in kind, with anger or silence or false cheer, will miss critical teaching opportunities.

The Art of Disagreement

MODELING IS VITAL TO HELP young people learn the how, when, and why of respectful disagreement. Consistently treating your teen with respect may not always earn immediate rewards but will establish a model for her interactions. When you become frustrated, it may help to remember that teaching a difficult lesson is often a difficult process.

If you find yourself thinking that you can't talk to your teen without arguing, don't worry. This phase will eventually pass. In addition to the communication ideas in Chapter 26 (see "Keeping Communication Open," page 352), you can help your teen learn the art of disagreeing without being disagreeable by teaching and reinforcing the following skills:

- *Self-control.* No discussion can be productive if one or all of the parties are out of control. When a teen is angry or refuses to talk, tell her that you will discuss the issue later, when you are both in a mood to listen. Be sure to follow through and raise the subject again, and try to start over with a clean slate. Apologize if you are the one who lost control and became angry.

- *Listening.* Learning to listen attentively is key to the art of disagreeing. A good listener is open to what other people actually say and conscious of verbal and nonverbal expression. Your teen is more likely to listen if she knows that you really listen to her. Teach her to listen by your model.

- *Organization and focus.* Respectful and effective argument requires mental organization, a skill learned through years of practice and trial and error. Keep conversations focused. Don't be drawn off the point into tangential issues or allow minor disagreements to escalate. (If your teen failed to complete a household chore, don't let the incident become an excuse to criticize the way she keeps her room.)

Humor Helps

A good sense of humor will help you survive your teenager's high school years. But a respectful parent never laughs *at* a teen or gives the impression that a teen's concerns are laughable. Find supportive friends with whom you can share feelings, anxieties, and "war stories." Among themselves, parents of teens often indulge in a kind of black humor that helps to relieve tension. When recounted in retrospect, the fights between parents and teens frequently reveal their funny side, and a parent can see more clearly where he or she was off base and which tactics work. Sharing stories with other parents can also help you sort out serious difficulties from normal parent–teen communication breakdowns. Do not reveal confidences shared by your teen or any information that would hurt if it got back to him. But allow yourself to let your hair down on occasion and share a laugh with a friend. You'll probably feel better about yourself and your teen.

- *Respect for the feelings of others.* No one wins an argument by name-calling or demeaning others for their ideas and opinions. You should challenge faulty opinions and at the same time model kindness and respect by steering clear of any hurtful personal remarks. Teens tend to be extremely sensitive, and simply addressing your teen by a childhood nickname or pet term can cause pain. Always be careful not to refer to others in pejorative terms, which sets a precedent for hurtful speech.

- *Providing accurate information.* If your daughter is arguing passionately that special driving restrictions discriminate against teens, you can agree with her basic premise, yet provide information about teen driving and accident rates that supports the policies she feels are unfair. Present facts as facts, not as demonstrations of a parent's superior knowledge.

- *Knowing when to quit.* There are some sure signs that a discussion or argument has gone on too long: when participants begin to repeat themselves or digress into other areas, when tempers flare or boredom sets in. It's time to stop the discussion for a while. Teens must learn that storming away is not a solution, but

What happens when your teenager is right and you are wrong? Parents and other adults are sometimes afraid to show weakness by backing down, but there are few more powerful examples of self-respect and respect for others than the willingness to admit error. The ability to adapt to better ideas and find compromises is a mark of maturity that you want your teen to emulate and master.

_____◄◄

that it is often necessary to call a respectful truce, give everyone time to calm down and contemplate, and return to the issue later.

Respect for Diversity

A TEENAGER'S CONFORMIST IMPULSES MAY put her at odds with those who do not conform to her standards. The division into groups that began in middle school continues in high school, and most teens will choose friends among teens who are like themselves. While social segmenting is part of forming a sense of personal identity, it can have the unfortunate effect of encouraging intolerance and disrespect for teens who are different and for diversity in general.

Intolerance may also appear when a teen has a run-in at school or on the job with a person of another ethnic or cultural background, sexual orientation, religion, or economic class. Out of anger or fear, she may conclude that all members of that group are unworthy or inferior. Attributing negative characteristics to an entire category, she may influence her peer group to share her bias.

Harsh Judgments

Although respect for peers with physical and mental disabilities has probably increased over recent generations—due to general societal changes and institutional efforts including mainstreaming—high schoolers can be very hard on other teens who look, speak, think, or behave differently.

Weight, height, speech problems such as stuttering, physical tics and mannerisms, lack of athletic prowess, style or cost of clothing—virtually anything that is perceived as different or odd can be the excuse for snubbing, teasing, or more aggressive forms of harassment. Sadly, simply

Like many adults, teens often have limited knowledge and understanding of history. Parents should provide information that explains why and how prejudices arise and why certain language (often pejorative terms that have crept into popular music and other media directed to young people) is unacceptable. A teen who uses racial or ethnic slurs may have little comprehension of the history of groups outside his own tradition. Without context, he cannot understand why language and attitudes that may be fairly common among his peers are disrespectful and wrong.

◄◄

being smart can bring peer rejection, and intellectually interesting teens may defend themselves by deliberately hiding their gifts in mediocre performance. Teasers and bullies may or may not understand the impact of their behavior on their victims, and without help from adults, these teens are unlikely to anticipate the long-term, occasionally tragic, consequences.

Be on the Alert

Prejudice, bigotry, teasing, and bullying may not be flagrant, but even a teenager's occasional use of an insulting term for an individual or group should be a warning. Calmly talk with your teen and discuss why she or her friends feel it necessary to do or say something hurtful to another person. Do what you have done for so long: appeal to her empathy and sense of right and wrong. Remind her of the Golden Rule and encourage her to think from the other person's point of view.

If hurtful words are the problem, find out if your teen really knows what the words mean. Teenagers are rarely as sophisticated as they and their parents think. They may have little more than a vague understanding of crude insults.

If a teen is involved in bullying or extreme teasing, parents must take action. Find out why a teen feels she has the right or need to harm others. The teen may well have an underlying problem, and parents should not hesitate to seek help from health-care providers and school psychologists and counselors.

Respect for the Opposite Sex

THE ETIQUETTE OF INTERACTIONS WITH the opposite sex boils down to one fundamental—*respect*. Genuine respect for the opposite sex is in large measure dependent on an individual's self-respect and family values and modeling. Teenagers who are reasonably secure with themselves and who have been reared in trusting and loving environments are generally better prepared for social interactions, including those with members of the opposite sex.

Parents can help teens understand that respect is demonstrated in all their day-to-day interactions—refusing to laugh at sexist jokes, not engaging in gender-based teasing, not stereotyping others based on gender and interests, and so on. A teen who is regularly exposed to healthy, courteous, and nonsexist role modeling among his family will be more inclined to regard and treat the opposite sex with genuine respect and courtesy.

Self-Image and Appearance

HIGH SCHOOL TEENS ARE STILL dealing with the physical changes of puberty. Most are also looking for tangible ways to express their identities and separate themselves from parents. They want to identify with their peers as they craft their self-image and choose how they want the rest of the world to see them. In general, parents are best advised to allow their teens leeway, within reason. Although each young person will react differently to parental "interference" in dressing and grooming issues, these recommendations should be useful:

- **Discuss and negotiate how your teen may dress.** Discuss how styles of dress not only convey an image but also express respect or disrespect for others. Talk about the meaning of appropriate dress. Jeans and tee shirts may be fine for the mall, sports events, and hanging out with friends. But such clothing choices are inappropriate for worship services, more formal public and private gatherings, job and college interviews—anywhere the clothes can demonstrate a lack of respect.

    Introduce the concept of *propriety* as dressing and behaving in a way that shows concern and consideration for the feelings of others. Think about your own priorities and be prepared to show flexibility. You can negotiate some specifics—coat, tie, and slacks or dress and hose are worn to church, for example. Be sure you are well acquainted with the current fashion trends in your area; your teen's style may not be as far out as you imagine.

- **Expect cleanliness and good grooming.** Teens should understand that even people who applaud creative, nontraditional dressing styles do not want to be around anyone who is dirty, smelly, and unkempt. Rather than fighting over styles of dress and hair, emphasize the fundamentals: daily bathing, shampooing, and use of deodorants; clean hands, feet, and nails; tooth brushing and use of mouthwash; fresh makeup; and so forth. Older teens may become obsessed with grooming, and their hours in the bathroom can become a serious nuisance. Negotiate what you can—especially if you have more than one teen in the house—and be ready to schedule and limit time in the bathroom if you must.

A Question for Peggy and Cindy

My husband insists that men should always open car doors for women. My son thinks the idea is silly and out-of-date. I'm on the fence and would appreciate another opinion.

The custom of men opening car doors and helping women out of cars is an updated version of ancient and chivalrous traditions. Today's women and girls, however, are not inclined to accept the underlying implication that women are weak and need a man's hand or arm to get to their feet. Rather than making opening car doors (and other traditional "manly" manners such as holding a woman's chair at the table and taking her arm when going up or down stairs) into a male–female issue, why not present it as a courtesy to anyone who needs assistance? Different circumstances call for different actions. A girl who normally hops out of the car on her own might appreciate the courtesy if she is wearing a full-skirted formal gown. A simple "Can I get the door for you?" is all your son has to say. He may encounter the occasional person who resents his offer, and he should not insist or take the rejection personally. There is one *always* that teens must learn, however. When anyone holds a door or offers assistance to them, *always* say "thank you."

- **Support school dress codes.** Many public schools are reinstating some form of dress restriction, and the movement for school uniforms is escalating. A dress code is generally imposed in order to encourage discipline, decrease distractions and disruptions in the classroom, and cut down on clothing rivalries that tend to favor affluent students. Dress codes also prepare young people for the expectations of employers. The darker side of dress codes involves safety issues such as preventing gang identification and eliminating clothes that can conceal weapons. Parents should be willing to back up the efforts of schools to develop reasonable dress codes and standards.

- **Talk about clothing budgets.** Your teen probably knows the exact price of the designer jeans that are the norm in her crowd, but has she ever bought her own underwear and pajamas? When she purchases an item labeled "Dry Clean Only," does she understand that someone must pay the dry cleaner every time the item is cleaned? You may or may not want to set up a clothing allowance for your teen, but either way, it's a good idea to introduce her to the real costs of clothing herself and the rest of the family. (See "The Meaning of Money," page 372.) A teen who is aware of the costs of dressing may become more sensitive to those whose wardrobes are less extensive or fashionable than hers.

- **Remember that good manners can say as much as bad clothes.** Most adults expect and often enjoy the eccentricities of youthful self-expression, but some hidebound souls refuse to give teens an inch of tolerance. Teens need encouragement to understand people who have negative preconceptions about unconventional styles. When your teen handles negative comments and criticism with good manners and poise, her behavior is much more important than her choice of clothes.

- **Pay compliments.** Teens like to hear that they look nice. Many are sensitive about their bodies and adopt dress, hair, and makeup styles to cover what they perceive to be physical flaws. Be sensitive and avoid backhanded compliments such as "That red shirt makes you look a lot less pale." Focus on your teen's strong points and look for positives. Who doesn't like to hear

Body Piercing and Tattoos

If your teen wants a nose ring, tongue stud, chest tattoo, or any variation on these themes, you have to talk seriously about your concerns. Your teen may not know about the potential dangers, including infection and serious disease such as hepatitis. Inform yourself; then inform your teen. Show him that your worries are based on respect for his safety and well-being. You may be able to negotiate some things—an extra ear piercing but no nose ring.

If your teen is unshakable, you still have the right and responsibility to insist that any procedure be done in a safe and healthy manner. Some procedures, such as tattooing, are illegal without the written permission of a parent or guardian. Check with your local public health service about laws and licensing. Your physician or health-care provider may do piercing or be able to refer you to another qualified provider. Be sure your teen understands that even seemingly simple procedures like ear piercing require aftercare, and make certain he takes all necessary precautions.

---

that she has a flair for style (though it may not be to your taste) or an eye for attractive colors?

Privacy Considerations

THE PRIVACY ISSUES RAISED WITH preteens and young teens (see "Privacy Issues," page 277) become even more important in the high school years. It can be easy to mistake the moodiness and reticence of teenagers for being "up to no good," when they simply need time to be alone. In general, teens are very protective of their privacy, and parents and caregivers should respect their wishes.

Exceptions can arise when parents suspect serious problems such as drug use. Teens should understand that their right to privacy is relinquished if they engage in dangerous, self-destructive, or illegal behavior. For parents, the challenge is not to become so fearful of what *might* be going on that they engage in preemptive snooping. Teens react differently when they feel they are under constant surveillance. Some become more adept at keeping their secrets, but others may rebel in ways that can be more dangerous than anything a parent dreams of. If a teen feels under siege, she may act out by doing precisely what her parents fear most. Besides, sneaking and snooping model the exact behavior the parent is trying to prevent.

Tacks to Take

Searching rooms and spying on activities are far less successful tactics than taking an interest in what a teen is doing, knowing her friends, and being discreetly but consistently observant. If you worry about your teen using drugs or alcohol when she goes out, stay up and greet her every time she returns home. Have a little chat. If you have acquainted yourself with the signs of drug and alcohol use, there will be no need to interrogate your teen; your five senses will tell you if there is a problem. It's also wise to welcome your teen's friends into your home. Parents who fear that their teen is involved with the "wrong crowd" should get to know her friends before making judgments. Showing respect for her friends may also enhance your relationship with your teen.

Your teen deserves to know how you define privacy and when you have the responsibility and obligation to step in. Teens often do not understand the legal jeopardy their actions pose for parents, guardians, and other family members. Nonconfrontational discussions of privacy issues will help your teen realize that everyone is entitled to the rights she demands for herself and that privacy is not an absolute right but a privilege earned through trust.

Good Sports, Good Leaders

BY NOW YOUR TEEN SHOULD be thoroughly steeped in the rules and expectations of fair play and have internalized the fundamentals of good sportsmanship. The next step is to move on to leadership roles. Teens may not realize that leadership doesn't apply just to the captain of the team or president of the club. True leadership means serving as a model for others and influencing positive behavior through the persuasive example of one's own actions and attitudes. Throughout life, people have countless opportunities to demonstrate leadership when in subordinate positions.

Leadership Qualities

Your teen may want to talk about the distinctions between being a leader and being popular and how leaders often risk popularity when

Introduce your teen to the meaning of money early. A good place to begin is the family budget. Explain how the family income is spent. Teens are often amazed to learn the true costs of mortgage or rent, utilities, food and clothing, automobiles, and insurance. When they see what must be paid out each month, they can better understand what is left over for discretionary spending.

If your teen has a job, take the opportunity to analyze his paycheck and explain the types and purposes of federal, state, and local taxes. Also talk about saving and investing and long-term versus short-term savings goals. Understanding the value of saving for the future—perhaps by learning about his college fund or your own retirement account—may encourage him to begin his own savings plan.

Be available to help your teen budget and manage his money, but don't bail him out every time he runs short. Reputable financial experts advise that parents carefully control use of their credit accounts and not give teens access to credit cards. A personal checking account or a debit card account is probably a better way for teens to learn that purchasing with paper or plastic is still spending and that the money must come from somewhere.

---

they make difficult decisions. She probably has plenty of questions and ideas based on her own experiences and observations. She may be especially conscious of unwarranted favoritism and bias shown toward some teens by adults and other teens. Frankly, there is often an extraordinary amount of unfairness in high school that can skew a teen's self-perceptions and hamper development of leadership capabilities. Parents and other adults can offer alternative views from their wider experience. Some of the characteristics of good leaders that you may want to talk about include:

- *Leading by example.* Real leaders set high standards for themselves and strive to meet those standards in part because they recognize their ability to influence others. Every day at school, older teens are modeling behavior for younger students. At work, a teen may not have the best job, but by being conscientious, courteous, and trustworthy, she will earn respect and perhaps lead others to follow her example.

- *Caring about others.* Real leaders never deliberately hurt others by their words or deeds. They give others a chance to be heard and value the contributions others make to team efforts. Leaders express appreciation for jobs well done and use constructive criticism to encourage improvement.

- *Knowing their limitations.* Effective leaders know what they can and cannot do, recognize the talents and skills of others, and are willing to delegate tasks and authority.

- *Honoring integrity above victory.* This gets back to basic good sportsmanship—playing by the rules and not taking unfair advantage. Teens can understand that a person's integrity requires lifelong commitment and cultivation. People of integrity are also willing to openly work for changes they believe are necessary and do not resort to cheating or deception to achieve their goals.

- *Losing with grace.* Leaders know that losing isn't the end of the world. Whether it's the big game, school election, or competition for a job, leaders don't blame others for their losses. A leader also understands that losing is an opportunity to learn and an incentive to try harder.

Finally, be sure your own expectations are realistic and you are not placing impossible demands on your teen. Being captain of the cheerleading squad or "most likely to succeed" in the high school yearbook is a highly unreliable predictor of future achievements.

The Power of Communication

-+-

LEARNING HOW TO COMMUNICATE EFFECTIVELY and to recognize and deal with communication breakdowns is critical to a young person's development. Your teen may be close-mouthed around you, but when he is with his friends, he is in an almost constant state of communication. His mind is teeming with new and more complex ideas, and he is struggling to express himself in more sophisticated ways.

He is trying to find his individual communication style—his own "voice"—as part of his overall identity. In school, he is learning the higher forms of language structure and use, but he also acquires a lot through osmosis, processing what he hears and adapting different styles and forms of communication to his own needs. The greater your teen's exposure to intelligent, vivid, lively, and courteous conversation, the better his communication skills will become.

At times, you will have to prod your teen to mind his communication manners—writing thank-you notes, for instance—and give help and instruction in forms that are new to him, such as writing cover letters for job applications. You will also be one of his primary resources for what to say in new circumstances. If he's facing an unfamiliar situation, such as introducing a guest in a school assembly or interviewing for a job, the old practice of role-playing may be just what he needs to gain confidence and poise.

Notes and Personal Letters

WRITING THANK-YOU NOTES IS LIKELY to become a fairly frequent obligation. Notes for gifts and special occasions should be an established habit by now, but your teen may need assistance as his notes become more sophisticated in both style and content. He will also need to know when and what kinds of thank-you gifts are appropriate.

The basics of gracious thank-you's discussed throughout this book all apply, including specific and enthusiastic reference to the gift, occasion, or service and personal references to the gift giver or host. Specific types of thank-you notes that teens may write include:

- Follow-up notes for interviews
- Thank-you notes for gifts received when the giver is not present, including gifts of money, mentioning the use planned for the funds
- Thank-you notes for special favors (references, college recommendations, and such)
- Notes on behalf of school and social organizations (thank-you's to guest speakers, financial contributors, volunteers)
- Notes of appreciation for services received (organizations providing employment assistance, college placement, or scholarship search services)

Notes should be sent as soon as possible after an occasion or receipt of a gift, but as a rule, even late thank-you notes are better than none except in the case of thanks for job interviews. Writing thank-you notes promptly after interviews is smart. So few applicants bother to follow up that employers tend to be impressed by the courtesy. A gracious note thanking an interviewer for her time and interest in an excellent way to affirm a good impression, show initiative, and demonstrate mannerly behavior.

Follow-Ups and Group Thanks

Sometimes, a second thank-you note is sent following the completion of a task or process. For example, your teen should write notes
immediately to everyone who agrees to supply a college recommendation. It is courteous to write another note to these people after he knows
which college he will attend. These second notes relate the outcome and
reiterate the teen's appreciation. The same goals can be accomplished
with a phone call, but a written note is especially appreciated.

When a teen writes a thank-you note on behalf of a group, he should
phrase the note in terms of the whole group, as in this example:

October 26, 2002
Dear Mr. Larue,
On behalf of the Bayview High School French Club, I want to thank
you for your fascinating presentation last night about study opportunities in France. Your talk has been the subject of lots of excited
conversation at school today, and several members are already
researching the programs in Arles and Paris that you mentioned.

We feel lucky that you were able to attend our meeting, and we
would very much like to invite you for another program, at your convenience.

Thank you again for your time and interest in our club.
Sincerely,
(Signature)
Jeremy Monroe
Corresponding Secretary

Thank-You Gifts

Gifts are often given to guest speakers and honorees at school and
public programs, even if the person receives a fee. These gifts need not
be expensive or elaborate. It's nice to give a token associated with the
sponsoring group or the event. Certificates or plaques are another
choice. Humorous gifts may be acceptable as long as the recipient is well
known and the gift is in good taste, but be sure the person will get the
joke and take it in good humor. Gifts are often presented during the
event, but can also be sent afterward with a thank-you note. In fact,
always send thank-you notes to a speaker or honoree, with or without a
gift.

It is inappropriate to give gifts to job interviewers or college personnel involved in college admissions. Gifts may be suspect in any situation when a teen (or an adult) is seeking attention or favor from someone.

In middle and high school, it is usually best to give gifts to teachers (if at all) only at the end of the school year. A "school's out" gift expresses gratitude after grades have been determined. Since students are not likely to give presents to all their teachers, giving at the end of the year avoids comparisons and possible hurt feelings among teachers who are left out. If holiday giving is the custom in your teen's school, holiday cards, charitable contributions in the teacher's name, or gifts for the classroom—a reference book or box of computer disks, for example—are practical options. Check with school administration about gift-giving policies.

Gifts from Houseguests

A gift for the host or hostess is expected when a teen is a houseguest. Gifts can be given on arrival or sent as soon as possible after the visit. The best choices are items that complement the host's or host family's interests and tastes. Teens may need a parent's suggestions when it comes to gift selection. Encourage your teen to think of what the recipient might like. The ability to select a fitting gift is a valuable social skill. In addition, your teen should always send a thank-you note after a visit.

Thank-you gifts and notes are not expected for overnights or routine visits to the homes of friends and family. But a gift out of the blue is always a treat. A teen might take a floral bouquet to his best friend's parents as an expression of thanks for their many kindnesses. Or he could mow his grandmother's lawn, free of charge, in gratitude for all the good times he has had at her house.

Get-Well Notes

Get-well notes, especially when the recipient is not seriously ill, tend to be brief and positive in tone. If the writer knows the person well, a note may include an offer of assistance, as this example illustrates:

Dear Malcolm,
I'm really sorry about your broken arm. Your sister said that you will be back at school next week, and I want to be the first to sign your

cast. If you need anything before then, please let me know. I'm making copies of my history and biology class notes for you.

Everyone misses you at school. See you next week.

Irene

Sympathy Letters

There is really only one rule when writing notes and letters of condolence after a death: Write what you feel. These letters are so personal that there is no right formula. Whether short or lengthy, condolence notes and letters should be the product of sincere feelings. A few guidelines, however, may help the teen who faces this difficult task.

- *Try not to dwell on the manner of the death.* Bereaved family members and friends do not need painful reminders.

- *Avoid remarks that imply that the death was a "blessing" or somehow a good thing.* Don't take this approach even if the death was a release from pain.

- *Focus on the life of the deceased person.* If a schoolmate has died, a teen might write about some aspect of the deceased per-

A Question for Peggy and Cindy

My daughter is conscientious about writing thank-you notes, but her handwriting is atrocious, and her notes are very hard to read. I haven't criticized her, but I was wondering if it is okay to type thank-you notes.

If your daughter's handwriting really is impossible to read, then yes, typing may be permissible, but notes must be signed by hand. Typed notes are not as personal and should be a last resort. Besides, very poor handwriting may be a bigger handicap. In college, for example, handwriting is required for tests, exams, and in-class essays, and instructors often will not grade what they cannot read. Before expressing concern, observe how your daughter writes. Investigate penmanship instruction. Speak with teachers or counselors who can probably suggest tutors, classes, or manuals for self-teaching. It will be easier to discuss the problem if you have some remedies to offer, and your daughter may be more receptive if you compliment her conscientiousness and the content of her writing. If she is willing to work on her penmanship, encourage her efforts and give her time to show improvement.

son's life that bereaved parents may not know about—her dedi-cation to a service club, for example, or her positive influence on younger students. The people who loved her will be comforted to learn what her life meant to her contemporaries.

- **Think about what you would like to say.** Then write it down. Don't worry about elegant language or eloquent phrases. Write from your heart.

- **Sign notes with your full name.** The person who receives the note is in a state of grief or shock and may not instantly recognize a first name, even though he knows the writer or sees her frequently.

Commercially printed condolence cards are an option, but should include at least a brief and personal handwritten expression of sympathy. When selecting a printed card, read the message carefully. The senti-ments should be appropriate to the situation and the person who has died and not include religious language that may offend the survivors.

Sympathy notes and letters are usually addressed to the person or people most closely related to the deceased: a parent or parents, spouse, eldest child if the deceased was a widow or widower. But notes can also be sent to the person whom the writer knows best. (If a teen's friend loses a parent, the teen will probably write directly to his friend.) If the writer did not know the deceased person but does know a surviving rela-tive, it is appropriate to send that person a note even though she may not be the closest relative.

Condolence notes and letters are generally sent around the time the death becomes known. But the news may be delayed when the deceased lived far away or an obituary was not published. It's never too late to express sympathy. A writer can briefly explain the delay ("I have just learned about the death of your mother last summer, and I wanted you to know how very sorry I am about your loss.") Then write as you would have done at the time of the death.

Replying to Condolences

When there is a death in a teen's family, the teen may be asked to help with acknowledgments of condolence notes. A teen probably won't write responses to notes addressed to his parents or older relatives but should reply to personal notes of condolence written to him. Response notes need not be long but should contain a heartfelt "thank you" to people who have expressed their sympathy.

Writing Business Letters

IN SCHOOL, YOUR TEEN IS likely to receive basic instruction in this essential form of communication, but unless he takes a technical secretarial course, his experience with the diverse types of business correspondence is probably limited. With each passing year, however, his opportunities to write business letters will increase—letters written for school and social groups; orders for consumer products; applications for employment; requests for information from colleges, universities, and technical training institutions; and cover letters to accompany applications and resumes. E-mail—though wonderful for casual communication—should be used sparingly and at the request of the recipient.

Composing Important Letters

Most business letters follow a streamlined formula, but they need not be stuffy or curt. The formats and etiquette of modern business correspondence have developed over time as a blend of efficiency and courtesy designed to accomplish the writer's and the reader's goals without a lot of fuss and bother.

The business section of bookstores, school and public libraries, and college and career counseling offices have guides with myriad examples of business correspondence including those all-important letters to colleges and potential employers. (Warn your teen not to copy a sample letter; business readers may have seen the same letter before and will recognize that it is not original.)

Business Letter Fundamentals

The fundamental principles listed here will serve as starting points for all effective and courteous business correspondence:

- *Brevity.* Business letters are generally short—usually no more than one page—in deference to the time and patience of the

There are times when sending a note is just a nice thing to do. If one of your teen's friends receives a special honor, it's courteous to send a note of congratulations. Or your teen might run across an article that will interest someone he knows. A note with the article enclosed is a pleasant way to say, "I am thinking of you."

These notes are often casual, quick messages—a few sentences to a couple of paragraphs in length. Writing a note like the example below demonstrates the writer's interest in and consideration for the person to whom he is writing.

Dear Kirstie,

I saw this article about your National Merit Scholarship and thought you might like an extra copy. I'm really proud of you and your achievements. This proves what we all know—that our friend Kirstie is one smart cookie.

Congratulations!

Doug

---

reader. Long, wordy letters are often put aside for later reading and then forgotten or even discarded.

- **Focus.** Business letters should be focused on a single point and should not digress into irrelevant issues. The subject of the letter should be introduced as quickly as possible and supported by information that makes the writer's case.

- **Clarity.** Business letters are not exercises in creative writing. Points are made and information is presented in clear, direct language—simple statements and questions that are easy to understand in a very quick reading. Don't use slang, overblown wording, or too many technical terms. It's a good idea to write a draft first, then read it aloud. Listen for any language that sounds unnatural, pretentious, or unclear.

The following example illustrates the key principles of brevity, focus, and clarity:

People rarely notice when their names are written correctly. But get it wrong, and the mistake almost jumps off the page. When writing business letters or sending e-mail, teens must check names, professional titles, courtesy titles, and even the gender of the person being addressed. If a company president or college dean is Pat J. Jones, don't assume that Pat is a man. Consult telephone listings, which may include full names (you can feel safe that P. Jane Jones is female); school or company directories; news articles; brochures; college handbooks and yearbooks; or annual business reports.

Alternatively, ask someone who knows the person, or call the person's office or business. Don't speak to the person directly; instead, ask a secretary or receptionist. Explain that you are writing to Pat J. Jones and don't know from the name if the person is a man or woman and that you would like the person's correct title. You can also inquire how the person prefers to be addressed: Miss, Mrs., Ms., Mr., Dr., Dean, or something else. Most personnel will be happy to help as long as you keep the call short and polite.

---

118 Crescent Court
Hilltop, Indiana 34567

October 9, 2002

Dr. Alice M. Carruthers,
Dean of Admissions
Upstate University
University City, Pennsylvania 12345

Dear Dean Carruthers:
I am a junior at Pleasant View High School in Hilltop, Indiana, and I plan to attend college in the fall of 2003. I am interested in learning more about Upstate University, especially your School of Engineering. I would also like to receive information about your early admission policies and application procedures.

Thank you very much for your help with my request. I look forward to reading more about the opportunities at Upstate.

Sincerely,
(Signature)
Jacob R. Huang

The writer has accomplished a great deal in just five sentences. He introduces himself and states his request politely but succinctly. He may well pique a university official's interest with the mention of a particular school and early admission. He concludes with polite expressions of appreciation and anticipation and ends with a courteous, professional closing.

- *Accuracy.* The information in any business letter must be checked and rechecked for accuracy and completeness.

- *Professionalism.* Business letters should be professional in tone and content. Inexperienced writers are often tempted to include unnecessary personal information and opinions or to relate lengthy stories that illustrate a point. Letters that bespeak professional courtesy often get attention before the rambling ones.

- *Grammar and spelling.* Perhaps the fastest way to lose out on a job opportunity or wind up at the bottom of the college applications is to write an ungrammatical, poorly worded letter with misspellings. Bad grammar and incorrect spelling call into question the writer's diligence, attention to detail, and seriousness of purpose.

A Teen's First Resume

A resume is a summary listing of a person's employment and education history. No one expects a teen to have a lengthy resume, but creating one now is good practice and can be helpful with job hunting. The resume begins with the writer's full name, address, and phone number at the top of the page. Jobs, then schools, are listed in chronological order beginning with the most recent. Information about sex, race, health status, and religious affiliation are not included, because employers cannot as a rule discuss these issues with applicants.

Since a teen has had little chance for formal employment, he should list jobs like babysitting and yard mowing and the names and addresses of his past employers. He can include volunteer service that is relevant. He should list his high school and middle school or schools and addresses. Under education history, the teen can include some of his memberships and honors.

Generally, business letters are typed or printed on good-quality white or cream paper (8½ by 11 inches), folded in thirds, and mailed in matching number 10 envelopes. Letters are always signed by hand, with the writer's full name typed below the signature. Letters can be handwritten as long as the handwriting is legible. When writing by hand, teens should avoid unprofessional flourishes (dotting I's with hearts or happy faces, for example, or using lots of exclamation points). Addresses on envelopes can be typed, printed, or handwritten. It is generally preferable for letters and envelopes to appear in the same format, but handwritten envelopes are acceptable. Whether written or printed, letters and envelopes should be clean, free of smudges, and unwrinkled.

It is common practice to include a "References available on request" notation at the bottom of the resume and leave it to an employer to ask for references or the names and phone numbers of people who can supply references.

Except when a resume is presented in an interview, it should always be accompanied by a cover letter—a brief and courteous business letter that explains why the resume is being sent. Teen resumes should be limited to one page, printed on good-quality white or cream paper, and easy to read. Studies have shown that employers and human resource personnel tend to spend less than a minute reviewing most resumes, so it's crucial that the information be clearly organized for easy scanning.

Letters of Reference

For college and job applications, your teen will probably need written references and recommendations from teachers, principals, clergy, club sponsors, coaches, volunteer organizers, and previous employers. Family friends can give recommendations, but their comments may carry less weight than those of people who have direct experience with a teen's work or study habits.

The etiquette of asking is simple: Talk to the person and explain that you would like a letter of reference. Tell the person how the letter will be used (sent out with applications, presented during or after interviews). Be sure the person understands that he or she may be contacted by an

Internet communications—e-mail, instant messaging, and chat rooms—are not very different from other forms of correspondence. Internet users should make their writing intelligible, refrain from using vulgarities and aggressive language, and never send harassing, threatening, or cruel messages. Most online communication is short and to the point, so save long jokes and stories for people you know well. Do not send or forward chain letters and solicitations. The ease of Internet communication lulls many users into verbal sloppiness, so check grammar, spelling, and punctuation before sending any messages. Always ask for permission before using someone else's computer equipment or Internet account, and never use another person's password.

Teens should know that Internet communications might not be private. Employers generally have the legal right to monitor communications generated on office computers. Despite security safeguards, it's easy to forward e-mail without the writer's permission, so don't write what you don't want the world to read. Guides to the specifics of "netiquette" are available and worth investigating.

---

employer or admissions office, so the letter should include an address and phone number.

Teens and parents should never pressure anyone to give a reference or dictate the contents. Some people simply do not like to write reference and recommendation letters but may be willing to be listed as a reference. Others are uncomfortable referring young people whom they have employed only briefly or do not know well. If a person is hesitant or refuses, be gracious. Don't demand to know his reasoning. Thank him for considering your request and let the matter drop.

High Schoolers and Speech

DURING A TEEN'S HIGH SCHOOL years, parents and primary care-givers should encourage the continued growth and refinement of spoken communication. You can help your teen expand his vocabulary and speaking skills through conversation about issues beyond the usual domestic subjects. Look for opportunities for adult-to-adult talk. (See

"Keeping Communication Open," page 352). Invite your teen to accompany you to the occasional lecture, speech, or play at which he can experience the power of language used well. Promote reading for pleasure, and try to guide your teen to both classical and contemporary literature that he will enjoy and learn from. Compliment his phrase-making and positive speaking and writing habits and even quote him when you have the chance. ("I like the way Hank refers to his car as 'the dream machine.' That's just how I felt when I bought my first car.")

At this age, young people are likely to use a lot of slang among themselves. But most teens are beginning to understand that different situations call for different levels of communication. Through instinct and a certain amount of trial and error, they quickly learn that slang is not acceptable when speaking to a college recruiter or an employer. They will also see that correct speech and writing create positive impressions and tend to achieve their desired results.

On the Phone

THE IMPORTANCE OF THE PHONE to teens cannot be understated. It is their lifeline, sanctuary, and escape route. Cognitively, a high schooler is better equipped than a preteen or young teen to discuss and negotiate limits that are mutually satisfactory. As he progresses through high school, his telephone use may actually decrease as his time is increasingly devoted to other interests. But some rules and limits must be enforced. It's a good idea to renegotiate phone use when your teen enters high school and revisit the issue as his pattern of phone use changes.

- **Timing.** Times for placing calls will probably remain a sensitive issue. High schoolers are often night owls, but consideration for others requires that times for calling be restricted. Exceptions can be made—if you know that your teen's best friend has a private line and that a ringing phone will not disturb the friend's family, then late calls might be open for negotiation. You have the right to restrict late calls into your home and to limit or restrict calls at other times—the dinner hour or weekend mornings—when peace and quiet are important to you. A teen who understands that your limits are reasonable will tell his friends not to call during those times.

Teens and many adults are prone to speech habits that mar their messages and distract and annoy listeners. Sometimes the habit is a sound—"um" or "er" or "huh." Or it may be a word or phrase—"like," "you know," "see what I mean"—or even a vulgarity. Many people use these sounds, words, or phrases repeatedly to fill in the natural pauses or gaps in ordinary speaking.

Annoying speech habits can spread like wildfire through a teen peer group. Parents can help by pointing out the problem. Be sensitive and don't refer to the speech habit around others. Explain that these speech "fillers" are very common and that most people (maybe even you) use them unconsciously. You might suggest that your teen tape some of his casual conversations and listen to his speech, which is an exercise that many speech teachers use. Often young people will begin to correct the habit when they become aware of it, so once you have raised the issue, give your teen a chance to work on it. If the filler is a vulgarity, however, correct him until he breaks the habit. Teach your teen that short, silent pauses in speech—like punctuation in sentences—assist the speaker to make his points clearly and help the listener to understand.

- **Duration.** Limits on the duration of calls may no longer be necessary, but a drop in grades or failure to complete household chores on a regular basis, for example, might be good reasons to restrict phone use (or non-school-related computer time) for a period. When imposing restrictions, talk seriously with your teen about time management and determining his priorities.

- **Messages.** The basic courtesies of answering and taking phone messages may need reinforcement. Teens, especially if they have their own phone line, may ignore calls that they know are not for them or fail to take or deliver messages. Be clear that when the phone rings and the answering machine isn't on, the person nearest the phone should pick up and answer politely, summon the person called, or offer to take a message. Unless he is at home alone, your teen shouldn't turn on the answering machine without your knowledge. When he takes a message, he must deliver it or put it where family members can find it easily, and others will do the same for him.

- **Call waiting.** If you have call waiting, your teen should know not to ignore incoming calls when he is on the phone. Review the polite ways to interrupt a conversation when there is a call waiting on the line. Be clear that when a call is for you or another adult, your teen is to end his call and hand over the phone unless you have given him other instructions. (See "Call Waiting," page 242).

- **Location.** Cordless phones are convenient, but it is rude for anyone to carry on a phone conversation where others are socializing, reading, or watching television. Your teen must also understand that he can't demand privacy when others are present; no one should be expected to leave a family area just because he wants to use the phone.

  It is also inconsiderate to talk to someone else while talking on the phone. If your teen has to speak to someone in the room, he should explain to the caller, excuse himself politely, and put the caller on hold or cover the phone mouthpiece. If the conversation with the person in the room is likely to last more than a minute or two, he should tell the person on the phone that he will call back, give a timeframe if possible, and make the return call without fail. On the other hand, when your teen must interrupt someone using the phone, he should signal or give the person a note, then wait quietly. You probably need to clarify what constitutes a real cause to interrupt. A kitchen fire is an emergency; a call to check in with his girlfriend is not.

Cell Phone Etiquette

Since your teen may now have legitimate reasons to use a cell phone—yours, his own, or possibly an employer's—rules are needed. Some issues may be negotiable, including when he will be allowed to have your cell phone and whether he will be responsible for all or part of his expenses. Because cell phone etiquette is a major issue, you may want to add other limits, but these basic courtesies are a place to start:

- Cell phones should always be turned off in public places and anywhere people are trying to pay attention, including private

Whenever someone is on the phone, children and teens should know not to hover or hang around. Often, a home phone is in a location where people naturally gather, and the person on the phone cannot easily get to a private spot. When a call comes in, others should lower their voices immediately, turn down music or television, and give the person on the phone some elbow room. When someone is using a public telephone, whether or not it is in an enclosed booth, people waiting to make calls and bystanders should stand at least several feet away from the caller and refrain from loud talking, noise making, or showing signs of impatience. Never honk horns, shout, or crank up the music when in line at a drive-up public phone.

social gatherings. The same consideration applies to beepers, watches with timers, and any other device that is likely to disturb others.

- Cell phones should not be taken into school or to work. If a cell phone is necessary for a job, the employer should provide one.

- When on public sidewalks, walkways, jogging paths, and the like, the caller should find an out-of-the-way place in order not to interfere with other people. Do not use cell phones on escalators and in elevators.

- Cell phones and car phones should not be used when driving except in real emergencies. Use phones only when the car is stopped and parked in a safe location.

Set the example, and encourage your teen to practice good cell phone manners at all times. Having a cell phone is not a sign of maturity; using it responsibly and with consideration is.

The Costs of Calling

Teens should understand that someone must pay whenever they make a call. When negotiating phone privileges, it's a good idea to get out your phone bills and go over the many types of charges for which you are responsible each month. Your teen will probably be surprised by the fees, taxes, and service charges on the average local-calling bill. If he is begging for a private line, he should understand that the basic costs for your current phone service will be doubled by the addition of

If you have more than one teen or preteen in the house, phone negotiations can be tricky. It may be best to talk with your children separately first and listen closely to what each has to say. These advance chats will enable you to anticipate problems. Siblings might want access to the phone at the same time, for instance, or one may need a disproportionate amount of time due to a special school or club responsibility. Knowing what might arise, you'll be better prepared to offer solutions.

When you begin to negotiate, make your expectations clear from the outset. If a younger child accuses you of favoritism, explain that phone privileges are related to age and responsibility. Your older teen may get more time on the phone, but he also has more duties at home. Have each child review the details of your agreement, so you will know that they understand their individual privileges and restrictions. Talk about "what if?" possibilities. What if one sibling is on the phone with a friend and the other needs to use the Internet or call for a school assignment? Discussing possibilities will encourage your teens to think through problems and settle conflicts between themselves. Be open to renegotiation as your children grow. Even when an older sibling goes away to college or moves out on his own, there will be times—holidays and other home visits—when phone privileges are again up for debate.

---

a new line. Faced with the financial facts, he might rethink his promise to pay for his own line and settle for an extension instead. Carefully review long-distance costs. Show him how charges are tallied by time of day, length of calls, and the distance between callers. Explain peak and low-rate times and the cost difference between direct and collect dialing.

You can continue the lesson by reviewing monthly phone bills together, checking that his long-distance calls have been charged correctly. (Do this particularly if he has agreed to pay for all or part of his long-distance use.) You might encourage your teen to keep a log of his calls. Logging for even a few weeks should give him a better idea of how much time he spends on the phone and promote consideration for others every time he makes a call.

Speaking in Public

SOME SCHOOLS MAINTAIN THE TRADITIONS of requiring oral reports and involving all students in school presentations or declamations. But most young people can escape even the most rudimentary public speaking until they reach college or hold jobs that require them to participate in presentations. Yet the ability to stand in front of others and speak with confidence is vital in higher education, the workplace, and civic and social life. Giving a toast to the bride and groom at a wedding reception or introducing a guest at the PTA meeting is as much an act of speech making as addressing Congress.

Public speaking is a skill learned and enhanced through practice. If your teen's school doesn't offer instruction, investigate your area's community college and nonprofit and commercial programs. Consider taking a course with your teen. A reputable provider will offer practice, positive reinforcement, and good advice about appropriate content, delivery styles, and the etiquette expectations for speakers, audience members, and event organizers.

CHAPTER 29

The Etiquette of Entertaining

YOUR TEEN HAS PROBABLY MASTERED the fundamentals of table manners, and you can now count on her to behave graciously when she dines out and you are not around. The time has arrived to teach the finer points of entertaining, both as host and guest. Successful entertaining is an art best learned through practice, so parents can help teens acquire the necessary skills by welcoming (but by no means forcing) opportunities to host various occasions.

When Teens Are Hosts

EXPLAIN TO YOUR TEEN THAT the primary goal of entertaining is providing for the pleasure and comfort of guests. Planning and effort are required, but no event should be so wearisome that the host or hostess is worn out; guests can't enjoy themselves when their host is clearly stressed or exhausted.

Casual parties may be the best way to start. A teen who gains confidence by entertaining friends in the comfort of home will be better equipped to take on more elaborate events in the future. You can introduce your teen to the demands of large gatherings and formal parties by letting her assist when you entertain and by involving her in preparations for school and social events such as academic and athletic banquets, alumni reunions, and fundraising events.

Ideas for Entertaining

For all their inventiveness, teenagers may hesitate to veer too far from the type of parties that everyone else is having. Parents can encourage some creative thinking, especially if their teen and her friends are growing bored with pizza-and-pop-music parties every weekend.

How about a picnic at home or a local park? A major TV event such as the Academy Awards can be a good excuse for a party. It's nice to follow a school-related activity, from a big game to the science fair, with a wrap-up party. You don't have to have a baseball diamond to host a sports party; volleyball, badminton, table tennis, even croquet are fun and don't require much athletic ability. Teens may be intrigued by a party idea associated with a worthy cause—come for dinner and bring an item of used clothing for the local homeless or abused women's shelter. Or plan lunch at your home before an afternoon of volunteer work.

Teens might enjoy a little formality occasionally—a sit-down luncheon or dinner. Holiday gatherings and teas or coffees are nice ways to introduce out-of-town visitors or to honor returning college friends. The traditional holidays can provide party themes, or your teen may be interested in a party that celebrates her ethnic heritage or the customs and foods of a country or culture that interests her.

Planning and Preparation

If your teen likes to cook, preparing food is a wonderful way for you to work together. Even a teen with little kitchen experience should be expected to help. Here are some ideas for sharing party duties and promoting personal responsibility:

- **Encourage your teen to plan the menu.** Get out the cookbooks and recipe files, and let her develop her ideas. Be ready to provide suggestions and some clear guidelines. Even teens who have never helped with meals at home can understand that feeding guests raises issues including cost, quantity, and scheduling of preparation time.

- **Work out a budget together.** Groceries are just one of the costs of throwing a party. Does she want to purchase flowers and decorations? What about napkins, paper plates, charcoal for grilling out, and bags of ice?

- **Let your teen do some or all of the shopping.** Work with her on how much to buy and how to select quality ingredients. Shopping for groceries is a good chance to introduce teens to food suppliers other than the supermarket—stores that specialize in foods from other cultures, health food stores, and bulk-item outlets—and to practice the discipline of sticking to a shopping list.

- **Avoid too many exotic or untried dishes.** Teen tastes tend to be conservative, so a complete menu of unfamiliar foods can be off-putting. Adding one or two new items to a familiar menu is better. Your teen might host an Italian dinner and introduce her guests to antipasti for starters but serve tried-and-true spaghetti Bolognese and garlic bread for the entree.

- **Let her do some of the cooking.** Help with the food preparation, but let your teen do as much of the cooking as she can manage. If she has school and other responsibilities to attend to, include a number of party dishes that can be completed or partially completed in advance.

Issuing Invitations

INVITATIONS SHOULD REFLECT THE NATURE of the event, from a phone call for a casual backyard barbecue to a printed or engraved third-person invitation to a graduation party or formal presentation ball. Informal invitations can be as creative as the host desires. Invitations by e-mail appeal to today's wired generation, but teens need to be considerate of friends who are not on the Internet. Whatever the look of the invitation, these basics are essential:

- Name or names of host or hosts. (If several teens are hosting, list the names alphabetically.)

Teens should take their friends' special food needs or restrictions into account when planning party menus. For vegetarians, your teen can include a hearty grain or vegetable casserole and an extra salad or have soy patties on hand for grilling. In advance of the party, he should ask a guest who follows a restricted diet about food choices, or parents can talk to the guest's parents.

What if your own teen has special food needs? If she is the only guest or one of a few, inform the host of any dietary restrictions. If your teen is attending a large party, the issue shouldn't be brought up. If your teen has any doubts about ingredients in food being served, she should ask what they are or refrain from eating the item.

There are some people a host can never please. Parents of persnickety eaters should encourage their teens to try everything and not to voice their complaints when they are someone's guest.

- Nature of the occasion, including any special expectations such as wearing costumes
- Location, date, and time of the event
- Request for reply (RSVP), if desired. Be sure to include the host's mailing address and/or telephone number and/or e-mail address or response card. Response cards are generally used only for very large events
- Any necessary instructions, such as written directions to the party location or a map

Invitations by phone should include all the preceding information. The invitee will usually accept or regret during the call (or soon afterward), so a written response isn't needed.

Inviting at School

Casual invitations can be issued at school, but parents need to discuss tact. As when they were younger, teens should not offer invitations during class time or whenever people who are not invited are around. There are usually opportunities during the school day to seek out invitees on their own. Written invitations should be mailed.

Invitations that are clever or hilarious to teens may be offensive to others. Without being intrusive, you should approve a sample invitation. If the issue of good taste arises, talk with your teen about the difference between wit and crudeness. Explain that any invitation he sends is also a reflection on you. Here's a good rule for teens to follow: Never send an invitation that can't be posted on the guest's refrigerator for the whole family to see.

Phoned invitations have their own etiquette considerations. It is important to present the invitation in a straightforward manner. ("Hi, Craig. This is Margy. I'm having a picnic at my house on Saturday afternoon, and I hope you can come. Please bring a date if you like.") Never open with a remark such as "What are you doing Saturday afternoon?" The invitee has no idea what the caller wants and, frankly, may answer quite differently to a party invitation than to a request to help clean the caller's garage.

Other invitation do's and don'ts include:

- **Don't pressure an invitee to say yes.** If the person has a potential conflict, ask him to let you know as soon as possible if he can attend. (If the invitation is very casual, good friends may leave an acceptance up in the air, but "come if you can" should be used sparingly.)

- **Do be clear when the invitee can bring a date or guest.** If a written invitation does not specify that guests are included, the invitee should know not to show up with anyone. In phone invitations, you can convey that dates are not included without being brusque. ("I'm giving a party next week, and it's just for us girls" or "I'm getting the guys together at my house Thursday afternoon for touch football and dinner.") Don't pressure an invitee to bring a date or to be set up with a partner if guests are invited.

- **Do provide suggestions about gifts if a guest asks.** Very rarely is gift information included in a written invitation, and teenagers may be confused about when a gift is expected. A host should never dictate gift giving, but it is permissible to offer suggestions when asked. Be conscious of other teens' financial limitations.

- **Do be clear when gifts are not expected.** If a teen hosts an event where gifts are traditional, such as a birthday party, let guests know if gifts are not expected.

- **Don't expect guests to bring food or other provisions.** If a guest asks to bring food or drinks, it's okay to suggest something that is not expensive or too elaborate. But if extra provisions are not needed, refuse the offer politely. If a guest really is anxious to help, you might suggest a reasonable alternative. ("We have all the food, but could you bring a couple of your rhythm-and-blues tapes?")

- **Do be clear about special requests and expectations.** If you want guests to wear costumes or bring music, for example, include the information in your invitation. Make sure that requests are reasonable and convenient. It is often best to make your requests optional. ("Don't forget your suit if you want to swim" for a pool party.) Special requests can be part of a printed invitation or added as a personal note.

When to Invite

As a rule, the timing of invitations depends on the amount of advance preparation required by guests (inviting a date, buying gifts, finding the right attire) and on the level of other activities at the time of the event. (Winter holiday calendars may be crowded with social events. National holidays and days of religious significance can also present social conflicts.) There are no exact rules, but it's important not to be too early or too late. If you mention an event to a friend months ahead of schedule, be sure to follow up with an invitation at the appropriate time.

Invitations issued within days of all but the most casual get-togethers are likely to result in a very short guest list. Custom and common practice in your community and the exact nature of the event will influence your deadlines. The following suggestions are intended as common-sense guidelines for popular teen occasions and not carved-in-stone rules:

TYPE OF EVENT	TIMEFRAME FOR SENDING INVITATIONS
Formal dinner party or dance	3 to 6 weeks
Informal dinner party or dance	A few days to 3 weeks
Holiday party	3 weeks to 1 month
Rite-of-passage parties (bar mitzvah, bat mitzvah, *quinceañera*, sweet sixteen, etc.)	1 month
Graduation party	3 to 6 weeks
Prom	3 to 6 weeks
Birthday party	A few days to 3 weeks
Luncheon or tea	A few days to 3 weeks
Picnic or pool party	Last minute to 2 weeks

The Duties of Hosting

THERE IS NO MAGIC FORMULA for successful entertaining. A host or hostess sets the tone; when she is being congenial, having a good time, and acting out of consideration for others, her guests will almost always follow suit and enjoy themselves. Yes, there will be times when a party does not go as expected—when the guests who your teen thought would get along so well don't hit it off, for example. But part of the fun of entertaining is a certain degree of unpredictability. Teens need experience as hosts in order to learn how to handle unanticipated problems with confidence. The following duties and responsibilities are fundamental, so review them with your teen.

- **Be ready.** When entertaining at home, the bulk of the food should be prepared and last-minute cooking and serving tasks assigned. Tables, place settings, and decorations should be ready well in advance. Parents can help teens list tasks that need to be completed before guests arrive and check off all details. A host or hostess should never be late, so plan time for dressing and a few extra minutes to relax before the doorbell begins to ring. Don't count on guests to arrive late.

- **Greet all guests personally.** A host or hostess should leave other guests—excusing herself politely but immediately—whenever

Whether a teen's response to an invitation is yea or nay, he should reply as soon as possible, preferably within forty-eight hours. There are two exceptions: (1) If the invitation includes a "Regrets Only" notation, a response is required only if the invitee cannot attend. (2) If the invitation includes no request for a reply, it is not necessary to respond, although it's considerate to inform the host if the invitee is unable to attend.

To reply, follow instructions included on the invitation. When an RSVP includes a mailing address, reply in writing. If a phone number is included, call. If an address, phone number, and perhaps an e-mail address are provided, the invitee has the option of replying by mail, phone call, or electronically. Generally a formal invitation requires a formal response (see "Accepting and Regretting," page 301, for more guidelines).

What if a teen can't reply immediately? Perhaps he has a tentative appointment for a college interview that will conflict with a friend's party, but the date may shift. He should call the host, explain the situation, and respond as soon as possible. If the host needs to know the precise number of guests attending, the teen may have to decline.

---

there is a knock or ring at the door. Even if someone else answers the door, your teen should be on the spot to meet and greet. Parents may be tempted to handle the greeting duties but shouldn't.

- *Make introductions.* Teens should be used to this courtesy by now, but in the rush of greeting many guests, they may forget or become preoccupied. When a person who doesn't know other guests arrives, it is nice to introduce the newcomer to one or two friends and ask those friends to continue making introductions. Think ahead, choose friends who are reliable and friendly, and prepare them in advance.

- *Be on the lookout for guests who are alone and on the sidelines.* The fundamental duty of hosting is to make every guest feel included and at ease. If a guest is on his own, the host should introduce him to others—even if you've made initial introductions—and draw him into conversation. Look for people with whom the guest may have common interests. ("Larry, have you met my cousin Randy? Randy is a first-string lineman

Parents should always be present but not obtrusive when teens host parties at home or in other locations. Helping in the kitchen or manning the barbecue grill is a good way to be available, visible, and inconspicuous. Offer to serve, but don't be offended if your teen prefers to handle service in his own way. Don't join the party unless your own teen extends the invitation, but be ready to talk with teens who seek you out. (Adult chaperones are often a safe refuge for shy or ill-at-ease teen guests.) The point is to let your teen and his guests know that you haven't abandoned your house to them. You can also help your teen deal with difficulties that may arise— from ordering extra pizzas to managing party crashers. Stay up to the end and remain alert. You have the right and the moral obligation to act quickly if you suspect real problems, such as alcohol or drug use or arguments that threaten to get out of control. As a nonnegotiable rule, be firm that your teen is not to entertain at home unless you or adults you designate are present.

for the Central High junior varsity. Maybe you guys have played each other.")

- **Be attentive to guests' comfort.** Put coats away. See that guests have food and drinks. Keep bowls of munchies filled, and clear away used glasses and containers. Politely and quietly point out bathrooms and periodically check and replenish bathroom supplies including soap, towels, toilet paper, and facial tissues. Make sure the music isn't too loud for conversation. (Parents may have to remind the host to lower the volume before it reaches disturbing-the-peace proportions.)

- **Keep the party on schedule.** Even in casual settings, meals should be served on time. A few minutes' delay is probably okay, but more than fifteen minutes is not.

  Give guests warning when the time to go is approaching. Unlike adults, teen hosts and their parents must be attentive to curfews. The host can announce one last song and then turn off the music when the song is done. Turning lights to bright is another signal that the party has come to its close. If a few guests seem determined to linger, the appearance of parents will usually hasten their departure.

- **See that guests leave safely.** Be sure that everyone has a ride home. If someone has managed to sneak in alcohol or to use drugs, do not let them drive. (Teens may or may not be able to handle an inebriated guest, so parents should be ready to take control.)

- **Clean up afterward.** Following an evening party, teens and parents may elect to do major cleaning the next day. But before going to bed, teen hosts should see that food is put away, dirty dishes removed to the kitchen, spills wiped up and stains treated if need be, trash and general clutter removed from family areas, and the house made habitable.

Being a Good Guest

GUESTS, LIKE HOSTS, HAVE OBLIGATIONS. Your teen has attended many parties over the years, but now she's ready for a new level of sophistication. You can still give etiquette reminders, but teens may ignore or take offense at too much instruction. Talk about party manners generally, including the following etiquette points, when you have the opportunity, but not five minutes before your teen is ready to leave for an event. Emphasize that good manners are expected no matter how well your teen knows the host or how familiar she is with the host's home.

- **Arrive on time.** If the party is scheduled to start "around six o'clock," don't show up at 5:45 when the host may still be in the shower. "Around six" means at six or a few minutes later. Arriving more than ten or fifteen minutes after the scheduled starting time is generally considered late. If you are late, apologize. If something happens that will detain you by more than a half-hour, such as a flat tire, call the host if you can. You don't want the host to become worried or to delay serving a meal because everyone is waiting for you.

- **Say "hello" to parents and chaperones.** More than likely, parents will be helping with cooking or serving, but they will enjoy a friendly greeting and brief chat. (If hired servers or caterers are present, be courteous and say "please" and "thank you," but don't try to engage employees in conversation. They have jobs to do.)

- **Enter into the spirit of the event.** Introduce yourself to guests you don't know. Join in conversation and include others. Make an effort to circulate rather than staying with the same people for the duration of the party. Never whisper, make disparaging remarks about others, or do anything to deliberately exclude other guests. You may not want to join in planned activities, but you can always be an enthusiastic bystander.

- **Be careful of property.** In other people's homes, guests have the responsibility to take care of furniture and possessions. Wipe wet or muddy feet before entering the house. At swimming parties or after sweaty activities, change into dry clothes before entering the main areas of the house; be careful about where you place wet bathing suits or towels. Don't put feet—with or without shoes—on tables or chairs. Avoid putting beverage glasses, bottles, or cans directly on furniture surfaces. Ask for a drink coaster or use a napkin under drink glasses. If your host needs to move furniture to clear space for dancing, pitch in and help. If you accidentally break a glass or drop food on the carpet, tell your host immediately, assist with the cleanup, and offer to replace the item or pay for replacement, repair, or cleaning. Just don't try to hide the damage.

- **Never smoke in someone else's home.** This rule applies even if you know that the host's parents smoke. In addition to the health hazards, cigarette smoke pollutes the environment, can inflame the allergies of other guests, and leaves behind unpleasant odors in drapes, carpets, and upholstery. If you must smoke, go outside; neatly and safely dispose of ashes and cigarette butts.

- **Never bring alcohol, illegal or dangerous substances, or weapons of any kind into someone else's home.** This is an absolute. No one has the right to put others in physical, moral, and legal jeopardy. Also, do not be tempted into any activity you

Being a guest in someone's home is not an invitation to investigate. No snooping in drawers, cabinets, closets, closed containers, and medicine chests. No opening closed doors or entering rooms that are clearly not part of the party area. No wandering outside when the party is inside. It's fine to look at what is in plain sight—magazines, books, the host's CD or video collection—but it's smart not to pick up fragile or valuable items. You can compliment the host family's collection of art or antiques, but don't ask about the cost. Good guests exercise common sense and don't intrude where they are not invited.

◀◆

know to be wrong. It's hard to tell on others, but you have a responsibility to inform your host when anything dangerous or illegal is taking place. Take the host or hostess aside and speak to her privately. If you can't bring yourself to name names, at least let her know what is happening. If your host is participating in the wrongdoing, your best choice is to make a graceful departure.

- **Ask permission to use the host's telephone.** Do not make long-distance calls unless you charge them to your home number or phone card or reverse the charges. Turn off your cell phone. Do not leave the host's phone number with other people (except your family) and expect the host to answer calls for you.

  If you must use a cell phone—to arrange for a ride home, for example—find a place where you won't disturb others. Guests who spend much time on the phone or use cell phones during a party are quite often showing off for others. They may be trying to make themselves look important, but the effect is to annoy others with their lack of consideration.

- **Mind the basic courtesies.** When your host or hostess announces that a meal is being served, proceed to the table or line up at the buffet or picnic table. If others are slow to respond, take the lead. Being first in a serving line doesn't mean that you are greedy; it signals that you know how to be polite. If you serve yourself at a meal, take reasonable—not heaping—portions of food. Hosts try to put out enough food for everyone to get a serving of everything on the first go-round. You can always return to the buffet or say "yes" to an offer of second helpings.

Another basic for guests involves bathroom manners. Rinse the sink after washing hands, hang hand towels unfolded on the towel rack, be sure paper towels are in the wastebasket, and lower the toilet seat and lid. Leave the bathroom tidy for the next guest.

- **Be conscious of noise levels.** Your host's neighbors do not want to hear loud music or yelling late into the evening. When you sense that the noise is getting out of control, tell your

---

A Question for Peggy and Cindy

Last week, my son Chris had to turn down an invitation to a buddy's seventeenth birthday party because we had planned a family vacation. But now we are postponing the trip. Chris really wants to go to the party, but he's worried his friend will think he changed his mind because a better option fell through. Is there a polite way to manage this kind of situation?

Indeed, there is. If the birthday party is going to be a casual affair and attending will not alter the host's plans, Chris should call his friend now, tell him about the postponed vacation, and ask if he can change his regret to an acceptance. Since your son isn't responsible for the change in plans, he has nothing to feel guilty about. Changing a reply from "no" to "yes" often depends on the nature of the occasion. When the party is a formal, catered affair or a seated dinner, the number of guests is limited; then it's best not to ask to be included after regretting.

On the other hand, illness or a real emergency is really the only excuse to cancel an acceptance to an event. Should teens have to change a "yes" to a "no," the polite procedure is to call the host immediately, explain, and express genuine regret.

---

friends to lower the volume. If your approach is a jovial and all-inclusive "Hey, we'd better pipe down before the neighbors complain," everyone should quiet down without much difficulty.

- **Leave on time.** Keep an eye on the time and be prepared to depart when the party ends. Your host may announce a last dance or song, but after that, guests should not beg for more. If the host is a good friend, you might offer to stay a little longer and help clean up, but don't insist. If you are driving other guests, be mindful of their curfews and plan enough time after leaving the party to get everyone home safely.

CHAPTER 30

The Challenging World

---------◄←

FOR ALL THEIR ASSERTIVENESS AND self-assurance, teenagers can be very fragile. Some of the best qualities of youth—idealism, trust in others, and openness to experimentation and change—can also make them vulnerable. But since older teens can't and won't be coddled, your job will shift from teaching explicit rules of mannerly behavior to preparing your teen for new situations, helping him adapt etiquette fundamentals to new experiences and apply the principles he has been learning to a much wider world of people and expectations. Since you often will not be at his side, your model and support will grow in importance. Confronted with challenging choices, some of which will be uncomfortable or dangerous, your teen can now turn to you in his mind and ask himself, "How would Mom handle this?" or "What would Dad do?" Your influence need not wane even when your physical presence does.

Licensed to Drive

GETTING A DRIVER'S LICENSE IS perhaps *the* symbol of adulthood to American teenagers—the first official recognition that the teen is no longer a child. Even teens who have little or no opportunity to drive may be anxious to get a license as a symbol of their new status.

Parents, however, often have mixed feelings. When a teen gets his license, he can take on more driving duties for himself and the family, and a parent's constant chauffeuring will taper off. But you will worry about his safety and possibly his competence. It's important not to let his driving sneak up on you. Begin talking with your teen about driving as soon as he shows interest and start preparing him for the responsibilities he will be accepting. To most teens, driving means freedom, and parents or primary caregivers must temper a young person's enthusiasm with some large doses of realism.

Some teens may need encouragement to take the big step, but parents should never push driving on a reluctant teen. You can ease a young person's anxiety by listening to his fears or worries, letting him learn at his own pace, and perhaps evaluating your own attitude. Are you an anxious driver, and is he picking up on your fears? Are you the best driving teacher, or might he benefit from more objective instruction?

Whether your teen is ready to show up at the motor vehicles station at dawn on his sixteenth birthday or prefers to delay, you will want him fully prepared for all his new obligations, including the essentials of on-the-road etiquette.

Who Teaches?

Although parents often harbor the dream of instructing their teen, many decide that the best teacher is someone else and turn to professionals. Driver's education is widely available through schools, and private instruction may also be an option.

If you choose someone else as primary teacher, you can still contribute to the process. Like any learned skill, driving requires practice, so be available to your teen. Help him find safe places for practice drives. Read your teen's driving manual; then go over the information with him and help him prepare for the written exam. There is a good chance that your state's driving laws and licensing restrictions have changed significantly since you were sixteen. Be sure your teen understands that driving is a privilege and not a right.

Driver's Ed Manners

Reinforce the seriousness of driver's education and other forms of vehicle instruction including motorbike and boat safety classes. Whoever is teaching, your teen should be expected to adhere to these manners guidelines:

- **Respect the instructor.** Professional driving teachers are too frequently the subject of ridicule among teens and in teen-oriented entertainment. But a teen with a positive attitude toward his driving teacher is more likely to benefit from the instruction and become a careful and courteous driver.

- **Pay attention to the instructor and follow directions.** Whatever teens may think, they do *not* know more than the instructor. Your teen should not insist on driving in ways or under conditions that he isn't ready for. Teens should feel free to ask for help but not to question the instructor's judgment.

- **Be prepared for lessons.** Dress comfortably but appropriately, wear proper shoes for driving, and be careful about personal hygiene and heavy scents. Teens who need glasses for driving should have the right eyewear with them.

- **Be quiet when others are driving.** Some teens suffer from over-confidence behind the wheel, but most are nervous and try hard to focus on both the road and their instructor. Cutting up is clearly not permissible. Talking in normal tones, asking questions, or whispering can be just as distracting to the instructor and another driver. Never comment on or joke about another's driving.

Your Rules of the Road

Getting a license does not make any driver proficient, and there are many situations that a teen's new license does not equip him to handle. Your principal concern will be the safety of your teen and anyone who rides with him. As with all discipline at this age, teens are more likely to agree to restrictions when expanded driving privileges are related to age and responsible behavior. Areas where parents will normally exercise their authority include:

It's extremely important to be punctual for driving lessons, whether your teen is the only student or one of a group. Showing up late for a class inconveniences the teacher and often means that other students do not receive their fair share of driving and instruction time. If your teen must be late or absent, he should notify the instructor as soon as possible. If you are teaching, be clear that your teen is not to leave you waiting and should always call if he is delayed. Show him the same consideration if you must be late for a planned lesson.

- **When your teen can drive.** Scheduling use of the family car can be a source of conflict if expectations are not clear from the outset. Teens should participate in scheduling discussions. Some parents limit a new driver's solo excursions to daylight hours and ride with their teen at night until they feel he is competent. (By restricting driving hours or night driving, a parent can also save a teen who is the first in his crowd to get his license from becoming the unpaid taxi driver for friends.)

- **What he can drive.** If you have more than one vehicle, decide which he may drive. Even if your teen has his own car, you will probably set limits on use and clarify expectations about proper care and maintenance of the vehicle. Agree on responsibilities including keeping gas in the tank, checking tire pressure, cleaning out the car after using it, keeping up with routine maintenance schedules, and so on.

- **Where he can drive.** Inexperienced drivers often do best by mastering familiar surroundings first. You may want to limit your new driver's range and accompany him in new situations. For example, if you live in a rural or suburban community, you probably want to be with him when he begins to drive in congested city traffic.

- **Vehicle safety rules.** A parent may assume that a teen has the rules down pat, but it's a good idea to review and reinforce your expectations: safety belts buckled at all times for the driver and *all* passengers, eyes on the road, defensive driving, and so forth. Discuss and clarify who and how many may ride with your teen.

When your teen is driving others, you have a right to know who will be in the car. Be very clear that your teen is not to allow anyone else to drive your or his car.

Passenger Guidelines for Teens

The minute one teen gets his driver's license or his own car, everyone in his crowd feels the freedom. Though usually well behaved when riding with adults, teens can become silly and raucous when a peer is driving. The combination of an inexperienced teen driver—who may be loath to correct his friends—and rambunctious passengers can have terrible consequences.

Be sure your teen understands that when riding with another teen, he is to act just as if you were driving the car. Until the novelty of independent driving and riding wears off—which may be quite some time in the future—parents should be prepared to do a good deal of reminding when it comes to these passenger considerations:

- *Safety comes first.* Always buckle up. No roughhousing, throwing objects, or making excessive noise that can distract the driver. Keep the volume on the radio, tape, and CD player to a reasonable level. Keep hands, arms, heads, and other body parts inside any moving vehicle.

- *The driver is always in control.* You will probably need to repeat and reinforce this basic rule. Be sure your teen understands that any driver, whether adult or teen, must have full control in a car.

- *Don't abuse the driver's privileges.* Teens should know not to ask or expect another teen to bend or break rules. If the teen driver must be home by a certain time or restrict his driving to a specific area, passengers should never tease, beg, or demand favors that will violate the driver's curfew and restrictions. Be considerate and do not ask for rides unless it is convenient for the driver.

- *Offer to pay for gasoline.* When teens spend a lot of time in other teens' vehicles, they should usually contribute to the costs. The offer to pay is not expected of dates and infrequent passengers, but a teen who regularly rides with another really ought to

Driving Under the Influence

Be firm; be clear. Driving under the influence of alcohol or drugs is never okay. Parents and teens should discuss this issue fully and often. Start talking long before your teen turns sixteen. Help her understand the danger to herself and others. How you approach the subject will depend in part on sensitivity to your teen's personality and previous behavior. (Is she a risk taker, for instance, or inclined to caution?) Keep in mind that highly responsible people can sometimes make bad choices. Parents want to discourage underage drinking and all drug use and to be clear about penalties for such behavior. But you also want your teen to know that *should* she drink or use drugs, she is never to drive.

This is a complex problem involving two issues: intoxication itself and driving while intoxicated. Strive for a balance. Be sure your teen understands the consequences for alcohol and drug use, but also be clear that you are ready to rescue her from a drinking/drug use and driving dilemma. She is more likely to call home and not drive (or not ride with someone under the influence) if she knows that you will come to her aid immediately and save the recriminations for later.

help with expenses. Teens can usually work out their own arrangements, but parents can advise if the young people aren't sure about a fair amount.

- **Don't litter.** Do not throw trash from the car or leave litter in someone else's car. Clean up any messes, which may mean paying for a trip to the car wash.

- **Be considerate of other drivers and pedestrians.** No yelling, whistling, or other behaviors that can distract people in other cars or on the street and cause accidents. Booming stereo players in cars are a serious annoyance, and if the car is equipped with one of these systems, cranking it up should be limited to wide-open spaces and times when people are not so likely to be disturbed.

When a teen is stopped for speeding or violating other traffic laws, she may be upset or frightened. But she will handle the situation better if she remains calm and behaves courteously. In general, anyone who is stopped by police should stay in the vehicle with hands in plain sight, on the steering wheel, until the officer approaches. Then roll down the window, let the officer speak, and follow instructions to the letter. Don't get out of the car unless the officer requests. Good manners and a respectful attitude are critical. Don't argue or launch into excuses. Don't make flippant remarks or try to flirt or cajole. Never make threats of any kind. If a teen thinks the officer is wrong, the place to argue is in traffic court. Answer all the officer's questions honestly and straightforwardly. If there are other passengers in the car, they should sit silently unless addressed by the officer. Statistics on teen driving indicate that the possibility of receiving a driving citation is fairly high. Parents can hope it never happens and at the same time prepare their teens for the day when the blue light flashes.

─◂─

On the Job

TURNING SIXTEEN BRINGS THE RIGHT to hold down a "real" job. The typical part-time job for teens may not be glamorous or well paid, but it involves responsibilities that teens are often eager to try. A part-time job can boost your child's confidence, expand his contacts with people of diverse ages and backgrounds, and help him master fundamental work habits and manners that will be essential throughout his working life. With your guidance, a job can be a powerful real-world lesson in business economics and personal money management. It should also open your child's eyes to the everyday roles of and difficulties facing employees and employers and encourage him to be a more considerate customer and consumer. Someday, he may remember his first jobs and be a more effective and more empathetic supervisor of others. (See "Joining the Workforce," page 343, for more on the benefits of teen jobs.)

You can help your teen prepare for the demands of the workplace and the eccentricities of employers and also supply the perspective needed when he is having difficulties. In areas where the well-being of your teen is at stake, it will be your responsibility to *anticipate* problems and take preventive measures.

Part-time employment is not the only option for high schoolers who want to experience the world of work. Some teens take the initiative and create their own jobs. If your child already has an established clientele for her babysitting, pet care, or tutoring services, she might want to keep her business going and even expand. Young people with a yen for responsibility may be able to turn their special expertise—whiz-bang computer skills, for example, or gourmet cooking—into a real business. Parents should be prepared to help (or find help for) budding entrepreneurs with the essentials of bookkeeping, taxes, codes and permits, payroll, and the like, and to monitor work hours closely.

How Much Work?

Teens often overestimate their ability to juggle work with school, extracurricular activities, and social life. Earning steady money can be seductive, especially if the teen is working toward a goal such as buying his own car or building up his college fund. Studies of teen work patterns, however, have shown that more than thirteen or fourteen work hours a week can adversely affect a teen's education and that the negative effects increase with the extra workload, cutting into normal and necessary activities and even damaging a teen's social relationships and friendships.

Your Involvement

It's important for parents to take an active interest in their teen's work life and oversee some aspects of his employment. This requires serious discussion and negotiation, if possible well before a teen begins job-seeking. Assure him that you are not trying to tell him how to do the job and that you won't be checking on his performance with his employer. But for his benefit, you do have the right and obligation to involve yourself in when and how long he works, and you will step in when his work conditions appear to be negatively affecting his life or taking a toll on others in the family. Be clear that you reserve the right to veto any job that puts your child's health and safety at risk or is inappropriate for a teenager.

Here are some other ways to involve yourself in your teen's first forays into employment:

- **Set limits on hours worked.** The recommended limit is thirteen or fourteen hours a week. Parents should keep a sharp eye out for increases. Teens may take on more hours gradually, or the occasional extra time at work may become habitual before a parent notices. A fall in grades, reports of poor school or class attendance, and dropping out of activities that your teen enjoys are usually clear signals that he is working too much. Employers do not always have a teen's best interests at heart, and a young person may fear losing the job or a promised promotion if he doesn't agree to work more hours. Parents must be willing to intervene.

- **Negotiate work schedules.** When a teen works may be as much a concern as the total number of hours, so discuss and negotiate the times your teen will be available to work. Working a single school night each week is preferable to three or four. Safety is a genuine concern, and you may not want your teen working late hours. When you negotiate, talk about the impact of his job hours on other family members. Will he need to use the family car? Will you or another family member be picking him up after work? And do you want to obligate yourself to several 10 or 11 P.M. pick-ups each week?

- **Promote weekend work.** A weekend job is often an ideal solution. Even a teen who has weekend homework assignments may be able to handle one full day or two half-days at his part-time job without too much trouble. After-school jobs are another option, leaving time for both schoolwork and sleep. A teen who wants to work longer hours may be more amenable to limits during the school year if he can take on more hours during the summer.

The Job Interview

Many well-qualified adults dread employment interviews, so it's not surprising if the prospect puts your teen on edge. Interviewing skills are learned through practice and trial and error. Parents can assist with practice and by explaining that a respectful demeanor and good manners will play an important part in impressing an interviewer.

Teens with jobs may think that their responsibilities at home should be lessened or eliminated, but it would be unfair to shift your teen's duties to others or take them on yourself. Perhaps an adjustment in the chore schedule will help your teen. Chores traditionally done in the afternoon may be as easily accomplished at night or on weekends. Or siblings might exchange chores to accommodate their differing schedules. (Be sure such exchanges are perceived as fair on both sides.) You might reassign chores in a way that takes advantage of your teen's work time. If she clerks at the grocery store, for instance, she could handle family shopping while someone else takes over her at-home jobs. Be as flexible as possible, but continue to teach that sharing chores shows consideration for the whole family.

The following advice is addressed to teens seeking jobs but applies as well to college and university interviews:

- *Make an appointment.* Teens may see a "Help Wanted" sign in a store or restaurant window and drop in expecting to talk with the manager. But a considerate applicant should always ask for an appointment at the convenience of the person who will conduct the interview. Requests can be made in person or by phone or letter (e-mail only at the hiring company's request). The etiquette is to let the interviewer set the day, time, and place. If the time conflicts with school or an important engagement, tell the interviewer and let her suggest alternatives. Interviews should be conducted during business hours and at business locations. Even if the interviewer has a home-based business, interviews outside normal working hours are not usual. If a potential employer suggests an after-hours interview or an inappropriate site, be extremely cautious and consult with parents.

- *Be prepared.* Have materials including resume, application forms, and letters of recommendation in order. (See "Writing Business Letters," page 380.) Know your Social Security number. It's also smart to do some advance research. An interviewer will almost always be impressed by a teen who has made the effort to learn something about the company or business.

- **Dress appropriately.** Think about the messages that clothing and accessories, jewelry, hairstyle, makeup, and personal hygiene can convey. Do not judge an interviewer's expectations by what you have seen employees wear. It is generally advisable to dress and accessorize conservatively. Neat and clean are mandatory; no heavy scents.

- **Be punctual.** Arriving late or missing an appointment will almost surely eliminate any chance of getting the job. In an emergency, call the interviewer as soon as possible, explain the problem briefly, and ask to reschedule. If it is impossible to call before the interview, contact the person later and apologize. Arrive for an interview five or ten minutes early. These few extra minutes give the interviewer a chance to clear his or her desk and also allow the interviewee to settle down, take some deep breaths, and survey the surroundings. Arriving too early may put the interviewer in the awkward position of keeping an applicant waiting or dropping other important business. If an interviewer is late, make no comment beyond accepting the interviewer's apology graciously.

- **Greet the interviewer politely.** An applicant must pay close attention and get the interviewer's name; the person doing the interview may not be the person you spoke to or corresponded with to set up the meeting. If you must introduce yourself, give your full name and the purpose of the greeting. ("Hello, Dr. Brightman. I'm Mike Spivak, and I'm here to interview for the part-time filing job.")

- **Listen carefully.** The interviewer will guide the meeting. But the job applicant has to listen carefully and be alert to nonverbal cues in order to follow the flow. If asked a question you don't understand, politely request clarification and be as specific as possible. ("I'm not sure I understand the question, Mrs. Sanchez. Do you want to know about my school record or past employment?")

- **Answer all questions honestly.** Never lie, exaggerate, or omit pertinent information. Falsehoods may be uncovered when the company contacts references or past employers. An applicant

People who hire teens do not expect them to be at the same level as adult job-seekers. They are looking for young employees who are conscientious, trustworthy, and respectful; ready and willing to learn; and motivated to work to the best of their abilities. A self-confident teen shows genuine interest in the job she is seeking and the opportunity (not just the money) being offered. She sits up straight during the interview, looks directly at the interviewer, shows respect by paying attention, uses correct language, and talks but doesn't try to dominate the conversation. When a person is confident that she can do the job, there's no need to be brash, pushy, or to indulge in tactics such as name dropping.

◄◄

may never know that he lost a job because he was caught in a lie, but he is establishing a reputation for dishonesty that can take years to undo. Volunteer to find any information you don't know and get back to the interviewer as soon as possible.

- **Conclude the interview graciously.** Be alert to the interviewer's verbal and nonverbal signals and be ready to leave when the interview is over. Don't try to make a few more points, and don't dash away. Thank the interviewer for his or her time and attention, and offer to shake hands. Sometimes, an applicant may leave an interview with a job offered and accepted. If so, be absolutely sure when and where to report for work or training and clarify other expectations such as on-the-job dress requirements and parking arrangements. The interviewer may simply thank you for coming and promise to get back to you within a few days. If the interviewer doesn't give a time, you can ask when you might expect to hear about the job. If the interviewer indicates a day and time to call back, be sure to call at that time, not sooner. Even if the interviewer makes it clear that no job is available, you should thank him courteously. It's fine to ask an interviewer to keep your resume on file should a similar job become available in the future.

- **Follow up an interview.** A smart interviewee will write down important information as quickly as possible after the interview. What is the name of the interviewer? When are you expected to call back or report for work? What further information did you promise to provide? Was anything said in the interview that you might want to refer to in your thank-you note to the interviewer? You should write within a day or two of the interview whether you got the job, didn't get it, or are waiting to hear. (See "Writing Business Letters," page 380.)

Going to Work

The fundamentals of good work habits are discussed in Chapter 25, and it's a good idea to review these basics before the job begins. Also talk to your teen about the qualities of a valued employee. Before he starts a new job, discuss concepts such as loyalty, commitment, and duty. Talk about the importance of keeping an employer's business confidential. Your teen should feel free to bring problems to you, but gossiping about work-related matters is unacceptable.

Pragmatic reasons for doing a good job abound. Teens may be receptive to the notion that these early jobs—despite the low pay—are the necessary starting places for more challenging and rewarding employment. Today's employer may become tomorrow's college or professional school reference. Co-workers as well as employers can become lifelong friends and supporters. No matter how menial, early jobs teach fundamental work and people skills, instill respect for the work of others, and require mannerly and considerate behaviors that are essential to later success and personal satisfaction in virtually every workplace.

You're Fired!

Getting fired from a part-time job can devastate a teenager. In the immediate aftermath, you can offer a shoulder to cry on. There's little need to get angry—your teen has probably punished herself enough as it is—and don't tell her that you understand how she feels unless you really do. It's also wise not to criticize the employer unless you know the facts and have good reason. Help your teen face up to whatever went wrong. Pay attention to her explanations and excuses because they may tell you a lot. Common reasons for a teen's firing include persistent lateness and absences, minor but consistent infractions of workplace rules, inattention or rudeness to customers, and failure to follow instructions. Usually a teen has been warned and given the opportunity to correct problems before losing a job, but many do not take the warnings seriously. Encourage your teen to analyze the situation, examine her work performance from the employer's point of view, and decide what she needs to do to keep her next job. If the cause of a firing is more serious—theft, damage to or misuse of property including company vehicles, physical or verbal aggression—the firing may be a warning of real antisocial problems, and parents should consider professional help for their teen.

The Benefits of Dating

THOUGH MORE CASUAL NOW THAN in past generations, dating still serves the basic purposes it did in days gone by: to ready young people for a world in which women and men interact daily in myriad ways and to prepare young people for successful, intimate adult relationships including marriage and parenthood. Dating is a form of social interaction with many benefits.

- *Friendship.* Dating helps young people distinguish between romantic fantasies and the real values of companionship and caring about someone else's feelings and comfort. Many teens are both surprised and happy to discover that dating friends can be lots of fun. Dating can help teens who have not had a lot of routine exposure to the opposite sex (young people who attend single-sex schools, for instance) develop new social skills and build self-confidence. Dating also raises issues of loyalty, personal responsibility, and integrity that a parent and family cannot duplicate.

- *Self-enhancement.* Dating conveys social status and boosts self-esteem, but as long as a teen is not dating someone solely for reflected glory or material gain, a little self-enhancement can't hurt.

- *Intimacy.* Although the term "intimacy" is used as a euphemism for sexual relations, its meaning is much broader. Intimacy implies closeness, commitment, and mutual respect in a personal relationship. Through dating, teens can learn a great deal about

It's not always easy to figure out why a teenager isn't interested in dating, but it's important to respect her decision. Dating can be rather low on a teen's list of priorities—well below academic preparation, career goals, jobs, sports, building a resume, and the like. Dating consumes time and energy that the teen may prefer to spend on other pursuits. Teens may also feel unready for one-on-one dating and choose to keep their interpersonal relations on the group level. As long as it's not part of a pattern of isolation, not dating is probably not a big problem. Parents shouldn't equate dating with sociability or popularity. Keep in mind that there's no precise timetable for social development, and allow your late-bloomer to blossom on his or her own schedule.

compromise and accommodating the needs of another person, balancing self-interest and self-sacrifice, sharing interests and setting common goals, open communication, fidelity and trust, and the importance of respectful manners in close relationships.

- **Rejection.** Breaking up is hard to do, but it will probably happen at least once to most teens. Being turned down for a date can also be a blow to a teen's ego. Rejection is a painful but inescapable part of life, and people need opportunities to develop their coping skills. Rejecting someone else can also be difficult, and teens should learn how to say "no" without equivocation but also with kindness and respect.

Dating Etiquette for Teens

DATING IN HIGH SCHOOL TAKES many forms. Group dates and pairing off within a group are likely to continue, though casual one-on-one dating becomes more frequent and some high schoolers enter steady relationships. Whether teens date on a regular basis or occasionally, there are some fundamental dating manners that they should understand and put into practice.

- **Ask in advance**—at least a day or two before a casual date and a week (or several weeks) in advance for more formal occasions.

A blind date can be a nice way to have a good time. It all depends on attitude. If a young person expects the date to be a disaster, there's a good chance it will be. Keep in mind that the goal of a blind date is to have a pleasant few hours getting to know someone new—not to find a soul mate.

When a teen or adult sets up a blind date for others, it's important to keep the "sales pitch" grounded in reality. Don't oversell either party. Focus on what you know about the people, especially common interests they may have. In case you don't know one or both people well (when, for instance, you are arranging a date for a childhood friend you haven't seen for years), it may be better to organize a group get-together or double date.

One important blind date warning: Teens should never accept dates with anyone they have met over the Internet, by telephone, or through correspondence only. Insist on meeting in a public place *with parents present*. If the person wants a private meeting, don't agree. This is a clear signal that his or her motives are suspect.

━━◂━

Last-minute arrangements for casual dates are common among good friends, but even your best friend deserves time to prepare for a big event like a prom. A last-minute invitation to someone you don't know well may be taken the wrong way.

- *Choose a good time to ask.* A call at dinnertime, too early in the morning, or too late at night can make a bad impression. Don't interrupt when the person is in conversation with a group or clearly busy with something important. Casual invitations by note or e-mail are best limited to people you know well.

- *Reply to invitations promptly.* It's always courteous to accept or turn down a date when asked. If you can't give an immediate response, explain the situation and promise to respond as quickly as you can. It is very inconsiderate to leave a person waiting for more than twenty-four hours.

- *Be kind when saying "no."* A date invitation is a high compliment, so there's no reason to cause hurt feelings. Be clear that you are saying "no" and thank the person for asking. If you would like to go out but can't, explain why and perhaps offer an alternative. ("I have band camp this weekend, so I can't go. But maybe we could do something next weekend.") You don't have to make specific plans, but convey the message that you would like another opportunity to get together.

Never make up excuses—even to save someone's feelings—because it is dishonest and disrespectful. When you turn down a date, don't talk about it to others. Gossiping in any way about a date you turn down is crass and immature and reflects poorly on the person who gossips rather than the subject of the talk. If someone you don't want to date is persistent, you'll probably have to be more direct. This can be difficult, but it's important to be both clear and as gracious as possible.

- **Address the details up front.** When making a date, be clear about all details: time, place, activity, transportation, and special considerations such as ordering tickets. It's fine to talk about money matters and decide who will pay for what. Be considerate: When asking someone out for the first time, don't expect him or her to finance an expensive evening.

- **Stick to your word when you accept a date.** Genuine illness and family emergencies are legitimate reasons for breaking a date. Going out with someone "better" or just having second thoughts is not. When you must cancel a date, offer to reschedule at a time that is reasonable.

- **Don't keep a date waiting.** Arrive on time if you are picking up a date, and be ready to go if you are being picked up. If you have an unavoidable delay, call your date as soon as possible, explain, and revise the date time. Expecting a person to cool his or her heels so that a date can make a grand entrance is self-indulgent and shows a basic lack of good manners.

- **Pick up a date in person.** Go to the door and greet parents courteously. If parents ask about plans and return time, answer fully and don't show impatience. If you meet your date at work or a friend's home, make a personal appearance. There may be occasions when you must wait for a date in the car or outside a place of business. Don't honk the horn, crank up the stereo, or yell for your date to come out. Patience is a virtue; making a spectacle that disturbs others is not.

Pay attention to curfews, and accompany your date to the door at the end of the occasion. Walking a date to the door may seem a little old-fashioned, but it is really an act of decency and respect that never goes out of style. Don't expect or push for a good-night kiss, and don't engage in public displays of affection on the doorstep.

- **Be ready to have a good time.** It takes two people to make a date enjoyable. It's normal to be nervous, especially on a first or second date, but a positive attitude can do a lot to calm the jitters.

Very Special Occasions

THOUGH A TEEN'S SOCIAL LIFE and parties are casual and freewheeling for the most part, there are a number of big events on the threshold to young adulthood.

Quinceañera

A coming-of-age tradition that originated in Latin America, a *quinceañera* (or *quince*) commemorates a girl's fifteenth birthday. Depending on the practices of the Roman Catholic Church in your area, the event may comprise a religious ceremony followed by a party or a party only. The *quinceañera* party is often a formal dance (black or white tie) with the young honoree wearing an elaborate gown. The invitation will indicate the degree of formality. (Formal invitations require formal replies.) Gifts are customary, and the type of gift often depends on local tradition. Although the *quinceañera* marks a birthday, gifts are not opened at a formal ball. A teen who attends a formal *quinceañera* and is not familiar with the customs can watch the honoree and her family and follow their lead. A *quinceañera* may also be celebrated much less lavishly with family and friends.

Sweet Sixteen Parties

Sixteen was once the age when youths were admitted to the society of adults, and the sweet sixteen party became a celebration of the end of childhood, especially for girls. Though the sweet sixteen tradition has faded in many places, a sixteenth birthday still has the aura of a mile-

When Your Teens Are Steadies

When teens begin to date exclusively, parents in particular may feel excluded from the charmed circle. Yet parents are naturally concerned about the seriousness of the relationship and may have fears for their children. You'll probably feel more confident if you get to know your teen's steady and his or her family. It's usually easier if the parents are acquainted, but don't hesitate to contact parents you don't know. The goal is to make contact and start building trust among the adults. Your teens are the first cause of any meeting, but they don't have to be the focus. By opening lines of communication, parents on both sides of a steady teen relationship should feel more comfortable just knowing that they can talk. Your teen may complain that you are interfering with his or her relationship but may also be secretly pleased that you care.

---

stone, and parents or other family members may want to celebrate with a special party. The format can vary from a pizza party or picnic to an elegant dinner and dance. Surprise parties are a traditional form of sweet sixteen. The invitation should be precise about the nature of the event. Birthday presents are expected. But if a guest is asked to bring a date and the date doesn't receive a separate invitation, then the invited teen brings the gift for both—gift-giving etiquette for all birthday parties and other occasions where gifts are presented.

High School Proms

Junior or senior proms are very exciting for many teens, and the prom buzz can begin months before the event. To be successful, prom nights generally require more planning and preparation than the social events a teen has attended in the past. In addition to the dating basics already discussed, here are some fundamental do's for prom-goers and one very important don't.

- **Do ask early.** Proms require preparation, so give your date plenty of time to accept and get his or her ducks in a row before the big night.

CORSAGES AND BOUTONNIERES

The custom of boys presenting corsages to their dates is alive and well. Before ordering flowers, check with your date about the color of her dress and ask if she prefers a corsage, wristlet, or nosegay (a small bouquet that is carried rather than worn). With this information, your florist can help you make an attractive choice. When presenting a corsage, a boy is not expected to pin it on. Simply give your date the flower box and let her decide where she wants to wear it. The traditional corsage is usually worn at the shoulder or waist or pinned to an evening purse. (When worn on a dress, the corsage is pinned so that the flowers turn upward, the way they grow in nature.)

A boutonniere is a single flower—usually a rose or carnation—presented by a girl to her date. The boutonniere is pinned to the lapel of his jacket where the buttonhole would be. The girl may pin it on or let her date handle this task.

- *Do think about money.* Proms and the associated activities can be costly, even when dates share expenses, but there are ways to economize. Rented tuxedos are an obvious choice. Instead of orchids, a corsage of fresh gardenias is lovely and less expensive. Dinner at a midrange restaurant will be just as much fun as expensive dining. Be creative with your prom budget; with thought, you can cut corners without appearing tightfisted.

- *Do make transportation plans well in advance if you want to rent a vehicle.* Limousines are very popular for proms, and some teens pool their funds to rent vans or buses. Be sure to make reservations early because limousines and other rented transportation may be in short supply at prom time. Call rental companies well ahead and get details including insurance information. There may be a security deposit, and a parent must make the actual rental agreement.

- *Do thank everyone who helped with the prom.* There's a great deal of work involved in creating a successful prom, so be sure to express appreciation to classmates, school officials, chaperones, and others who gave their time to make the evening special.

- **Do use common sense about after-party activities.** Prom night should become a wonderful memory, not a night of regrets. It's usually best to plan after-dance parties, especially all-nighters, at a classmate's home with parents and chaperones present. Prom night is not an excuse for any behaviors, including pranks and vandalism, that can cause harm to you and others. Young people and their reputations can be hurt just by their presence in situations that are inappropriate (an all-night party in a hotel room, for example) and when others misbehave.

- **Don't use alcohol or drugs.** It's that simple. *Make a commitment to be responsible.* You cannot control what others do, but you can control yourself and behave with maturity. You may be able to influence others by making your own commitment clear and sticking to it. You can step in if someone who is intoxicated tries to drive or becomes aggressive, but do not engage in physical confrontation. Call on adults to help.

A Question for Peggy and Cindy

My daughter, who is finishing her freshman year, has been invited to the senior prom. This is a social coup for her, but I'm not sure whether to allow her to go. I worry that she may be out of her depth with seniors. Am I being too protective?

You are right to be concerned. You will want to ask yourself and your daughter a number of questions. How well do you know the boy? How well does she know him? The date may be more acceptable if he is a good friend. You definitely should know what is planned. If there are all-night activities, you'll probably want your daughter to attend the dance only. Who will be driving? Does your locality have curfew laws that affect your daughter but not her escort? Is there a likelihood that alcohol or drugs will be present? Ask your daughter if any of her freshman friends will be attending; you may want to talk with their parents. Some high schools have age policies about prom dates, so check with your daughter's school to see if freshmen are allowed to attend.

If you decide not to let your daughter accept, be clear about your reasons, but avoid turning it into a matter of not trusting your daughter or the boy. The key issues are appropriateness and safety. Your daughter may be angry and resentful, but there's a possibility she may be relieved. (It can be easier to say "no" to an older teen if she can use a parent as her excuse.) Whatever you decide, do so quickly. If your answer is "no," the boy needs time to get another date for his big event.

Graduation Parties

High school graduation is the happy culmination of many people's efforts, and parents, family, and friends often want to honor the proud graduate. There is no explicit time limit on when graduation parties can be held, but it should be within a couple of months of the graduation. Often several parents and grandparents host the event for their young graduates. Following morning or afternoon ceremonies, a brunch, luncheon, or supper party is a nice way to celebrate. These events may be held at the home of parents or family members. A local restaurant or club can be a good choice.

Graduation parties can be as lavish or intimate as you desire, but it's always a good idea to consult with the guest of honor. It is not appropriate to hold a graduation party before the guest of honor has actually graduated.

Parties held on graduation night, however, can present problems. After so much anticipation, teens often want to kick up their heels when their diplomas are finally handed over. Parents should trust their teens but also stay involved to protect their children and other graduates from dangerous and self-destructive behaviors. Holding a party at a parent's home, providing plenty of food and soft drinks, and letting the teens party safely but in their own way may be the best option.

Graduation night parties require thoughtful planning. If you agree to hold a party in your home, be sure to have other responsible adult chaperones in attendance. Since the noise level is likely to rise into the wee hours, inform neighbors about the party and ask for their indulgence. Local law enforcement is often out in force on graduation and prom nights, and you may want to let the police know that there will be a party at your home so that they can patrol your area. You can't control the guest list, but you can expect your teen to tell you who is invited. Watch out for gate-crashers, and pay close attention to young teens who may be brought as dates.

Do not serve liquor (including beer) and keep a sharp eye out for teens who are drinking alcohol or using drugs. Never let a teen who has been drinking or using drugs drive. Some parents make the surrender of car keys a condition of attending an all-night graduation bash.

There are now local and national organizations, composed mostly of parents, that provide excellent advice for arranging and managing safe graduation night activities. Try an Internet search or check with your school principal's office for suggestions. When parents and teens talk about plans well in advance and expectations on all sides are clear, graduation night is much more likely to be the perfect cap to this major milestone occasion.

GRADUATION INVITATIONS AND GIFTS

Since invitations to graduations are often limited in number, they should generally be sent to the people who mean the most to the graduate: grandparents, close family, godparents, and supportive friends. It's unnecessary to invite school faculty or the parents of students in a teen's graduating class.

Traditionally, parents give their graduating teen a gift of special value and personal significance. For others, there are no rules about gifts, but it is nice to select a present that reflects the special nature of graduation. Fine pen-and-pencil sets, monogrammed stationery and address books, leatherbound books, picture frames, silver cuff links or tie tacks, framed works of art or photography, luggage—all say welcome to the adult world. Gift certificates and money gifts are appropriate, especially if the giver is not sure about the teen's tastes and interests.

Thank-you notes must be written for every gift. Graduates should also write notes to anyone who entertains for them or does special favors.

Fine Points of Restaurant Dining

HIGH SCHOOL STUDENTS USUALLY HAVE opportunities to dine in nice restaurants without parents present. Eating in a middle- to top-tier restaurant requires self-confidence and a bit more knowledge of dining manners and customs. These dining-out specifics can boost a teen's self-assurance:

- *Call in advance for reservations, indicate how many people will be dining, and specify smoking or nonsmoking section.* If the occasion is special, such as a birthday or prom night, tell the person who takes the reservation; you may get a better table or an extra courtesy. Arrive on time, or you may lose your reservation.

- *If the restaurant has valet parking service, let the valet park the car.* Don't forget to leave the keys with the valet or in the car. The restaurant has some responsibility for security, but it's smart to lock any valuable items in the trunk. Valet parking attendants are usually tipped. (See "Concerning Tipping," page 431.) If you don't want to use the service, park near the restaurant but not in the area designated for valet parking.

- *It's okay to ask politely for a better table if you are shown to one in a noisy or busy spot.* If the restaurant is very crowded and another table is not available, you can ask to wait for an opening, if you have the time. If the seating is really not tolerable, you can leave, though you must pay for anything you have ordered.

- *If the restaurant has a checkroom, leave your coat and hat if you choose.* It's a good idea to check bulky coats and items such as umbrellas that can inconvenience you or others at the table. There should be no charge for checking coats, but checkroom attendants receive a tip when items are retrieved.

- *In fine restaurants, a headwaiter and servers will often hold chairs for women.* Otherwise, everyone should seat themselves. (Holding a chair for a woman or girl and waiting for women to be seated first are gentlemanly traditions and still gracious as long as they seem to be welcomed by the females in your party.)

- *Diners usually place their own orders with the server.* If the meal is Dutch treat, order what you want and can afford. When someone else is paying, it's courteous to stick to the middle range of prices or to be guided by what the host and others order. You might get a hint by asking the host what he would recommend. Even if a host says to have whatever you like, common decency dictates not ordering the most expensive items on the menu. There may be occasions when you do ask a host to order for you, as when the restaurant offers a foreign cuisine and you have no idea what to try.

- **If you drop a utensil, napkin, or bit of food, leave it on the floor unless it falls in the aisle and might cause someone to trip or slip.** Signal to a server, and he or she will remove whatever has been dropped and bring a fresh item. A hand signal or even a glance is usually sufficient to attract a waiter's attention. Be considerate if your server is very rushed or serving another table.

- **Empty paper or cellophane packets for sweeteners and crackers are placed under the rim of the dinner plate, on the salad plate, or in an unused ashtray.**

- **Do not comb hair or reapply makeup at the table.** Freshening lipstick may be okay as long as you are not too obvious. No toothpicks or tooth care, including flossing, at the table. All personal grooming really should be done in the rest room.

- **If you can't finish your meal, it's fine to ask for a container for the remainder.** What was once called a "doggie bag" (because people were too embarrassed to ask for their leftovers and requested the scraps for their dog) is now an accepted custom even in very expensive restaurants. Ask for what you have left on your plate—a substantial portion of steak or chicken, for example, or the dessert you just couldn't make room for—not a bit of salad or vegetable or items that will melt and not an extra portion.

- **When dining Dutch treat, organize your method of payment well before the bill arrives.** If you want separate checks for everyone, be sure to tell your server *before* he or she takes orders. If everyone will be ordering meals of approximately the same value, you might pool funds before you enter the restaurant and designate one person to handle the check. When you receive a single bill for several diners, you can divide the total amount equally and sort out the differences later. Don't quibble over a few cents or a dollar, and don't argue about the bill or tip in the restaurant.

Teens and adults are likely to come across unfamiliar menu items when dining out. If you don't know what a food is, ask someone at the table or your server. It's fun to try unusual or exotic dishes when dining out, but find out the key ingredients before ordering. Escargot sounds delicious, but are you ready for snails? If you aren't sure how to eat an exotic item such as an artichoke or lobster, servers are usually happy to provide discreet instructions.

- **When the bill is delivered on a small tray, that's a signal to pay the server at the table.** Place money or your credit/debit card on the tray, and the server will return with your change or the credit slip for your signature. When the bill alone is left on the table beside the host, this usually means to pay the cashier. If you aren't sure, ask your server.

- **It's always gracious to thank servers and the headwaiter after a meal.** If the food was very good, tell your server, and he or she will pass your compliments to the chef.

Concerning Tipping

OTHER THAN MOST FAST-FOOD CHAINS, restaurants in the United States generally pay waiters and waitresses no more and often less than minimum wage. From the local family eatery to the most expensive restaurants, people who serve meals make their income primarily through tips. Knowing this fact of life, Americans tend to tip for most food service. (Tipping is a reward for service, not the quality of the food.)

A 15 percent tip is standard, though it may be 20 percent in some areas and at high-priced restaurants. The tip is calculated on the before-tax amount of the bill. Tips can be left in cash or added to a credit-card payment. In some restaurants, the tip is already included in the cost and should be indicated on the bill. If you are not sure whether a tip, or gratuity, has been included, ask your server. Although tipping is generally expected, you have some control. You may want to tip more for excellent service and a little below the standard for poor or discourteous treatment. You are not expected to tip restaurant personnel other than servers, but a dollar or two is appropriate for coat room, rest room, and valet parking attendants.

Tipping in other situations depends on local custom. In some areas, customers are expected to tip the people who take groceries to the car at the food market but not cashiers. Tipping barbers and beauticians is commonplace, as is tipping taxi and limousine drivers and luggage porters in hotels and transportation terminals. In general, tipping is for personal service, but in this computerized, mechanized age, it can be difficult to determine who is providing personal service and who is simply pressing a button. When you aren't sure, ask someone who knows, though not the person who will receive the tip. If you forget to leave a tip that was deserved, you can always go back or double the tip the next time you use the service.

Getting to College

AS YOU ATTEND TO THE official requirements for college admission, etiquette should never be forgotten. Competition can be stiff, and believe it or not, good manners can give a student the edge. These fundamentals apply to teens and their parents:

- **Be courteous to everyone.** Whenever you have contact with a college—via written correspondence, phone calls, or in person— your manners and demeanor will be on display. The woman on the phone could be the director of admissions, and the young fellow in jeans and sandals whom you brush by during a campus visit might be a department chairman. Treat everyone with respect.

- **Be on your best behavior when on campus.** High schoolers may have informal, unchaperoned visits—attending social functions or visiting a friend and staying in a dorm. College students who conduct official tours are selected by the college and report back to admissions staff. A pragmatic rule is never to do anything that you don't want recounted to an admissions officer. Even large universities are like small towns; word of immature behaviors (including underage drinking), rudeness, and lack of consideration circulates quickly.

- **Be considerate of officials' time.** Colleges and universities often have thousands of requests and applications to process and a relatively small number of staff. When you call or correspond, be mannerly, but stick to your point. (See "Writing Business Letters," page 380.) Don't ask for information that the college has already provided; most questions are covered in brochures, handbooks, and on college websites.

- **Be scrupulously honest.** Never lie or exaggerate. Assume from the outset that any fabrication will be caught. The discovery that a college student has falsified application information is grounds for expulsion, so don't even "puff up" an application— claiming to be an officer of a high school organization when you are only a member or adding volunteer jobs you never had. Parents should take care that financial information for loan and scholarship applications is complete and accurate.

- *Follow instructions and meet every deadline.* If a college application form or personal essay is to be typed, type it. Mail applications and other materials several days in advance of deadlines. Check and recheck every submission for accuracy, and keep copies as well as postal and express service receipts to verify mailing dates in case a document is lost. Use e-mail and fax only at the college's request. Attention to detail is just as important after you have been accepted: Read all materials carefully; note dates for enrollment, payments, orientation; follow instructions exactly.

- *Be interested and interesting.* In interviews, on campus tours, and when meeting recruiters, be ready to talk about more than your own needs and goals. Colleges are looking for bright, intellectually curious students who can discuss ideas and concepts, so don't be afraid to converse about an interesting subject when the opportunity is presented. Express interest in the college itself. Never indicate that a college is your second or fall-back choice.

- *Write thank-you notes promptly after college tours and interviews.* Send your note to the person with whom you met. (Check titles and spelling of names.) If a student conducted your campus tour, thank that person as well as the college officials who arranged the tour.

- *Respond to all notices of acceptance, rejection, or wait-listing.* You will immediately confirm your acceptance when you get into the college of your choice. You should also quickly inform other schools you've applied to; letting them know that you won't attend is a courtesy to the schools and other students whose applications are pending. If you receive a rejection, it's wise to write a short note of thanks for the school's consideration. (You may want to reapply in the future.) Be sure to write if you are wait-listed for a college you wish to attend. Don't beg for admission, but do reaffirm your sincere desire to attend. Expressing genuine commitment at this stage could tip the scale in your favor and lessen your waiting time. All follow-up letters should be addressed to the person who signed the official notification, even if you haven't met this person. Also send a copy to the college counselor with whom you worked.

Index

Emily Post 1873 to 1960

EMILY POST BEGAN HER CAREER as a writer at the age of thirty-one. Her romantic stories of European and American society were serialized in *Vanity Fair, Collier's, McCall's,* and other popular magazines. Many were also successfully published in book form.

Upon its publication in 1922, her book, *Etiquette,* topped the nonfiction bestseller list, and the phrase "according to Emily Post" soon entered our language as the last word on the subject of social conduct. Mrs. Post, who as a girl had been told that well-bred women should not work, was suddenly a pioneering American career woman. Her numerous books, a syndicated newspaper column, and a regular network radio program made Emily Post a figure of national stature and importance throughout the rest of her life.

"Good manners reflect something from inside—an innate sense of consideration for others and respect for self."—Emily Post